FOREIGN AFFAIRS

Special Collection

Essays for the Presidency

A Century's Worth of Candidates and Their Advisers Make Their Cases

Gideon Rose   SEPTEMBER 22, 2015

The United States is an indirect democracy rather than a direct one; citizens rarely choose policies, but instead choose representatives to do that for them. But how can voters know what their representatives will do once elected, in order to make an informed choice? In part, by looking to their clearest and most authoritative policy manifestos. Foreign Affairs has long been the place for aspiring presidents and their advisers to present their foreign policy visions, and so with the 2016 campaign well under way, we decided to provide some context for it by pulling together nearly a century's worth of campaign-related articles from our archives.

In this collection, you'll find everybody, from all the major candidates in 2008—including Barack Obama, Hillary Clinton, John McCain, Mitt Romney, and Mike Huckabee—to crucial historical figures such as Colonel House, Franklin Roosevelt, John F. Kennedy, Richard Nixon, and many more. The more than 60 essays it includes represent a unique trove of political Americana, a time machine that can transport you back to any election you want and see how things looked to the players themselves, in real time. It's a great volume to keep close at hand as you watch the election unfold—even as you keep an eye on the magazine and Foreign Affairs.com for essays by current candidates, along with continuous coverage of U.S. foreign policy and the world at large.

Rebooting Republican Foreign Policy

Daniel W. Drezner   JANUARY/FEBRUARY 2015

A man carries a cut-out of Republican presidential candidate Mitt Romney in New Delhi.

This past fall was not kind to U.S. President Barack Obama's foreign policy. It became increasingly clear that Afghan security forces were not going to be ready for the 2014 transition. *The New York Times* highlighted the administration's failure to persuade the Iraqi government to allow a residual U.S. force to stay in the country, leaving Baghdad ever more at the mercy of Tehran. Obama and Israeli Prime Minister Benjamin Netanyahu fought publicly over how to respond to Iran's advancing nuclear program. The administration's much-touted "pivot" to the Pacific seemed like more talk than action, as the United States passively watched tensions rise between China and Japan. And then, the administration tripped over itself repeatedly in trying to explain the fiasco in Benghazi, Libya.

Yet despite all this, Obama not only won the election in November but was more trusted by the public than Mitt Romney, the Republican candidate, on foreign policy and national security issues. The Pew Research Center's last preelection poll, for example, found that more voters trusted Obama than Romney on foreign affairs, by 50 percent to 42 percent, and CBS/*New York Times* and NBC/*Wall Street Journal* surveys showed similar figures. Tracking polls suggested that the foreign policy debate helped halt whatever momentum Romney had.

This was all a big change from the past. Republicans had previously possessed a decades-long advantage on foreign policy. Exit polls have shown that voters consistently trusted Republican presidential candidates over Democratic ones on foreign policy from the Vietnam era until 2012. So Obama's edge cannot be chalked up simply to incumbency. And if this exception becomes a trend, it will pose a serious problem for the Republican Party, significantly altering the political landscape. Foreign policy is rarely the decisive issue in presidential campaigns, but it does matter: even voters who profess not to care about the rest of the world need to feel comfortable that their candidate can be the next commander in chief. A candidate's command of foreign policy acts as a proxy for assessing broader leadership abilities. As of right now, far too many Republicans flunk that test.

So how did the party of Dwight Eisenhower and Ronald Reagan get itself into this mess? Simply put, GOP leaders stopped being smart foxes and devolved into stupid hedgehogs. During the Cold War, the party of Eisenhower, Richard Nixon, and Reagan was strongly anticommunist, but these presidents took foreign policy seriously and executed their grand strategies with a healthy degree of tactical flexibility. Since 9/11, however, Republicans have known only one big thing—the "global war on terror"—and have remained stubbornly committed to a narrow militarized approach. Since the fall of Baghdad, moreover, this approach has produced at least as much failure as success, leading the American public to be increasingly skeptical of the bellicosity that now defines the party's foreign policy.

Republicans need to start taking international relations more seriously, addressing the true complexities and requirements of the issues rather than allowing the subject to be a plaything for right-wing interest groups. And if they don't act quickly, they might cede this ground to the Democrats for the next generation.

BUILDING THE BRAND

Republican presidents from the 1950s through the early 1990s had variegated records, but they had one thing in common: they left behind favorable legacies on foreign policy. Eisenhower stabilized the rivalry with the Soviet Union, preventing it from escalating into a violent conflagration. He dramatically improved the U.S. foreign-policy-making process, strengthened domestic infrastructure, extricated the United States from the Korean War, and limited U.S. involvement in Vietnam. Nixon improved relations with the Soviet Union, opened relations with China, and extricated the United States from Vietnam. Reagan spoke truth to power by railing against the Soviet Union as an "evil empire," but when faced with a genuine negotiating partner in Mikhail Gorbachev, he did not hesitate to sign numerous treaties, reduce Cold War tensions, and cut nuclear stockpiles. George H. W. Bush adroitly seized the opportunities afforded by the end of the Cold War to expand the West's liberal order to the world at large, as well as overseeing German reunification, rebuffing Iraq's invasion of Kuwait, and locking in Mexico's path toward economic liberalization.

Each president built his reputation as a foreign policy hawk, and none was afraid to talk tough or act forcefully when dealing with adversaries. But the key to their success was the ability to combine principled beliefs at the strategic level with prudence and flexibility at the tactical level. Eisenhower took great care to prevent small crises from distracting the United States from its main goal of containing the Soviet Union. Nixon built his political career on anti-communism but recognized the strategic advantage of opening relations with Maoist China. Reagan talked tough on terrorism, but after 241 U.S. marines were killed in a suicide attack in Beirut, he did not hesitate to draw down U.S. forces from a peripheral conflict in Lebanon. And rather than do a sack dance at the end of the Cold War, Bush 41 took care to respond tactfully and nimbly, pocketing and building on an extraordinary strategic windfall.

To be sure, they all had their foreign policy blemishes, too. But their strengths outweighed their weaknesses, especially when compared with Democratic counterparts such as Lyndon Johnson and Jimmy Carter. Republican presidents during the Cold War skillfully combined the idealpolitik of American exceptionalism with the realpolitik necessary to navigate a world of bipolarity, nuclear deterrence, and Third World nationalism. They relied on a string of steady-handed professionals, such as John Foster Dulles, Henry Kissinger, George Shultz, James Baker, and Brent Scowcroft, to help manage their administrations. Indeed, so great was the legacy this era bequeathed that in 2000, exit polls showed that the public viewed the neophyte George W. Bush as stronger on foreign policy than Al Gore, the sitting vice president. Gore's considerable experience was neutralized by public trust in the Republican foreign policy "Vulcans" advising his opponent.

... THEN SQUANDERING IT

For a brief time, it looked as though Bush 43 would be able to carry on the legacy. In the wake of 9/11, the neoconservatives in his administration supplied a clear and coherent grand strategy of using unilateral military action to destroy terrorist bases and remake the Middle East, and after quickly toppling hostile regimes in Afghanistan and Iraq, it seemed to be working.

Over the next several years, however, the Bush administration's strategic miscalculations became apparent. The administration focused on a mythical "axis of evil," lumping disparate actors into a single anti-American threat. It displayed little tactical flexibility and no ability to plan for the consequences of its actions. The initial swift success in Afghanistan was marred by a failure to capture or kill al Qaeda's senior leadership, and when the administration pivoted almost immediately to Iraq, it took its eye off the ball in South Asia and allowed a short-term victory to deteriorate into a long-term quagmire.

Iraq, meanwhile, turned into nothing short of a disaster. There, too, the invasion went well, but the postwar planning was so slap-dash that it sabotaged any chance of a stable occupation. A growing insurgency crippled Washington's ability to project power in the region and consumed an appalling amount of American and Iraqi blood and treasure. And the failure to discover weapons of mass destruction—the existence of which had been the central rationale for the war—undermined the United States' reputation for both competence and honesty. Late in Bush's second term, a well-executed course correction helped stabilize the situation and ultimately permit a U.S. withdrawal with some measure of dignity. But the chief beneficiary of the whole affair turned out to be Iran— the United States' main adversary in the region.

The failures in Afghanistan and Iraq compounded other errors that the administration committed. The Bush team pushed for free and fair elections across the Middle East but seems never to have thought about what would happen if the elections were won by radical Islamists—as was the case with Hamas in Gaza in 2006. And an obsession with the "war on terror" alienated allies in Europe, Latin America, and the Pacific Rim, allowing a rising China to gain increasing influence.

The administration did have some successes—getting Libya to abandon its weapons of mass destruction, developing a warm relationship with India, and providing generous support for AIDS relief in Africa. But by the end of the Bush years, global attitudes toward the United States had reached an all-time low, and the American public noticed. A 2008 survey by the Chicago Council on Global Affairs showed that 83 percent of Americans polled placed the highest priority on "improving America's standing in the world"—a higher figure than for the traditional top priority of protecting American jobs.

John McCain, the 2008 Republican presidential candidate, had neither the desire nor the ability to distance himself much from Bush's unpopular foreign policy record and was overwhelmed by the outbreak of the financial crisis during the final stages of the campaign. And after the GOP was evicted from the White House, the party's foreign policy approach grew even more problematic, with McCain's running mate, Sarah Palin, heralding the future.

It is always difficult for a party out of power to craft a coherent worldview, in part because of the lack of a dominant figure able to impose order on the discussion, and this time was no exception. Freed from the burden of executive-branch responsibility after the 2008 defeat, Republicans began to lose touch with the real world of foreign policy. Some libertarians advocated a radical and impractical reduction of the United States' overseas presence. Most others moved in the opposite direction, toward jingoism and xenophobia.

Unbowed by Iraq, prominent neoconservatives called for aggressive military action against Iran. Popular party figures strongly opposed the construction of a mosque in Manhattan. Major Republican politicians held congressional hearings about whether American Muslims could be trusted. Right-wing columnists demanded that the Obama administration resuscitate the use of torture. Leading Senate Republicans opposed any new international treaty as a matter of principle, resisting the relatively uncontroversial New START treaty with Russia and flatly opposing the Law of the Sea Treaty, despite endorsements from every living former Republican secretary of state, big business, and the U.S. Navy. A few, such as Senator Richard Lugar of Indiana, placed country over party and tried to find some common ground with Obama. The reward for his troubles was a primary challenge by a Tea Party favorite, who managed to defeat Lugar before self-destructing during the general election.

BOTTOMING OUT

The 2012 presidential campaign devalued Republican foreign policy thinking even further. Most of the GOP candidates displayed a noxious mix of belligerent posturing and stunning ignorance. Representative Michele Bachmann of Minnesota mistakenly praised China's regulatory framework and warned against Hezbollah's role in Cuba. Representative Ron Paul of Texas insisted that the global economy could be fixed by a return to the gold standard. Former Representative Newt Gingrich of Georgia became obsessed with the minute chances of an electromagnetic pulse targeting the United States, even as he disputed the actual threats posed by climate change. The business executive Herman Cain repeatedly flubbed questions on China, Israel, and Libya and proudly defended his ignorance in interviews, explaining that it was irrelevant whether or not a candidate knew who the "president of Ubeki-beki-beki-beki-stan-stan" was.

Compared with this crew during the primaries, Romney sounded reasonable. After securing the nomination, however, his musings lost focus. Romney's primary foreign policy criticism of Obama dealt not with any actual policy dispute but with a vague tonal issue, represented by the president's alleged "apology tour" around the world. Romney claimed that Russia was the number one geopolitical threat to the United States, a statement 25 years out of date. And at various points during the campaign, Romney insulted the Japanese, the Italians, the Spanish, the British, and the Palestinians. His own campaign advisers repeatedly complained that he never engaged deeply on international affairs. The few times that he did talk about foreign policy—in reference to the case of the Chinese civil rights activist Chen Guangcheng; during his July overseas trip to the United Kingdom, Israel, and Poland; and in the aftermath of the attacks on U.S. installations in Cairo and Benghazi—Romney used rhetoric that was ham-handed and politicized. And in picking Representative Paul Ryan (R-Wis.) to be his running mate, Romney guaranteed that his ticket would have the least foreign policy gravitas of any GOP presidential campaign in 60 years.

The 2012 election was the nadir of the GOP's decadelong descent. By the time Romney was selected as the nominee,

Republicans had come to talk about foreign policy almost entirely as an offshoot of domestic politics or ideology. What passed for discussion consisted of a series of tactical gestures designed to appease various constituencies in the party rather than responses to actual issues in U.S. relations with the world. The resulting excess of unchecked pablum and misinformation depressed not only outside observers but also many of the more seasoned members of the Republican foreign policy community who took the subject seriously. This palpable disdain of old GOP foreign policy hands helped further tarnish the Republican brand.

Increasingly, moreover, the Republican rhetoric clashed with the instincts of the public at large. Most Americans have always been reluctant to use force except in the service of vital interests, and a decade of war and recession had reinforced such feelings. A 2009 Pew survey showed that isolationist sentiments had reached an all-time high in the United States, and a 2012 PIPA (Program on International Policy Attitudes) poll found that Americans would strongly prefer to cut defense spending rather than Medicare or Social Security. A 2012 Pew survey noted that "defending against terrorism and strengthening the military are given less priority today than over the course of the past decade," and the 2012 Chicago Council on Global Affairs survey showed "a strong desire to move on from a decade of war, scale back spending, and avoid major new military entanglements." The Chicago survey also showed that independents had drifted toward Democrats and away from Republicans on most major foreign policy issues. As the GOP's rhetoric was tacking hawkish, in other words, a war-weary public was moving in the opposite direction.

The Obama administration exploited this divergence and pushed its foreign policy advantage throughout the 2012 campaign. In response to the malapropisms of the GOP primary, Vice President Joseph Biden started taunting Republican challengers, noting, "There's a minimum threshold any man or woman has to cross on national security and foreign policy for the American people to think you're remotely eligible to be president. And these guys have a long way to go." At the Democratic National Convention, speaker after speaker gleefully mocked the GOP's ignorance and hyperbole about the rest of the world. The administration could weather its own shortcomings because it knew how the American people would judge the two parties relative to each other: the Republicans were responsible for getting the United States stuck in Afghanistan and Iraq; the Democrats were responsible for moving to close out both wars and killing Osama bin Laden.

HOW TO GET BACK ON TRACK

It is conceivable that major screwups during Obama's second term could hand the advantage on foreign policy back to the Republicans without any effort of their own, but the reverse is more likely. Every additional year the party is locked out of the executive branch, the experience and skills of GOP foreign-policy makers will atrophy, while those of their Democratic counterparts will grow. It took the Democratic Party a generation to heal politically from the foreign policy scars of Vietnam and several years in office during the Clinton administration to develop new cadres of competent midcareer professionals. And public inattention to the subject doesn't help, offering few major opportunities for rebranding. So the GOP has its work cut out for it.

The key to moving forward is for Republicans to stop acting like hedgehogs and start thinking like foxes again, moving beyond crude single-minded objectives and relearning flexibility and nuance. They need to quit overhyping threats and demanding military solutions. After 9/11, the political logic for threat inflation was clear: politicians would be punished far more for downplaying a real security threat than for exaggerating a false one. But the GOP has taken this calculation too far and twisted it to serve other party interests.

Republicans continually attempt to justify extremely high levels of defense spending, for example, on the grounds that the United States supposedly faces greater threats now than during the Cold War. Romney claimed during the campaign that the world was more "dangerous, destructive, chaotic" than ever before. And Republican hawks warn that Armageddon will ensue if defense expenditures fall below four percent of GDP, even though they are vague about the connection between such an abstract figure and actual defense policy challenges.

A reality check is necessary. Precisely because Republican presidents during the Cold War took the Soviet threat seriously, they were careful not to escalate tensions needlessly. Today's threats may be more numerous and varied, but even combined, they are significantly smaller and less grave. As Micah Zenko and Michael Cohen have argued in these pages, long-term trends suggest that the world has become more, not less, safe for the United States over the past decade. U.S. deaths from terrorism are declining, and even with the global financial crisis, the world has not become more conflictual.

This is not to say that the United States should let its guard down. For Republicans, however, the political costs of overhyping threats now exceed the benefits. To echo Montesquieu, useless warnings weaken necessary warnings. Since the knee-jerk Republican response has been to call for military action anywhere and everywhere trouble breaks out, the American people have tuned out the GOP's alarmist rhetoric. It will be hard for any leader to mobilize a war-weary public into taking even necessary military action in the near future, and the GOP's constant crying of wolf will make this task much harder. A good grand strategy prioritizes threats and interests, and that is a habit the Republicans need to relearn.

The GOP must also develop a better appreciation for the full spectrum of foreign policy tools and stop talking only about military action. Indeed, George W. Bush's greatest foreign policy accomplishments came not in the military realm but in rethinking economic statecraft. He signed more free-trade agreements than any other president. Through the Millennium Challenge Corporation and the President's Emergency Plan for AIDS Relief, the Bush administration devised innovative ways of advancing U.S. interests and values abroad. In developing the architecture for improved financial coercion, the administration paved the way for the sanctions that are now crippling Iran's economy. Force can be an essential tool of statecraft, but it should rarely be the first tool used, and sometimes it can be most effective if never used at all. Republicans understand the power of the free market at home; they need to revive their enthusiasm for the power of the market abroad, as well.

Finally, Republicans need to avoid the problem of rhetorical blowbackbeing ensnared in unwanted commitments as the result of the use of absolutistic foreign policy language. Being out of power, the GOP is judged by its words rather than by its actions. And black-and-white statements on issues such as immigration, antiterrorism, and multilateralism only delegitimize the party. The best foreign policy presidents were able to combine the appealing rhetorical vision of an American world order with the realistic recognition that international relations is messier in practice than in theory.

George H. W. Bush was able to build a broad multilateral coalition, including the United Nations, to fight Iraq because he both took diplomacy seriously and could deploy the implicit threat of acting outside un auspices. Too many of his successors in the party, however, have embraced a "my way or the highway" approach to friends and allies. Their logic is that the rest of the world is attracted to strength, clarity, and resolve, and so if the United States projects those qualities, all will be well. But this bandwagoning logic has little basis in reality, and if anything, in recent years the rest of the world has seemed to be balancing against the GOP. A BBC poll of the populations of ten close U.S. allies during the campaign revealed that respondents preferred Obama to Romney by an average of 45 percentage points. Strength, clarity, and resolve are important foreign policy virtues, obviously, but so are an appreciation of complexity and the ability to compromise and play well with others, qualities that have been in short supply on the Republican side of the aisle recently.

TOWARD 2016

The Republican Party has a long and distinguished foreign policy lineage that currently lies in tatters. The ghosts of Iraq haunt the GOP's foreign policy mandarins, and the antics of right-wing pundits and politicians have further delegitimized the party. As a result, the GOP has frittered away a partisan advantage in foreign policy and national security that took half a century to accumulate.

Absent an Obama foreign policy fiasco—a real one that commands the country's attention, not the sort of trumped-up ones that resonate only on Fox News and in the fever swamps of the Republican base—the only way to repair the damage will be for the GOP to take foreign policy seriously again, in Congress and in the 2016 election. This does not mean railing against the isolationists in the party; in truth, their numbers are small. Nor does it mean purging the neoconservatives or any other ideological faction; no group has a lock on sense or wisdom, and there will and should be vigorous policy debate within both parties.

Rather, it means rejecting the ideological absolutism that has consumed the GOP's foreign policy rhetoric in recent years. It means recognizing that foreign policy has nonmilitary dimensions as well as military ones. And it means focusing on the threats and priorities that matter, rather than hyping every picayune concern. Most of all, it means that Republican politicians need to start caring about foreign policy because it is important, not because it is a cheap way to rally their supporters. The GOP has a venerated tradition of foreign policy competence; it is long past time to discover that tradition anew.

DANIEL W. DREZNER is Professor of International Politics at the Fletcher School of Law and Diplomacy at Tufts University and the editor of *Avoiding Trivia: The Role of Strategic Planning in American Foreign Policy*. Follow him on Twitter @dandrezner.

Getting the GOP's Groove Back

Bret Stephens   MARCH/APRIL 2013

Republican presidential nominee Mitt Romney walks across the tarmac at the airport in Des Moines, Iowa October 26, 2012.

I t is the healthy habit of partisans on the losing side of a U.S. presidential election to spend some time reflecting on the reasons for their defeat. And it is the grating habit of partisans on the winning side to tell the losers how they might have done better. Most of their advice is self-serving, none of it is solicited, and little of it is ever heeded. Yet still people pile on.

So it has been following Mitt Romney's defeat by President Barack Obama in last November's election. On domestic policy, pundits have instructed Republicans to moderate their positions on social issues and overcome their traditional opposition to higher taxes. On foreign policy, they are telling them to abandon their alleged preference for military solutions over diplomatic ones, as well as their reflexive hostility to multilateral institutions, their Cold War mentality toward Russia, their "denialism" on climate change, their excessive deference to right-wing Israelis, and so on. Much of this advice is based on caricature, and the likelihood of any of it having the slightest impact on the GOP's leadership or rank and file is minimal: the United States does not have a competitive two-party system so that one party can define for the other the terms of reasonable disagreement.

Put aside, then, fantasies about saving the GOP from itself or restoring the statesmanlike ways of George H. W. Bush, Ronald Reagan, Richard Nixon, or Dwight Eisenhower (all of whom were derided as foreign policy dunces or extremists when they held office). Instead, take note of the more consequential foreign policy debate now taking shape within the heart of the conservative movement itself. This is the debate between small-government and big-military conservatives. Until recently, the two camps had few problems traveling together. Yet faced with the concrete political choices raised by last year's budget sequester—which made large cuts in nondefense discretionary spending contingent on equally large cuts in the Pentagon's budget—the coalition has begun to show signs of strain.

On the one side, Republican leaders such as Senator John McCain of Arizona have effectively conceded that higher tax rates are a price worth paying to avoid further defense cuts. On the other, one finds politicians such as Senator Johnny Isakson of Georgia, who, when asked in 2010 about what government programs should get cut, said, "There's not a government program that shouldn't be under scrutiny, and that begins with the Department of Defense." However one may feel about these differences, it is important to understand each side as it understands itself. Then, perhaps, it might be possible to see how the differences can be bridged.

LAND OF LIBERTY—OR LIBERATORS?

For big-military conservatives, a supremely powerful U.S. military isn't just vital to the national interest; it defines what the

Republican presidential nominee Mitt Romney walks across the tarmac at the airport in Des Moines, Iowa October 26, 2012.

United States is. Part of this stance might owe to circumstantial factors, such as a politician's military background or large military constituency. But it is also based on an understanding of the United States as a liberator—a country that won its own freedom and then, through the possession and application of overwhelming military might, won and defended the freedom of others, from Checkpoint Charlie to the demilitarized zone on the Korean Peninsula.

This is a heroic view of the United States' purpose in the world—and an expensive one. It implies that if freedom isn't being actively advanced in the world, it risks wobbling to a standstill and even falling down, like a rider peddling a bicycle too slowly. It is also a view that is not unfriendly to at least some parts of a big-government agenda and certainly not to the de facto industrial policy that is the Pentagon's procurement system.

On the other side are those conservatives who, while not depreciating the United States' historic role as a liberator, mainly cherish its domestic tradition of liberty—above all, liberty from the burdens of excessive federal debt, taxation, regulation, and intrusion.

These Republicans are by no means hostile to the military, and most believe it constitutes one of the few truly legitimate functions of government. Still, they tend to view the Pentagon as another overgrown and wasteful government bureaucracy. Some have also drawn the lesson from the wars in Afghanistan and Iraq that well-meaning attempts to reengineer foreign societies will succumb to the law of unintended consequences just as frequently as well-meaning attempts to use government to improve American society do. Far from being a heroic view of the United States' role, theirs is a more prudential, and perhaps more parochial, one. It also contains a sneaking sympathy for Obama's refrain that the United States needs to do less nation building abroad and more at home, even if these conservatives differ sharply with the president on the matter of means.

The differences between these two groups are ones that most Republicans would gladly paper over for the party's long-term political good. Republicans fear that Obama's ultimate political ambition is to break the back of the modern GOP, and the defense budget is the ultimate wedge issue to do the job. Republican leaders understand this and will do what they can to hold their party together. Small-government conservatives don't want to turn the Republican Party into a rump faction, capable of winning elections at the congressional or state level but locked out of the presidency. And big-military conservatives aren't eager to become an appendage of big-government liberalism, in the way that Blue Dog Democrats were instruments of the Reagan agenda in the 1980s.

Yet the philosophical differences between the two camps run deep—and may soon run deeper. Ask a big-military conservative to name the gravest long-term threat to U.S. security, and his likely answer will be Iran, or perhaps China. These countries are classic strategic adversaries, for which military calculations inevitably play a large role. By contrast, ask a small-government conservative to name the chief threat, and he will probably say Europe, which has now become a byword among conservatives for everything they fear may yet beset the United States: too much unionization, low employment rates, permanently high taxes, politically entrenched beneficiaries of state largess, ever-rising public debts, and so on.

In the ideal conservative universe, avoiding a European destiny and facing up to the threat of Iran and other states would not be an either-or proposition. As most conservatives see it, supply-side tax cuts spur economic growth, reduce the overall burden of debt, increase federal tax revenues, and thus fund defense budgets adequate for the United States' global strategic requirements. This policy prescription may look like a fantasy, but it has worked before. "Our true choice is not between tax reduction, on the one hand, and the avoidance of large federal deficits on the other. It is increasingly clear that no matter what party is in power, so long as our national security needs keep rising, an economy hampered by restrictive tax rates will never produce enough revenues to balance our budget—just as it will never produce enough jobs or enough profits." That was President John F. Kennedy speaking to the Economic Club of New York in 1962. Following the Kennedy tax cut (enacted in 1964), federal tax receipts roughly doubled over six years and military spending rose by some 25 percent, yet defense spending as a share of GDP rose only modestly and never went above ten percent.

Kennedy's words could have just as easily been spoken by Reagan. The problem for conservatives, however, is that neither Kennedy nor Reagan is president today. In the world as it is, Obama has been handily reelected, Democrats maintain control of the Senate, tax rates are going up on higher incomes, and the Supreme Court has turned back the central legal challenge to the Affordable Care Act. What Republicans might be able to achieve politically remains to be seen, although it will be limited. But it is not too soon for the party to start thinking about how it might resolve some of its internal policy tensions, including on foreign policy.

DISASTROUS OSCILLATIONS

Henry Kissinger once observed that U.S. foreign policy in the twentieth century was characterized by "disastrous oscillations between overcommitment and isolation." The oscillation was especially pronounced for Republicans in the first half of the century—from President Theodore Roosevelt's Great White Fleet of 1907–9 to Secretary of State Charles Evans Hughes' Washington Naval Treaty in 1922 and from Senator Robert Taft's isolationism before World War II to Senator Arthur Vandenberg's 1945 conversion to internationalism—although the internal differences became much less pronounced in the second half. Now that the pendulum appears to be swinging again, Republicans have an interest in seeing that it doesn't do so wildly.

How to do that? Every type of persuasion—moral, political, policy—carries with it the temptation of extremes. Contrary to the stereotype, big-military conservatives (along with neoconservatives) do not want to bomb every troublesome country into submission, or rebuild the U.S. armed forces to their 1960s proportions, or resume the Cold War with Russia. Nor is the problem that big-military conservatives somehow fail to appreciate the limits of American power. Of course they appreciate the limits—but they also understand that the United States is nowhere near reaching them. Even at the height of the Iraq war, U.S. military spending constituted a smaller percentage of GDP (5.1 percent in 2008) than it did during the final full year of the Carter administration (six percent in 1980). The real limits of American power haven't been seriously tested since World War II.

Instead, the problem with big-military conservatives is that they fail to appreciate the limits of American will—of Washington's capacity to generate broad political support for military endeavors that since 9/11 have proved not only bloody and costly but also exceedingly lengthy. Taking a heroic view of America's purpose, these conservatives are tempted by a heroic view of the American public, emphasizing its willingness to pay any price and bear any burden. Yet there is a wide gap between what the United States can achieve abroad, given unlimited political support, and what Americans want to achieve, as determined by the ebb and flow of the political tides in a democracy innately reluctant to wage war.

Small-government conservatives have their own temptations when it comes to foreign policy. At the far extreme, there is the insipid libertarianism of Ron Paul, the former Texas representative, who has claimed that Marine detachments guarding U.S. embassies count as examples of military overstretch. Paul showed remarkable strength in the last GOP presidential primary and has, in his son Rand Paul, the junior senator from Kentucky, a politically potent heir.

Most small-government conservatives aren't about to jump off the libertarian cliff: they may want to reduce the United States' footprint in the world, at least for the time being, but they don't want to erase it completely. Yet the purism that tends to drive the small-government view of the world also has a way of obscuring its vision. "If we don't take defense spending seriously, it undermines our credibility on other spending issues," Mick Mulvaney, the conservative South Carolina congressman, told *Politico* in December.

The heart of the United States' spending issue, however, has increasingly little to do with the defense budget (which constituted 19 percent of overall federal outlays in 2012, down from 49 percent in 1962) and increasingly more to do with entitlement programs (62 percent in 2012, up from 31 percent half a century ago). Just as the Obama administration cannot hope to erase the federal deficit by raising taxes on the rich but wants to do so anyway out of a notion of social justice, small-government conservatives cannot hope to contain runaway spending through large cuts to the defense budget. But ideological blinders get in the way.

More broadly, small-government conservatives are too often tempted to treat small government as an end in itself, not as a means to achieve greater opportunity and freedom. They make a fetish of thrift at the expense of prosperity. They fancy that a retreat from the United States' global commitments could save lives without storing trouble. The record of the twentieth century tells a different story. Republicans should not wish to again become the party of such isolationists as Taft and Charles Lindbergh.

Bret Stephens

A CONSERVATIVE BALANCE

Fortunately, there is a happy medium. It's not what goes today under the name "realism"—a term of considerable self-flattery and negligible popular appeal. Republicans, in particular, will never stand for any kind of foreign policy that lacks a clear moral anchor. And Americans would not take well to a would-be Richelieu at the State Department. As it is, the GOP does not need a total makeover; what it needs is a refurbished modus vivendi between small-government and big-military conservatives, two sides that need not become antagonists and have valuable things to teach each other.

Small-government conservatives, for their part, can teach their big-military friends that the Pentagon doesn't need more money. What it needs desperately is a functional procurement system. The costs of U.S. jet fighters, for example, have skyrocketed: the F-4 Phantom, introduced in 1960, cost $16 million (in inflation-adjusted 2010 dollars) per plane, excluding research and development, whereas the equivalent figure for the F-35 Lightning II, in development now, is $120 million. The result is an underequipped air force that invests billions of dollars for the research-and-development costs of planes, such as the B-2 bomber and the F-22 fighter, that it can afford to procure only in inadequate numbers. The result is not just the ordinary waste, fraud, and abuse of any bureaucracy but also deep and lasting damage to the country's ability to project power and wage war.

Another lesson small-government conservatives have to offer is that nobody hates a benefactor as much as his beneficiary. From Somalia to Afghanistan, conservatives should look far more skeptically at military ventures in which the anticipated payoff is gratitude. Americans should go to war for the sake of their security, interests, and values. But they should never enter a popularity contest they are destined to lose.

Small-government conservatives also realize that Americans will stomach long wars only when national survival is clearly at stake. Since modern counterinsurgency is time-intensive by nature, the public should look askance at future counterinsurgency operations. Although he later disavowed his own words, former Defense Secretary Robert Gates was largely right when he told West Point cadets in 2011 that "any future defense secretary who advises the president to again send a big American land army into Asia or into the Middle East or Africa should 'have his head examined,' as General MacArthur so delicately put it." That's not because the wars are unwinnable from a military standpoint. It's because they are unfinishable from a political one.

Finally, those in the small-government camp understand that unlike authoritarian states, democratic ones will not indefinitely sustain large militaries in the face of prolonged economic stagnation or contraction. Except in moments of supreme emergency, when it comes to a choice, butter always beats guns. Big-military conservatives, therefore, cannot stay indifferent to issues of long-term economic competitiveness and the things that sustain it, not least of which is a government that facilitates wealth creation at home, promotes free trade globally, is fundamentally friendly to immigrants, and seeks to live within its means.

Then there are the things big-military conservatives can teach their small-government friends. First, they should make clear that a robust military is a net economic asset to the United States. A peaceful, trading, and increasingly free and prosperous world has been sustained for over six decades thanks in large part to a U.S. military with the power to make good on U.S. guarantees and deter real (or would-be) aggressors. And although the small-government purist might dismiss as corporate welfare the jobs, skills, and technology base that the so-called military-industrial complex supports, there are some industries that no great power can allow to wither or move offshore.

Big-military conservatives also correctly argue that a substantially weaker U.S. military will ultimately incur its own long-term economic costs. Former Secretary of Defense Donald Rumsfeld was right when he said that "weakness is provocative." China's ambition to establish what amounts to a modern-day Greater East

Asia Co-prosperity Sphere may ultimately succeed unless places such as Taiwan, Vietnam, and the Philippines can be reasonably sure that the United States will serve as a regional military counterweight to China's growing navy. Much the same may go for Iran's efforts to become the Middle East's dominant player, especially if its neighbors—not just Afghanistan and Iraq but also small states such as Bahrain and Kuwait—ose their remaining faith in U.S. security guarantees. That would go double should Iran acquire a nuclear weapons capability.

As big-military conservatives also know, shrinking the defense budget is a costly short-term solution to a difficult long-term problem. Small-government conservatives imagine that the United States can stomach steep temporary defense cuts to help bring deficits into line. But as European countries have belatedly discovered, without structural reforms, the overspending problem remains even after defense budgets have been slashed. The result is a continent that is nearly bankrupt and nearly defenseless at the same time.

Finally, small-government conservatives need to remember that there is no reliable guarantor of global order besides the United States. When the United Kingdom realized in 1947 that it could no longer afford to honor its security commitments to Greece and Turkey, it could at least look westward to the United States, which was prepared to shoulder those responsibilities. But when the United States looks westward, it sees only China. President Abraham Lincoln's "last, best hope" remains what it always was— perhaps more so, given the deep economic disarray in other corners of the developed world.

These observations ought to remind Republicans about the necessity of preponderant U.S. power. But they also ought to remind them that U.S. power will be squandered when it isn't used decisively, something that in turn requires great discrimination given Americans' reluctance to support protracted military actions. Ultimately, there are few things so damaging to countries as large and wasted efforts.

KEEPING NIGHTMARES AT BAY

In retooling its foreign policy, the Republican Party should heed lessons from both types of conservatives. What does this mean in practice? Consider China, where an atavistic nationalism, emboldened by an increasingly modern military, threatens to overtake the rational economic decision-making that largely characterized the tenures of Deng Xiaoping and Jiang Zemin. U.S. policymakers need to restrain the former and encourage the latter.

But labeling Beijing a "currency manipulator" and raising trade barriers against it, as Romney proposed to do from day one of his administration, will have the opposite effect. Modern China is often compared with Wilhelmine Germany because of its regional ambitions, and in many ways the comparison is apt. But for now, China remains more of a competitor than an outright adversary, and one that is increasingly aware of its political brittleness and economic vulnerability.

That status means that the United States can create a policy that is a genuine synthesis between small-government and big-military conservatism. Big-military conservatives are right to worry about China's growing military adventurism and right to advocate a larger overall U.S. naval presence in the region and arms sales to skittish allies such as Taiwan. But that is only one side of the coin. The other is the opportunity to demonstrate to Beijing that an adversarial relationship is not inevitable: that the United States will desist from constantly thwarting efforts by Chinese companies to expand overseas and that Washington is interested in deepening economic cooperation with China, not fighting endless trade skirmishes. The United States should want China to become an economic colossus—so long as it doesn't also become a regional bully. That differs from the Obama administration's policy, which has been mostly a muddle: a military "pivot" that so far has been more rhetorical than substantive, as well as a pattern of engaging in unhelpful, albeit relatively minor, trade skirmishes with Beijing.

Now take Iran, where the Obama administration has combined two feckless policy options—diplomacy and sanctions—to produce the most undesirable outcome possible: diminished U.S. regional credibility, a greater likelihood of U.S. or Israeli military action, and an Iran that has more incentive to accelerate its nuclear program than to stop it. Along with most left-leaning liberals, many small-government conservatives instinctively look askance at the thought of military action against Iran. More broadly, they would like to reduce U.S. involvement in the Middle East as much as possible, something the discovery of vast domestic U.S. energy reserves has made conceivable for the first time in decades.

Yet the surest way to embroil the United States in intractable Middle Eastern problems for another generation is to acquiesce to an Iranian nuclear capability. Among the many reasons why it's a bad idea to try to contain a nuclear Iran is that containment entails two things most Americans don't like: long-term effort and high cost. The United States has a strong stake in a Middle East that is no longer the focus of its security concerns. But getting there depends on reducing the region's centrality as a source of both energy and terrorism. A nuclear Iran would make that goal far less achievable, which means that a credible policy of prevention is essential. Obama also claims to believe in prevention, but the administration's mixed messages on the viability of military strikes have undercut its credibility.

Finally, there is the Arab Spring, which seemed at its outset to be a vindication of President George W. Bush's "freedom agenda" but has, after two years, come to seem more like a rebuke of it. The results of elections in Gaza, Tunis, Rabat, and Cairo are powerful reminders that the words "liberal" and "democracy" don't always travel together, that the essence of freedom is the right to choose political and social options radically different from the standard American ones. In this sense, small-government conservatives, with their innate suspicion of any grand Washington project to reengineer the moral priorities of a society, are being proved right.

But like it or not, the United States will still have to deal with the consequences of the upheavals in the Middle East. It would be a fool's gambit for Washington to attempt, for example, to steer political outcomes in Cairo or once again roll the boulder up the hill of an Arab-Israeli peace settlement. At the same time, the United States maintains a powerful interest in making sure certain things do not happen. Among them: chemical munitions getting loose in Syria, the abrupt collapse of the Hashemite dynasty in Jordan, a direct confrontation between Israel and Egypt over the Sinai, and (further afield) the Taliban's return to Kabul.

Preventing those outcomes means taking on the negative task of keeping nightmare scenarios at bay, not the positive one of realizing a more progressive and tolerant world. Yet if conservatives of any stripe can agree on anything, it's that utopianism has no place in policymaking. And when it comes to foreign policy, the American people will ultimately reward not the party with the most ambitious vision but the party with the most sober and realistic one.

BRET STEPHENS is Deputy Editorial Page Editor and Foreign Affairs Columnist at The Wall Street Journal.

The Clinton Legacy

Michael Hirsh   MAY/JUNE 2013

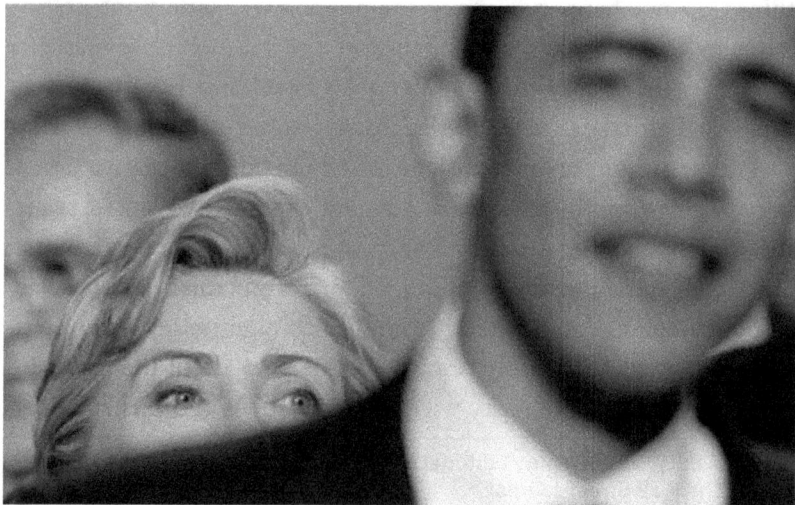

Overshadowed: Hillary Clinton, Washington, D.C., January 2007.

In late January, only a few days after his second inauguration, U.S. President Barack Obama delivered a surprisingly fond fare-well to his old political rival Hillary Clinton. Sitting for a joint interview with the outgoing secretary of state on *60 Minutes*, Obama lauded their "great collaboration." He continued: "I just wanted to have a chance to publicly say thank you, because I think Hillary will go down as one of the finest secretaries of state we've had."

The president had reason to be grateful. His Lincolnesque effort to create a team of rivals had paid off, thanks largely to Clinton's own efforts at reconciliation. During her four years in office, Clinton, displaying impressive humility and self-discipline for an ambitious politician, managed to put one of the fiercest presidential primary battles in U.S. history behind her. Once the runaway favorite to win her party's nomination, Clinton transformed herself into a loyal messenger and passionate defender of the Obama faith.

But neither Obama's gratitude nor Clinton's graciousness should cloud history's judgment. By any standard measure of diplomacy, Clinton will be remembered as a highly competent secretary of state, but not a great one. Despite her considerable star power around the world, her popularity at home, and her reputation for being on the right side of most issues, she left office without a signature doctrine, strategy, or diplomatic triumph. It is a stretch to include Clinton in the company of John Quincy Adams, George Marshall, Dean Acheson, and Henry Kissinger—some of the great secretaries of state who profoundly changed U.S. foreign policy. Although she has avoided all talk of what comes next, it may well be that Clinton's tenure as diplomat in chief will someday be viewed as a steppingstone to the presidency, as it was for Thomas Jefferson and Adams.

It is not that Clinton can't point to some notable and enduring achievements. Because of her worldwide popularity and tireless travel—she set a new record for a secretary of state by visiting 112 countries—Clinton helped undo the damage that the habitual unilateralism of the George W. Bush administration had done to the global image of the United States. As Clinton put it to me in a 2010 interview, "My big-picture commitment is to restore American leadership, and I think that's about as big a job as you can get. And everything I've done is in furtherance of that."

This goal was shared by the whole administration. In his first term, Obama faced the daunting task of winding down two major wars in Iraq and Afghanistan. He needed to contend with the reduction in U.S. leverage and prestige following the strategic mistakes and economic collapse of the Bush years. As a result, the administration was keen on emphasizing the "soft" diplomacy of U.S. image building and values promotion over "hard," or coercive, diplomacy, which necessitates direct involvement in conflicts.

Despite her frustrations with a White House that often did not heed her advice, Clinton elevated this effort to levels unseen in

Michael Hirsh

previous administrations. Indeed, her most lasting legacy will likely be the way that she thrust soft diplomacy to the forefront of U.S. foreign policy. By speaking out about Internet freedom, women's rights, public health, and economic issues everywhere she went, Clinton sought to transcend traditional government-to-government contacts. She set out to create—or at least dramatically expand in scope—a new kind of people-to-people diplomacy, one designed to extend Washington's influence in an Internet-driven world in which popular uprisings, such as the Arab Spring, could quickly uproot the traditional relationships between governments.

Beyond that, Clinton often played the realist hawk in an administration that started with overconfidence about its president's transformational powers. In 2009, she allied with Defense Secretary Robert Gates to press for a 30,000-troop surge to address the chaos in Afghanistan, even though the president's instincts were for a far smaller escalation. Later that year, when Obama had nothing to show for offering an outstretched hand to Tehran (a policy that Clinton had encouraged), she prodded the president into imposing unprecedentedly severe sanctions on Iran. In 2011, she corralled a troupe of advisers, including Susan Rice, the U.S. ambassador to the United Nations, to convince Obama to support a NATO-led intervention in Libya. And it was Clinton's State Department that was mainly responsible for the administration's attempt at a strategic "pivot" to Asia, designed largely to counter China's growing influence. Clinton personally led the way with a historic trip that brought long-isolated Myanmar (also called Burma) into the fold of American partners, with a deft mix of realpolitik and democracy promotion. Clinton also became the caretaker of major relationships with other heads of state with whom the somewhat aloof U.S. president engaged only sporadically.

The effectiveness of Clinton's approach is as yet unclear. The outcome of the Arab Spring appears to be increasingly Islamist and anti-American, and among the legacies Clinton bequeathed to her successor, John Kerry, is a resurgent jihadist movement in the Arab world—including an al Qaeda that is "on the rise," as she admitted only days before her departure. U.S. relations are deteriorating with Pakistan and Russia, and it did not help that Clinton avoided involvement in direct negotiations with those countries over critical issues that divided them from Washington. Nevertheless, a global Pew Research Center poll and other international surveys have shown a substantial improvement in U.S. standing in world opinion, especially among Europeans. So there can be little doubt that Clinton restored some luster to an American brand badly tarnished by the previous administration.

GOING SOFT

Like George Shultz, Ronald Reagan's revered secretary of state, Clinton regularly stressed that diplomacy and economic development must go hand in hand. She preached that helping partner countries achieve social stability—built on progress on health, food security, and women's rights—would create stronger alliances and new paths to solving traditional foreign policy problems. In a January 2011 speech in Qatar, just as the early signs of the Arab Spring were starting to appear, Clinton issued what now looks like a prescient admonition to Arab leaders, taking them to task for failing to "build a future that your young people will believe in, stay for, and defend." She said that the Arab people had "grown tired of corrupt institutions and a stagnant political order," and she warned the regimes that their "foundations [were] sinking into the sand."

Clinton then took her message directly to the people in the countries she visited. She held regular town-hall meetings abroad, speaking not just to the international press but also to local citizens and local media, an approach that may have helped ease some anti-Americanism in Islamic countries (although few polls show it yet). "I think that really is new," her former policy-planning chief, the Princeton scholar Anne-Marie Slaughter, told me in a recent interview. "She's the one who kept saying, 'You've got to have government-to-government, government-to-people, and people-to-people contacts.' She's been very clear that the people of different countries are not just the object of policies; they are active agents of change and evolution. And, above all, of problem solving."

A test case for whether the Clinton model of diplomacy can work going forward may be the current turmoil in Egypt, where President Hosni Mubarak's successor, the Muslim Brotherhood's Mohamed Morsi, appears to be wavering in his commitment to democracy. Although Washington deals mainly with Morsi's government and the Egyptian military, the State Department has fostered ties between nongovernmental organizations in the United States and Egypt that focus on education and development. "One way to think about it is that because of her integrated framework, we always have someone to call," said Slaughter. "Mubarak fell and the Muslim Brotherhood is in power, but now we have contacts with women's groups, techies, and entrepreneurs through various programs. If diplomacy is building relationships that you can call on in a crisis, then she has developed the frame." Now, a power-grabbing Morsi finds himself under pressure to moderate his actions not just from U.S. government officials but also from grass-roots pro-democracy organizations supported or trained by Washington.

Even as she helped design the realpolitik pivot to Asia, Clinton also pushed this people-to-people approach with China. She promoted the 100,000 Strong Initiative, a program aimed at dramatically increasing the number of Americans studying at Chinese universities (ten times as many Chinese study in the United States). She emphasized economic development in Central and South Asia, where she sought to stabilize Afghanistan and counter Pakistani recalcitrance by proposing a "New Silk Road" that would promote new trade routes in order to induce Islamabad to cooperate more with Kabul. And when Obama announced in February his plan to negotiate a transatlantic free-trade pact with Europe, he was embracing a proposal pushed by his former secretary of state.

Yet in the end, although Clinton excelled at soft diplomacy, she shied away from the kind of hard diplomacy that traditionalists identify with foreign policy greatness. One thinks of Adams' authorship of the Monroe Doctrine and the Transcontinental Treaty with Spain, Acheson's aggressive championing of containment, Kissinger's shuttle diplomacy between the Arabs and the Israelis and his clever exploitation of the Sino-Soviet split. Some critics have interpreted Clinton's more modest agenda as stemming from political caution. In a recent assessment, the journalist David Rohde quoted a State Department official who suggested that Clinton's hesitation to get personally involved in conflicts was related to her future presidential ambitions.

Indeed, Clinton consistently avoided getting her hands dirty with direct mediation. She happily agreed to leave key negotiations in crisis spots to special envoys, charging George Mitchell with overseeing the Israeli-Palestinian portfolio and relying on Richard Holbrooke to bring about a political settlement in Afghanistan and Pakistan. She rarely stepped in as each of them failed to make much headway. Other pressing issues, such as North Korea's nuclear program, she simply put off. Her policy of "strategic patience" with North Korea, under which Washington refused to offer any new incentives to Pyongyang in the hopes of restarting nuclear disarmament talks, did not work. The problem festered for four years, and as soon as Clinton left office, the North Korean leader Kim Jong Un greeted her successor with yet another nuclear test.

It may be unfair to fault Clinton for the deadly attack on U.S. personnel in Benghazi, Libya, which occurred last September. Nonetheless, she became the first secretary of state to lose an ambassador in the field since Adolph Dubs was killed in 1979, while Cyrus Vance held the office. And Clinton does deserve some blame for what she herself admitted in Senate testimony about the incident: that she and her State Department colleagues were taken by surprise by the rise of new jihadist groups in Libya and the region. "We've got to have a better strategy," she said. "The Arab Spring has ushered in a time when al Qaeda is on the rise." Clinton thus appeared to concede what the former Republican presidential candidate Mitt Romney had relentlessly argued during the 2012 campaign: that the terrorist group responsible for 9/11 and its off-shoots are not close to being defeated.

In her farewell testimony, Clinton spoke of the "Pandora's box" of weapons flowing through countries in the Middle East and North Africa. And that Pandora's box may yield even worse ills on Kerry's watch. The post-Qaddafi chaos in Libya, the civil war in Syria, the emergence of a terrorist sanctuary in northern Mali—all these developments have taken the Obama administration by surprise. Some U.S. officials now fear that these countries could break up or turn into permanently strife-ridden lands that resemble the postcolonial countries of Africa, such as Somalia or the Democratic Republic of the Congo, where tribes and ethnic groups never stop warring even though the countries' borders remain superficially intact.

The spreading violence in the Middle East and North Africa could come to be seen as one of Clinton's grimmest legacies. It all but ensures that however much Kerry tries to focus on Asia, he will likely get pulled back into the Middle Eastern mire that the Obama administration's first-term national security team left him. Indeed, if any one situation demonstrates the potential costs of the administration's caution in the region, it is that in Syria, where the president's decision to avoid arming the rebels has struck critics as inaction in the face of a terrible humanitarian crisis and a conflict that could destabilize the entire region.

IMPROV DRAMA

On a number of critical issues, anything resembling a larger strategy was often hard to find in Obama's first term. In a recent conversation with me, Zbigniew Brzezinski, the dean of the Democratic national security establishment, criticized the administration's foreign policy for being "improvisational." To be fair, the improvisation was sometimes effective. In one case, Obama and Clinton barged into a meeting at the 2009 global climate change talks in Copenhagen and forced the Chinese president to agree to a nonbinding pact under which rich and poor countries alike pledged to curb their carbon emissions.

And last year, Clinton displayed cleverness and agility in negotiating the release of the Chinese dissident Chen Guangcheng, who had taken refuge in the U.S. embassy in Beijing. But those were rare instances of successful impromptu mediation.

At other times when Obama's foreign policy team was forced to act on its feet, the results were not as impressive. The administration failed to anticipate the increasingly Islamist bent of the countries whose regimes were ousted in the Arab Spring, and it has been slow in formulating a coordinated response to the abuses against democracy by Morsi and other Islamist leaders. Instead, Obama appears to be approaching Morsi in much the same realpolitik way he once dealt with Mubarak—paying lip service to democracy and human rights but essentially leaving Egypt's internal chaos to sort itself out. The democracy expert Larry Diamond told me in an interview that he saw "very little sign—to be blunt, no sign—of any coherent strategy to try to defend and sustain the very, very tentative democratic progress in Egypt or to . . . create a more facilitating environment." Clinton's State Department did not develop a strategic framework for addressing the Islamist middle phase that the Arab world appears to be undergoing on its way to modernization and democracy—a transition that was entirely predictable given Islam's traditionally dominant role in Arab society. In her final testimony before the Senate, commenting on the new wave of jihadism in the region, Clinton said, "We've got to get our act together." It was a helpless remark that recalled former U.S. Defense Secretary Donald Rumsfeld's notorious lament from a decade ago: "We lack the metrics to know if we are winning or losing the global war on terror."

Still, one must ask: Could any secretary of state realistically have done a better job grappling with such unexpected unrest? Probably not. "Anybody would be improvising now," Reuel Marc Gerecht, a conservative Middle East analyst, told me. "I wouldn't fault the administration too much." Clinton's defenders question how any overarching strategy could have addressed something as chaotic and complex as the Arab uprisings. James Steinberg, a former deputy secretary of state and former Clinton aide, has invoked the famous line attributed to the former Chinese leader Zhou Enlai, who, when asked in the 1970s about the significance of the French Revolution, supposedly replied, "It's too soon to tell." "Traditional ideas about grand strategy don't really capture the challenge of dealing with broad popular movements," Steinberg said to me in a recent interview. "It's less about a strategy and more about how do you position the U.S. to positively take advantage of it?"

It's a fair point. The diplomatic world keeps pining for the next George Kennan, someone who might sum up the country's overall mission in a strategic concept as simple as containment. But Kennan, in truth, had things relatively easy compared with today's policymakers. He faced a bipolar world consisting of two utterly opposed ideological systems and an adversary whose strengths and weaknesses could be analyzed in a static way. Twenty-first-century strategists confront a far more complex and multidimensional world, one in which a lone terrorist or hacker can threaten a superpower.

To its detractors, the Obama administration has looked consistently weak and indecisive in its response to the Arab Spring. But these critics generally fail to offer appealing alternatives. Obama and Clinton have had good reasons, for example, to avoid a large-scale intervention in Syria. After a decade of war, Washington cannot afford to look like it is interfering, yet again, in a region that has already seen far too much Western meddling. Obama's concerns that U.S.-supplied weapons would find their way to jihadist militants are equally valid.

WHO IS OBAMA'S KISSINGER?

For four years, Clinton had to spend a lot of time and energy simply making herself heard on Pennsylvania Avenue. It was often as hard for her to persuade the White House to take her advice as it was to deal with foreign governments. Although Clinton sometimes got her way and served as the administration's public face,

Obama and a coterie of devoted national security aides—including Denis McDonough, Obama's former deputy national security adviser and now the White House chief of staff—were the main authors of the administration's foreign policy. And despite Obama's kind parting words, Clinton never really developed warm personal ties to her former rival. This gap made her job much harder, since in Washington, real power is measured in presidential face time, and a close relationship between the White House and the State Department is critical to a secretary of state's success. (Acheson, fortunate enough to be Harry Truman's alter ego, used to say that he had "a constituency of one.")

Her distance from Obama, by most accounts, was a source of frustration and disappointment for Clinton, especially at the beginning of her tenure. She likely felt shortchanged by the difference between her original job description and the reality that emerged. In the fall of 2008, when Obama surprised Clinton by asking her to take the job, he told her that he had his hands full with the collapsing economy and needed someone of her global stature to take care of foreign policy. The implication was that Clinton would be the dominant figure.

But that never happened. Early in Obama's first term, a senior aide to Clinton told me that "the biggest issue still unresolved in the Obama administration is, can there be more than one star?" The answer, it soon became clear, was no; the only star was going to be Obama himself. Despite his short tenure as a senator, Obama prided himself on his grass-roots knowledge of foreign affairs, having grown up partly in Indonesia with a foreign stepfather, and he had developed his own definite worldview. As the aide put it, "If you ask, 'Who is Barack Obama's Henry Kissinger?' the answer, of course, is that it's Barack Obama."

When Clinton did appear to get out ahead of the White House, she was quickly reined in. In 2009, Clinton hinted that she was developing a policy to unite the Arab autocracies in an anti-Tehran bloc, and she gave a speech calling for Arab regimes to join a Cold War–style "defense umbrella" to protect against Iran's nuclear program. *The New York Times* soon quoted a "senior White House official" as saying that Clinton was speaking for herself. That was the last mention of a defense umbrella. Later, she tentatively supported a CIA plan to arm the Syrian rebels, but Obama shot down that idea as well.

Clinton also suffered from the same problem that former Secretary of State Colin Powell confronted in George W. Bush's first term: the presence of an influential vice president who constituted a separate power center on foreign policy. In Powell's case, that was Dick Cheney; for Clinton, it was Joseph Biden, the deeply experienced former chair of the Senate Foreign Relations Committee.

In 2009, for example, top administration officials were split over how to handle the quagmire in Afghanistan. Biden counseled the president to scale down the U.S. presence there and rely on a policy of counterterrorism, carried out by special operations units and drone strikes. Although Clinton and Gates' call for a troop surge won the day, by 2012, Obama began siding with Biden and started accelerating the U.S. withdrawal. The Iraq withdrawal plan, too, was handed over to Biden and his team. A senior administration official described what happened at an early meeting in 2009: "All of sudden, Obama stopped. He said, 'Joe will do Iraq. Joe knows more about Iraq than anyone.'"

Despite the lack of a singular triumph to her name, however, there is a case to be made that the impact Clinton had on U.S. foreign policy will be felt long after she has left office. In an interview midway through her tenure, I asked Clinton how she assessed her effectiveness and why she hadn't "taken a big issue and totally owned it." She responded that she had "inherited such a range of problems and deficits across the world that it would be a luxury to say, 'I'm going to focus on this and this alone.'" Like Obama, Clinton set out to repair the damage that Bush had done to the country's stature around the world, and in that, she had some noteworthy success. As she put it, "We've worked very hard to restore relations with allies, and I think we've made a lot of progress in doing so . . . and frankly taking situations that had badly deteriorated, especially

Russia and China, and turning them around to be able to put them on a much more positive footing." Asked what she most enjoyed about the job, she replied, "A lot of it is not the headline stuff. It's the slow and steady progress that I think provides a much firmer footing for us."

Slow and steady progress is not necessarily the stuff of greatness. But it is valuable nonetheless, and it may be what, in the end, the world will remember most about Clinton's tenure as the country's top diplomat.

MICHAEL HIRSH is Chief Correspondent for *National Journal*.

Renewing American Leadership

Barack Obama JULY/AUGUST 2007

U.S. President Barack Obama celebrates on stage as confetti falls after his victory speech during his election rally in Chicago, November 6, 2012.

COMMON SECURITY FOR OUR COMMON HUMANITY

At moments of great peril in the last century, American leaders such as Franklin Roosevelt, Harry Truman, and John F. Kennedy managed both to protect the American people and to expand opportunity for the next generation. What is more, they ensured that America, by deed and example, led and lifted the world—that we stood for and fought for the freedoms sought by billions of people beyond our borders.

As Roosevelt built the most formidable military the world had ever seen, his Four Freedoms gave purpose to our struggle against fascism. Truman championed a bold new architecture to respond to the Soviet threat—one that paired military strength with the Marshall Plan and helped secure the peace and well-being of nations around the world. As colonialism crumbled and the Soviet Union achieved effective nuclear parity, Kennedy modernized our military doctrine, strengthened our conventional forces, and created the Peace Corps and the Alliance for Progress. They used our strengths to show people everywhere America at its best.

Today, we are again called to provide visionary leadership. This century's threats are at least as dangerous as and in some ways more complex than those we have confronted in the past. They come from weapons that can kill on a mass scale and from global terrorists who respond to alienation or perceived injustice with murderous nihilism. They come from rogue states allied to terrorists and from rising powers that could challenge both America and the international foundation of liberal democracy. They come from weak states that cannot control their territory or provide for their people. And they come from a warming planet that will spur new diseases, spawn more devastating natural disasters, and catalyze deadly conflicts.

To recognize the number and complexity of these threats is not to give way to pessimism. Rather, it is a call to action. These threats demand a new vision of leadership in the twenty-first century—a vision that draws from the past but is not bound by outdated thinking. The Bush administration responded to the unconventional attacks of 9/11 with conventional thinking of the past, largely viewing problems as state-based and principally amenable to military solutions. It was this tragically misguided view that led us into a war in Iraq that never should have been authorized and never should have been waged. In the wake of Iraq and Abu Ghraib, the world has lost trust in our purposes and our principles.

After thousands of lives lost and billions of dollars spent, many Americans may be tempted to turn inward and cede our leadership in world affairs. But this is a mistake we must not make. America cannot meet the threats of this century alone, and the world cannot meet them without America. We can neither retreat from the world nor try to bully it into submission. We must lead the world, by deed and by example.

Such leadership demands that we retrieve a fundamental insight of Roosevelt, Truman, and Kennedy—one that is truer now than ever before: the security and well-being of each and every American depend on the security and well-being of those who live beyond our borders. The mission of the United States is to provide global leadership grounded in the understanding that the world shares a common security and a common humanity.

The American moment is not over, but it must be seized anew. To see American power in terminal decline is to ignore America's great promise and historic purpose in the world. If elected president, I will start renewing that promise and purpose the day I take office.

MOVING BEYOND IRAQ

To renew American leadership in the world, we must first bring the Iraq war to a responsible end and refocus our attention on the broader Middle East. Iraq was a diversion from the fight against the terrorists who struck us on 9/11, and incompetent prosecution of the war by America's civilian leaders compounded the strategic blunder of choosing to wage it in the first place. We have now lost over 3,300 American lives, and thousands more suffer wounds both seen and unseen.

Our servicemen and servicewomen have performed admirably while sacrificing immeasurably. But it is time for our civilian leaders to acknowledge a painful truth: we cannot impose a military solution on a civil war between Sunni and Shiite factions. The best chance we have to leave Iraq a better place is to pressure these warring parties to find a lasting political solution. And the only effective way to apply this pressure is to begin a phased withdrawal of U.S. forces, with the goal of removing all combat brigades from Iraq by March 31, 2008—a date consistent with the goal set by the bipartisan Iraq Study Group. This redeployment could be temporarily suspended if the Iraqi government meets the security, political, and economic benchmarks to which it has committed. But we must recognize that, in the end, only Iraqi leaders can bring real peace and stability to their country.

At the same time, we must launch a comprehensive regional and international diplomatic initiative to help broker an end to the civil war in Iraq, prevent its spread, and limit the suffering of the Iraqi people. To gain credibility in this effort, we must make clear that we seek no permanent bases in Iraq. We should leave behind only a minimal over-the-horizon military force in the region to protect American personnel and facilities, continue training Iraqi security forces, and root out al Qaeda.

The morass in Iraq has made it immeasurably harder to confront and work through the many other problems in the region—and it has made many of those problems considerably more dangerous. Changing the dynamic in Iraq will allow us to focus our attention and influence on resolving the festering conflict between the Israelis and the Palestinians—a task that the Bush administration neglected for years.

For more than three decades, Israelis, Palestinians, Arab leaders, and the rest of the world have looked to America to lead the effort to build the road to a lasting peace. In recent years, they have all too often looked in vain. Our starting point must always be a clear and strong commitment to the security of Israel, our strongest ally in the region and its only established democracy. That commitment is all the more important as we contend with growing threats in the region—a strengthened Iran, a chaotic Iraq, the resurgence of al Qaeda, the reinvigoration of Hamas and Hezbollah. Now more than ever, we must strive to secure a lasting settlement of the conflict with two states living side by side in peace and security. To do so, we must help the Israelis identify and strengthen those partners who are truly committed to peace, while isolating those who seek conflict and instability. Sustained American leadership for peace and security will require patient effort and the personal commitment of the president of the United States. That is a commitment I will make.

Throughout the Middle East, we must harness American power to reinvigorate American diplomacy. Tough-minded diplomacy, backed by the whole range of instruments of American power—political, economic, and military—could bring success even when dealing with long-standing adversaries such as Iran and Syria. Our policy of issuing threats and relying on intermediaries to curb Iran's nuclear program, sponsorship of terrorism, and regional aggression is failing. Although we must not rule out using military force, we should not hesitate to talk directly to Iran. Our diplomacy should aim to raise the cost for Iran of continuing its nuclear program by applying tougher sanctions and increasing pressure from its key trading partners. The world must work to stop Iran's uranium-enrichment program and prevent Iran from acquiring nuclear weapons. It is far too dangerous to have nuclear weapons in the hands of a radical theocracy. At the same time, we must show Iran—and especially the Iranian people—what could be gained from fundamental change: economic engagement, security assurances, and diplomatic relations. Diplomacy combined with pressure could also reorient Syria away from its radical agenda to a more moderate stance—which could, in turn, help stabilize Iraq, isolate Iran, free Lebanon from Damascus' grip, and better secure Israel.

REVITALIZING THE MILITARY

To renew American leadership in the world, we must immediately begin working to revitalize our military. A strong military is, more than anything, necessary to sustain peace. Unfortunately, the U.S. Army and the Marine Corps, according to our military leaders, are facing a crisis. The Pentagon cannot certify a single army unit within the United States as fully ready to respond in the event of a new crisis or emergency beyond Iraq; 88 percent of the National Guard is not ready to deploy overseas.

We must use this moment both to rebuild our military and to prepare it for the missions of the future. We must retain the capacity to swiftly defeat any conventional threat to our country and our vital interests. But we must also become better prepared to put boots on the ground in order to take on foes that fight asymmetrical and highly adaptive campaigns on a global scale.

We should expand our ground forces by adding 65,000 soldiers to the army and 27,000 marines. Bolstering these forces is about more than meeting quotas. We must recruit the very best and invest in their capacity to succeed. That means providing our servicemen and servicewomen with first-rate equipment, armor, incentives, and training—including in foreign languages and other critical skills. Each major defense program should be reevaluated in light of current needs, gaps in the field, and likely future threat scenarios. Our military will have to rebuild some capabilities and transform others. At the same time, we need to commit sufficient funding to enable the National Guard to regain a state of readiness.

Enhancing our military will not be enough. As commander in chief, I would also use our armed forces wisely. When we send our men and women into harm's way, I will clearly define the mission, seek out the advice of our military commanders, objectively evaluate intelligence, and ensure that our troops have the resources and the support they need. I will not hesitate to use force, unilaterally if necessary, to protect the American people or our vital interests whenever we are attacked or imminently threatened.

We must also consider using military force in circumstances beyond self-defense in order to provide for the common security that underpins global stability—to support friends, participate in stability and reconstruction operations, or confront mass atrocities. But when we do use force in situations other than self-defense, we should make every effort to garner the clear support and participation of others—as President George H. W. Bush did when we led the effort to oust Saddam Hussein from Kuwait in 1991. The consequences of forgetting that lesson in the context of the current conflict in Iraq have been grave.

HALTING THE SPREAD OF NUCLEAR WEAPONS

To renew American leadership in the world, we must confront the most urgent threat to the security of America and the world—the spread of nuclear weapons, material, and technology and the risk that a nuclear device will fall into the hands of terrorists. The explosion of one such device would bring catastrophe, dwarfing the devastation of 9/11 and shaking every corner of the globe.

As George Shultz, William Perry, Henry Kissinger, and Sam Nunn have warned, our current measures are not sufficient to meet the nuclear threat. The nonproliferation regime is being challenged, and new civilian nuclear programs could spread the means to make nuclear weapons. Al Qaeda has made it a goal to bring a "Hiroshima" to the United States. Terrorists need not build a nuclear weapon from scratch; they need only steal or buy a weapon or the material to assemble one. There is now highly enriched uranium—some of it poorly secured—sitting in civilian nuclear facilities in over 40 countries around the world. In the former Soviet Union, there are approximately 15,000–16,000 nuclear weapons and stockpiles of uranium and plutonium capable of making another 40,000 weapons—all scattered across 11 time zones. People have already been caught trying to smuggle nuclear material to sell on the black market.

As president, I will work with other nations to secure, destroy, and stop the spread of these weapons in order to dramatically reduce the nuclear dangers for our nation and the world. America must lead a global effort to secure all nuclear weapons and material at vulnerable sites within four years—the most effective way to prevent terrorists from acquiring a bomb.

This will require the active cooperation of Russia. Although we must not shy away from pushing for more democracy and accountability in Russia, we must work with the country in areas of common interest—above all, in making sure that nuclear weapons and material are secure. We must also work with Russia to update and scale back our dangerously outdated Cold War nuclear postures and de-emphasize the role of nuclear weapons. America must not rush to produce a new generation of nuclear warheads. And we should take advantage of recent technological advances to build bipartisan consensus behind ratification of the Comprehensive

Test Ban Treaty. All of this can be done while maintaining a strong nuclear deterrent. These steps will ultimately strengthen, not weaken, our security.

As we lock down existing nuclear stockpiles, I will work to negotiate a verifiable global ban on the production of new nuclear weapons material. We must also stop the spread of nuclear weapons technology and ensure that countries cannot build—or come to the brink of building—a weapons program under the auspices of developing peaceful nuclear power. That is why my administration will immediately provide $50 million to jump-start the creation of an International Atomic Energy Agency-controlled nuclear fuel bank and work to update the Nuclear Nonproliferation Treaty. We must also fully implement the law Senator Richard Lugar and I passed to help the United States and our allies detect and stop the smuggling of weapons of mass destruction throughout the world.

Finally, we must develop a strong international coalition to prevent Iran from acquiring nuclear weapons and eliminate North Korea's nuclear weapons program. Iran and North Korea could trigger regional arms races, creating dangerous nuclear flashpoints in the Middle East and East Asia. In confronting these threats, I will not take the military option off the table. But our first measure must be sustained, direct, and aggressive diplomacy—the kind that the Bush administration has been unable and unwilling to use.

COMBATING GLOBAL TERRORISM

To renew American leadership in the world, we must forge a more effective global response to the terrorism that came to our shores on an unprecedented scale on 9/11. From Bali to London, Baghdad to Algiers, Mumbai to Mombasa to Madrid, terrorists who reject modernity, oppose America, and distort Islam have killed and mutilated tens of thousands of people just this decade. Because this enemy operates globally, it must be confronted globally.

We must refocus our efforts on Afghanistan and Pakistan—the central front in our war against al Qaeda—so that we are confronting terrorists where their roots run deepest. Success in Afghanistan is still possible, but only if we act quickly, judiciously, and decisively. We should pursue an integrated strategy that reinforces our troops in Afghanistan and works to remove the limitations placed by some NATO allies on their forces. Our strategy must also include sustained diplomacy to isolate the Taliban and more effective development programs that target aid to areas where the Taliban are making inroads.

I will join with our allies in insisting—not simply requesting—that Pakistan crack down on the Taliban, pursue Osama bin Laden and his lieutenants, and end its relationship with all terrorist groups. At the same time, I will encourage dialogue between Pakistan and India to work toward resolving their dispute over Kashmir and between Afghanistan and Pakistan to resolve their historic differences and develop the Pashtun border region. If Pakistan can look toward the east with greater confidence, it will be less likely to believe that its interests are best advanced through cooperation with the Taliban.

Although vigorous action in South Asia and Central Asia should be a starting point, our efforts must be broader. There must be no safe haven for those who plot to kill Americans. To defeat al Qaeda, I will build a twenty-first-century military and twenty-first-century partnerships as strong as the anticommunist alliance that won the Cold War to stay on the offense everywhere from Djibouti to Kandahar.

Here at home, we must strengthen our homeland security and protect the critical infrastructure on which the entire world depends. We can start by spending homeland security dollars on the basis of risk. This means investing more resources to defend mass transit, closing the gaps in our aviation security by screening all cargo on passenger airliners and checking all passengers against a comprehensive watch list, and upgrading port security by ensuring that cargo is screened for radiation.

To succeed, our homeland security and counterterrorism actions must be linked to an intelligence community that deals effectively with the threats we face. Today, we rely largely on the same institutions and practices that were in place before 9/11. We need to revisit intelligence reform, going beyond rearranging boxes on an organizational chart. To keep pace with highly adaptable enemies, we need technologies and practices that enable us to efficiently collect and share information within and across our intelligence agencies. We must invest still more in human intelligence and deploy additional trained operatives and diplomats with specialized knowledge of local cultures and languages. And we should institutionalize the practice of developing competitive assessments of critical threats and strengthen our methodologies of analysis.

Finally, we need a comprehensive strategy to defeat global terrorists—one that draws on the full range of American power, not just our military might. As a senior U.S. military commander put it, when people have dignity and opportunity, "the chance of extremism being welcomed greatly, if not completely, diminishes." It is for this reason that we need to invest with our allies in strengthening weak states and helping to rebuild failed ones.

In the Islamic world and beyond, combating the terrorists' prophets of fear will require more than lectures on democracy. We need to deepen our knowledge of the circumstances and beliefs that underpin extremism. A crucial debate is occurring within Islam. Some believe in a future of peace, tolerance, development, and democratization. Others embrace a rigid and violent intolerance of personal liberty and the world at large. To empower forces of moderation, America must make every effort to export opportunity—access to education and health care, trade and investment—and provide the kind of steady support for political reformers and civil society that enabled our victory in the Cold War. Our beliefs rest on hope; the extremists' rest on fear. That is why we can—and will—win this struggle.

REBUILDING OUR PARTNERSHIPS

To renew American leadership in the world, I intend to rebuild the alliances, partnerships, and institutions necessary to confront common threats and enhance common security. Needed reform of these alliances and institutions will not come by bullying other countries to ratify changes we hatch in isolation. It will come when we convince other governments and peoples that they, too, have a stake in effective partnerships.

Too often we have sent the opposite signal to our international partners. In the case of Europe, we dismissed European reservations about the wisdom and necessity of the Iraq war. In Asia, we belittled South Korean efforts to improve relations with the North. In Latin America, from Mexico to Argentina, we failed to adequately address concerns about immigration and equity and economic growth. In Africa, we have allowed genocide to persist for over four years in Darfur and have not done nearly enough to answer the African Union's call for more support to stop the killing. I will rebuild our ties to our allies in Europe and Asia and strengthen our partnerships throughout the Americas and Africa.

Our alliances require constant cooperation and revision if they are to remain effective and relevant. NATO has made tremendous strides over the last 15 years, transforming itself from a Cold War security structure into a partnership for peace. But today, NATO's challenge in Afghanistan has exposed, as Senator Lugar has put it, "the growing discrepancy between NATO's expanding missions and its lagging capabilities." To close this gap, I will rally our NATO allies to contribute more troops to collective security operations and to invest more in reconstruction and stabilization capabilities.

And as we strengthen NATO, we must build new alliances and partnerships in other vital regions. As China rises and Japan and South Korea assert themselves, I will work to forge a more effective framework in Asia that goes beyond bilateral agreements, occasional summits, and ad hoc arrangements, such as the six-party talks on North Korea. We need an inclusive infrastructure with the countries in East Asia that can promote stability and prosperity and help confront transnational threats, from terrorist cells in the

Philippines to avian flu in Indonesia. I will also encourage China to play a responsible role as a growing power—to help lead in addressing the common problems of the twenty-first century. We will compete with China in some areas and cooperate in others. Our essential challenge is to build a relationship that broadens cooperation while strengthening our ability to compete.

In addition, we need effective collaboration on pressing global issues among all the major powers—including such newly emerging ones as Brazil, India, Nigeria, and South Africa. We need to give all of them a stake in upholding the international order. To that end, the United Nations requires far-reaching reform. The UN Secretariat's management practices remain weak. Peacekeeping operations are overextended. The new UN Human Rights Council has passed eight resolutions condemning Israel—but not a single resolution condemning the genocide in Darfur or human rights abuses in Zimbabwe. Yet none of these problems will be solved unless America rededicates itself to the organization and its mission.

Strengthened institutions and invigorated alliances and partnerships are especially crucial if we are to defeat the epochal, man-made threat to the planet: climate change. Without dramatic changes, rising sea levels will flood coastal regions around the world, including much of the eastern seaboard. Warmer temperatures and declining rainfall will reduce crop yields, increasing conflict, famine, disease, and poverty. By 2050, famine could displace more than 250 million people worldwide. That means increased instability in some of the most volatile parts of the world.

As the world's largest producer of greenhouse gases, America has the responsibility to lead. While many of our industrial partners are working hard to reduce their emissions, we are increasing ours at a steady clip—by more than ten percent per decade. As president, I intend to enact a cap-and-trade system that will dramatically reduce our carbon emissions. And I will work to finally free America of its dependence on foreign oil—by using energy more efficiently in our cars, factories, and homes, relying more on renewable sources of electricity, and harnessing the potential of biofuels.

Getting our own house in order is only a first step. China will soon replace America as the world's largest emitter of greenhouse gases. Clean energy development must be a central focus in our relationships with major countries in Europe and Asia. I will invest in efficient and clean technologies at home while using our assistance policies and export promotions to help developing countries leapfrog the carbon-energy-intensive stage of development. We need a global response to climate change that includes binding and enforceable commitments to reducing emissions, especially for those that pollute the most: the United States, China, India, the European Union, and Russia. This challenge is massive, but rising to it will also bring new benefits to America. By 2050, global demand for low-carbon energy could create an annual market worth $500 billion. Meeting that demand would open new frontiers for American entrepreneurs and workers.

BUILDING JUST, SECURE, DEMOCRATIC SOCIETIES

Finally, to renew American leadership in the world, I will strengthen our common security by investing in our common humanity. Our global engagement cannot be defined by what we are against; it must be guided by a clear sense of what we stand for. We have a significant stake in ensuring that those who live in fear and want today can live with dignity and opportunity tomorrow.

People around the world have heard a great deal of late about freedom on the march. Tragically, many have come to associate this with war, torture, and forcibly imposed regime change. To build a better, freer world, we must first behave in ways that reflect the decency and aspirations of the American people. This means ending the practices of shipping away prisoners in the dead of night to be tortured in far-off countries, of detaining thousands without charge or trial, of maintaining a network of secret prisons to jail people beyond the reach of the law.

Citizens everywhere should be able to choose their leaders in climates free of fear. America must commit to strengthening the pillars of a just society. We can help build accountable institutions that deliver services and opportunity: strong legislatures, independent judiciaries, honest police forces, free presses, vibrant civil societies. In countries wracked by poverty and conflict, citizens long to enjoy freedom from want. And since extremely poor societies and weak states provide optimal breeding grounds for disease, terrorism, and conflict, the United States has a direct national security interest in dramatically reducing global poverty and joining with our allies in sharing more of our riches to help those most in need. We need to invest in building capable, democratic states that can establish healthy and educated communities, develop markets, and generate wealth. Such states would also have greater institutional capacities to fight terrorism, halt the spread of deadly weapons, and build health-care infrastructures to prevent, detect, and treat deadly diseases such as HIV/AIDS, malaria, and avian flu.

As president, I will double our annual investment in meeting these challenges to $50 billion by 2012 and ensure that those new resources are directed toward worthwhile goals. For the last 20 years, U.S. foreign assistance funding has done little more than keep pace with inflation. It is in our national security interest to do better. But if America is going to help others build more just and secure societies, our trade deals, debt relief, and foreign aid must not come as blank checks. I will couple our support with an insistent call for reform, to combat the corruption that rots societies and governments from within. I will do so not in the spirit of a patron but in the spirit of a partner—a partner mindful of his own imperfections.

Our rapidly growing international AIDS programs have demonstrated that increased foreign assistance can make a real difference. As part of this new funding, I will capitalize a $2 billion Global Education Fund that will bring the world together in eliminating the global education deficit, much as the 9/11 Commission proposed. We cannot hope to shape a world where opportunity outweighs danger unless we ensure that every child everywhere is taught to build and not to destroy.

There are compelling moral reasons and compelling security reasons for renewed American leadership that recognizes the inherent equality and worth of all people. As President Kennedy said in his 1961 inaugural address, "To those people in the huts and villages of half the globe struggling to break the bonds of mass misery, we pledge our best efforts to help them help themselves, for whatever period is required—not because the communists may be doing it, not because we seek their votes, but because it is right. If a free society cannot help the many who are poor, it cannot save the few who are rich." I will show the world that America remains true to its founding values. We lead not only for ourselves but also for the common good.

RESTORING AMERICA'S TRUST

Confronted by Hitler, Roosevelt said that our power would be "directed toward ultimate good as well as against immediate evil. We Americans are not destroyers; we are builders." It is time for a president who can build consensus here at home for an equally ambitious course.

Ultimately, no foreign policy can succeed unless the American people understand it and feel they have a stake in its success—unless they trust that their government hears their concerns as well. We will not be able to increase foreign aid if we fail to invest in security and opportunity for our own people. We cannot negotiate trade agreements to help spur development in poor countries so long as we provide no meaningful help to working Americans burdened by the dislocations of a global economy. We cannot reduce our dependence on foreign oil or defeat global warming unless Americans are willing to innovate and conserve. We cannot expect Americans to support placing our men and women in harm's way if we cannot show that we will use force wisely and judiciously. But if the next president can restore the American people's trust—if they know that he or she is acting with their best interests at heart, with prudence and wisdom and some measure of humility—then I believe the American people will be eager to see America lead again.

I believe they will also agree that it is time for a new generation to tell the next great American story. If we act with boldness and foresight, we will be able to tell our grandchildren that this was the time when we helped forge peace in the Middle East. This was the time we confronted climate change and secured the weapons that could destroy the human race. This was the time we defeated global terrorists and brought opportunity to forgotten corners of the world. And this was the time when we renewed the America that has led generations of weary travelers from all over the world to find opportunity and liberty and hope on our doorstep.

It was not all that long ago that farmers in Venezuela and Indonesia welcomed American doctors to their villages and hung pictures of JFK on their living room walls, when millions, like my father, waited every day for a letter in the mail that would grant them the privilege to come to America to study, work, live, or just be free.

We can be this America again. This is our moment to renew the trust and faith of our people—and all people—in an America that battles immediate evils, promotes an ultimate good, and leads the world once more.

BARACK OBAMA is a Democratic Senator from Illinois and a candidate for the Democratic presidential nomination.

Rising to a New Generation of Global Challenges

Mitt Romney JULY/AUGUST 2007

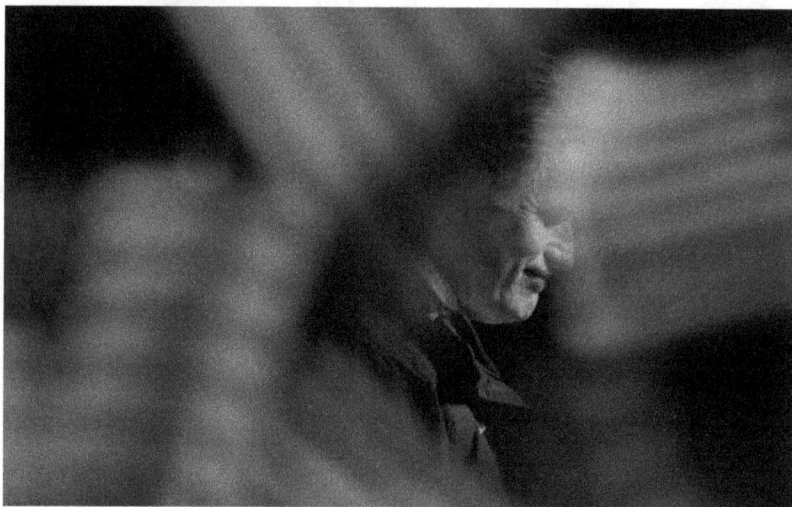

Republican presidential nominee Mitt Romney pauses while speaking at a campaign rally in Newport News, Virginia November 4, 2012.

WASHINGTON DIVIDED

Less than six years after 9/11, Washington is as divided and con-flicted over foreign policy as it has been at any point in the last 50 years. Senator Arthur Vandenberg once famously declared that "politics stops at the water's edge"; today, the chair of the House Foreign Affairs Committee declares that our major political parties should carry out two separate foreign policies. The Senate unani-mously confirmed General David Petraeus, who pledged to imple-ment a new strategy, as the commander of U.S. forces in Iraq. Yet just weeks later, the Senate began crafting legislation specifically designed to stop that new strategy. More broadly, lines have been drawn be-tween those labeled "realists" and those labeled "neoconservatives."

Yet these terms mean little when even the most committed neoconservative recognizes that any successful policy must be grounded in reality and even the most hardened realist admits that much of the United States' power and influence stems from its values and ideals.

In the midst of these divisions, the American people—and many others around the world—have increasing doubts about the United States' direction and role in the world. Indeed, it seems that concern about Washington's divisiveness and capability to meet today's challenges is the one thing that unites us all. We need new thinking on foreign policy and an overarching strategy that can unite the United States and its allies—not around a particular political camp or foreign policy school but around a shared understanding of how to meet a new generation of challenges.

A GENERATION'S LEGACY OF LEADERSHIP

Today's challenges are daunting. They include the conflict in Iraq, the resurgence of the Taliban, and global terrorist networks made even more menacing by the threat of nuclear proliferation. While Iran's leaders relentlessly pursue nuclear weapons capabilities and spout genocidal threats against Israel, the world largely stands silent, unable to agree on effective sanctions even as each day the danger grows. Genocide ravages Darfur even as the world stands frozen. In Latin America, leaders such as Venezuelan President Hugo Chávez seek to reverse the spread of freedom and return to failed authoritarian policies. AIDS and potential new pandemics threaten us in an interconnected world. The economic rise of China and other countries across Asia poses a different type of challenge. It is easy to understand why Americans—and many others around the world—feel so much unease and uncertainty. Yet although we face fundamentally different issues today, the United States has a history of rising to meet even greater challenges. Indeed, we need not look to ancient history, but only to the courage and determination of our parents and grandparents to see a stark contrast with the confusion and infighting of Washington today. Just over 60 years ago, we were in the midst of a global war that would take the lives of tens of millions.

The outcome was far from certain. General Dwight Eisenhower drafted a short note before the D-day landings at Normandy accepting full responsibility "in case of failure."

The invasion did not fail. Yet no sooner had we defeated fascism than we were engaged in a 50-year struggle with communism. Those whom the journalist Tom Brokaw memorialized as "the greatest generation" made the tough choices that allowed us to prevail in these struggles. And it was not just our Washington leaders who were decisive. In the 1940s, Americans rationed and saved, and mothers and daughters enlisted to work in factories. Together with the GIs who returned home, they built this country's prosperity and fueled a sense of optimism. In the 1960s, 1970s, and 1980s, America pursued learning and innovation to lead the world in space, technology, and productivity—outcompeting the Soviets and driving them to an economic bankruptcy that matched their moral bankruptcy.

In the aftermath of World War II and with the coming of the Cold War, members of "the greatest generation" united America and the free world around shared values and actions that changed history. They unified U.S. military and security efforts, creating the Department of Defense and the National Security Council. They rethought U.S. approaches to the world, building the U.S. Agency for International Development, the Office of the U.S. Trade Representative, and the Peace Corps. They forged alliances, such as NATO, that magnified the power of freedom and created a world trading system that helped launch the greatest expansion of economic and political freedom and development in history. Our times call for equally bold leadership and for a renewed sense of service and shared sacrifice among Americans and our allies around the world.

A NEW GENERATION OF CHALLENGES

Today, the nation's attention is focused on Iraq. All Americans want U.S. troops to come home as soon as possible. But walking away now or dividing Iraq up into parts and walking away later would present grave risks to the United States and the world. Iran could seize the Shiite south, al Qaeda could dominate the Sunni west, and Kurdish nationalism could destabilize the border with Turkey. A regional conflict could ensue, perhaps even requiring the return of U.S. troops under far worse circumstances. There is no guarantee that the new strategy pursued by General Petraeus will ultimately succeed, but the stakes are too high and the potential fallout too great to deny our military leaders and troops on the ground the resources and the time needed to give it an opportunity to succeed.

Many still fail to comprehend the extent of the threat posed by radical Islam, specifically by those extremists who promote violent jihad against the United States and the universal values Americans espouse. Understandably, the nation tends to focus on Afghanistan and Iraq, where American men and women are dying. We think in terms of countries because countries were our enemies in the last century's great conflicts. The congressional debate in Washington has largely, and myopically, focused on whether troops should be redeployed from Iraq to Afghanistan, as if these were isolated issues. Yet the jihad is much broader than any one nation, or even several nations. It is broader than the conflicts in Afghanistan and Iraq, or that between the Israelis and the Palestinians. Radical Islam has one goal: to replace all modern Islamic states with a worldwide caliphate while destroying the United States and converting all nonbelievers, forcibly if necessary, to Islam. This plan sounds irrational, and it is. But it is no more irrational than the policies pursued by Nazi Germany in the 1930s and 1940s and Stalin's Soviet Union during the Cold War. And the threat is just as real.

In the current conflict, the balance of forces is not nearly as close as during the early days of World War II and at critical points during the Cold War. There is no comparison between the economic, diplomatic, technological, and military resources of the civilized world today and those of the terrorist organizations and states that threaten it. Perhaps most important is the incredible resourcefulness of the American people and their unmatched education, inventiveness, and dedication. But today's threats are fundamentally different from those we grew used to confronting during World War II and the Cold War. Our enemies now have sleeper cells rather than armies. They use indiscriminate terror rather than tanks. Their soldiers—as well as their victims—include children. They count radical clergy among their generals. They communicate via the Internet. They recruit in schools, houses of worship, and prisons. They pursue nuclear weapons not as a strategic deterrent but as an offensive tool of terror.

The jihadist threat is the defining challenge of our generation and is symptomatic of a range of new global realities. It is common to the point of cliché to talk about how much the world has changed since 9/11. Our president led a dramatic response to the events of that day and has taken action to protect the U.S. homeland. Yet if one looks at our tools of national power, what is surprising is not how much has changed since then but how little. While we wage wars in Afghanistan and Iraq, U.S. troop levels and our investment in the military as a percentage of GDP remain lower than at any time of major conflict since World War II. Decades after the oil shocks of the 1970s highlighted the United States' vulnerability, we remain dangerously dependent on foreign oil. Many of our instruments of national security were created not only before most Americans had access to the Internet and cell phones but also before they had televisions. Our difficulties in Iraq and Afghanistan, along with disturbing gaps in our intelligence, are well known. A growing number of experts question whether we have the capabilities to meet various transnational challenges, ranging from pandemic diseases to international terrorism. And while the United Nations has stood impotent in the face of genocide in Sudan and has been unable to address Iran's rush to build dangerous nuclear capabilities, we have done little more than tweak international alliances and antiquated institutions.

While the difficult struggle in Iraq dominates the political debate, we cannot let current polls and political dynamics drive us to repeat mistakes the United States has made at critical moments of doubt and uncertainty about our role in the world. Twice in the last several decades, following the end of U.S. military involvement in Vietnam and the end of the Cold War in the 1990s, the United States became dangerously unprepared. Today, among our main challenges are an Iranian regime and an al Qaeda network that developed while we let down our defenses. Whether or not the current "surge" in troop levels in Iraq succeeds, the United States and our allies need to be prepared to deal not only with the struggle against jihadists but with a new generation of challenges that go far beyond any single nation or conflict.

We need an honest debate about what policies and what sacrifices will ensure a strong America and a safe world. As President Ronald Reagan once observed, "There have been four wars in my lifetime. None of them came about because the United States was too strong." A strong America requires a strong military and a strong economy. And we need to take further action if we are to remain strong and if we are to build a safe world, with peace, prosperity, freedom, and dignity. Doing so will be controversial, and it will be strongly resisted because it will require dramatic changes to Cold War institutions and approaches. The Cold War is over, and the world that too many of our current capabilities and alliances were created to address no longer exists. We cannot remain mired in the past.

Change is difficult in and of itself. And it is especially hard to summon the will necessary to set a new course in the absence of a clear and convincing crisis. Look at how long it took the U.S. government to confront the reality of jihadism. Extremists bombed our marines in Lebanon. They bombed our embassies in East Africa. They bombed the U.S.S. Cole. They even set off a bomb in the basement of the World Trade Center before we truly saw the threat they posed.

Change will require sacrifice from the American people. But I believe America is ready for the challenge. To meet it, we need to focus on four key pillars of action.

BUILDING U.S. MILITARY AND ECONOMIC STRENGTH

First, we need to increase our investment in national defense. This means adding at least 100,000 troops and making a long-overdue investment in equipment, armament, weapons systems, and strategic defense. The need to support our troops is repeated like a mantra in Washington. Yet little has been said about the commitment of resources needed to make this more than an empty phrase.

After President George H. W. Bush left office, in 1993, the Clinton administration began to dismantle the military, taking advantage of what has been called a "peace dividend" from the end of the Cold War. It took a dividend, but we did not get the peace. It seems that our leaders had come to believe that war and security threats were gone forever; as Charles Krauthammer observed, we took a holiday from history. Meanwhile, we lost about 500,000 military personnel and about $50 billion a year in military spending. The U.S. Army lost four active divisions and two reserve divisions. The U.S. Navy lost almost 80 ships. The U.S. Air Force saw its active personnel decrease by 30 percent. The Marines' personnel dropped by 22,000.

And we purchased only a small fraction of the equipment needed to maintain our strength, living off the assets that had been purchased in prior decades. The equipment and armament gap continues to this day. Even as we have increased defense spending to meet the challenges in Iraq and Afghanistan, our budgets for procurement and modernization have lagged behind. This is a troubling scenario for the future, and it puts our country and our troops—present and future—at risk, as we wring the life out of old and inadequate equipment.

The Bush administration has proposed an increase in defense spending for next year. This is an important first step, but we are going to need at least an additional $30-$40 billion annually over the next several years to modernize our military, fill gaps in troop levels, ease the strain on our National Guard and Reserves, and support our wounded soldiers. Looking at military spending over time as a percentage of GDP provides an interesting perspective.

During World War II, the United States made huge sacrifices, investing more than a third of its economic activity to fight the war. As we confronted different enemies, such as those in Korea, our investment in defense responded accordingly. Since then, slowly but surely, it has decreased significantly. Through the buildup under President Reagan, it reached six percent of GDP in 1986 and helped turn the tide against the Soviet Union. Yet during the Clinton years, defense spending was dangerously reduced. More recently, although spending has increased, less than four percent of our GDP has been devoted to baseline defense spending. These ebbs and flows stemming from political dynamics have increased the costs and the uncertainty of our military preparedness.

The next president should commit to spending a minimum of four percent of GDP on national defense. Increased spending should not mean increased waste, however. A team of private-sector leaders and defense experts should carry out a stem-to-stern analysis of military purchasing. Accounts need to be thoroughly scrutinized to eliminate excessive contractor and supplier charges and prevent deals for equipment and programs that do more for politicians' popularity in their home districts than for the nation's protection. Congress needs to set stricter lobbying rules and keep a far more watchful eye on self-serving politicians, current and past, in regard to these matters.

The United States' strength goes beyond its military capacity. Indeed, a nation cannot remain a military superpower if it has a second-tier economy. The weakness of the Soviet economy was a vulnerability that President Reagan exploited. Our ability to influence the world also vitally depends on our ability to maintain our economic lead through policies such as smaller government, lower taxes, better schools and health care, greater investment in technology, and the promotion of free trade, while maintaining the strength of America's families, values, and moral leadership.

ENERGY INDEPENDENCE

Second, the United States must become energy independent. This does not mean no longer importing or using oil. It means making sure that our nation's future will always be in our hands. Our decisions and destiny cannot be bound to the whims of oil-producing states.

We use about 25 percent of the world's oil supply to power our economy, but according to the Department of Energy, we possess only 1.7 percent of the world's crude oil reserves. Our military and economic strength depend on our becoming energy independent—moving past symbolic measures to actually produce as much energy as we use. This could take 20 years or more; and, of course, we would continue to purchase fuel after that time. Yet we would end our strategic vulnerability to oil shutoffs by nations such as Iran, Russia, and Venezuela and stop sending almost $1 billion a day to other oil-producing nations, some of which use the money against us. At the same time, we may well be able to rein in our greenhouse gas emissions.

Energy independence will require technology that allows us to use energy more efficiently in our cars, homes, and businesses. It will also mean increasing our domestic energy production with more drilling offshore and in the Arctic National Wildlife Refuge, more nuclear power, more renewable energy sources, more ethanol, more biodiesel, more solar and wind power, and a fuller exploitation of coal. Shared investments or incentives may be required to develop additional and alternative sources of energy.

We need to initiate a bold, far-reaching research initiative—an energy revolution—that will be our generation's equivalent of the Manhattan Project or the mission to the moon. It will be a mission to create new, economical sources of clean energy and clean ways to use the sources we have now. We will license our technology to other nations, and, of course, we will employ it at home. It will be good for our national defense, it will be good for our foreign policy, and it will be good for our economy. Moreover, even as scientists still debate how much human activity impacts the environment, we can all agree that alternative energy sources will be good for the planet. For any and all of these reasons, the time for energy independence has come.

RETHINKING AND REENERGIZING CIVILIAN CAPABILITIES

Third, we need to dramatically and fundamentally transform our civilian capabilities to promote peace, security, and freedom around the world. After World War II, America created capabilities and structures—such as the National Security Council, the Department of Defense, and the U.S. Agency for International Development—to meet the challenges of a world that was radically different from that of the 1930s. In the Reagan era, the Goldwater-Nichols Act helped tear down bureaucratic boundaries that were undermining our military effectiveness, fostered unified efforts across military services, and established "joint commands," with an individual commander fully responsible for everything going on within his or her geographic region. We need the same level of dramatic rethinking and reform that took place at these critical junctures.

Today, there is no such unity among our international nonmilitary resources. There is no clear leadership and no clear line of authority. Too often, we struggle to integrate our nonmilitary instruments into coherent, timely, and effective operations. For instance, even as we face the need to strengthen the democratic underpinnings of a country such as Lebanon, our resources in education, health, banking, energy, commerce, law enforcement, and diplomacy are spread across separate bureaucracies and are under separate leadership. As a result, we have had to look on as Hezbollah has brought health care and schools to areas of Lebanon. And guess who the people followed when the conflict between Israel and Lebanon broke out last summer? Likewise, the popularity of Hamas in Gaza and the West Bank should be no surprise given that the group has provided Palestinians with the basic services that neither the international community nor the Palestinian government could deliver.

The problem has been just as evident in Iraq. In 2003, while the U.S. military moved in rapid order to topple Saddam Hussein, many of our nonmilitary resources seemed stuck in tar. Then, even as we were taking casualties and spending over $7 billion a month on the war, U.S. civilian authorities were fighting over which agency was going to pay their employees' $11 daily food allowance. In response to these problems, the White House has sought to give to a single individual the authority to oversee all the agencies operating in Iraq and Afghanistan. Yet broad interagency challenges remain and continue to stymie our efforts not only in these areas but around the world.

It is time to move beyond the current limited approaches that call for "transformation" and truly transform our interagency and civilian capabilities. We need to fundamentally change the cultures of our civilian agencies and create dynamic, flexible, and task-based approaches that focus on results rather than bureaucracy. We need joint strategies and joint operations that go beyond the Goldwater-Nichols Act to mobilize all areas of our national power. Just as the military has divided the world into regional theaters for all of its branches, the work of our civilian agencies should be organized along common geographic boundaries. For every region, one civilian leader should have authority over and responsibility for all the relevant agencies and departments, similar to the single military commander who heads U.S. Central Command. These new leaders should be heavy hitters, with names that are recognized around the world. They should have independent objectives, budgets, and oversight. Their performance should be evaluated according to their success in promoting America's political, military, diplomatic, and economic interests in their respective regions and building the foundations of freedom, democracy, security, and peace.

REVITALIZING AND STRENGTHENING ALLIANCES

Finally, we need to strengthen old partnerships and alliances and inaugurate new ones to meet twenty-first-century challenges. The inaction, if not the breakdown, of many Cold War institutions has made many Americans skeptical of multilateralism. Nothing shows the failures of the current system more clearly than the UN Human Rights Council, an entity that has condemned the democratic government of Israel nine times while remaining virtually silent on the serial human rights abuses of the governments of Cuba, Iran,

Myanmar, North Korea, and Sudan. In the face of such hypocrisy, it is understandable that some Americans would be tempted to favor unilateralism. But such failures should not obscure the fact that the United States' strength is amplified when it is combined with the strength of other nations. Whether diplomatically, militarily, or economically, the United States is stronger when its friends stand alongside it.

In the changing world we face, our alliances and engagement must change, too. Clearly, the United Nations has not been able to fulfill its founding purpose of providing collective security against aggression and genocide. Thus, we need to continue to push for reform of the organization. Yet where institutions are fundamentally incapable of meeting a new generation of challenges, the United States does not have to go it alone. Instead, we must examine where existing alliances can be strengthened and reinvigorated and where new alliances need to be forged. I agree with former Spanish Prime Minister José María Aznar that we should build on the NATO alliance to defeat radical Islam. We need to work with our allies to pursue Aznar's call for greater coordination in military, homeland security, and nonproliferation efforts.

The challenges we now face—especially terrorism, genocide, and the spread of weapons of mass destruction—require global networks of intelligence and law enforcement. We should also look for new ways to strengthen regional cooperation and security partnerships with responsible actors in order to confront challenges such as the genocide in Darfur. And if the UN Human Rights Council continues to be inactive or behave hypocritically, we should unite with nations that share our commitment to defending human rights in order to promote change.

In no area is our leadership more important and more urgently needed than the Islamic world. Today, the Middle East is facing a demographic crisis: over half the population there is under 22 years old, and the GDP of all Arab nations put together remains lower than that of Spain. A growing population and a lack of jobs create fertile ground for radical Islam. The Marshall Plan showed our deep understanding that winning the Cold War would depend on far more than the strength of our military. The situation we face today is dramatically different from the one we faced in the wake of World War II. Yet it requires the same type of political attention and resolve we exhibited then. Today, thousands of Americans, such as former Senator Bill Frist, are helping to alleviate problems in the vulnerable parts of Africa and the Middle East, showing that we are a compassionate people. And other leaders in this effort, such as the musician Bono, have highlighted the need to address problems far from one's borders in today's interconnected world. Recent government efforts such as the Middle East Partnership Initiative, the Broader Middle East and North Africa Initiative of the G-8, and the Forum for the Future are a start, but they have garnered nowhere near the degree of attention, resources, and commitment necessary to address such serious problems.

If elected, one of my first acts as president would be to call for a summit of nations to address these issues. In addition to the United States, the countries convened would include other leading developed nations and moderate Muslim states. The objective of the summit would be to create a worldwide strategy to support moderate Muslims in their effort to defeat radical and violent Islam. I envision that the summit would lead to the creation of a Partnership for Prosperity and Progress: a coalition of states that would assemble resources from developed nations and use them to support public schools (not Wahhabi madrasahs), microcredit and banking, the rule of law, human rights, basic health care, and free-market policies in modernizing Islamic states. These resources would be drawn from public and private institutions and from volunteers and nongovernmental organizations.

A critical part of this effort would involve creating new trade and economic opportunities for the Middle East that could be powerful forces, not only economically, but also in breaking down barriers to cooperation on even the most intractable problems. Muslim countries pursuing free-trade agreements with the United States, for example, have dismantled all aspects of the Arab

League's boycott of Israel. The power of trade to break down bar-riers and build ties is also seen in the Qualified Industrial Zone program that grants U.S. free-trade benefits to Egyptian products that incorporate materials from Israel. When the program was first suggested, some Egyptian officials balked, saying that trade with Israel would spark protests. When the program was launched, there were indeed protests—from Egyptians who were excluded from the program and wanted to participate.

Congress must give the president the authority to move for-ward with these efforts so that we can expand and integrate our existing free-trade agreements in the region. A critical part of the economic resurgence and peace of postwar Europe was the United States' support for a unified market and U.S. engagement in cross-country ties. Today, we must push for more integration and cross-border cooperation in the Middle East. As a group of experts working on the Princeton Project on National Security noted recently, "The history of Europe since 1945 tells us that institutions can play a constructive role in building a framework for cooperation, channeling nationalist sentiments in a positive direction, and fostering economic development and liberaliza-tion. Yet the Middle East is one of the least institutionalized re-gions in the world."

Few would have thought before 1945 that the war-torn and di-vided nations of Europe could achieve the stability and economic growth that these states know today. Some have called for develop-ing in the Middle East a regional organization based on the Orga-nization for Security and Cooperation in Europe, which would build cooperation and encourage political, economic, and security reforms and integration. How these efforts would be institutional-ized is a question that we must address in partnership with our friends in the region and key allies. Yet we cannot wait to address this problem.

Merely closing our eyes and hoping that jihadism will go away is not an acceptable solution. U.S. military action alone cannot change the hearts and minds of hundreds of millions of Muslims.

In the end, only Muslims themselves can defeat the violent radicals. But we must work with them. The consequences of ignoring this challenge—such as a radicalized Islamic actor possessing nuclear weapons—are simply unacceptable.

MOVING FORWARD

The new generation of challenges we face may seem daunting. Yet confronting challenges has always made the United States stronger. The confusion and pessimism that prevail in Washington today in no way reflect the United States' legacy or underlying strengths. I believe our current generation can match the courage, dedication, and vision of "the greatest generation." I recently had the privilege of spending some time with Shimon Peres, the former prime minister of Israel. Someone asked him about the conflict in Iraq, and he said, "You need to put this in context. America is unique in the history of the world. During this last century, there was only one nation that laid down hundreds of thousands of lives of its own sons and daughters and asked for nothing for itself." He explained that in the history of the world, whenever there has been a war, winning nations have taken the land of losing ones. "America is unique," he added. "You took no land from the Germans, no land from the Japanese. All you asked for was enough land to bury your dead."

We are a unique nation, and there is no substitute for our leadership. The difficulties we face in Iraq should neither cause us to lose faith in the United States' strength and role in the world nor blind us to the new challenges we face. Our future and that of generations to come depend on our resolve to move beyond the divisiveness in Washington today and unite America and our allies to confront a new generation of global challenges.

MITT ROMNEY, Governor of Massachusetts from 2003 to 2007, is a candidate for the Republican presidential nomination.

Reengaging With the World

John Edwards

SEPTEMBER/OCTOBER 2007

U.S. Democratic presidential candidate former Senator John Edwards arrives at the Democratic Presidential debate in Johnston, Iowa, December 13, 2007.

At the dawn of a new century and on the brink of a new presidency, the United States today needs to reclaim the moral high ground that defined our foreign policy for much of the last century.

We must move beyond the wreckage created by one of the greatest strategic failures in U.S. history: the war in Iraq. Rather than alienating the rest of the world through assertions of infallibility and demands of obedience, as the current administration has done, U.S. foreign policy must be driven by a strategy of reengagement. We must reengage with our history of courage, liberty, and generosity. We must reengage with our tradition of moral leadership on issues ranging from the killings in Darfur to global poverty and climate change. We must reengage with our allies on critical security issues, including terrorism, the Middle East, and nuclear proliferation. With confidence and resolve, we must reengage with those who pose a security threat to us, from Iran to North Korea. And our government must reengage with the American people to restore our nation's reputation as a moral beacon to the world, tapping into our fundamental hope and optimism and calling on our citizens' commitment and courage to make this possible. We must lead the world by demonstrating the power of our ideals, not by stoking fear about those who do not share them.

The last century saw tremendous advances in the human condition—from increased economic prosperity to the spread of human rights and the emergence of a truly global community. But the century also brought two devastating world wars, the death of millions, and a Cold War that lasted two generations and risked the end of humanity. The new century, too, will bring both promise and peril. We can look forward to incredible technological advances in communications and medicine and an expanding world economy that will lift millions out of poverty while raising the standards of living for working people at home and abroad.

But we must also prepare for a world filled with new risks: the increasing reach of nonstate actors who reject our very way of life, the consequences of global climate change, and the possibility that dangerous technology will fall into the wrong hands. We can lead the world through these challenges, just as the United States led the world through the challenges of the previous century. But we can only do so if we reclaim the trust and respect of those countries whose cooperation we need but whose will we cannot compel.

RESTORING AMERICA'S REPUTATION

This century's first test of our leadership arrived with terrible force on September 11, 2001. When the United States was attacked, the entire world stood with us. We could have pursued a broad policy of reengagement with the world, yet instead we squandered this broad support through a series of policies that drove away our friends and allies. A recent Pew survey showed the United States' approval ratings plummeting throughout the world between 2000 and 2006. This decline was especially worrisome in Muslim countries of strategic importance to the United States, such as Indonesia, where approval dropped from 75 percent to 30 percent, and Turkey, where it fell from 52 percent to 12 percent. Perceptions of America's efforts to promote democracy have suffered as well. In 33 of the 47 countries surveyed by the Pew Research Center, majorities or pluralities expressed dislike for American ideas of democracy.

We need a new path, one that will lead to reengagement with the world and restoration of the United States' moral authority in the community of nations. President Harry Truman once said, "No one nation alone can bring peace. Together, nations can build a strong defense against aggression and combine the energy of free men everywhere in building a better future for all." For 50 years, presidents from Truman and Dwight Eisenhower to Ronald Reagan and Bill Clinton built strong alliances and deepened the world's respect for us. We gained that respect by viewing our military strength not as an end in itself but as a means to protect a system of laws and institutions that gave hope to billions across the globe. In avoiding the temptation to rule as an empire, we hastened the fall of a corrupt and evil one in the Soviet Union. The lesson is that we cannot only be warriors; we must be thinkers and leaders as well.

And so as we contemplate a national security policy for a new century, we must ask ourselves far-reaching questions: Are we truly denying our enemies what they seek? Are we doing all we can to win the war not only of weapons but also of ideas? Are we battling the fear our enemies sow by planting seeds of hope instead?

This is about much more than convincing people to like us. There was a time when a president did not speak just to Americans—he spoke to the world. People thousands of miles away would gather to listen to someone they called, without irony, "the leader of the free world." Men and women in Nazi-occupied

Europe would huddle around shortwave radios to listen to President Franklin Roosevelt. Millions cheered in Berlin when President John F. Kennedy stood with them and said, "Ich bin ein Berliner." Millions of people imprisoned behind the Iron Curtain silently cheered the day President Reagan declared, "Mr. Gorbachev, tear down this wall!" Even if these ordinary men and women did not always agree with our policies, they looked to our president and saw a person—and a nation—they could trust. Today, under the current administration, this is no longer the case. At the dawn of a new century, it is vital that we win the war of ideas in the world. We need to reach out to ordinary men and women from Egypt to Indonesia and convince them, once again, that the United States is a force to be admired.

BEYOND THE "WAR ON TERROR"

There is no question that we must confront terrorist groups such as al Qaeda with the full force of our military might. As commander in chief, I will never hesitate to apply the full extent of our security apparatus to protect our vital interests, take measures to root out terrorist cells, and strike swiftly and forcefully against those who seek to harm us.

But I believe we must stay on the offensive against both terrorism and its causes. The "war on terror" approach has backfired, straining our military to the breaking point while allowing the threat of terrorism to grow. "War on terror" is a slogan designed for politics, not a strategy to make the United States safe. It is a bumper sticker, not a plan. Worst of all, the "war on terror" has failed. Instead of making the United States safer, it has spawned even more terrorism—as we have seen so tragically in Iraq—and left us with fewer allies.

There is no question that we are less safe today as a result of this administration's policies. The Bush administration has walked the United States right into the terrorists' trap. By framing this struggle against extremism as a war, it has reinforced the jihadists' narrative that we want to conquer the Muslim world and that there is a "clash of civilizations" pitting the West against Islam. From Guantï¿½namo to Abu Ghraib, the "war on terror" has tragically become the recruitment poster al Qaeda wanted. Instead of reengaging with the peoples of the world, we have driven too many into the terrorists' arms. In fact, defining the current struggle against radical Islamists as a war minimizes the challenge we face by suggesting that the fight against Islamist extremism can be won on the battlefield alone.

For these reasons, many generals and national security experts have criticized the president's "war on terror" approach. Retired Marine General Anthony Zinni has said that the "war on terror" is a counterproductive doctrine. So has the government of one of our closest allies; the new British prime minister, Gordon Brown, has distanced himself from the term. Admiral William Fallon—President George W. Bush's new chief of U.S. Central Command (CENTCOM)—has instructed his staff to stop saying that we are in a "long war." These leaders know that we need substance, not slogans.

Leading Republicans have echoed such views. The president's own former secretary of defense, Donald Rumsfeld, said last March that the doctrine was one of his regrets. "It is not a war on terror," he flatly told an interviewer. Meanwhile, former New York City Mayor Rudolph Giuliani curiously seems to have forgotten that he said in March that we should abandon the "war on terror" approach because, in his words, "America is seen as a country by too many that wants to have war, or exercises its power too much, pushes its weight around too much."

Yet the politics of fear remains tempting. Some have chosen to pillory those who dare question the concept of a "war on terror" as somehow weak. But these attacks unmask the slogan for what it is: a political sledgehammer used to stifle debate and justify policies that would otherwise be utterly unacceptable.

Our enemies are taking advantage of the United States' declining popularity. According to a recent article by the former CIA official Bruce Riedel in this magazine, al Qaeda has expanded its reach not only across Afghanistan, Iraq, and Pakistan but even in

Europe. And a recent report by the National Counterterrorism Center found that al Qaeda's operational capabilities have returned to levels unseen since just before 9/11. Iran has been emboldened by the Bush administration's ineffective policies and has announced plans to expand its nuclear program. Meanwhile, other powers are benefiting, too. China is capitalizing on the United States' current unpopularity to project its own "soft power." And Russia is bullying its neighbors while openly defying the United States and Europe.

Our law enforcement, security, and intelligence professionals are to be congratulated and honored for stopping plots such as the recent conspiracy to attack John F. Kennedy International Airport, in New York City. However, we must not let our enthusiasm for these tactical victories cloud a broader view of the threat environment. In April, the State Department released a report stating that terrorism had increased 29 percent worldwide between 2005 and 2006, with most attacks occurring in Iraq and Afghanistan. We need to refocus our national security policy on the mission of protecting Americans from twenty-first-century threats rather than pursuing discredited ideological agendas. What we need is not more slogans but a comprehensive strategy to respond to terrorism and prevent it from taking root in the first place. This strategy should transcend the familiar divide between "hard power" and "soft power." Instead, we need to place "smart power" at the center of our national security policy.

NEW CENTURY, NEW CHALLENGES

Confronting the challenges of the new century will require strength, creativity, and moral leadership. The century ahead will bring new efforts by nonstate actors, ranging from terrorist groups to ethnically based local and regional movements, to redefine the boundaries of states, the jurisdiction of multilateral organizations, and the authority of international law. We will also face instability generated by weak and failing states. And we will face continuing challenges to our efforts to promote democracy. Elections alone are not enough; new democracies need to cultivate constitutionalism, strong institutions, pluralism, and a respect for a free press and the rule of law. Finally, a host of twenty-first-century developments from climate change to pandemics will likely impose additional stresses. A report issued in April by a group of 11 retired military officers, including General Gordon Sullivan, the former army chief of staff, and General Zinni, the former CENTCOM commander, described the potential of climate change to ignite a chain reaction leading to global instability. It could trigger conflicts over shrinking natural resources, weaken states through the creation of climate refugees, and hasten the spread of diseases and famine. We must act aggressively against this threat.

We should begin our reengagement with the world by bringing an end to the Iraq war. Iraq's problems are deep and dangerous, but they cannot be solved by the U.S. military. For over a year, I have argued for an immediate withdrawal of 40,000 to 50,000 U.S. combat troops from Iraq, followed by an orderly and complete withdrawal of all combat troops. Once we are out of Iraq, the United States must retain sufficient forces in the region to prevent a genocide, a regional spillover of the civil war, or the establishment of an al Qaeda safe haven. We will most likely need to retain quick-reaction forces in Kuwait and a significant naval presence in the Persian Gulf. We will also need some security capabilities in Baghdad, inside the Green Zone, to protect the U.S. embassy and U.S. personnel. Finally, we will need a diplomatic offensive to engage the rest of the world—including Middle Eastern nations and our allies in Europe—in working to secure Iraq's future. All of these measures will finally allow us to close this terrible chapter and move on to the broader challenges of the new century.

We must confront these challenges not only through our military but also through diplomacy. Few areas deserve the United States' moral leadership more urgently than Sudan. The African Union peacekeeping troops stationed in Darfur have acted bravely in a difficult situation. But these 7,000 troops have been unable to protect civilians or enforce a 2004 cease-fire, and security has deteriorated dramatically. I believe President Bush should convene an emergency meeting of NATO's leadership to provide assistance to a UN deployment of 3,000 troops, backed by logistical, operational, and financial support. NATO must establish a no-fly zone over the region to cut off supplies to the brutal Janjaweed militias and end the Sudanese government's bombing of civilians in Darfur. NATO member states should also impose a new round of multilateral sanctions on the Sudanese government and freeze the foreign assets of individuals complicit in the genocide. The United States must make a decisive new commitment to employ the extraordinary assets of the U.S. military—our airlift capabilities, logistical support, and intelligence systems—to assist UN and African Union peacekeeping efforts in Darfur. And we must continue to pressure other countries with influence in the region, such as China, to meet their own responsibilities to help end this conflict.

We also need to renew our commitment to engagement and diplomacy in order to solve problems before they occur, rather than scrambling to deal with crises after they have erupted. With engagement comes far greater knowledge and the potential for progress and even trust. Presidents Kennedy and Reagan talked with Soviet leaders at the height of the Cold War, in both cases turning back major threats to our national security. We need to do the same with Iranian and North Korean leaders.

Iran presents a complicated challenge for the United States. President Mahmoud Ahmadinejad is a dangerous radical and a strong supporter of Hezbollah and Hamas. He has said repeatedly that Israel should be "wiped off the map" and last December sponsored a conference for Holocaust deniers in Tehran. Iran cannot be allowed to possess nuclear weapons.

Unfortunately, the situation in Iran has only worsened under this administration. With a threat so serious, no U.S. president should take any option off the table—diplomacy, sanctions, engagement, or even military force. When we say something is unacceptable, however, we must mean it, and that requires developing a strategy that delivers results, not just rhetoric. Instead of saber rattling about military action, we should employ an effective combination of carrots and sticks. For example, right now we must do everything we can to isolate Iran's leader from the moderate forces within the country. We need to contain Iran's nuclear ambitions through diplomatic measures that will, over time, force Iran to finally understand that the international community will not allow it to possess nuclear weapons. Every major U.S. ally agrees that the advent of a nuclear Iran would be a threat to global security. We should continue to work with other great powers to offer Tehran economic incentives for good behavior. At the same time, we must use much more serious economic sanctions to deter Ahmadinejad's government when it refuses to cooperate. To do this, we will have to deal with Iran directly. Such diplomacy is not a gift, nor is it a concession. The current administration recently managed to have one single-issue meeting with Iran to discuss Iraq. It simply makes no sense for the administration to engage Iran on this subject alone and avoid one as consequential as nuclear proliferation.

In North Korea, the recent agreement to shut down the Yongbyon nuclear reactor in exchange for the release of frozen assets is encouraging—though long overdue. It is a sign that the carrots-and-sticks approach can work. Pyongyang's words, however, are not enough. We must require a commitment to future action. We must engage the North Korean government directly, through the six-party framework, placing economic and political incentives on the table in exchange for the verified, complete elimination of North Korea's nuclear weapons capabilities.

Indeed, new leadership is needed for a broader, more systematic approach to confronting the most dangerous threat of the new century: the proliferation of weapons of mass destruction (WMD). In working toward the goal of a nuclear-free world, the United States must lead the effort to strengthen the international nonproliferation institutions, not cast them aside. The rules and institutions we rely on to stymie and isolate bad actors, while providing strong leverage and instruments for measuring progress, are increasingly riddled with loopholes and gaps. We should create a new

Global Nuclear Compact to bolster the Nuclear Nonproliferation Treaty, which would support peaceful nuclear programs, improve security for existing stocks of nuclear materials, and ensure more frequent verification that materials are not being diverted and nuclear facilities are not being misused. We must also halt the trade of the most dangerous technologies by the most dangerous states and increase the amount of money we spend on cooperative threat-reduction programs in the former Soviet republics. Finally, we should strengthen our nation's capacity to identify and respond to WMD threats by reforming the ways the U.S. government collects and analyzes intelligence and by giving the intelligence community the resources it needs.

The tsunami that hit Southeast Asia in 2004, the troubled status of the government in Afghanistan, and the need for a functioning infrastructure in Iraq all have something in common: they present a new set of challenges for which the United States will need to prepare. In the coming years, we will most likely see an increasing need to stabilize weak and failing states and provide humanitarian assistance to the victims of disasters across the world.

These missions are demanding, dangerous, and expensive. They require a wide range of resources and sources of knowledge, from experts in water purification to medical technicians, judges to corrections officers, bankers to stock-market analysts. In most cases, the help of thousands of such specialists is required. Yet for years, the U.S. government has not been properly prepared for these kinds of missions. As a result, when these situations arise, the government turns repeatedly to the only existing institution with the required logistical capabilities and a sufficiently broad range of skills: the military. But the military lacks many of the resources that are required to conduct these missions successfully. To resolve these problems, I will establish a Marshall Corps during my first year in office, named for our greatest secretary of state, General George Marshall. The Marshall Corps, patterned after the military reserves, will consist of at least 10,000 civilian experts who could be deployed abroad to serve in reconstruction, stabilization, and humanitarian missions. They will be on the frontline in the United States' reengagement with the world.

REENGAGING WITH THE WORLD'S MAJOR POWERS

In the new century, a number of emerging or already major powers will pose new challenges to the United States. We will have to continue integrating rising powers into a peaceful international system by convincing them that they can both benefit from and contribute to the system's strength. This means adapting our most important international leadership organizations, such as the G-8, to include these new major players. We must also strive to maintain our strong partnerships with longtime allies, including the United Kingdom, Japan, and the transforming European Union, as well as work to rebuild the long-neglected relationships with our neighbors throughout Latin America. Finally, we must stand by our ally and partner Israel, ensuring its security while doing everything in our power to bring peace and stability to the region.

China, Russia, and India, among others, will test U.S. leadership. China is developing a unique political system and economy with both authoritarian and free-market elements. The nation is economically important to the United States, heavily invested in our Treasury bonds, and a significant trading partner. But China is also a growing economic competitor, particularly in its dealings with nations possessing rich energy resources, which can lead to conflicting perspectives on security issues. China's approach to Iran and Sudan are prime examples. In sum, the U.S.-Chinese relationship is a delicate one, which has not been well managed by the current administration. In the coming years, China's influence and importance will only continue to grow. On issues such as trade, climate change, and human rights, our overarching goal must be to get China to commit to the rules that govern the conduct of nations.

Russia presents a very different challenge. The situation in Russia is deteriorating, and democracy is on the wane. President Vladimir Putin has also initiated a worrisome pattern of bellicose rhetoric against the United States and has threatened to withdraw from arms control treaties. The presidential transition scheduled for next year will be a critical test of Russia's commitment to democracy and the rule of law. Despite these concerns, Russia also offers substantial opportunities for the United States, both as an economic partner and as a stabilizing influence over other, more overtly hostile nations, such as Iran. Last year, in a Council on Foreign Relations task force I co-led with former Republican Congressman Jack Kemp, we concluded that the United States ought to initiate a new era of selective cooperation with Russia on particular issues, such as Iran, energy, and nuclear nonproliferation, while preserving our ability to disagree and push for change on other issues, such as our concerns about increasing authoritarianism in Russia and potential Russian-Chinese cooperation. Our most important goal is to draw Russia into the Western political mainstream through continued engagement and, when necessary, diplomatic and economic pressure.

I have seen for myself that India is one of the world's richest treasures. With its great history, tremendous people, and rich culture, India has truly overwhelming potential. The United States is fortunate to count India as a partner, and we must cultivate our friendship to advance our common values. India is a country that knows both the positive and the negative aspects of our globalized world. It has achieved remarkable economic growth, benefiting from access to technology and information. Yet the nation also grapples with threats that refuse to respect borders—the AIDS pandemic, extreme poverty, and terrorists, such as those who struck New Delhi late in 2005. The United States and India are natural allies, and the U.S.-Indian strategic partnership will help shape the twenty-first century. We must therefore strengthen our relationship using both national and international tools: reforming the UN so that there is a place for India on the Security Council and working with India to help it achieve a credible and transparent plan to permanently separate its civilian and military nuclear programs. The United States could then more easily work with India to address its energy needs—another step that would deepen the U.S.-Indian friendship.

BUILDING A STRONG DEFENSE

The past few years have brought the biggest crisis in civil-military relations in a generation. The mismanagement of the military has been so severe that many of our most decorated retired officers are speaking out. I will reengage with our military through a basic doctrine of national security management that has been demolished by the current administration: military professionals will have primary responsibility in matters of tactics and operations, while civilian leaders will have authority over political decisions and in all matters of broad strategy.

The force structure of our military should match its missions. We must be very clear about the military's purpose. The U.S. armed forces have three important missions: deterring or responding to those who wish to do us harm, ensuring that the problems of weak and failing states do not create dangers for the United States, and maintaining our strategic advantage over major competitor states, in part so that they choose to cooperate with us, rather than challenge our interests militarily.

The current administration's mismanagement of the military has gone far beyond these missions, leading to a very dangerous situation for our troops, their families, and our nation. We are sending some troops back to Iraq with less than a year's rest. Military leaders are warning about "breaking" the force. It is tempting for politicians to respond to this situation by trying to outbid one another on the number of troops they would add to the military. Some have fallen right in line behind President Bush's recent proposal to add 92,000 troops between now and 2012, giving little rationale for exactly why we need this many men and women, particularly with a likely withdrawal from Iraq. But the problem of our force structure is not best dealt with by a numbers game. We must be more thoughtful about what the troops would actually be used for. Any troops we add now would take a number of years to recruit and train, and they would therefore not help us today in Iraq.

As president, I will rebalance our forces to ensure that the size and capabilities of our military match its missions. We must have enough troops to rebuild from the debacle in Iraq, to bolster deterrence, to decrease our heavy reliance on National Guard and Reserve members in overseas missions, to provide additional support for our brave troops fighting in Afghanistan, and to deploy to other trouble spots when necessary. I will double the budget for recruitment and raise the standards for the recruitment pool so that we can reduce our reliance on felony waivers and other exceptions. In addition, I will increase our investment in the maintenance of our equipment for the safety of our troops.

Our all-volunteer military is the best in the world, and its servicemen and servicewomen have done everything their leaders have asked them to do—and more. They and their families have stayed strong through an increasing number of deployments and the administration's unconscionable decision to extend tours from 12 to 15 months—and in the future, perhaps longer. U.S. soldiers, sailors, air force personnel, and marines and their families are the ones suffering the most from the administration's failures, including poor planning, equipment shortages, and inadequate training.

As commander in chief, I will do everything I can to repair the sacred contract with our active-duty personnel and veterans. Central to this sacred contract is a simple and solemn pledge to every man and woman who risks his or her life for our country: we will take care of you as you have taken care of us. My administration will guarantee quality health care for our servicemen and servicewomen and every generation of veterans, provide families with the support they need to withstand the strain of separations, and ensure that returning troops have access to the education and opportunities necessary to succeed in civilian life.

The military budget itself also needs substantial reform. Today, dozens of agencies perform overlapping tasks. There is no central, overall accounting of all the security activities performed by all the relevant agencies. There are nuclear nonproliferation programs in the Defense, State, and Energy Departments and more than 15 different security assistance programs running out of both the State Department and the Pentagon. As president, I will create a national security budget that will include all security programs at the Pentagon and the Department of Energy, as well as our homeland security, intelligence, and foreign affairs agencies. The national security budget will eliminate wasteful and counterproductive overlaps and gather all of our resources behind a unified strategy.

RESTORING AMERICA'S MORAL LEADERSHIP

When it comes to reengaging with the world, there is no task more critical than restoring our moral leadership. We must begin to create a world in which the despair that breeds radical terrorism is overwhelmed by the hope that comes with universal education, democracy, and economic opportunity. By exercising this sort of leadership, we can transform a generation of potential enemies into a generation of friends.

We can begin by leading the fight to eradicate global poverty and provide universal primary education. At first glance, these areas might not seem directly related to our self-interest. But they are in fact intimately tied to our present and future national security. Unsurprisingly, we see radicalism rising today in unstable countries such as Pakistan, Saudi Arabia, Somalia, and, of course, Iraq and Afghanistan. This illuminates the importance of foreign and national security policies that seek to prevent terrorism, not just respond to it.

Education is one of the most critical ways we can reverse the effects of poverty. According to UNICEF (the United Nations Children's Fund), the mortality rate for children under five years of age decreases by half if their mothers have received a primary school education. As president, I will increase our funding for global primary education sixfold, with a $3 billion annual effort to educate poor children in countries with a history of violent extremism. Through the U.S. Agency for International Development and multilateral aid organizations, I will also pursue reform of the school systems in developing countries, working to eliminate school fees and required expenses for books and uniforms, which effectively bar millions of children from enrolling; investing in teacher education, classroom expansion, and teaching materials; and helping to provide safe and hygienic facilities for all students. Finally, as president, I will lead an effort to increase opportunity for millions of people by adding $750 million annually for micro-credit programs.

Clean water and sanitation are also necessary to improve health, education, and economic prosperity. Women and children bear the burden of poverty and disease in the developing world. Women in the poorest countries have a ten percent chance of dying during childbirth. More than ten million children die each year from preventable diseases. Developing countries suffer enormously from the top three killer diseases: AIDS, tuberculosis, and malaria.

As president, I will concentrate on reversing the spread of these three deadly diseases by guaranteeing universal access to preventive drugs and treatment by 2010. I will also substantially increase U.S. funding for clean-water programs. Finally, I will direct U.S. agencies to lead an international effort to dramatically increase preventive care, beginning with increased vaccinations and the provision of sterile equipment and basic medications.

Despite the urgency of these programs, the same redundancy that plagues our national security activities exists in our foreign assistance programs. Over 50 separate U.S. government entities are currently involved in the delivery of foreign aid. We need to return to President Kennedy's vision. He said in 1961 that the American system was fragmented, awkward, and slow and that improvement was necessary because "the nation's interest and the cause of political freedom require it." Kennedy reformed the American foreign-aid system, and we need a similar fundamental restructuring today. As president, I will create a new cabinet-level position to coordinate global development policies across the government. I will also replace Kennedy's Foreign Assistance Act of

1961 with a Global Development Act to modernize and consolidate development assistance, and I will ask Congress to improve its oversight and revamp its committee structure so that it can be a more effective partner in this effort. With measures like these, we can reclaim our historic role as a moral leader of the world while at the same time making the world safer and more secure for the United States.

THE WAY FORWARD

In 1945, it would have been easy enough for us to glance at the devastation in Europe and look the other way. But leaders such as President Truman and General Marshall understood that it would require more than the United States' military might to rebuild Europe. Keeping post-World War II Europe safe from tyrants who would prey on poverty and resentment called for our ingenuity, our allies, and our generosity. General Marshall made a momentous decision to engage with the world in order to build a brighter, more hopeful future. In his 1953 speech accepting the Nobel Peace Prize for rebuilding Europe, General Marshall explained that military power was "too narrow a basis on which to build a dependable, long-enduring peace." He was right. Today's peaceful and prosperous Europe is a testament to his wisdom and foresight.

Our nation now stands at the pinnacle of its power, but it also faces serious challenges. Today, we need a national security policy for the twenty-first century that will not only respond to threats but apply all our resources to the critical goal of preventing such threats in the first place. We can be strong, secure, and good, and we can build a more hopeful future. Our national security policy should be designed to reach these goals. We must do everything in our power to reclaim the United States' historic role as a beacon for the world and become, once again, a shining example for other nations to follow.

JOHN EDWARDS, a former U.S. Senator from North Carolina, is a candidate for the Democratic presidential nomination.

Toward a Realistic Peace

Rudolph W. Giuliani   SEPTEMBER/OCTOBER 2007

Republican presidential candidate and former New York City Mayor Rudy Giuliani pauses while speaking at the Institute of Politics at Saint Anselm College in Manchester, New Hampshire, November 5, 2007.

We are all members of the 9/11 generation. The defining challenges of the twentieth century ended with the fall of the Berlin Wall. Full recognition of the first great challenge of the twenty-first century came with the attacks of September 11, 2001, even though Islamist terrorists had begun their assault on world order decades before. Confronted with an act of war on American soil, our old assumptions about conflict between nation-states fell away. Civilization itself, and the international system, had come under attack by a ruthless and radical Islamist enemy.

America and its allies have made progress since that terrible day. We have responded forcefully to the Terrorists' War on Us, abandoning a decadelong—and counterproductive—strategy of defensive reaction in favor of a vigorous offense. And we have set in motion changes to the international system that promise a safer and better world for generations to come.

But this war will be long, and we are still in its early stages. Much like at the beginning of the Cold War, we are at the dawn of a new era in global affairs, when old ideas have to be rethought and new ideas have to be devised to meet new challenges.

The next U.S. president will face three key foreign policy challenges. First and foremost will be to set a course for victory in the terrorists' war on global order. The second will be to strengthen the international system that the terrorists seek to destroy. The third will be to extend the benefits of the international system in an ever-widening arc of security and stability across the globe. The most effective means for achieving these goals are building a stronger defense, developing a determined diplomacy, and expanding our economic and cultural influence. Using all three, the next president can build the foundations of a lasting, realistic peace.

Achieving a realistic peace means balancing realism and idealism in our foreign policy. America is a nation that loves peace and hates war. At the core of all Americans is the belief that all human beings have certain inalienable rights that proceed from God but must be protected by the state. Americans believe that to the extent that nations recognize these rights within their own laws and customs, peace with them is achievable. To the extent that they do not, violence and disorder are much more likely. Preserving and extending American ideals must remain the goal of all U.S. policy, foreign and domestic. But unless we pursue our idealistic goals through realistic means, peace will not be achieved.

Idealism should define our ultimate goals; realism must help us recognize the road we must travel to achieve them. The world is a dangerous place. We cannot afford to indulge any illusions about the enemies we face. The Terrorists' War on Us was encouraged by unrealistic and inconsistent actions taken in response to terrorist attacks in the past. A realistic peace can only be achieved through strength.

A realistic peace is not a peace to be achieved by embracing the "realist" school of foreign policy thought. That doctrine defines America's interests too narrowly and avoids attempts to reform the international system according to our values. To rely solely on this type of realism would be to cede the advantage to our enemies in the complex war of ideas and ideals. It would also place too great a hope in the potential for diplomatic accommodation with hostile states. And it would exaggerate America's weaknesses and downplay America's strengths. Our economy is the strongest in the developed world. Our political system is far more stable than those of the world's rising economic giants. And the United States is the world's premier magnet for global talent and capital.

Still, the realist school offers some valuable insights, in particular its insistence on seeing the world as it is and on tempering our expectations of what American foreign policy can achieve. We cannot achieve peace by promising too much or indulging false hopes. This next decade can be a positive era for our country and the world so long as the next president realistically mobilizes the 9/11 generation for the momentous tasks ahead.

WINNING THE EARLY BATTLES OF THE LONG WAR

The first step toward a realistic peace is to be realistic about our enemies. They follow a violent ideology: radical Islamic fascism, which uses the mask of religion to further totalitarian goals and aims to destroy the existing international system. These enemies wear no uniform. They have no traditional military assets. They rule no states but can hide and operate in virtually any of them and are supported by some.

Above all, we must understand that our enemies are emboldened by signs of weakness. Radical Islamic terrorists attacked the World Trade Center in 1993, the Khobar Towers facility in Saudi Arabia in 1996, our embassies in Kenya and Tanzania in 1998, and the U.S.S. Cole in 2000. In some instances, we responded inadequately. In others, we failed to respond at all. Our retreat from Lebanon in 1983 and from Somalia in 1993 convinced them that our will was weak.

We must learn from these experiences for the long war that lies ahead. It is almost certain that U.S. troops will still be fighting in Iraq and Afghanistan when the next president takes office. The purpose of this fight must be to defeat the terrorists and the insurgents in Iraq and Afghanistan and to allow these countries to become members of the international system in good standing. We must be under no illusions that either Iraq or Afghanistan will quickly attain the levels of peace and security enjoyed in the developed world today. Our aim should be to help them build accountable, functioning governments that can serve the needs of their populations, reduce violence within their borders, and eliminate the export of terror. As violence decreases and security improves, more responsibility can and should be turned over to local security forces. But some U.S. forces will need to remain for some time in order to deter external threats.

We cannot predict when our efforts will be successful. But we can predict the consequences of failure: Afghanistan would revert to being a safe haven for terrorists, and Iraq would become another one—larger, richer, and more strategically located. Parts of Iraq would undoubtedly fall under the sway of our enemies, particularly Iran, which would use its influence to direct even more terror at U.S. interests and U.S. allies than it does today. The balance of power in the Middle East would tip further toward terror, extremism, and repression. America's influence and prestige—not just in the Middle East but around the world—would be dealt a shattering blow. Our allies would conclude that we cannot back up our commitments with sustained action. Our enemies—both terrorists and rogue states—would be emboldened. They would see further opportunities to weaken the international state system that is the primary defense of civilization. Much as our enemies in the 1990s concluded from our inconsistent response to terrorism then, our enemies today would conclude that America's will is weak and the civilization we pledged to defend is tired. Failure would be an invitation for more war, in even more difficult and dangerous circumstances.

America must remember one of the lessons of the Vietnam War. Then, as now, we fought a war with the wrong strategy for several years. And then, as now, we corrected course and began to show real progress. Many historians today believe that by about 1972 we and our South Vietnamese partners had succeeded in defeating the Vietcong insurgency and in setting South Vietnam on a path to political self-sufficiency. But America then withdrew its support, allowing the communist North to conquer the South. The consequences were dire, and not only in Vietnam: numerous deaths in places such as the killing fields of Cambodia, a newly energized and expansionist Soviet Union, and a weaker America. The consequences of abandoning Iraq would be worse.

Our goal is to see in Iraq and Afghanistan the emergence of stable governments and societies that can act as our allies against the terrorists and not as breeding grounds for expanded terrorist activities. Succeeding in Iraq and Afghanistan is necessary but not sufficient. Ultimately, these are only two battlegrounds in a wider war. The United States must not rest until the al Qaeda network is destroyed and its leaders, from Osama bin Laden on down, are killed or captured. And the United States must not rest until the global terrorist movement and its ideology are defeated.

Much of that fight will take place in the shadows. It will be the work of intelligence operatives, paramilitary groups, and Special Operations forces. It will also require close relationships with other governments and local forces. The next U.S. president should direct our armed forces to emphasize such work, in part because local forces are best able to operate in their home countries and in part in order to reduce the strain on our own troops.

A STRONGER DEFENSE

For 15 years, the de facto policy of both Republicans and Democrats has been to ask the U.S. military to do increasingly more with increasingly less. The idea of a post-Cold War "peace dividend" was a serious mistake—the product of wishful thinking and the opposite of true realism. As a result of taking this dividend, our military is too small to meet its current commitments or shoulder the burden of any additional challenges that might arise. We must rebuild a military force that can deter aggression and meet the wide variety of present and future challenges. When America appears bogged down and unready to face aggressors, it invites conflict.

The U.S. Army needs a minimum of ten new combat brigades. It may need more, but this is an appropriate baseline increase while we reevaluate our strategies and resources. We must also take a hard look at other requirements, especially in terms of submarines, modern long-range bombers, and in-flight refueling tankers. Rebuilding will not be cheap, but it is necessary. And the benefits will outweigh the costs.

The next U.S. president must also press ahead with building a national missile defense system. America can no longer rely on Cold War doctrines such as "mutual assured destruction" in the face of threats from hostile, unstable regimes. Nor can it ignore the possibility of nuclear blackmail. Rogue regimes that know they can threaten America, our allies, and our interests with ballistic missiles will behave more aggressively, including by increasing their support for terrorists. On the other hand, the knowledge that America and our allies could intercept and destroy incoming missiles would not only make blackmail less likely but also decrease the appeal of ballistic missile programs and so help to slow their development and proliferation. It is well within our capability to field a layered missile defense capable of shielding us from the arsenals of the world's most dangerous states. President George W. Bush deserves credit for changing America's course on this issue. But progress needs to be accelerated.

An even greater danger is the possibility of a terrorist attack on U.S. soil with a chemical, biological, radiological, or nuclear weapon. Every effort must be made to improve our intelligence capabilities and technological capacities to prevent this. Constellations of satellites that can watch arms factories everywhere around the globe, day and night, above- and belowground, combined with more robust human intelligence, must be part of America's arsenal. The laudable and effective Proliferation Security Initiative, a global effort to stop the shipment of weapons of mass destruction and related materials, should be expanded and strengthened. In particular, we must work to deter the development, transfer, or use of weapons of mass destruction. We must also develop the capability to prevent an attack—including a clandestine attack—by those who cannot be deterred. Rogue states must be prevented from handing nuclear materials to terrorist groups. Our enemies must know that they cannot murder our citizens with impunity and escape retaliation.

We must also develop detection systems to identify nuclear material that is being imported into the United States or developed by operatives inside the country. Heightened and more comprehensive security measures at our ports and borders must be enacted as rapidly as possible. And our national security agencies must work much more closely with our homeland security and law enforcement agencies. We must preserve the gains made by the U.S.A. Patriot Act and not unrealistically limit electronic surveillance or legal interrogation. Preventing a chemical, biological, radiological, or nuclear attack on our homeland must be the federal government's top priority. We must construct a technological and intelligence shield that is effective against all delivery methods.

Military victories are essential, but they are not enough. A lasting, realistic peace will be achieved when more effective diplomacy, combined with greater economic and cultural integration, helps the people of the Middle East understand that they have a stake in the success of the international system.

DETERMINED DIPLOMACY

To achieve a realistic peace, some of what we need to do can and must be accomplished through our own efforts. But much more requires international cooperation, and cooperation requires diplomacy.

In recent years, diplomacy has received a bad name, because of two opposing perspectives. One side denigrates diplomacy because it believes that negotiation is inseparable from accommodation and almost indistinguishable from surrender. The other seemingly believes that diplomacy can solve nearly all problems, even those involving people dedicated to our destruction. When such efforts fail, as they inevitably do, diplomacy itself is blamed, rather than the flawed approach that led to their failure.

America has been most successful as a world leader when it has used strength and diplomacy hand in hand. To achieve a realistic peace, U.S. diplomacy must be tightly linked to our other strengths: military, economic, and moral. Whom we choose to talk to is as important as what we say. Diplomacy should never be a tool that our enemies can manipulate to their advantage. Holding serious talks may be advisable even with our adversaries, but not with those bent on our destruction or those who cannot deliver on their agreements.

Iran is a case in point. The Islamic Republic has been determined to attack the international system throughout its entire existence: it took U.S. diplomats hostage in 1979 and seized British sailors in 2007 and during the decades in between supported terrorism and murder. But Tehran invokes the protections of the international system when doing so suits it, hiding behind the principle of sovereignty to stave off the consequences of its actions. This is not to say that talks with Iran cannot possibly work. They could—but only if we came to the table in a position of strength, knowing what we wanted.

The next U.S. president should take inspiration from Ronald Reagan's actions during his summit with Soviet leader Mikhail Gorbachev in Reykjavík in 1986: he was open to the possibility of negotiations but ready to walk away if talking went nowhere. The lesson is never talk for the sake of talking and never accept a bad deal for the sake of making a deal. Those with whom we negotiate— whether ally or adversary—must know that America has other options. The theocrats ruling Iran need to understand that we can wield the stick as well as the carrot, by undermining popular support for their regime, damaging the Iranian economy, weakening Iran's military, and, should all else fail, destroying its nuclear infrastructure.

For diplomacy to succeed, the U.S. government must be united. Adversaries naturally exploit divisions. Members of Congress who talk directly to rogue regimes at cross-purposes with the White House are not practicing diplomacy; they are undermining it. The task of a president is not merely to set priorities but to ensure that they are pursued across the government. It is only when they are—and when Washington can negotiate from a position of strength—that negotiations will yield results. As President John F. Kennedy said in his inaugural address, "Let us never negotiate out of fear. But let us never fear to negotiate."

Another step in rebuilding a strong diplomacy will be to make changes in the State Department and the Foreign Service. The time has come to refine the diplomats' mission down to their core purpose: presenting U.S. policy to the rest of the world. Reforming the State Department is a matter not of changing its organizational chart—although simplification is needed—but of changing the way we practice diplomacy and the way we measure results. Our ambassadors must clearly understand and clearly advocate for U.S. policies and be judged on the results. Too many people denounce our country or our policies simply because they are confident that they will not hear any serious refutation from our representatives. The American ideals of freedom and democracy deserve stronger advocacy. And the era of cost-free anti-Americanism must end.

Since leaving the New York City mayor's office, I have traveled to 35 different countries. It is clear that we need to do a better job of explaining America's message and mission to the rest of the world, not by imposing our ideas on others but by appealing to their enlightened self-interest. To this end, the Voice of America program must be significantly strengthened and broadened. Its surrogate stations, such as Radio Free Europe and Radio Liberty, which were so effective at inspiring grass-roots dissidents during the Cold War, must be expanded as well. Our entire approach to public diplomacy and strategic communications must be upgraded and extended, with a greater focus on new media such as the Internet. We confront multifaceted challenges in the Middle East, the Pacific region, Africa, and Latin America. In all these places, effective communication can be a powerful way of advancing our interests. We will not shy away from any debate. And armed with honest advocacy, America will win the war of ideas.

STRENGTHENING THE INTERNATIONAL SYSTEM

The next U.S. president will share the world stage with a new generation of leaders, few of whom were in office when the attacks of 9/11 occurred but all of whom have been influenced by their impact. This will be a rare opportunity for American leadership to make the case that our common interest lies in defeating the terrorists and strengthening the international system.

Defeating the terrorists must be our principal priority in the near future, but we do not have the luxury of focusing on it to the exclusion of other goals. World events unfold whether the United States is engaged or not, and when we are not, they often unfold in ways that are against our interests. The art of managing a large enterprise is to multitask, and so U.S. foreign policy must always be multidimensional.

A primary goal for our diplomacy—whether directed toward great powers, developing states, or international institutions— must be to strengthen the international system, which most of the world has a direct interest in seeing function well. After all, the system helps keep the peace and provide prosperity. Some theorists say that it is outmoded and display either too much faith in globalization or assume that the age of the sovereign state is coming to a close. These views are naive. There is no realistic alternative to the sovereign state system. Transnational terrorists and other rogue actors have difficulty operating where the state system is strong, and they flourish where it is weak. This is the reason they try to exploit its weaknesses.

We should therefore work to strengthen the international system through America's relations with other great powers, both long established and rising. We should regard no great power as our inherent adversary. We should continue to fully engage with Europe, both in its collective capacity as the European Union and through our special relationship with the United Kingdom and our traditional diplomatic relations with France, Germany, Italy, and other western European nations. We highly value our ties with the states of central and eastern Europe and the Baltic and Balkan nations. Their experience of oppression under communism has made them steadfast allies and strong advocates of economic freedom.

America is grateful to NATO for the vital functions it is performing in Afghanistan and elsewhere. Yet NATO's role and character should be reexamined. For almost 60 years, it has been a vital bond connecting the United States and Europe. But its founding rationale dissolved with the end of the Cold War, and the alliance should be transformed to meet the challenges of this new century. NATO has already expanded to include former adversaries, taken on roles for which it was not originally conceived, and acted beyond its original theater. We should build on these successes and think more boldly and more globally. We should open the organization's membership to any state that meets basic standards of good governance, military readiness, and global responsibility, regardless of its location. The new NATO should dedicate itself to confronting significant threats to the international system, from territorial aggression to terrorism. I hope that NATO members will see the wisdom in such changes. NATO must change with the times, and its members must always match their rhetorical commitment with action and investment. In return, America can assure them that we will be there for them in times of crisis. They stood by America after 9/11, and America will never forget.

As important as America's Western alliances are, we must recognize that America will often be best served by turning also to its other friends, old and new. Much of America's future will be linked to the already established and still rising powers of Asia. These states share with us a clear commitment to economic growth, and they must be given at least as much attention as Europe. Our alliance with Japan, which has been strengthened considerably under this administration, is a rock of stability in Asia. South Korea has been a key to security in Northeast Asia and an important contributor to international peace. Australia, our distant but long-standing ally, continues to assume a greater role in world affairs and acts as a steadfast defender of international standards and security. U.S. cooperation with India on issues ranging from intelligence to naval patrols and civil nuclear power will serve as a pillar of security and prosperity in South Asia.

U.S. relations with China and Russia will remain complex for the foreseeable future. Americans have no wish to return to the tensions of the Cold War or to launch a new one. We must seek common ground without turning a blind eye to our differences with these two countries. Like America, they have a fundamental stake in the health of the international system. But too often, their governments act shortsightedly, undermining their long-term interest in international norms for the sake of near-term gains. Even as we work with these countries on economic and security issues, the U.S. government should not be silent about their unhelpful behavior or human rights abuses. Washington should also make clear that only if China and Russia move toward democracy, civil liberties, and an open and uncorrupted economy will they benefit from the vast possibilities available in the world today.

Our relationships with other American nations remain of primary importance. Canada and Mexico, our two closest neighbors, are our two largest trading partners. With them, we share a continent, a free-trade agreement, and a commitment to peace, prosperity, and freedom. Latin America faces a choice between the failures of the past and the hopes of the future. Some look to the governments of Bolivia and Venezuela, and their mentor in Cuba, and see an inevitable path to greater statism. But elections in Colombia, Mexico, and Peru show that the spirit of free-market reform is alive and well among our southern neighbors. Cuba has long stood out in Latin America, first as one of the region's most successful economies, later as its only communist police state. The death of Fidel Castro may begin a new chapter in Cuban history. But America should take nothing for granted. It must stand ready to help the Cuban people reclaim their liberty and resist any step that allows a decrepit, corrupt regime from consolidating its power under Raúl Castro. Only a commitment to free people and free markets will bring a prosperous future to Cuba and all of Latin America.

More people in the United States need to understand how helping Africa today will help increase peace and decency throughout the world tomorrow. The next president should continue the Bush administration's effort to help Africa overcome AIDS and malaria. The international community must also learn from the mistakes that allowed the genocide in Darfur to begin and have prevented the relevant international organizations from ending it. The world's commitment to end genocide has been sidestepped again and again. Ultimately, the most important thing we can do to help Africa is to increase trade with the continent. U.S. government aid is important, but aid not linked to reform perpetuates bad policies and poverty. It is better to give people a hand up than a handout.

Finally, we need to look realistically at America's relationship with the United Nations. The organization can be useful for some humanitarian and peacekeeping functions, but we should not expect much more of it. The UN has proved irrelevant to the resolution of almost every major dispute of the last 50 years. Worse, it has failed to combat terrorism and human rights abuses. It has not lived up to the great hopes that inspired its creation. Too often, it has been weak, indecisive, and outright corrupt. The UN's charter and the speeches of its members' leaders have meant little because its members' deeds have frequently fallen short. International law and institutions exist to serve peoples and nations, but many leaders act as if the reverse were true—that is, as if institutions, not the ends to be achieved, were the important thing.

Despite the UN's flaws, however, the great objectives of humanity would become even more difficult to achieve without mechanisms for international discussion. History has shown that such institutions work best when the United States leads them. Yet we cannot take for granted that they will work forever and must be prepared to look to other tools.

EXTENDING THE INTERNATIONAL SYSTEM'S BENEFITS

Most of the problems in the world today arise from places where the state system is broken or has never functioned. Much of the Middle East, Africa, and Latin America remains mired in poverty, corruption, anarchy, and terror. But there is nothing inevitable about this. For all these troubled cases, there are many more success stories that deserve to be celebrated. The number of functioning democracies in the world has tripled since the 1970s. The poverty rate in the developing world has been cut by roughly one-third since the end of the Cold War. Millions of people have been liberated from oppression and fear. Progress is not only possible, it is real. And it must continue to be real.

America has a clear interest in helping to establish good governance throughout the world. Democracy is a noble ideal, and promoting it abroad is the right long-term goal of U.S. policy. But democracy cannot be achieved rapidly or sustained unless it is built on sound legal, institutional, and cultural foundations. It can only work if people have a reasonable degree of safety and security. Elections are necessary but not sufficient to establish genuine democracy. Aspiring dictators sometimes win elections, and elected leaders sometimes govern badly and threaten their neighbors. History demonstrates that democracy usually follows good governance, not the reverse. U.S. assistance can do much to set nations on the road to democracy, but we must be realistic about how much we can accomplish alone and how long it will take to achieve lasting progress.

The election of Hamas in the Palestinian-controlled territories is a case in point. The problem there is not the lack of statehood but corrupt and unaccountable governance. The Palestinian people need decent governance first, as a prerequisite for statehood. Too much emphasis has been placed on brokering negotiations between the Israelis and the Palestinians—negotiations that bring up the same issues again and again. It is not in the interest of the United States, at a time when it is being threatened by Islamist terrorists, to assist the creation of another state that will support terrorism. Palestinian statehood will have to be earned through sustained good governance, a clear commitment to fighting terrorism, and a willingness to live in peace with Israel. America's commitment to Israel's security is a permanent feature of our foreign policy.

The next president must champion human rights and speak out when they are violated. America should continue to use its influence to bring attention to individual abuses and use a full range of inducements and pressures to try to end them. Securing the rights of men, women, and children everywhere should be a core commitment of any country that counts itself as part of the civilized world. Whether with friends, allies, or adversaries, democracy will always be an issue in our relations and part of the conversation. And so the better a country's record on good governance, human rights, and democratic development, the better its relations with the United States will be. Those countries that want our help in moving toward these ideals will have it.

USING ECONOMIC AND CULTURAL INFLUENCE

Economic development and engagement are proven, if not fail-safe, engines for successfully moving countries into the international system. America's robust domestic economy is one of its greatest strengths. Other nations have found that following the U.S. model—with low taxes, sensible regulations, protections for private property, and free trade—brings not only national wealth but also national strength. These principles are not ascendant everywhere, but never has it been clearer that they work.

Ever more open trade throughout the world is essential. Bilateral and regional free-trade agreements are often positive for all involved, but we must not allow them to become special arrangements that undermine a truly global trading system. Foreign aid can help overcome specific problems, but it does not lead to lasting prosperity because it cannot replace trade. Private direct investment is the best way to promote economic development. The next U.S. president should thus revitalize and streamline all U.S. foreign-aid activities to support—not substitute for—private investment in other countries.

Our cultural and commercial influence can also have a positive impact. They did during the Cold War. The steadfast leadership of President Reagan, working alongside British Prime Minister Margaret Thatcher and Pope John Paul II, helped the Soviet Union understand that it could not bully the West into submission. Although such leadership was essential, alone it might not have toppled the Soviet Union in the time that it did. But it was effective because it came with Western economic investment and cultural influence that inspired people in the Soviet Union and the Warsaw Pact countries. Companies such as Pepsi, Coca-Cola, McDonald's, and Levi's helped win the Cold War by entering the Soviet market. Cultural events, such as Van Cliburn's concerts in the Soviet Union and Mstislav Rostropovich's in the United States, also hastened change.

Today, we need a similar type of exchange with the Muslim countries that we hope to plug into the global economy. Jordan, Kuwait, Qatar, and the United Arab Emirates are pointing the way by starting to interpret Islam in ways that respect the distinctiveness of their local cultures but are consistent with the global marketplace. Some of these states have coeducational schools, allow women to serve in government, and count shopping malls that sell Western and Arab goods side by side. Their leaders recognize that modernization is their ticket to the global marketplace. And the global marketplace can build bridges between the West and the Islamic world in a way that promotes mutual respect and mutual benefit.

Economic investment and cultural influence work best where civil society already exists. But sometimes America will be compelled to act in those parts of the world where few institutions function properly—those zones that lack not only good governance but any governance—and in states teetering on the edge of conflict or recovering from it. Faced with a choice between leaving a troubled zone to anarchy or helping build functioning civil societies with accountable governments that can serve as bulwarks against barbarism, the American people will choose the latter.

To assist these missions, the next U.S. president should restructure and coordinate all the agencies involved in that process. A hybrid military-civilian organization—a Stabilization and Reconstruction Corps staffed by specially trained military and civilian reservists—must be developed. The agency would undertake tasks such as building roads, sewers, and schools; advising on legal reform; and restoring local currencies. The United States did similar work, and with great success, in Germany, Japan, and Italy after World War II. But even with the rich civic traditions in these nations, the process took a number of years. We must learn from our past if we want to win the peace as well as the war.

PRINCIPLED STRENGTH

Civilization must stand up and combat the current collapse of governance, the rise of violence, and the spread of chaos and fear in many parts of the world. To turn back this tide of terror and defeat the violent forces of disorder wherever they appear, America must play an even more active role to strengthen the international state system.

In this decade, for the first time in human history, half of the world's population will live in cities. I know from personal experience that when security is reliably established in a troubled part of a city, normal life rapidly reestablishes itself: shops open, people move back in, children start playing ball on the sidewalks again, and soon a decent and law-abiding community returns to life. The same is true in world affairs. Disorder in the world's bad neighborhoods tends to spread. Tolerating bad behavior breeds more bad behavior. But concerted action to uphold international standards will help peoples, economies, and states to thrive. Civil society can triumph over chaos if it is backed by determined action.

After the attacks of 9/11, President Bush put America on the offensive against terrorists, orchestrating the most fundamental change in U.S. strategy since President Harry Truman reoriented American foreign and defense policy at the outset of the Cold War. But times and challenges change, and our nation must be flexible. President Dwight Eisenhower and his successors accepted Truman's framework, but they corrected course to fit the specific challenges of their own times. America's next president must also craft polices to fit the needs of the decade ahead, even as the nation stays on the offensive against the terrorist threat.

The 9/11 generation has learned from the history of the twentieth century that America must not turn a blind eye to gathering storms. We must base our trust on the actions, rather than the words, of others. And we must be on guard against overpromising and underdelivering. Above all, we have learned that evil must be confronted—not appeased—because only principled strength can lead to a realistic peace.

RUDOLPH W. GIULIANI, former Mayor of New York City, is a candidate for the Republican presidential nomination.

Security and Opportunity in the Twenty-first Century

Hillary Rodham Clinton   NOVEMBER/DECEMBER 2007

Hillary Rodham Clinton waves to the crowd after addressing the National League of Cities 2007 Congressional City Conference in Washington, March 13, 2007.

To lead, a great nation must command the respect of others. America has been respected in the past as a powerful nation, a purposeful nation, and a generous and warm-hearted nation. In my travels around the world as senator and as first lady, I have met people from all walks of life. I have seen firsthand how many of our past policies have earned us respect and gratitude.

The tragedy of the last six years is that the Bush administration has squandered the respect, trust, and confidence of even our closest allies and friends. At the dawn of the twenty-first century, the United States enjoyed a unique position. Our world leadership was widely accepted and respected, as we strengthened old alliances and built new ones, worked for peace across the globe, advanced nonproliferation, and modernized our military. After 9/11, the world rallied behind the United States as never before, supporting our efforts to remove the Taliban in Afghanistan and go after the al Qaeda leadership. We had a historic opportunity to build a broad global coalition to combat terror, increase the impact of our diplomacy, and create a world with more partners and fewer adversaries.

But we lost that opportunity by refusing to let the UN inspectors finish their work in Iraq and rushing to war instead. Moreover, we diverted vital military and financial resources from the struggle against al Qaeda and the daunting task of building a Muslim democracy in Afghanistan. At the same time, we embarked on an unprecedented course of unilateralism: refusing to pursue ratification of the Comprehensive Nuclear Test Ban Treaty, abandoning our commitment to nuclear nonproliferation, and turning our backs on the search for peace in the Middle East. Our withdrawal from the Kyoto Protocol and refusal to participate in any international effort to deal with the tremendous challenges of climate change further damaged our international standing.

Our nation has paid a heavy price for rejecting a long-standing bipartisan tradition of global leadership rooted in a preference for cooperating over acting unilaterally, for exhausting diplomacy before making war, and for converting old adversaries into allies rather than making new enemies. At a moment in history when the world's most pressing problems require unprecedented cooperation, this administration has unilaterally pursued policies that are widely disliked and distrusted.

Yet it does not have to be this way. Indeed, our allies do not want it to be this way. The world still looks to the United States for leadership. American leadership is wanting, but it is still wanted. Our friends around the world do not want the United States to retreat. They want once again to be allied with the nation whose values, leadership, and strength have inspired the world for the last century.

To reclaim our proper place in the world, the United States must be stronger, and our policies must be smarter. The next president will have a moment of opportunity to restore America's global standing and convince the world that America can lead once again. As president, I will seize that opportunity by reintroducing ourselves to the world. I will rebuild our power and ensure that the United States is committed to building a world we want, rather than simply defending against a world we fear.

We should aim to lead our friends and allies in building a world of security and opportunity. America has long been the land of opportunity. But as we know at home and as we see today in Iraq and Afghanistan, opportunity cannot flourish without basic security. We must build a world in which security and opportunity go hand in hand, a world that will be safer, more prosperous, and more just.

We need more than vision, however, to achieve the world we want. We must face up to an unprecedented array of challenges in the twenty-first century, threats from states, nonstate actors, and nature itself. The next president will be the first to inherit two wars, a long-term campaign against global terrorist networks, and growing tension with Iran as it seeks to acquire nuclear weapons. The United States will face a resurgent Russia whose future orientation is uncertain and a rapidly growing China that must be integrated into the international system. Moreover, the next administration will have to confront an unpredictable and dangerous situation in the Middle East that threatens Israel and could potentially bring down the global economy by disrupting oil supplies. Finally, the next president will have to address the looming long-term threats of climate change and a new wave of global health epidemics.

To meet these challenges, we will have to replenish American power by getting out of Iraq, rebuilding our military, and developing a much broader arsenal of tools in the fight against terrorism. We must learn once again to draw on all aspects of American power, to inspire and attract as much as to coerce. We must return to a pragmatic willingness to look at the facts on the ground and make decisions based on evidence rather than ideology.

POWER AND PRINCIPLE

Leadership requires a blend of strategy, persuasion, inspiration, and motivation. It is based on respect more than fear. America's founders wrote the Declaration of Independence to explain our actions to the world out of a decent respect for the opinions of mankind. Gaining the respect of other nations today requires that we harness our might to a set of guiding principles.

Avoid false choices driven by ideology. The Bush administration has presented the American people with a series of false choices: force versus diplomacy, unilateralism versus multilateralism, hard power versus soft. Seeing these choices as mutually exclusive reflects an ideologically blinkered vision of the world that denies the United States the tools and the flexibility it needs to lead and succeed. There is a time for force and a time for diplomacy; when properly deployed, the two can reinforce each other. U.S. foreign policy must be guided by a preference for multilateralism, with unilateralism as an option when absolutely necessary to protect our security or avert an avoidable tragedy.

Use our military not as the solution to every problem but as one element in a comprehensive strategy. As president, I will never hesitate to use force to protect Americans or to defend our territory and our vital interests. We cannot negotiate with individual terrorists; they must be hunted down and captured or killed. Nor can diplomacy alone stop the perpetrators of genocide and crimes against humanity in places such as Darfur. But soldiers are not the answer to every problem. Using force in lieu of diplomacy compels our young men and women in uniform to carry out missions that they may not be trained or prepared for. And it ignores the value of simply carrying a big stick, rather than using it.

Make international institutions work, and work through them when possible. Contrary to what many in the current administration appear to believe, international institutions are tools rather than traps. The United States must be prepared to act on its own to defend its vital interests, but effective international institutions make it much less likely that we will have to do so. Both

Republican and Democratic presidents have understood this for decades. When such institutions work well, they enhance our influence. When they do not work, their procedures serve as pretexts for endless delays, as in the case of Darfur, or descend into farce, as in the case of Sudan's election to the UN Commission on Human Rights. But instead of disparaging these institutions for their failures, we should bring them in line with the power realities of the twenty-first century and the basic values embodied in such documents as the Universal Declaration of Human Rights.

Ensure that democracy delivers on its promises. Gnawing hunger, poverty, and the absence of economic prospects are a recipe for despair. Globalization is widening the gap between the haves and the have-nots within societies and between them. Today, there are more than two billion people living on less than $2 a day. These people risk becoming a vast permanent underclass. Calls for expanding civil and political rights in countries plagued by mass poverty and ruled by tiny wealthy elites will fall on deaf ears unless democracy actually delivers enough material benefits to improve people's lives. The Bush administration's policy in Iraq has temporarily given democracy a bad name, but over the long term the value of democracy will continue to inspire the world.

Stand for and live up to our values. The values that our founders embraced as universal have shaped the aspirations of millions of people around the world and are the deepest source of our strength—but only as long as we live up to them ourselves. As we seek to promote the rule of law in other nations, we must accept it ourselves. As we counsel liberty and justice for all, we cannot support torture and the indefinite detention of individuals we have declared to be beyond the law.

A STRONGER AMERICA

Ending the war in Iraq is the first step toward restoring the United States' global leadership. The war is sapping our military strength, absorbing our strategic assets, diverting attention and resources from Afghanistan, alienating our allies, and dividing our people. The war in Iraq has also stretched our military to the breaking point. We must rebuild our armed services and restore them body and soul.

We must withdraw from Iraq in a way that brings our troops home safely, begins to restore stability to the region, and replaces military force with a new diplomatic initiative to engage countries around the world in securing Iraq's future. To that end, as president, I will convene the Joint Chiefs of Staff, the secretary of defense, and the National Security Council and direct them to draw up a clear, viable plan to bring our troops home, starting within the first 60 days of my administration.

While working to stabilize Iraq as our forces withdraw, I will focus U.S. aid on helping Iraqis, not propping up the Iraqi government. Financial resources will go only where they will be used properly, rather than to government ministries or ministers that hoard, steal, or waste them.

As we leave Iraq militarily, I will replace our military force with an intensive diplomatic initiative in the region. The Bush administration has belatedly begun to engage Iran and Syria in talks about the future of Iraq. This is a step in the right direction, but much more must be done. As president, I will convene a regional stabilization group composed of key allies, other global powers, and all the states bordering Iraq. Working with the newly appointed UN special representative for Iraq, the group will be charged with developing and implementing a strategy for achieving a stable Iraq that provides incentives for Iran, Saudi Arabia, Syria, and Turkey to stay out of the civil war.

Finally, we need to engage the world in a global humanitarian effort to confront the human costs of this war. We must address the plight of the two million Iraqis who have fled their country and the two million more who have been displaced internally. This will require a multibillion-dollar international effort under the direction of the Office of the UN High Commissioner for Refugees. Meanwhile, the United States, along with governments in Europe and the Middle East, must agree to accept asylum seekers and help them return to Iraq when it is safe for them to do so.

As we redeploy our troops from Iraq, we must not let down our guard against terrorism. I will order specialized units to engage in targeted operations against al Qaeda in Iraq and other terrorist organizations in the region. These units will also provide security for U.S. troops and personnel in Iraq and train and equip Iraqi security services to keep order and promote stability in the country, but only to the extent that such training is actually working. I will also consider leaving some forces in the Kurdish area of northern Iraq in order to protect the fragile but real democracy and relative peace and security that have developed there, but with the clear understanding that the terrorist organization the PKK (Kurdistan Workers' Party) must be dealt with and the Turkish border must be respected.

Getting out of Iraq will enable us to play a constructive role in a renewed Middle East peace process that would mean security and normal relations for Israel and the Palestinians. The fundamental elements of a final agreement have been clear since 2000: a Palestinian state in Gaza and the West Bank in return for a declaration that the conflict is over, recognition of Israel's right to exist, guarantees of Israeli security, diplomatic recognition of Israel, and normalization of its relations with Arab states. U.S. diplomacy is critical in helping to resolve this conflict. In addition to facilitating negotiations, we must engage in regional diplomacy to gain Arab support for a Palestinian leadership that is committed to peace and willing to engage in a dialogue with the Israelis. Whether or not the United States makes progress in helping to broker a final agreement, consistent U.S. involvement can lower the level of violence and restore our credibility in the region.

To help our forces recover from Iraq and prepare them to confront the full range of twenty-first-century threats, I will work to expand and modernize the military so that fighting wars no longer comes at the expense of deployments for long-term deterrence, military readiness, or responses to urgent needs at home. As the only senator serving on the Transformation Advisory Group established by the U.S. Joint Forces Command, I have had the chance to explore these issues in detail. Ongoing military innovation is essential, but the Bush administration has undermined this goal by focusing obsessively on expensive and unproven missile defense technology while making the tragically misguided assumption that light invasion forces could not only conquer the Taliban and Saddam Hussein but also stabilize Afghanistan and Iraq.

Our brave soldiers who are wounded in Afghanistan and Iraq must receive the health care, benefits, training, and support they deserve. The treatment of wounded soldiers at the Walter Reed Army Medical Center was a travesty. Those convalescing or struggling to build new lives after grievous injuries need an expanded version of the Family and Medical Leave Act to enable their families to provide the support they need. Beyond health care, it is also time to develop a modern GI Bill of Rights in order to expand professional and entrepreneurial opportunities as well as access to education and home ownership.

WINNING THE REAL WAR ON TERROR

We must be unrelenting in the prosecution of the war on al Qaeda and a growing number of like-minded extremist organizations. These terrorists are as determined as ever to strike the United States. If they think they can carry out another 9/11, I have no doubt that they will try. To stop them, we must use every tool we have.

In the cities of Europe and Asia—such as Hamburg and Kuala Lumpur, which were the springboards for 9/11—terrorist cells are preparing for future attacks. We must understand not only their methods but their motives: a rejection of modernity, women's rights, and democracy, as well as a dangerous nostalgia for a mythical past. We must develop a comprehensive strategy focusing on education, intelligence, and law enforcement to counter not only the terrorists themselves but also the larger forces fueling support for their extremism.

The forgotten frontline in the war on terror is Afghanistan, where our military effort must be reinforced. The Taliban cannot be allowed to regain power in Afghanistan; if they return, al Qaeda will return with them. Yet current U.S. policies have actually weakened President Hamid Karzai's government and allowed the Taliban to retake many areas, especially in the south. A largely unimpeded heroin trade finances the very Taliban fighters and al Qaeda terrorists who are attacking our troops. In addition to engaging in counternarcotics efforts, we must seek to dry up recruiting opportunities for the Taliban by funding crop-substitution programs, a large-scale road-building initiative, institutions that train and prepare Afghans for honest and effective governance, and programs to enable women to play a larger role in society.

We must also strengthen the national and local governments and resolve the problems along Afghanistan's border. Terrorists are increasingly finding safe havens in the Federally Administered Tribal Areas of Pakistan. Redoubling our efforts with Pakistan would not only help root out terrorist elements there; it would also signal to our NATO partners that the war in Afghanistan and the broader fight against extremism in South Asia are battles that we can and must win. Yet we cannot succeed unless we design a strategy that treats the entire region as an interconnected whole, where crises overlap with one another and the danger of a chain reaction of disasters is real.

Combating terrorism around the world will require better intelligence and a clandestine service that is out on the street, not sitting behind desks. As president, I will work to restore morale in our intelligence community, increase the number of agents and analysts proficient in Arabic and other key languages, and raise the profile and status of intelligence analysis. Most of the terrorists apprehended for plotting attacks against the United States, both before and after 9/11, were arrested in other countries as a result of cooperation between intelligence and law enforcement agencies.

To maximize our effectiveness, we have to rebuild our alliances. The problem we face is global; we must therefore be attentive to the values, concerns, and interests of our allies and partners. That means doing a better job of building counterterrorist capacity around the world. We must help strengthen police, prosecutorial, and judicial systems abroad; improve intelligence; and implement more stringent border controls, especially in developing countries.

We must also keep our guard up at home. As a senator from New York, I have long advocated full investment in our first responders and in protecting our critical infrastructure. I have pushed for new strategies and new technologies, such as a new federal interoperable communications and safety system. After years of Bush administration neglect, 80 percent of the 9/11 Commission's recommendations on homeland security have now been enacted, principally as a result of the Democratic Congress' work. But there is more to do. We must match the resources to the stakes and help the most vulnerable and at-risk cities prepare for an attack. We must improve health-care delivery systems in order to manage the consequences of attacks. Finally, we must improve the security of chemical plants and safeguard the transportation of hazardous materials so that terrorists do not have easy targets.

SECURITY THROUGH STATESMANSHIP

The Bush administration has opposed talks with our adversaries, seeming to believe that we are not strong enough to defend our interests through negotiations. This is a misleading and counterproductive strategy. True statesmanship requires that we engage with our adversaries, not for the sake of talking but because robust diplomacy is a prerequisite to achieving our aims.

The case in point is Iran. Iran poses a long-term strategic challenge to the United States, our NATO allies, and Israel. It is the country that most practices state-sponsored terrorism, and it uses its surrogates to supply explosives that kill U.S. troops in Iraq. The Bush administration refuses to talk to Iran about its nuclear program, preferring to ignore bad behavior rather than challenge it. Meanwhile, Iran has enhanced its nuclear-enrichment capabilities, armed Iraqi Shiite militias, funneled arms to Hezbollah, and subsidized Hamas, even as the government continues to hurt its own citizens by mismanaging the economy and increasing political and social repression.

As a result, we have lost precious time. Iran must conform to its nonproliferation obligations and must not be permitted to build or acquire nuclear weapons. If Iran does not comply with its own commitments and the will of the international community, all options must remain on the table.

On the other hand, if Iran is in fact willing to end its nuclear weapons program, renounce sponsorship of terrorism, support Middle East peace, and play a constructive role in stabilizing Iraq, the United States should be prepared to offer Iran a carefully calibrated package of incentives. This will let the Iranian people know that our quarrel is not with them but with their government and show the world that the United States is prepared to pursue every diplomatic option.

Like Iran, North Korea responded to the Bush administration's effort to isolate it by accelerating its nuclear program, conducting a nuclear test, and building more nuclear weapons. Only since the State Department returned to diplomacy have we been able, belatedly, to make progress.

Neither North Korea nor Iran will change course as a result of what we do with our own nuclear weapons, but taking dramatic steps to reduce our nuclear arsenal would build support for the coalitions we need to address the threat of nuclear proliferation and help the United States regain the moral high ground. Former Secretaries of State George Shultz and Henry Kissinger, former Defense Secretary William Perry, and former Senator Sam Nunn have called on the United States to "rekindle the vision," shared by every president from Dwight Eisenhower to Bill Clinton, of reducing reliance on nuclear weapons.

To reassert our nonproliferation leadership, I will seek to negotiate an accord that substantially and verifiably reduces the U.S. and Russian nuclear arsenals. This dramatic initiative would send a strong message of nuclear restraint to the world, while we retain enough strength to deter others from trying to match our arsenal. I will also seek Senate approval of the Comprehensive Test Ban Treaty by 2009, the tenth anniversary of the Senate's initial rejection of the agreement. This would enhance the United States' credibility when demanding that other nations refrain from testing. As president, I will support efforts to supplement the Nuclear Nonproliferation Treaty. Establishing an international fuel bank that guaranteed secure access to nuclear fuel at reasonable prices would help limit the number of countries that pose proliferation risks.

In the Senate, I have introduced legislation to accelerate and reinvigorate U.S. efforts to prevent nuclear terrorism. As president, I will do everything in my power to ensure that nuclear, biological, and chemical weapons and the materials needed to make them are kept out of terrorists' hands. My first goal would be to remove all nuclear material from the world's most vulnerable nuclear sites and effectively secure the remainder during my first term in office.

Statesmanship is also necessary to engage countries that are not adversaries but that are challenging the United States on many fronts. Russian President Vladimir Putin has thwarted a carefully crafted UN plan that would have put Kosovo on a belated path to independence, attempted to use energy as a political weapon against Russia's neighbors and beyond, and tested the United States and Europe on a range of nonproliferation and arms reduction issues. Putin has also suppressed many of the freedoms won after the fall of communism, created a new class of oligarchs, and interfered deeply in the internal affairs of former Soviet republics.

It is a mistake, however, to see Russia only as a threat. Putin has used Russia's energy wealth to expand the Russian economy, so that more ordinary Russians are enjoying a rising standard of living. We need to engage Russia selectively on issues of high national importance, such as thwarting Iran's nuclear ambitions, securing loose nuclear weapons in Russia and the former Soviet republics, and reaching a diplomatic solution in Kosovo. At the same time, we must make clear that our ability to view Russia as a genuine partner depends on whether Russia chooses to strengthen democracy or return to authoritarianism and regional interference.

Our relationship with China will be the most important bilateral relationship in the world in this century. The United States and China have vastly different values and political systems, yet even though we disagree profoundly on issues ranging from trade to human rights, religious freedom, labor practices, and Tibet, there is much that the United States and China can and must accomplish together. China's support was important in reaching a deal to disable North Korea's nuclear facilities. We should build on this framework to establish a Northeast Asian security regime.

But China's rise is also creating new challenges. The Chinese have finally begun to realize that their rapid economic growth is coming at a tremendous environmental price. The United States should undertake a joint program with China and Japan to develop new clean-energy sources, promote greater energy efficiency, and combat climate change. This program would be part of an overall energy policy that would require a dramatic reduction in U.S. dependence on foreign oil.

We must persuade China to join global institutions and support international rules by building on areas where our interests converge and working to narrow our differences. Although the United States must stand ready to challenge China when its conduct is at odds with U.S. vital interests, we should work for a cooperative future.

STRENGTHENING ALLIANCES

It is important to engage our adversaries but even more important to reassure our allies. We must reestablish our traditional relationship of confidence and trust with Europe. Disagreements are inevitable, even among the closest friends, but we can never forget that on most global issues we have no more trusted allies than those in Europe. The new administration will have a chance to reach out across the Atlantic to a new generation of leaders in France, Germany, and the United Kingdom. When America and Europe work together, global objectives are within our means.

In Asia, India has a special significance both as an emerging power and as the world's most populous democracy. As co-chair of the Senate India Caucus, I recognize the tremendous opportunity presented by India's rise and the need to give the country an augmented voice in regional and international institutions, such as the UN. We must find additional ways for Australia, India, Japan, and the United States to cooperate on issues of mutual concern, including combating terrorism, cooperating on global climate control, protecting global energy supplies, and deepening global economic development.

At our peril, the Bush administration has neglected our neighbors to the south. We have witnessed the rollback of democratic development and economic openness in parts of Latin America. We must return to a policy of vigorous engagement; this is too critical a region for the United States to stand idly by. We must support the largest developing democracies in the region, Brazil and Mexico, and deepen economic and strategic cooperation with Argentina and Chile. We must also continue to cooperate with our allies in Colombia, Central America, and the Caribbean to combat the interconnected threats of drug trafficking, crime, and insurgency. Finally, we must work with our allies to provide sustainable-development programs that promote economic opportunity and reduce inequality for the citizens of Latin America.

Equally important are the growing ranks of democracies in Africa—some established, some new—which will be the engines of Africa's future. We should target these countries for aid and other forms of support and work with them to strengthen regional institutions such as the African Union. The AU seeks to emulate the European Union by requiring and supporting democracy among its members, but it has a long way to go. It has thus far failed even to denounce the blatant political corruption and brutality of Zimbabwe's Robert Mugabe. It must also develop the ability to act with sufficient strength and speed to stop mass atrocities, such as those in Darfur.

Our interests in Africa are strategic, not just humanitarian. They include al Qaeda's efforts to seek safe havens in failed states in the Horn of Africa and the growing competition with other global players, including China, for Africa's natural resources. The long-term solution, for us as well as for Africa, is to help Africans develop both the will and the capability to address their own problems and help the continent live up to its vast potential.

BUILDING THE WORLD WE WANT

To build the world we want, we must begin by speaking honestly about the problems we face. We will have to talk about the consequences of our invasion of Iraq for the Iraqi people and others in the region. We will have to talk about Guantánamo and Abu Ghraib. We will also have to take concrete steps to enhance security and spread opportunity throughout the world.

Education is the foundation of economic opportunity and should lie at the heart of America's foreign assistance efforts. More than 100 million children in the developing world are not in school. Another 150 million drop out before they finish grade school. By failing these children, we sow the seeds of lost generations. As president, I will press for quick passage of the Education for All Act, which would provide $10 billion over a five-year period to train teachers and build schools in the developing world. This program would channel funds to those countries that provide the best plans for how to use them and rigorously measure performance to ensure that our dollars deliver results for children.

The fight against HIV/AIDS, tuberculosis, malaria, and other dreaded diseases is both a moral imperative and a practical necessity. These diseases have created a generation of orphans and set back economic and political progress by decades in many countries.

These problems often seem overwhelming, but we can solve them with the combined resources of governments, the private sector, nongovernmental organizations, and charities such as the Bill and Melinda Gates Foundation. We can set specific targets in areas such as expanding access to primary education, providing clean water, reducing child and maternal mortality, and reversing the spread of HIV/AIDS and other diseases. We can strengthen the International Labor Organization in order to enforce labor standards, just as we strengthened the World Trade Organization to enforce trade agreements. Such policies demonstrate that by doing good we can do well. This sort of investment and diplomacy will yield results for the United States, building goodwill even in places where our standing has suffered.

We must also take threats and turn them into opportunities. The seemingly overwhelming challenge of climate change is a prime example. Far from being a drag on global growth, climate control represents a powerful economic opportunity that can be a driver of growth, jobs, and competitive advantage in the twenty-first century. As president, I will make the fight against global warming a priority. We cannot solve the climate crisis alone, and the rest of the world cannot solve it without us. The United States must reengage in international climate change negotiations and provide the leadership needed to reach a binding global climate agreement. But we must first restore our own credibility on the issue. Rapidly emerging countries, such as China, will not curb their own carbon emissions until the United States has demonstrated a serious commitment to reducing its own through a market-based cap-and-trade approach.

We must also help developing nations build efficient and environmentally sustainable domestic energy infrastructures. Two-thirds of the growth in energy demand over the next 25 years will come from countries with little existing infrastructure. Many opportunities exist here as well: Mali is electrifying rural communities with solar power, Malawi is developing a biomass energy strategy, and all of Africa can provide carbon credits to the West.

Finally, we must create formal links between the International Energy Agency and China and India and create an "E-8" international forum modeled on the G-8. This group would be comprised of the world's major carbon-emitting nations and hold an annual summit devoted to international ecological and resource issues.

The world we want is also a world where human rights are respected. By surrendering our values in the name of our safety, the Bush administration has left Americans wondering whether its rhetoric about freedom around the world still applies back home. We have undercut international support for fighting terrorism by suggesting that the job cannot be done without humiliation, infringements on basic rights to privacy and free speech, and even torture. We must once again make human rights a centerpiece of U.S. foreign policy and a core element of our conception of democracy.

Human rights will never truly be realized as long as a majority of the world's population is still treated as second-class citizens. Twelve years ago, the UN convened a historic conference on women in Beijing, where I was proud to represent our country and to proclaim that women's rights are human rights. Since then, women have been elected heads of state in countries on nearly every continent. Thanks to the United States, many, but not yet all, Afghan women have been liberated from one of the most tyrannical and repressive regimes of our day and are now in schools, in the work force, and in parliament.

Yet progress in key areas has lagged, as evidenced by the continuing spread of trafficking in women, the ongoing use of rape as an instrument of war, the political marginalization of women, and persistent gender gaps in employment and economic opportunity. U.S. leadership, including a commitment to incorporate the promotion of women's rights in our bilateral relationships and international aid programs, is essential not just to improving the lives of women but to strengthening the families, communities, and societies in which they live.

REVIVING THE AMERICAN IDEA

Seasoned, clear-eyed leadership can take us far. We must draw on all the dimensions of American power and reject false choices driven by ideology rather than facts. An America that rebuilds its strength and recovers its principles will be an America that can spread the blessings of security and opportunity around the world.

In 1825, 50 years after the Battle of Bunker Hill, the great secretary of state Daniel Webster laid the cornerstone of the Bunker Hill Monument that stands today in Boston. He exulted in the simple fact that America had survived and flourished, and he celebrated "the benefit which the example of our country has produced, and is likely to produce, on human freedom and human happiness." He gloried not in American power but rather in the power of the American idea, the idea that "with wisdom and knowledge men may govern themselves." And he urged his audience, and all Americans, to maintain this example and "take care that nothing may weaken its authority with the world."

Two centuries later, our economic power and military might have grown beyond anything that our forefathers could have imagined. But that power and might can only be sustained and renewed if we can regain our authority with the world, the authority not simply of a large and wealthy nation but of the American idea. If we can live up to that idea, if we can exercise our power wisely and well, we can make America great again.

HILLARY RODHAM CLINTON, a U.S. Senator from New York, is a candidate for the Democratic presidential nomination.

An Enduring Peace Built on Freedom

John McCain   NOVEMBER/DECEMBER 2007

Supporters cheer for U.S. Republican presidential nominee Senator John McCain at a campaign rally in Dayton, Ohio, October 27, 2008.

Since the dawn of our republic, Americans have believed that our nation was created for a purpose. We are, as Alexander Hamilton said, "a people of great destinies." From the American Revolution to the Cold War, Americans have understood their duty to serve a cause greater than self-interest and to keep faith with the eternal and universal principles of the Declaration of Independence. By overcoming threats to our nation's survival and to our way of life, and by seizing history's great opportunities, Americans have changed the world.

Now it is this generation's turn to restore and replenish the world's faith in our nation and our principles. President Harry Truman once said of America, "God has created us and brought us to our present position of power and strength for some great purpose." In his time, that great purpose was to erect the structures of peace and prosperity that provided safe passage through the Cold War. In the face of new dangers and opportunities, our next president will have a mandate to build an enduring global peace on the foundations of freedom, security, opportunity, prosperity, and hope.

America needs a president who can revitalize our country's purpose and standing in the world, defeat terrorist adversaries who threaten liberty at home and abroad, and build enduring peace. There is an enormous amount to do. Our wars in Iraq and Afghanistan have been costly in blood and treasure and in other less tangible ways as well. Our next president will need to rally nations across the world around common causes as only America can. There will be no time for on-the-job training. Given the present dangers, our country cannot afford the kind of malaise, drift, and fecklessness that followed the Vietnam War. The next president must be prepared to lead America and the world to victory—and to seize the opportunities afforded by the unprecedented liberty and prosperity in the world today to build a peace that will last a century.

WINNING THE WAR ON TERROR

Defeating radical Islamist extremists is the national security challenge of our time. Iraq is this war's central front, according to our commander there, General David Petraeus, and according to our enemies, including al Qaeda's leadership.

The recent years of mismanagement and failure in Iraq demonstrate that America should go to war only with sufficient troop levels and with a realistic and comprehensive plan for success. We did not do so in Iraq, and our country and the people of Iraq have paid a dear price. Only after four years of conflict did the United States adopt a counterinsurgency strategy, backed by increased force levels, that gives us a realistic chance of success. We cannot get those years back, and now the only responsible action for any presidential candidate is to look forward and outline the strategic posture in Iraq that is most likely to protect U.S. national interests.

So long as we can succeed in Iraq—and I believe that we can—we must succeed. The consequences of failure would be horrific: a historic loss at the hands of Islamist extremists who, after having defeated the Soviet Union in Afghanistan and the United States in Iraq, will believe that the world is going their way and that anything is possible; a failed state in the heart of the Middle East providing sanctuary for terrorists; a civil war that could quickly develop into a regional conflict and even genocide; a decisive end to the prospect of a modern democracy in Iraq, for which large Iraqi majorities have repeatedly voted; and an invitation for Iran to dominate Iraq and the region even more.

Whether success grows closer or more distant over the coming months, it is clear that Iraq will be a central issue for the next U.S. president. Democratic candidates have promised to withdraw U.S. troops and "end the war" by fiat, regardless of the consequences. To make such decisions based on the political winds at home, rather than on the realities in the theater, is to court disaster. The war in Iraq cannot be wished away, and it is a miscalculation of historic magnitude to believe that the consequences of failure will be limited to one administration or one party. This is an American war, and its outcome will touch every one of our citizens for years to come.

That is why I support our continuing efforts to win in Iraq. It is also why I oppose a preemptive withdrawal strategy that has no Plan B for the aftermath of its inevitable failure and the greater problems that would ensue.

What happens in Iraq will also affect Afghanistan. There has been progress in Afghanistan: over two million refugees have returned, the welfare of Afghan citizens has meaningfully improved, and historic elections took place in 2004. The Taliban's recent resurgence, however, threatens to lead Afghanistan to revert to its pre-9/11 role as a sanctuary for terrorists with global reach. Our recommitment to Afghanistan must include increasing NATO forces, suspending the debilitating restrictions on when and how those forces can fight, expanding the training and equipping of the Afghan National Army through a long-term partnership with NATO to make it more professional and multiethnic, and deploying significantly more foreign police trainers. It must also address the current political deficiencies in judicial reform, reconstruction, governance, and anticorruption efforts.

Success in Afghanistan is critical to stopping al Qaeda, but success in neighboring Pakistan is just as vital. We must continue to work with President Pervez Musharraf to dismantle the cells and camps that the Taliban and al Qaeda maintain in his country. These groups still have sanctuaries there, and the "Talibanization" of Pakistani society is advancing. The United States must help Pakistan resist the forces of extremism by making a long-term commitment to the country. This would mean enhancing Pakistan's ability to act against insurgent safe havens and bring children into schools and out of extremist madrasahs and supporting Pakistani moderates.

Our counterterrorism efforts cannot be limited to stateless groups operating in safe havens. Iran, the world's chief state sponsor of terrorism, continues its deadly quest for nuclear weapons and the means to deliver them. Protected by a nuclear arsenal, Iran would be even more willing and able to sponsor terrorist attacks against any perceived enemy, including the United States and Israel, or even to pass nuclear materials to one of its allied terrorist networks. The next president must confront this threat directly, and that effort must begin with tougher political and economic sanctions. If the United Nations is unwilling to act, the United States must lead a group of like-minded countries to impose effective multilateral sanctions, such as restrictions on exports of refined gasoline, outside the UN framework. America and its partners should also privatize the sanctions effort by supporting a disinvestment campaign to isolate and delegitimize the regime in Tehran, whose policies are already opposed by many Iranian citizens. And military action, although not the preferred option, must remain on the table: Tehran must understand that it cannot win a showdown with the world.

Meanwhile, in view of the increased threats to Israel—from Iran, Hezbollah, Hamas, and others—the next U.S. president must continue America's long-standing support for Israel, including by providing needed military equipment and technology and ensuring that Israel maintains its qualitative military edge. The long-elusive quest for peace between Israel and the Palestinians must remain a priority. But the goal must be genuine peace, and so Hamas must be isolated even as the United States intensifies its commitment to finding an enduring settlement.

Defeating the terrorists who already threaten America is vital, but just as important is preventing a new generation of them from joining the fight. As president, I will employ every economic, diplomatic, political, legal, and ideological tool at our disposal to aid moderate Muslims—women's rights campaigners, labor leaders, lawyers, journalists, teachers, tolerant imams, and many others—who are resisting the well-financed campaign of extremism that is tearing Muslim societies apart. My administration, with its partners, will help friendly Muslim states establish the building blocks of open and tolerant societies. And we will nurture a culture of hope and economic opportunity by establishing a free-trade area from Morocco to Afghanistan, open to all who do not sponsor terrorism.

DEFENDING THE HOMELAND

In 1947, the Truman administration launched a massive overhaul of the nation's foreign policy, defense, and intelligence agencies to meet the challenges of the Cold War. Today, we must do the same to meet the challenges of the twenty-first century. Our armed forces are seriously overstretched and underresourced. As president, I will increase the size of the U.S. Army and the Marine Corps from the currently planned level of roughly 750,000 troops to 900,000 troops. Enhancing recruitment will require more resources and will take time, but it must be done as soon as possible.

Along with more personnel, our military needs additional equipment in order to make up for its recent losses and modernize. We can partially offset some of this additional investment by cutting wasteful spending. But we can also afford to spend more on national defense, which currently consumes less than four cents of every dollar that our economy generates—far less than what we spent during the Cold War. We must also accelerate the transformation of our military, which is still configured to fight enemies that no longer exist.

America needs not simply more soldiers but more soldiers with the skills necessary to help friendly governments and their security forces resist common foes. I will create an Army Advisory Corps with 20,000 soldiers to partner with militaries abroad, and I will increase the number of U.S. personnel available to engage in Special Forces operations, civil affairs activities, military policing, and military intelligence. We also need a nonmilitary deployable police force to train foreign forces and help maintain law and order in places threatened by state collapse.

Today, understanding foreign cultures is not a luxury but a strategic necessity. As president, I will launch a crash program in civilian and military schools to prepare more experts in critical languages such as Arabic, Chinese, Farsi, and Pashto. Students at our service academies should be required to study abroad. I will enlarge the military's Foreign Area Officer program and create a new specialty in strategic interrogation in order to produce more interrogators who can obtain critical knowledge from detainees by using advanced psychological techniques, rather than the kind of abusive tactics properly prohibited by the Geneva Conventions.

I will set up a new agency patterned after the erstwhile Office of Strategic Services. A modern-day OSS could draw together specialists in unconventional warfare, civil affairs, and psychological warfare; covert-action operators; and experts in anthropology, advertising, and other relevant disciplines from inside and outside government. Like the original OSS, this would be a small, nimble, can-do organization. It would fight terrorist subversion around the world and in cyberspace. It could take risks that our bureaucracies today rarely consider taking—such as deploying infiltrating agents without diplomatic cover in terrorist states and organizations—and play a key role in frontline efforts to rebuild failed states.

As we increase our military capacity, we must also enhance our civilian capacity. As president, I will energize and expand our post-conflict reconstruction capabilities so that any military campaign would be complemented by a civilian "surge" that would build the political and economic foundations of peace. To better coordinate our disparate military and civilian operations, I will ask Congress for a civilian follow-on to the 1986 Goldwater-Nichols Act, which fostered a culture of joint operations within the military services. The new act would create a framework for civil servants and military forces to train and work together in order to facilitate cooperation in postconflict reconstruction.

We must also revitalize our public diplomacy. In 1998, the Clinton administration and Congress mistakenly agreed to abolish the U.S. Information Agency and move its public diplomacy functions to the State Department. This amounted to unilateral disarmament in the war of ideas. I will work with Congress to create a new independent agency with the sole purpose of getting America's message to the world—a critical element in combating Islamic extremism and restoring the positive image of our country abroad.

UNITING THE WORLD'S DEMOCRACIES

Our organizations and partnerships must be as international as the challenges we confront. Today, U.S. soldiers are serving in Afghanistan with British, Canadian, Dutch, German, Italian, Lithuanian, Polish, Spanish, and Turkish soldiers from the NATO alliance. They are also serving alongside forces from Australia, Japan, New Zealand, the Philippines, and South Korea—all democratic allies or close partners of the United States. But these troops are not all part of a common structure. They do not work together systematically or meet regularly to develop diplomatic and economic strategies to meet the common challenges they face.

NATO has begun to fill this gap by promoting partnerships be-tween the alliance and great democracies in Asia and elsewhere. We should go further by linking democratic nations in one com-mon organization: a worldwide League of Democracies. This would be unlike Woodrow Wilson's doomed plan for the universal-membership League of Nations. Instead, it would be similar to what Theodore Roosevelt envisioned: like-minded nations work-ing together for peace and liberty. The organization could act when the UN fails—to relieve human suffering in places such as Darfur, combat HIV/AIDS in sub-Saharan Africa, fashion better policies to confront environmental crises, provide unimpeded market ac-cess to those who endorse economic and political freedom, and take other measures unattainable by existing regional or universal-membership systems.

This League of Democracies would not supplant the UN or other international organizations but complement them by har-nessing the political and moral advantages offered by united demo-cratic action. By taking steps such as bringing concerted pressure to bear on tyrants in Burma (renamed Myanmar by its military government in 1989) or Zimbabwe, uniting to impose sanctions on Iran, and providing support to struggling democracies in Serbia and Ukraine, the League of Democracies would serve as a unique handmaiden of freedom. If I am elected president, during my first year in office I will call a summit of the world's democracies to seek the views of my counterparts and explore the steps necessary to realize this vision—just as America led in creating NATO six de-cades ago.

REVITALIZING THE TRANSATLANTIC PARTNERSHIP

The United States did not single-handedly win the Cold War; the transatlantic alliance did, in concert with partners around the world. The bonds we share with Europe in terms of history, values, and interests are unique. Unfortunately, they have frayed. As presi-dent, one of my top foreign policy priorities will be to revitalize the transatlantic partnership.

Americans should welcome the rise of a strong, confident European Union. The future of the transatlantic relationship lies in confronting the challenges of the twenty-first century worldwide: developing a common energy policy, creating a transatlantic common market tying our economies more closely together, and institutionalizing our cooperation on issues such as climate change, foreign assistance, and democracy promotion.

A decade and a half ago, the Russian people threw off the tyranny of communism and seemed determined to build a democracy and a free market and to join the West. Today, we see in Russia diminishing political freedoms, a leadership dominated by a clique of former intelligence officers, efforts to bully democratic neighbors, such as Georgia, and attempts to manipulate Europe's dependence on Russian oil and gas. We need a new Western approach to this revanchist Russia. We should start by ensuring that the G-8, the group of eight highly industrialized states, becomes again a club of leading market democracies: it should include Brazil and India but exclude Russia. Rather than tolerate Russia's nuclear blackmail or cyberattacks, Western nations should make clear that the solidarity of NATO, from the Baltic to the Black Sea, is indivisible and that the organization's doors remain open to all democracies committed to the defense of freedom. We must also increase our programs supporting freedom and the rule of law in Russia and emphasize that genuine partnership remains open to Moscow if it desires it but that such a partnership would involve a commitment to being a responsible actor, internationally and domestically.

More broadly, America needs to revive the democratic solidarity that united the West during the Cold War. We cannot build an enduring peace based on freedom by ourselves. We must be willing to listen to our democratic allies. Being a great power does not mean that we can do whatever we want whenever we want, nor should we assume that we have all the wisdom, knowledge, and resources necessary to succeed. When we believe international action—whether military, economic, or diplomatic—is necessary, we must work to persuade our friends and allies that we are right.

And we must also be willing to be persuaded by them. To be a good leader, America must be a good ally.

SHAPING THE ASIA-PACIFIC CENTURY

Power in the world today is moving east; the Asia-Pacific region is on the rise. If we grasp the opportunities present in the unfolding world, this century can become safe and both American and Asian, both prosperous and free.

Asia has made enormous strides in recent decades. Its economic achievements are well known; less known is that more people live under democratic rule in Asia than in any other region of the world. Japan's former prime minister spoke of an "arc of freedom and prosperity" stretching across Asia. India's prime minister has called liberal democracy "the natural order of social and political organization in today's world." Asian countries are drawing closer together, striking trade and security agreements with one another and with other states.

North Korea's totalitarian regime and impoverished society buck these trends. It is unclear today whether North Korea is truly committed to verifiable denuclearization and a full accounting of all its nuclear materials and facilities, two steps that are necessary before any lasting diplomatic agreement can be reached. Future talks must take into account North Korea's ballistic missile programs, its abduction of Japanese citizens, and its support for terrorism and proliferation.

The key to meeting this and other challenges in a changing Asia is increasing cooperation with our allies. The linchpin to the region's promise is continued American engagement. I welcome Japan's international leadership and emergence as a global power, encourage its admirable "values-based diplomacy," and support its bid for permanent membership in the UN Security Council. As president, I will tend carefully to our ever-stronger alliance with Australia, whose troops are fighting shoulder to shoulder with ours in Afghanistan and Iraq. I will seek to rebuild our frayed partnership with South Korea by emphasizing economic and security cooperation and will cement our growing partnership with India.

In Southeast Asia, I will seek an elevated partnership with Indonesia and continue to expand defense cooperation with Malaysia, the Philippines, Singapore, and Vietnam while working with willing regional partners to promote democracy; defeat the threats of terrorism, crime, and the narcotics trade; and end Burma's deplorable human rights abuses. The United States should participate more actively in Asian regional organizations, including those led by members of the Association of Southeast Asian Nations. As president, I will seek to institutionalize the new quadrilateral security partnership among the major Asia-Pacific democracies: Australia, India, Japan, and the United States.

Dealing with a rising China will be a central challenge for the next American president. Recent prosperity in China has brought more people out of poverty faster than during any other time in human history. China's newfound power implies responsibilities. It raises legitimate expectations that internationally China will behave as a responsible economic partner by developing a transparent code of conduct for its corporations, assuring the safety of its exports, adopting a market approach to currency valuation, pursuing sustainable environmental policies, and abandoning its go-it-alone approach to world energy supplies.

China could also bolster its claim that it is "peacefully rising" by being more transparent about its significant military buildup. When China builds new submarines, adds hundreds of new jet fighters, modernizes its arsenal of strategic ballistic missiles, and tests antisatellite weapons, the United States legitimately must question the intent of such provocative acts. When China threatens democratic Taiwan with a massive arsenal of missiles and warlike rhetoric, the United States must take note. When China enjoys close economic and diplomatic relations with pariah states such as Burma, Sudan, and Zimbabwe, tension will result. When China proposes regional forums and economic arrangements designed to exclude America from Asia, the United States will react.

China and the United States are not destined to be adversaries. We have numerous overlapping interests. U.S.-Chinese relations can benefit both countries and, in turn, the Asia-Pacific region and the world. But until China moves toward political liberalization, our relationship will be based on periodically shared interests rather than the bedrock of shared values.

The United States should set the standard for trade liberalization in Asia. Completing free-trade agreements with Malaysia and Thailand, realizing the full potential of our new trade agreement with South Korea, and institutionalizing economic partnerships with India and Indonesia so that they build on existing agreements with Australia and Singapore should set the stage for an ambitious Pacific-wide effort to liberalize trade. Such trade liberalization would benefit Americans and Asians alike.

BUILDING A HEMISPHERE OF PEACE AND PROSPERITY

John F. Kennedy described the people of Latin America as our "firm and ancient friends, united by history and experience and by our determination to advance the values of American civilization." The countries of Latin America are our natural partners, but U.S. inattention has harmed our relationships. We must enhance U.S. relations with Mexico to control illegal immigration and defeat drug cartels, and with Brazil, a partner whose leadership in the UN peacekeeping force in Haiti is a model for fostering regional security. My administration would give these and other great democratic Latin American nations a strong voice in the League of Democracies—a voice they are denied in the UN Security Council.

We must also work together to counter the propaganda of demagogues who threaten the security and prosperity of the Americas. Hugo Chávez has overseen the dismantling of Venezuela's democracy by undermining the parliament, the judiciary, the media, free labor unions, and private enterprises. His regime is acquiring advanced military equipment. And it is trying to build a global anti-American axis. My administration will work to marginalize such nefarious influences. It will also prepare immediately for Cuba's transition to democracy by developing a plan with regional and European partners for a post-Castro Cuba so as to be ready to spark rapid change in that long-suffering country when the time comes. We must build on the passage of the Central America Free Trade Agreement by ratifying pending trade agreements with Colombia, Panama, and Peru and move the process of completing a Free Trade Area of the Americas forward.

AIDING AN AFRICAN RENAISSANCE

Africa's problems—poverty, corruption, disease, and instability—are well known. Less discussed is the promise offered by many countries on that continent. My administration will seek to engage on a political, economic, and security level with friendly governments across Africa. Many African nations will not reach their true potential without external assistance to combat the entrenched problems, such as HIV/AIDS, that afflict Africans disproportionately. I will establish the goal of eradicating malaria—the number one killer of African children under the age of five—on the continent. In addition to saving millions of lives in the world's poorest regions, such a campaign would do much to add luster to America's image in the world. These and other efforts, including enhancing trade and investment, would assist Africans in sparking a renaissance that would enable the continent's people to achieve their potential.

Africa continues to offer the most compelling case for humanitarian intervention. With respect to the Darfur region of Sudan, I fear that the United States is once again repeating the mistakes it made in Bosnia and Rwanda. In Bosnia, we acted late but eventually saved countless lives. In Rwanda, we stood by and watched the slaughter and later pledged that we would not do so again. The genocide in Darfur demands U.S. leadership. My administration will consider the use of all elements of American power to stop the outrageous acts of human destruction that have unfolded there.

PREVENTING NUCLEAR PROLIFERATION

The nuclear nonproliferation regime is broken for one clear reason: the mistaken assumption behind the Nuclear Nonproliferation Treaty (NPT) that nuclear technology can spread without nuclear weapons eventually following. The next U.S. president must convene a summit of the world's leading powers—none of which have an interest in seeing a world full of nuclear-armed states—with three agenda items. First, the notion that non-nuclear-weapons states have a right to nuclear technology must be revisited. Second, the burden of proof for suspected violators of the NPT must be reversed. Instead of requiring the International Atomic Energy Agency board to reach unanimous agreement in order to act, as is the case today, there should be an automatic suspension of nuclear assistance to states that the agency cannot guarantee are in full compliance with safeguard agreements. Finally, the IAEA's annual budget of $130 million must be substantially increased so that the agency can meet its monitoring and safeguarding tasks.

SECURING ENERGY AND SAVING THE ENVIRONMENT

America's dependence on foreign oil constitutes a critical strategic vulnerability. America accounts for 25 percent of global demand for oil but possesses less than three percent of the world's proven reserves. Most of the world's known reserves are in the Persian Gulf, in the hands of dictators or nationalized oil companies. Terrorists understand our vulnerability: had it succeeded, the attempted suicide attack on a Saudi refinery in February 2006 would have driven the world price of oil above $150 per barrel. The transfer of American wealth to the Middle East through continued oil purchases helps sustain the conditions under which extremism breeds, and the burning of oil and other fossil fuels spurs global warming, a gathering danger to our planet.

John McCain

My national energy strategy will amount to a declaration of independence from our reliance on oil sheiks and our vulnerability to their troubled politics. This strategy will include employing technology to achieve new efficiencies in energy extraction and consumption, enforcing conservation, creating market incentives to encourage the development of alternative sources of energy and hybrid vehicles, and expanding sources of renewable energy. I will also greatly increase the use of nuclear power, a zero-emission energy source. Given the proper incentives, our innovators, scientists, entrepreneurs, and workers have the capability to lead the world in achieving energy security; given the stakes, they must.

I have proposed a bipartisan plan in the U.S. Senate to address the problem of climate change and ensure a sustainable future for humankind. My market-based approach will set reasonable caps on emissions of carbon dioxide and other greenhouse gases, provide industries with tradable emissions credits, and create other incentives for the deployment of new and better energy sources and technologies. It is time for America to lead the world in protecting the environment for future generations.

PREPARING TO LEAD

As president, I will make America's economic leadership in the globalized world of the twenty-first century a centerpiece of its engagement in foreign affairs. Today, from Singapore to South Africa, more people than ever before have embraced our liberal capitalist model of economic freedom and our culture of opportunity. Some Americans see globalization and the rise of economic giants such as China and India as a threat. We should reform our job training and education programs to more effectively help displaced American workers find new jobs that take advantage of trade and innovation. But we should continue to promote free trade, as it is vital to American prosperity. Americans will thrive in a world of economic freedom because our products and services remain the best and because our country draws strength from the forces shaping the new global economy, ranging from inflows of foreign investment to new businesses created by highly skilled immigrants. Americans can be confident that a world of economic and political freedom will sustain our global leadership by promoting our values and enhancing our prosperity. To unite us with friends and allies in a common prosperity, as president I will aggressively promote global trade liberalization at the World Trade Organization and expand America's free-trade agreements to friendly nations on every continent.

American leadership has helped build a world that is more secure, more prosperous, and freer than ever before. Our unique form of leadership—the antithesis of empire—gives us moral credibility, which is more powerful than any show of arms. We are rich in people and resources but richer still in ideals and vision—and the means to realize them. Yet today much of the world has come to challenge our actions and doubt our intentions. Polls indicate that the United States is more unpopular now than at any time in history and increasingly viewed as pursuing its narrow self-interest. The people who hold these views are wrong. We are a special nation, the closest thing to a "shining city on a hill" ever to have existed. But it is incumbent on us to restore our mantle as a global leader, reestablish our moral credibility, and rebuild those damaged relationships that once brought so much good to so many places.

As president, I will seek the widest possible circle of allies through the League of Democracies, NATO, the UN, and the Organization of American States. During President Ronald Reagan's deployment of intermediate-range nuclear missiles and President George H. W. Bush's Gulf War, the United States was joined by vast coalitions despite considerable opposition to American policies among foreign publics. These alliances came about because America had carefully cultivated relationships and shared values with its friends abroad. Working multilaterally can be a frustrating experience, but approaching problems with allies works far better than facing problems alone.

Almost two centuries ago, James Madison declared that "the great struggle of the Epoch" was "between liberty and despotism."

Many thought that this struggle ended with the Cold War, but it did not. It has taken on new guises, such as Islamist terrorists using our technological advances for their murderous designs and resurgent autocrats reminiscent of the nineteenth century. International terrorists capable of inflicting mass destruction are a new phenomenon. But what they seek and what they stand for are as old as time. They are part of a worldwide political, economic, and philosophical struggle between the future and the past, progress and reaction, liberty and despotism. Our security, our prosperity, and our democratic way of life depend on the outcome of that struggle.

Thomas Jefferson argued that America was the "solitary republic of the world, the only monument of human rights, and the sole depository of the sacred fire of freedom and self-government, from hence it is to be lighted up in other regions of the earth, if other regions of the earth shall ever become susceptible of its benign influence." Since that time two centuries ago when the United States was the "solitary republic of the world," more people than ever before have come under the "benign influence" of liberty. The protection and promotion of the democratic ideal, at home and abroad, will be the surest source of security and peace for the century that lies before us. The next U.S. president must be ready to lead, ready to show America and the world that this country's best days are yet to come, and ready to establish an enduring peace based on freedom that can safeguard American security for the rest of the twenty-first century. I am ready.

A New Realism

Bill Richardson JANUARY/FEBRUARY 2008

Democratic Presidential candidates and U.S. Senator Barack Obama; Bill Richardson, governor of New Mexico; and U.S. Senator Hillary Clinton stand for the National Anthem during the 30th annual Harkin Steak Fry in Indianola, Iowa, September 16, 2007.

Sixty years ago, in the pages of this magazine, George Kennan presented a compelling case for U.S. global engagement and leadership to contain Soviet power. His strategic vision laid the foundation for a realistic and principled foreign policy that, despite mistakes and setbacks, united the United States and its allies for the duration of the Cold War.

In the wake of the Bush administration's failed experiment with unilateralism, the United States needs once again to construct a foreign policy that is based on reality and loyal to American values. Such a policy must address the challenges of our time with effective actions rather than naive hopes. And it must unite us because it is inspired by the ideals of our nation rather than by the ideology of a president.

In his July 1947 "X" article, Kennan argued that the United States must meet Soviet power with American power and communist ideology with credible democratic leadership. He understood that containing Soviet communism would require strong American international leadership and that such leadership would depend on the power of our military, the dynamism of our economy, and the courage of our convictions. This strategic vision—because it was based on fundamental realities and fundamental American values—informed the policies not only of Harry Truman and Dwight Eisenhower but also of every president, Democratic or Republican, for two generations.

America is a great nation that knows how to defend itself. But its greatness is built on foundations more solid than self-absorption. We defend ourselves best when we lead others, and the key to our history of effective leadership has been our willingness to seek and find common ground, to blend our interests with the interests of others. Truman and Eisenhower understood that defending Europe and America from the Soviets required a strong military, but they also understood that we could not lead our allies if they did not wish to follow.

These and subsequent American presidents knew the importance of moral leadership. While our remarkable military and prosperous economy gave us the power to lead, our commitment to human dignity—including our willingness to struggle against our own prejudices—inspired others to follow. If America is to lead again, we need to remember this history and to rebuild our overextended military, revive our alliances, and restore our reputation as a nation that respects international law, human rights, and civil liberties.

Today, we are at the beginning of a new era of unprecedented global opportunities and global threats. New challenges demand that we chart a new strategic course. To do so, we must reject easy ideological recipes and examine carefully the assumptions that guided us in the twentieth century. We must assess what it means to be America in the world of today—a world of rapid economic and technological change, grave and worsening energy and environmental risks, and the simultaneous emergence of new world powers and asymmetric security challenges.

In the twenty-first century, globalization in all its forms is eroding the significance of national boundaries. Many of the greatest challenges that we face—from jihadism to nuclear proliferation to global warming—are not faced only by us. Urgent problems that once were national are now global, and dangers that once came only from states now come also from societies—not from hostile governments but from hostile individuals or impersonal social trends, such as the consumption of fossil fuels.

American foreign policy must be able to cope effectively with these realities. We must reject both isolationist fantasies of retreat from global engagement and neoconservative fantasies of transforming other countries through the unilateral application of American military power. Our policy also must go beyond the balance-of-power realism of the last century. In this new, interdependent world, we need a New Realism—one driven by an understanding that to defend our national interests, we must, more than ever, find common ground with others, so that we can lead them toward our common purposes.

Looking reality in the face also requires recognizing that because of the failures of the Bush administration, U.S. influence and prestige are at all-time lows. The damage is extensive: in an age of terrorism, when we need all the friends we can get, we find ourselves isolated. The Bush administration's policies have weakened our alliances, emboldened our enemies, depleted our treasury, exhausted our armed forces, and fueled global anger against us. From global warming to weapons of mass destruction (WMD) to the number of troops that would be needed to pacify Iraq, this president has preferred ideology to evidence. He has been unwilling to accept that leadership requires not just the power to destroy but also the power to persuade. Rather than doing the hard, patient, necessary work of strategic diplomacy, he has indulged the fantasy that he could reorder the world through unilateralism and bullying.

The Bush administration's foreign policy also has lacked sound principles. The president has regularly employed the rhetoric of the virtuous, but his actions have not matched his words. Moralizing has substituted for moral leadership, lecturing others about democracy has substituted for respecting democratic values. George W. Bush has claimed to be championing democracy, but the rest of the world sees a great nation diminished by secret prisons, torture, and warrantless wiretapping. And every day that we remain mired in Iraq, the world is reminded of the folly, the dishonesty, and the disregard for the opinions of others that got us there.

The next president needs to send a clear signal to the world that America has turned the corner and will once again be a leader rather than a unilateralist loner. To do this, the new president must first end the Iraq war. We need to withdraw all our troops and embrace a decisive new political strategy that engages all the nations of the region, as well as the international donor community. Only when we have done this can we begin the hard work of rebuilding our military and our alliances and restoring our tarnished reputation—so that we can move forward and lead the world in addressing urgent global problems.

THE NEW CHALLENGES OF A NEW CENTURY

Getting out of Iraq and restoring our reputation and leadership capacities are necessary first steps toward a new strategy of U.S. global engagement and leadership. But these steps alone are not enough. To address new problems effectively, we must first understand them in all of their complexity. We must question old assumptions, break old paradigms, and embrace new approaches equal to our new tasks. Six trends are transforming the world today.

The first trend is fanatical jihadism bursting from an increasingly unstable and violent greater Middle East. This trend had been growing for years, but the invasion and collapse of Iraq have greatly fueled its rise. A second trend transforming the world (in ways still not well understood by the public) is the growing power and sophistication of criminal networks capable of disrupting the global economy and trafficking in WMD.

Together, these two trends raise the frightening specter of nuclear terrorism. We know that al Qaeda has tried to acquire nuclear weapons and that the Pakistani nuclear scientist A. Q. Khan sold nuclear technology to rogue states. We know that parts of the former Soviet nuclear arsenal still are not secure and that nuclear materials are scattered around the world in dozens of countries and hundreds of locations, some of them no more secure than a grocery store. The proliferation of nuclear weapons to new countries, especially North Korea, has further increased the opportunities for jihadists to obtain them, as has the diffusion of nuclear energy technologies that can be converted for use in weapons programs. Iran, a nation with close ties to the world's most skilled terrorist organization, Hezbollah, is enriching uranium. And al Qaeda has said that it wishes to kill four million Americans, including two million children. In its madness, it claims that such a slaughter of innocents would "balance the scales of justice" for crimes that it alleges we have committed against Muslims. We would be mad not to take it at its word.

A third trend transforming the world is the rapid rise of Asian economic and military power. India and China are destined to be global powers in the decades ahead—one as a democracy, the other not. And a fourth trend is the reemergence of Russia as an assertive global and regional player with a large nuclear arsenal and control over energy resources—and one tempted by authoritarianism and militant nationalism. The rise of India and China and the reemergence of Russia call for U.S. strategic leadership to integrate these powerful nuclear-armed nations into a stable global order.

A fifth trend transforming our world is the increase in global economic interdependence and financial imbalances without the sufficient growth of institutional capacities to manage these realities. Globalization has made every country's economy more vulnerable to resource constraints and financial shocks that originate beyond its borders. A global energy crisis or a sudden collapse of the U.S. dollar could do great damage to the world economy.

The sixth trend we face is that of grave global environmental and health problems. Climate change and pandemics such as AIDS do not respect national borders. Poverty, ethnic conflict, and overpopulation spill over national boundaries, feeding into a growing underground economy of money launderers, counterfeiters, and smugglers of drugs, arms, and human beings.

Together, these six trends present us with problems that are international and societal in their origins—and that, accordingly, will require international and societal solutions. They also demand political leadership that only the United States, the sole superpower, can provide. If the world succeeds in defeating jihadism, preventing nuclear terrorism, integrating rising powers into a stable order, protecting the stability of global financial markets, and fighting global environmental and health threats, the United States will deserve much of the credit. If the world fails to meet these challenges, the United States will deserve much of the blame.

A NEW REALISM

To cope with this new world, we need a New Realism in our foreign policy—an ethical, principled realism that harbors no illusions about the importance of a strong military in a dangerous world but that also understands the importance of diplomacy and multilateral cooperation. We need a New Realism based on the understanding that what goes on inside of other countries profoundly impacts us—but that we can only influence, not control, what goes on inside of other countries. A New Realism for the twenty-first century must understand that to solve our own problems, we need to work with other governments that respect and trust us.

To be effective in the coming decades, America must set the following priorities. First and foremost, we must rebuild our alliances. We cannot lead other nations toward solutions to shared problems if they do not trust our leadership. We need to restore respect and appreciation for our allies—and for the democratic values that unite us—if we are to work with them to solve global problems. We must restore our commitment to international law and to multilateral cooperation. This means respecting both the letter and the spirit of the Geneva Conventions and joining the International Criminal Court (ICC). It means expanding the United Nations Security Council to include Germany, India, Japan, a country from Latin America, and a country from Africa as permanent members.

We must be impeccable in our own respect for human rights. We should reward countries that live up to the Universal Declaration of Human Rights, as we negotiate, constructively but firmly, with those who do not. And when genocide or other grave human rights violations begin, the United States should lead the world to stop them. History teaches that if the United States does not take the lead on ending genocide, no one else will. The norm of absolute territorial sovereignty is moot when national governments partner with those who rape, torture, and kill masses of people. The United States should lead the world toward acceptance of a greater norm of respect for basic human rights—and toward enforcing that norm through international institutions and multilateral measures.

We need to start taking human rights in Africa particularly seriously, because the two worst genocides in recent history have taken place there, in Rwanda and now in Darfur. We failed to stop the killing in Rwanda, and for years we have failed to stop the killing in Darfur. America must hold itself to a higher standard of leadership. The United States should have sent a special envoy as soon as the mass killings began in Darfur. We could still do more to mobilize multilateral pressure on the Sudanese government and on China, which has great influence over Sudan. It is shameful that the Bush administration continues to wring its hands over Darfur when it is within our power to do something.

In the long run, I believe that the most important tool to stop human rights violators will be the ICC. If the United States joined the ICC and supported it enthusiastically, the calculus of leaders who engage in or allow crimes against humanity to take place would change. A strong ICC would hold criminal leaders accountable. When all else fails, the United States also should take the lead in providing military support to local and regional forces opposing genocide and in assembling multilateral interventions to stop the killing.

The United States must also be the leader, not the laggard, in global efforts to reduce greenhouse gas emissions. We must embrace the Kyoto Protocol on global warming and then go well beyond it. We must lead the world with a man-on-the-moon effort to improve energy efficiency and to commercialize clean, alternative technologies. We must implement an ambitious national cap-and-trade system to cut our fossil fuel consumption dramatically and negotiate an equally ambitious and binding global agreement to get others, most urgently China and India, to follow us into a sustainable-energy future. I have developed these ideas in detail in my energy plan, which environmental groups agree is the most ambitious plan presented by any presidential candidate.

The United States needs to stop considering diplomatic engagement with others to be a reward for good behavior. The Bush administration's long refusal to engage diplomatically regimes such as Pyongyang and Tehran only encouraged and strengthened their most paranoid and hard-line tendencies. Both governments, not surprisingly, responded to Washington's snubs and threats about "regime change" by intensifying their nuclear programs.

THE REAL THREATS

Most urgently, we need to focus on the real security threats from which Iraq has so dangerously diverted our attention. This means doing the hard work to build strong coalitions to infiltrate and destroy terrorist networks, to stop nuclear proliferation, and to keep nuclear weapons out of the hands of terrorists. In the twenty-first century, a nuclear threat will come not from a missile but from a suitcase or a cargo hull. In such a world, nuclear security will not be achieved with missile defense or a new generation of nuclear weapons. It will come through tough, patient, determined diplomacy to secure fissile material worldwide.

Nuclear terrorism is the most serious security threat we face: nothing will stop suicidal jihadists from using a nuclear bomb if they get their hands on one. Some good things are already being done to improve global nuclear security. The nuclear agreement with India, if the Indian Parliament approves it, will help bring a great democracy, a natural ally of the United States, into the global nuclear regime. The Nunn-Lugar Cooperative Threat Reduction Program has reduced the danger from Russian loose nukes. Its budget should be increased and its timetable accelerated. The Proliferation Security Initiative is also an effective program. But the ease with which A. Q. Khan was able to obtain and distribute nuclear technology demonstrates that the danger from loosely guarded nuclear materials is global and will require a comprehensive, global solution.

The United States, as the leading nuclear power, must immediately lead a comprehensive, global effort to reduce the number of nuclear weapons and the amount of bomb-grade fissile material in the world, to consolidate and secure that which remains, and to consolidate nuclear enrichment worldwide in a limited number of highly secure facilities through a global-fuel-banking agreement. A comprehensive strategy also must prevent the construction of any new power plants that use highly enriched uranium.

If we want other countries to cooperate with us, we need to show that we are willing to do our part. We should reaffirm the commitment we made to the long-term goal of a nuclear-weapons-free world when we signed the Nuclear Nonproliferation Treaty. We should offer to reduce our arsenal to a few hundred weapons—enough to deter any attack—if other nuclear nations reduce their arsenals, too, and if non-nuclear-weapons powers agree to stronger global safeguards and the consolidation of nuclear enrichment.

We must engage China and Russia more effectively, strategically, and systematically, making nuclear security our top priority, especially with Russia. One of the few occasions on which President Bush tried to engage Russian President Vladimir Putin on this issue was at a February 2005 conference in Bratislava, Slovakia. During these negotiations, the United States rightly sought to include Russia's conversion of civilian reactors that use highly enriched uranium. When Russia demurred, however, this item was omitted. The conference was used to berate Russia about human rights violations rather than to pressure it to safeguard its tactical nuclear weapons and fissile material. We should be concerned about creeping authoritarianism in Russia, which is a potential long-term danger to our national security. But we also need to realize that even superpowers have limited leverage over the internal politics of other states and that we should prioritize matters we actually can influence. The top priority of the U.S. president must be preventing a nuclear 9/11.

Fighting nuclear trafficking will require better human intelligence and better international intelligence and law enforcement coordination. And it will require tough and persistent U.S. diplomacy to unite the world, including China and Russia, behind efforts to contain the nuclear ambitions of Iran and North Korea, even as we provide these nations with incentives and face-saving ways to permanently renounce nuclear weapons. We should remember that no nation has ever been forced to renounce nuclear weapons but that many nations have been convinced to renounce them. The case of Libya shows that even regimes with terrorist pasts can be persuaded to give up their nuclear weapons ambitions. In a rare resort to diplomacy, and building on connections begun by President Bill Clinton, the Bush administration convinced Libya's Muammar al-Qaddafi to abandon his plans to develop WMD and to end his support for terrorism. Rather than threatening regime change, we convinced Qaddafi that by coming out of the cold, he would have a secure future. After years of delay, progress is now finally being made with North Korea as well.

We should approach Iran the same way. We need to stop the saber rattling and instead work tirelessly with the international community to impose severe multilateral sanctions. The Iranians must know that they have no future as a nuclear weapons power: the international community will stand united behind painful sanctions. But they also must know that they will receive benefits similar to those that Libya received if they renounce uranium enrichment. If they meet international security standards, sanctions will end, and they will have guaranteed access to fuel enriched and banked elsewhere.

We must also open an ideological front in the war against jihadism. There is a civil war within Islam between extremists and moderates—and we have been inadvertently helping our enemies in that civil war. We need to start showing, both through our words and through our deeds, that we are not embroiled, as the jihadists claim, in a clash of civilizations. Rather, the clash is between civilization and barbarity. Our enemy is not Islam: most Muslims reject terrorism. Even most Muslims who do not share our liberal democratic values do share our commitment to peace. To enlist them as partners, we need to respect our differences and to present them with a vision that is better than the apocalyptic fantasy of the jihadists—a vision of peace, prosperity, tolerance, and respect for human dignity.

We should support democracies and democrats around the world, but we should give up on the failed policy of promoting democracy at gunpoint. We must recognize that democratization is a complicated, difficult, long-term project. It took decades or centuries for today's democracies to consolidate themselves. I believe that all nations would benefit from democracy, but we need to recognize that democratization does not happen overnight, especially in nations with deep ethnic or religious divisions or weak civil societies.

COOL EYES AND ARDENT PRINCIPLES

The United States' reputation as a model of freedom and human dignity is one of our greatest resources. We tarnish it at our peril. In the wake of the Bush administration's violations of our values, a skillful public diplomacy effort will be needed to convince the world that the United States has rediscovered itself. Such public diplomacy should include radio and television broadcasts in local languages, as well as expanded educational and exchange programs.

For such efforts to be credible, however, we really need to live up to our own ideals every day. If we want others to value civil liberties, we need to stop spying on our own citizens. Prisoner abuse, torture, secret prisons, denials of habeas corpus, and evasions of the Geneva Conventions must never again have a place in our policy. We should start by closing our prison at Guantánamo Bay, Cuba, and explaining clearly to the world why we have done so.

We must reengage the Middle East peace process with the determination to succeed, so that we can deprive the jihadists of their most effective propaganda tool. We must use all our sticks and carrots to strengthen Palestinian moderates and to achieve a two-state solution that guarantees Israel's security. I would ask Bill Clinton to serve as a high-level full-time envoy to help broker a final settlement. We should also engage discreetly in Kashmir, the tinderbox of Asia.

We are spending more than $2 billion per week on Iraq, but we are not doing nearly enough to protect our cities, nuclear power plants, shipping lanes, and ports from a terrorist attack. We must spend more to recruit, equip, and train more first responders, and we must drastically improve our public health facilities, which more than six years after 9/11 are not ready for a biological attack. And we need to allocate federal homeland security dollars to the places where they are needed—the population centers and facilities that we know al Qaeda targets.

The United States of America also needs to start paying attention to the Americas. We need better border security and comprehensive immigration reform. And to reduce both illegal immigration and anti-American populism in Latin America, we must work with reform-minded governments there to alleviate poverty and promote equitable development. We need to strengthen energy cooperation in the region and foster democracy and fair trade. Our efforts to promote democracy must include Cuba. We should reverse the Bush administration's policies restricting remittances to and travel to visit loved ones in Cuba, and we should respond to steps toward liberalization there with steps toward ending the embargo.

Finally, the United States should lead the global fight against poverty, which is the basis of so much violence. Through example and diplomacy, we must encourage all developed countries to honor their commitments to the UN Millennium Development Goals. A commission on the implementation of sustainable-development goals, composed of world leaders and prominent experts, should recommend ways of meeting those commitments. The United States should lead donors on debt relief, increase assistance to very poor countries, and focus aid programs more on primary health care and affordable vaccines. We should double our development assistance and encourage other rich nations to do the same. We need a World Bank focused on poverty reduction and an International Monetary Fund that has a more flexible approach to preserving and building social safety nets. We must promote equitable multilateral and bilateral trade agreements that create jobs in all the countries involved and that protect workers and the environment. We should encourage the expanded use of generic drugs in poor countries, and we should stimulate public-private partnerships to reduce the costs of and enhance access to HIV antiretroviral drugs, antimalaria drugs, and bed nets.

Most important, the United States should lead a multilaterally funded Marshall Plan for Afghanistan, the Middle East, and Africa. For a small fraction of the cost of the Iraq war, which has made us so many enemies, we could make many friends. A crucial effort in fighting terrorism must be support for public education in the Muslim world, which is the best way to mitigate the role of those madrasahs that foment extremism. Development alleviates the injustice and lack of opportunity that proponents of violence and terrorism exploit.

The challenges facing us today are unprecedented. We need to learn from the mistakes of the Bush administration and adopt twenty-first-century strategies to solve twenty-first-century problems. We need to see the world as it really is—so that we can lead others to make it a better, safer place. This is the New Realist vision of an enlightened and effective policy for the challenges of a new era: a realistic, principled policy that looks at the world through cool eyes but is inspired by ardent principles.

BILL RICHARDSON, Governor of New Mexico, is a candidate for the Democratic presidential nomination.

America's Priorities in the War on Terror

Michael D. Huckabee   JANUARY/FEBRUARY 2008

U.S. Republican presidential candidate and former Arkansas Governor Mike Huckabee campaigns in Appleton, Wisconsin February 18, 2008.

The United States, as the world's only superpower, is less vulnerable to military defeat. But it is more vulnerable to the animosity of other countries. Much like a top high school student, if it is modest about its abilities and achievements, if it is generous in helping others, it is loved. But if it attempts to dominate others, it is despised.

American foreign policy needs to change its tone and attitude, open up, and reach out. The Bush administration's arrogant bunker mentality has been counterproductive at home and abroad. My administration will recognize that the United States' main fight today does not pit us against the world but pits the world against the terrorists. At the same time, my administration will never surrender any of our sovereignty, which is why I was the first presidential candidate to oppose ratification of the Law of the Sea Treaty, which would endanger both our national security and our economic interests.

A more successful U.S. foreign policy needs to better explain Islamic jihadism to the American people. Given how Americans have thrived on diversity—religious, ethnic, racial—it takes an enormous leap of imagination to understand what Islamic terrorists are about, that they really do want to kill every last one of us and destroy civilization as we know it. If they are willing to kill their own children by letting them detonate suicide bombs, then they will also be willing to kill our children for their misguided cause. The Bush administration has never adequately explained the theology and ideology behind Islamic terrorism or convinced us of its ruthless fanaticism. The first rule of war is "know your enemy," and most Americans do not know theirs. To grasp the magnitude of the threat, we first have to understand what makes Islamic terrorists tick. Very few Americans are familiar with the writings of Sayyid Qutb, the Egyptian radical executed in 1966, or the Muslim Brotherhood, whose call to active jihad influenced Osama bin Laden and the rise of al Qaeda. Qutb raged against the decadence and sin he saw around him and sought to restore the "pure" Islam of the seventh century through a theocratic caliphate without national borders. He saw nothing decadent or sinful in murdering in order to achieve that end. America's culture of life stands in stark contrast to the jihadists' culture of death.

The United States' biggest challenge in the Arab and Muslim worlds is the lack of a viable moderate alternative to radicalism. On the one hand, there are radical Islamists willing to fight dictators with terrorist tactics that moderates are too humane to use. On the other, there are repressive regimes that stay in power by force and through the suppression of basic human rights—many of which we support by buying oil, such as the Saudi government, or with foreign aid, such as the Egyptian government, our second-largest recipient of aid.

Although we cannot export democracy as if it were Coca-Cola or KFC, we can nurture moderate forces in places where al Qaeda is seeking to replace modern evil with medieval evil. Such moderation may not look or function like our system—it may be a benevolent oligarchy or more tribal than individualistic—but both for us and for the peoples of those countries, it will be better than the dictatorships they have now or the theocracy they would have under radical Islamists. The potential for such moderation to emerge is visible in the way that Sunni tribal leaders in Iraq have turned against al Qaeda to work with us; they could not stand the thought of living under such fundamentalism and brutality. The people of Afghanistan turned against the Taliban for the same reason. To know these extremists is not to love them.

As president, my goal in the Arab and Muslim worlds will be to calibrate a course between maintaining stability and promoting democracy. It is self-defeating to attempt too much too soon: doing so could mean holding elections that the extremists would win. But it is also self-defeating to do nothing. We must first destroy existing terrorist groups and then attack the underlying conditions that breed them: the lack of basic sanitation, health care, education, jobs, a free press, fair courts—which all translates into a lack of opportunity and hope. The United States' strategic interests as the world's most powerful country coincide with its moral obligations as the richest. If we do not do the right thing to improve life in the Muslim world, the terrorists will step in and do the wrong thing.

IF FORCE, THEN OVERWHELMING

For too long, we have been constrained because our dependence on imported oil has forced us to support repressive regimes and conduct our foreign policy with one hand tied behind our back. I will free that hand from its oil-soaked rope and reach out to moderates in the Arab and Muslim worlds with both. I want to treat Saudi Arabia the way we treat Sweden, and that will require the United States to be energy independent. The first thing I will do as president is send Congress my comprehensive plan for achieving energy

independence within ten years of my inauguration. We will explore, we will conserve, and we will pursue all types of alternative
energy: nuclear, wind, solar, ethanol, hydrogen, clean coal, biomass,
and biodiesel.

Supporting Islamic moderates and moving toward energy independence will not protect us from the terrorists who already exist.
These enemies, who plot and train in small, scattered cells, can be
tracked down and eliminated by the CIA, U.S. Special Forces, and
the military forces of the coalition countries united to rid the world
of this scourge. We can achieve a tremendous amount with swift
and surgical air strikes and commando raids by our elite units. But
these operations demand first-rate intelligence. When the Cold
War ended, we cut back our human intelligence, just as we cut back
our armed forces, and these reductions have come back to haunt us.
I will strengthen both.

The "peace dividend" from the fall of the Soviet Union has become a war deficit with the rise of Islamic terrorism. We did not
send enough troops to Iraq initially. We still do not have enough
troops in Afghanistan and are losing hard-won gains there as foreign fighters pour in and the number of Iraq-style suicide attacks
increases. Our current active armed forces simply are not large
enough. We have relied far too heavily on the National Guard and
the Reserves and worn them out.

The Bush administration plans to increase the size of the U.S.
Army and the Marine Corps by about 92,000 troops over the next
five years. We can and must do this in two to three years. I recognize the challenges of increasing our enlistments without lowering
standards and of expanding training facilities and personnel, and
that is one of the reasons why we must increase our military budget. Right now, we spend about 3.9 percent of our GDP on defense, compared with about six percent in 1986, under President
Ronald Reagan. We need to return to that six percent level. And
we must stop using active-duty forces for nation building and return to our policy of using other government agencies to build
schools, hospitals, roads, sewage treatment plants, water filtration

systems, electrical facilities, and legal and banking systems. We must marshal the goodwill, ingenuity, and power of our governmental and nongovernmental organizations in coordinating and implementing these essential nonmilitary functions.

If I ever have to undertake a large invasion, I will follow the Powell Doctrine and use overwhelming force. The notion of an occupation with a "light footprint," which was our model for Iraq, is a contradiction in terms. Liberating a country and occupying it are two different missions. Our invasion of Iraq went well militarily, but the occupation has destroyed the country politically, economically, and socially. In the former Yugoslavia, we sent 20 peacekeeping soldiers for every thousand civilians. In Iraq, an equivalent ratio would have meant sending a force of 450,000 U.S. troops. Unlike President George W. Bush, who marginalized General Eric Shinseki, the former army chief of staff, when he recommended sending several hundred thousand troops to Iraq, I would have met with Shinseki privately and carefully weighed his advice. Our generals must be independent advisers, always free to speak without fear of retribution or dismissal.

SECURING IRAQ

As president, I will not withdraw U.S. troops from Iraq any faster than General David Petraeus, the top U.S. commander there, recommends. I will bring our troops home based on the conditions on the ground, not the calendar on the wall. It is still too soon to reduce the U.S. counterterrorism mission and pass the torch of security to the Iraqis. If we do not preserve and expand population security, by maintaining the significant number of forces required, we risk losing all our hard-won gains. These are significant but tenuous.

Seeing Iraqi Sunnis in Anbar, Diyala, and parts of Baghdad reject al Qaeda and join our forces, often at tremendous risk to themselves, has been a truly extraordinary shift. Those who once embraced al Qaeda members as liberators now see them for what these radicals are: brutal oppressors who want to take Iraq back to the seventh century. And this development is serving as a model for turning Shiite tribes against their militants. Despite what the gloomy Democrats in the United States profess, reconciliation is happening in Iraq, only it is bottom up rather than top down, and since it comes directly from the people, it can end the violence faster. Benchmarks are being reached in fact, if not in law. As Ryan Crocker, the U.S. ambassador to Iraq, told Congress last September, oil revenues are being distributed, de-Baathification is being reversed, and the Shiite-dominated government is giving financial resources to the provinces, including Sunni areas.

The Kurdish north is the most peaceful and prosperous part of Iraq. We must not allow the PKK (Kurdistan Workers' Party), the Kurdish Marxist terrorist group responsible for almost 40,000 deaths since the mid-1980s, to jeopardize that achievement. The PKK is losing support among mainstream Turkish Kurds: they have made great strides economically, culturally, and politically in the past decade, and many are renouncing violence. We must encourage Turkey to continue to improve life for its Kurds, and we must encourage the Turkish Kurds to address their grievances through the political process, including through the 20 deputies currently representing them in parliament. On the Iraqi side of the border, Turkey provides 80 percent of the foreign investment in the Kurdish region, and the Iraqi Kurds do not want to jeopardize that relationship.

I support providing the Turks with actionable intelligence to go after the PKK with limited air strikes and commando raids but would prefer to train and equip Iraqi Kurds to fight the PKK and rid themselves of this menace. I regret that it took the deployment of 100,000 Turkish troops to the border with Iraq, and the PKK problem becoming a crisis, for the Bush administration to give the issue the attention it deserves. We should have put more pressure on the Iraqi government, including the Kurdish authorities, to deal with the PKK earlier. Our special envoy on the issue, retired General Joseph Ralston, quit his post last October out of frustration over the passivity of both the U.S. and the Iraqi governments. Some crises cannot be averted; this one could and should have been.

Withdrawing from Iraq before the country is stable and secure would have serious strategic consequences for us and horrific humanitarian consequences for the Iraqis. Iraq's neighbors on all sides would be drawn into the war and face refugee crises as a result of fleeing Iraqis. Iraq is the crossroads where Arabs meet Persians and Kurds, and Sunnis meet Shiites. When we deposed Saddam Hussein, we emphasized the potentially dramatic upside of Iraq's centrality in the region: the country could be a prime place to establish democracy and have it spread from. Today, we face the dramatic downside: Iraq's centrality makes the country the perfect place for terrorists to create anarchy and have it spread. Those who say that we do not owe the Iraqis anything more are ignoring what we owe our own children and grandchildren in terms of security.

CONTAINING IRAN

Americans have urgent concerns about Iran's military and financial support for Shiite militants in Iraq, the Taliban in Afghanistan, Hezbollah in Lebanon, and Hamas in the Palestinian territories. And we have urgent concerns about Iran's development of nuclear weapons, especially since more is at stake than just Iran's progress: faced with a nuclear Shiite Persian power, Sunni Arab regimes will feel the need to match it.

The Bush administration has properly said that it will not take the military option for dealing with Iran off the table. Neither will I. But if we do not put other options on the table, eventually a military strike will become the only viable one. And nothing would make bin Laden happier than this outcome; he would welcome war between the United States and Iran. Indeed, al Qaeda and Iran seek control of the same territory: what Iran envisions as its Shiite crescent is a large part of what would be the Sunni caliphate that al Qaeda seeks to create from Spain to Indonesia. Both Iran and al Qaeda seek not just to dominate Israel but to destroy it and control the Palestinians. And I will not waver in standing by our ally Israel. The main difference between these two enemies is that al Qaeda is a movement that must be destroyed, whereas Iran is a nation that just has to be contained.

In order to contain Iran, it is essential to win in Iraq. When we overthrew Saddam, whose regime was a bulwark against Iran, we upset the regional balance of power. Now, we must stabilize and strengthen Iraq not just for its own security but for the security of its neighbors, the region, and ourselves. We cannot allow Iran to push its theocracy into Iraq and then expand it further west.

Another way to contain Iran is through diplomacy. We must be as aggressive diplomatically as we have been militarily since 9/11. We must intensify our diplomatic efforts with China, India, Russia, South Korea, and European states and persuade them to put more economic pressure on Iran. These countries have been far more interested in pursuing profit than preventing proliferation. They must realize that if the United States does end up taking military action, they will bear some responsibility for having failed to maximize peaceful options.

I welcome the Bush administration's new sanctions against Iran and its decision to designate Iran's Revolutionary Guards as a proliferator of weapons of mass destruction and its al Quds force as a supporter of terrorism. (The Democrats who claim that such measures are a step toward war are deluded: these moves are an attempt to use economic power instead of, not as a prelude to, using military power.) We must also put more of our money where our mouth is and encourage our state and private pension funds to divest themselves of Iran-related assets.

Since the United States does no business directly with Iran, these sanctions will have an impact only if other countries honor them. United Nations sanctions will have to remain weak if China and Russia are to support them, but I have greater hope for tougher ones from the European Union, Iran's biggest trading partner. With Nicolas Sarkozy as president of France, we now have a much more willing ally.

I am less hopeful that Russia will be helpful. Since Russia benefits from high energy prices, President Vladimir Putin has more incentives to keep energy markets jittery than to resolve the crisis with Iran. Russia also profits handsomely from selling weapons to Iran, mostly air defense systems intended to protect Iran from possible U.S. air strikes. I support going forward with the current plan to set up ten missile interceptors in Poland and a radar system in the Czech Republic to protect Europe from Iranian missiles. Putin opposes an antimissile system in the former Soviet satellite states (even though we have offered to share the technology with the Russians) and our potential use of Azerbaijan, a former Soviet republic, as a staging ground for an attack on Iran.

We must remember that with the collapse of the Soviet Union came the revival of Russia, which has always had both imperialist ambitions and an inferiority complex vis-à-vis the West. Tsarist history is a case study in the struggle between westernizers and Slavophiles. The push and pull will continue, bringing good days and bad in our relations with Russia. Overall, things will be better than during the Cold War because, much as we do not want another 9/11, Putin does not want another terrorist attack like the 2004 school siege in Beslan. But I see him for what he is: a staunch nationalist in a country that has no democratic tradition. He will do everything he can to reassert Russia's power—militarily, economically, diplomatically.

Sun-tzu's ancient wisdom is relevant today: "Keep your friends close and your enemies closer." Yet we have not had diplomatic relations with Iran in almost 30 years; the U.S. government usually communicates with the Iranian government through the Swiss embassy in Tehran. When one stops talking to a parent or a friend, differences cannot be resolved and relationships cannot move forward. The same is true for countries. The reestablishment of diplomatic ties will not occur automatically or without the Iranians' making concessions that serve to create a less hostile relationship.

Our experience in Iraq offers a valuable lesson for how to proceed in Iran. Since we overthrew Saddam, we have learned that we invaded an imaginary country, because we relied at the time on information that was out of date and on longtime exiles who exaggerated the good condition of Iraq's infrastructure, the strength of its middle class, and the secular nature of its society. We would have received better information if we had had our own ambassador in Baghdad. Before we put boots on the ground elsewhere, we had better have wingtips there first.

Many Iranians are well disposed toward us. On 9/11, there was dancing in the streets in parts of the Muslim world but candlelit vigils and mourning in Tehran. When we invaded Afghanistan, Iran helped us, especially in our dealings with the Northern Alliance. Hoping for better bilateral relations, Tehran wanted to join us against al Qaeda. The CIA and the State Department supported this partnership, but some in the White House and the Pentagon did not. After President Bush included Iran in the "axis of evil," everything went downhill fast.

Whereas there can be no rational dealings with al Qaeda, Iran is a nation-state seeking regional clout and playing the game of power politics we understand and can skillfully pursue. We cannot live with al Qaeda, but we might be able to live with a contained Iran. Iran will not acquire nuclear weapons on my watch. But before I look parents in the eye to explain why I put their son's or daughter's life at risk, I want to do everything possible to avoid conflict. We have substantive issues to discuss with Tehran. Recent direct negotiations about Iraq have not been productive because they have not explored the full range of issues. We have valuable incentives to offer Iran: trade and economic assistance, full diplomatic relations, and security guarantees.

TOUGH LOVE FOR PAKISTAN

Whereas our failure to tackle Iran seems to be leading inexorably to our attacking it, our failure to tackle al Qaeda in Pakistan seems to be leading inexorably to its attacking us again.

When we let bin Laden escape at Tora Bora, a region along the Afghan-Pakistani border, in December 2001, we played Brer Fox to his Brer Rabbit. We threw him into the perfect briar patch, under the direct protection of tribal leaders who do not consider their land part of Pakistan and under the indirect protection of the Pakistani government, which believes that it is. On September 12, 2001, Pakistani President Pervez Musharraf agreed to sever his relationship with the Taliban and let us fight al Qaeda inside Pakistan. But distracted by Iraq, we have since allowed him to go back on his word.

Despite the Bush administration's continued claims that the U.S. military will pursue "actionable targets," according to a July 2007 article in The New York Times based on interviews with a dozen current and former military and defense officials, a classified raid targeting bin Laden's top deputy, Ayman al-Zawahiri, in Pakistan was aborted in early 2005. Then Defense Secretary Donald Rumsfeld called off the attack at the very last minute, as Navy Seals in parachutes were preparing in C-130s in Afghanistan, because he felt he needed Musharraf's permission to proceed. Why did Rumsfeld, instead of President Bush, call off the attack? Did he ask for Musharraf's permission or assume he would not get it? When I am president, I will make the final call on such actions.

This missed opportunity was especially costly because in September 2006 Musharraf agreed to a cease-fire with frontier tribal leaders (which lasted until last July), allowing al Qaeda and the Taliban to gain strength and operate more easily and freely. With that, Pakistan's halfhearted efforts against the terrorists in the region bordering Afghanistan stopped altogether.

Iraq may be the hot war, but Pakistan is where the cold, calculating planning is going on. If al Qaeda strikes us tomorrow, the attack will be postmarked "Pakistan." And the American people, not understanding why a supposed U.S. ally refused to help and our government put up with it, will justifiably be outraged that bin Laden and his top people got away. In fact, we almost did suffer that next attack: the plot to blow up ten airliners over the Atlantic that the British government foiled in 2006 was hatched in Pakistan, as was an attack against U.S. targets in Germany that was planned to coincide with the sixth anniversary of 9/11.

Rather than wait for the next strike, I prefer to cut to the chase by going after al Qaeda's safe havens in Pakistan. As commander in chief, the U.S. president must balance threats and risks in calculating how best to protect the American people. We are living on borrowed time. The threat of an attack on us is far graver than the risk that a quick and limited strike against al Qaeda would bring extremists to power in Pakistan.

To be sure, Pakistan is an inherently unstable country that has never had a constitutional change of government in its 60 years of existence. It has alternated between military and civilian rule, punctuated by assassinations and coups. Even during times of nominal civilian rule, the army and its affiliated intelligence service, the Inter-Services Intelligence, or ISI, were the country's most powerful institutions. But in the name of stability, the U.S. government has erred on the side of protecting Musharraf. We have an unfortunate tendency to confuse leaders with their countries and their citizens and to back them for too long, with too few questions asked and too few strings attached. As the Bush administration scrambled to cope with Musharraf's state of emergency last November, it became clear that we had no Pakistan policy, only a Musharraf policy.

Musharraf's top priority is not the United States' survival but his own, physical and political. Musharraf has done his best to convince the Bush administration that the United States' destiny and his are inextricably interwoven—after him, the deluge. But this is not true. He has not kept extremists from seizing power in Pakistan; they have not seized it simply because they have not had the strength or the support to do so. He claims that he declared the state of emergency because of the threat of extremism to Pakistan. In fact, he was responding to a threat not to the country but to himself and not from extremists but from Pakistan's Supreme Court, which was about to invalidate his recent reelection.

This puts into sharp relief what a waste, what a setback the United States' Pakistan policy has been over the last few years. Al Qaeda and the Taliban have grown stronger; Pakistan's native extremists have expanded east from their frontier strongholds and spread to the cities; the moderate secular parties led by former Prime Ministers Benazir Bhutto and Nawaz Sharif have languished. Musharraf has spent far more energy and enthusiasm sidelining the moderate Pakistani forces we must strengthen than he has going after religious extremists and terrorists. As of this writing, he is arresting the people who share our values and whom we need to empower: leaders and supporters of moderate parties, judges, lawyers, human rights activists, and journalists. He is on a collision course with his own people and with us.

Since 9/11, the United States has given Pakistan about $10 billion, including some $5.6 billion to pay for counterterrorism activities against al Qaeda and the Taliban. Less than $1 billion has gone to projects that directly help the Pakistani people by providing them with schools, food, or medical aid. The lack of schools creates demand for the madrasahs that produce terrorists. We have wasted money on counterterrorism that has not happened and spent precious little on projects to win hearts and minds.

Much of the aid is made up of cash transfers that are not monitored by any U.S. government agency; we must improve transparency and accountability in this area. If we consider cutting aid to Pakistan, we must distinguish among different kinds of funds. We should not cut money for projects that alleviate poverty. Money designated for counterterrorism must be spent for that purpose and with quantifiable results. Money designated for weapons not suited to fighting terrorists should be used as a carrot to reward the Pakistani government for demonstrated progress in strengthening moderate forces, improving its citizens' quality of life, and fighting terrorism.

It is not enough for Musharraf to appoint a caretaker government, give up his post as army chief, and hold elections in early January, as he has promised: such elections cannot possibly be free and fair with the state of emergency still in effect, opposition politicians and their supporters under arrest, the media censored, assembly forbidden, and the judiciary packed. Opposition party leaders rightly threaten

167

to boycott such sham elections, which would have no legitimacy in the eyes of the Pakistani people. Bhutto and Sharif must be allowed to move freely about the country. Whatever happens in Pakistan next, the country's policy toward the United States is unlikely to change significantly. General Ashfaq Kiyani, the deputy chief of staff of the army and Musharraf's most likely successor, is a moderate who wants the military less involved in politics. As prime minister, Sharif would sound more anti-American, and Bhutto more pro-American. But in any event, our problems with al Qaeda and the Taliban will not be magically solved for us. They are our problems, and we must face up to them.

I will assure the Pakistanis that we are with them for the long haul. When the Russians left Afghanistan in the late 1980s, we quickly lost interest in Pakistan. Many Pakistanis fear the same will happen when al Qaeda and the Taliban are no longer around to keep us engaged. They should not. Pakistan, like Iraq, is a regional problem rather than an isolated one. We must use our friendly ties with India to encourage and help it improve its relationship with Pakistan and to push for increased trade and cooperation between the two countries, all to bring greater stability to the South Asian region.

"The process will not be quick," Ambassador Crocker told Congress of the progress in Iraq last fall. "It will be uneven, punctuated by setbacks as well as achievements, and it will require substantial U.S. resolve and commitment." Does this sound familiar? To me, the statement could also have applied to the American Revolution, the American Civil War, World War I, or World War II. We paid a heavy price in each of those conflicts, but we prevailed. And we will prevail now. Our history, from the snows of Valley Forge to the flames of 9/11, has been one of perseverance. I understand the threats we face today. When I am president, America will look this evil in the eye, confront it, defeat it, and emerge stronger than ever. It is easy to be a peace lover; the challenging part is being a peacemaker.

MICHAEL D. HUCKABEE, former Governor of Arkansas, is a candidate for the Republican presidential nomination.

Bridges, Bombs, or Bluster?

Madeleine K. Albright   SEPTEMBER/OCTOBER 2003

Madeleine Albright in Prague, January 12, 2010.

EITHER, OR

> Every nation, in every region, now has a decision to make. Either you are with us, or you are with the terrorists.

> There are only two powers now in the world. One is America, which is tyrannical and oppressive. The other is a warrior who has not yet been awakened from his slumber and that warrior is Islam.

> Make no mistake about it: the choice for sure is between two visions of the world.

Few readers will fail to identify the first quotation cited above: it was uttered by President George W. Bush, speaking soon after the September 11, 2001, terrorist attacks. Few readers, similarly, will be surprised to learn that the second quote came from a Sunni Muslim cleric in Baghdad, Imam Mouaid al-Ubaidi. The third quote, however, may be a bit harder to identify: it was spoken by French

Foreign Minister Dominique de Villepin, describing the different world views now held by Washington and Paris. And it should remind us that not everyone divides the world along the same lines as the United States.

Framing choices is central to national security policy. Since World War II, no nation has played a more influential role in defining such alternatives than the United States. Today, however, the Bush administration purports to be redefining the fundamental choice "every nation, in every region" must make. America's radical adversaries—eager to promote themselves as the United States' chief nemeses—are echoing the attempt. Those caught in the middle, however, suggest the choices before them may not be quite so simple.

For President Bush, September 11 came as a revelation, leading him to the startled conclusion that the globe had changed in ways gravely hazardous to the security—indeed, the very survival—of the United States. This conclusion soon led Bush to a fateful decision: to depart, in fundamental ways, from the approach that has characterized U.S. foreign policy for more than half a century. Soon, reliance on alliance had been replaced by redemption through preemption; the shock of force trumped the hard work of diplomacy, and long-time relationships were redefined.

In making these changes, Bush explicitly rejected the advice offered by one senior statesman who warned, "this most recent surprise attack [should] erase the concept in some quarters that the United States can somehow go it alone in the fight against terrorism, or in anything else, for that matter." So said George H.W. Bush, the United States' 41st president. But his son, the 43rd president, offered his own perspective shortly before going to war with Iraq: "At some point, we may be the only ones left. That's okay with me. We are America."

The second Bush administration, believing that its perception of the meaning of September 11 is self-evidently right, has failed to make a sustained effort to persuade the rest of the world to share it. As a result, the world does not in fact subscribe to the same view. Certainly, most of the world does not agree with Bush that September 11 "changed everything." This is not to say the attacks were met by indifference. On the contrary, NATO, for the first time in its history, declared the crimes to be acts of aggression against the entire alliance. Almost every government in the Muslim world, including Iran and the Palestinian Authority, condemned the strikes. U.S. allies, from Canada to Japan to Australia, rushed to aid or complement the American military campaign against al Qaeda and the Taliban in Afghanistan. Pakistan, properly confronted by the administration with a stark choice, chose to cooperate as well. Even China and Russia, plagued by Muslim separatists, pledged solidarity. For months after September 11, it seemed the Bush administration would harness these reactions to unite the world in opposition to a common threat.

The president began well, emphasizing the array of nationalities victimized in the Twin Towers attacks and gathering broad support for the military operation he directed at the perpetrators. Al Qaeda's Taliban protectors were pushed from power, its training camps were destroyed, arms caches were seized, and many of its leaders were captured or killed. But instead of single-mindedly building on these gains, the Bush administration has since steadily enlarged and complicated its own mission.

In his 2002 State of the Union address, for example, President Bush focused not on al Qaeda and the work remaining in Afghanistan, but rather on the so-called axis of evil. In public remarks later that year, he emphasized not the value of building an antiterror coalition, but rather his unilateral intention to maintain U.S. "military strength beyond challenge, thereby making the destabilizing arms races of other eras pointless." He then asked Congress for the authority to explore new uses for nuclear weapons, creating the perception overseas that he was lowering the threshold for nuclear strikes—despite the United States' vast conventional military superiority and the risks posed to U.S. security by the proliferation of weapons of mass destruction (WMD).

When the administration published its 2002 National Security Strategy last September, it took this process even further, transforming anticipatory self-defense—a tool every president has quietly held in reserve—into the centerpiece of its national security policy. This step, however, was dangerously easy to misconstrue. (Do we really want a world in which every country feels entitled to attack any other that might someday threaten it?) And when Bush did discuss the pursuit of al Qaeda, he portrayed it less as a global struggle against a global threat than as an effort to bring terrorists to "American justice"—as if justice alone were not enough.

Finally, in 2003, Washington did begin once more to rally world support—but this time against Iraq, not al Qaeda. To bolster the decision to oust Saddam Hussein, administration officials lumped his regime together with al Qaeda, describing them as complementary halves of the same existential threat. U.S. officials declared that America would act against such threats when and wherever necessary, regardless of international law, notwithstanding the doubts of allies, and without concern for the outrage of those who might misunderstand U.S. actions. America, said the president, had no choice but to go to war to prevent its enemies from obtaining more weapons or growing more powerful. And so the United States duly went to war against Iraq, despite having convinced only four members of the UN Security Council to back the action.

NEITHER, NOR

Many observers see in the Bush administration's policies an admirable demonstration of spine in confronting those who threaten the safety of the American people. I would join the applause—if only those policies were safeguarding U.S. citizens more effectively.

But they are not. Moreover, I remain convinced that had Al Gore been elected president, and had the attacks of September 11 still happened, the United States and NATO would have gone to war in Afghanistan together, then deployed forces all around that country and stayed to rebuild it. Democrats, after all, confess support for nation building, and also believe in finishing the jobs we start. I also believe the United States and NATO together would have remained focused on fighting al Qaeda and would not have pretended—and certainly would not have been allowed to get away with pretending—that the ongoing failure to capture Osama bin Laden did not matter. As for Saddam, I believe the Gore team would have read the intelligence information about his activities differently and concluded that a war against Iraq, although justifiable, was not essential in the short term to protect U.S. security. A policy of containment would have been sufficient while the administration pursued the criminals who had murdered thousands on American soil.

The Bush administration's decision to broaden its focus from opposing al Qaeda to invading Iraq and threatening military action against others has had unintended and unwelcome consequences. According to the recent findings of the Pew Global Attitudes Project, which surveyed 16,000 people in 20 countries and the Palestinian territories in May, the percentage of those who have a favorable view of the United States has declined sharply (15 percentage points or more) in nations such as Brazil, France, Germany, Jordan, Nigeria, Russia, and Turkey. In Indonesia, the world's most populous Muslim-majority state, the view of the United States plunged from 75 percent favorable to 83 percent negative between 2000 and 2003. Support for the U.S.-led war on terror has declined in each of the countries listed above, along with pivotal Pakistan, where it stands at a disheartening 20 percent. The citizens of such NATO allies as the United Kingdom, France, Germany, and Italy rated Russia's Vladimir Putin more highly as a world leader than Bush. Significant majorities of those interviewed in Russia and in 7 of 8 predominantly Muslim countries (Kuwait being the exception) claimed to be somewhat or very worried about the potential threat to their societies posed by the U.S. military. I never thought the day would come when the United States would be feared by those it has neither the intention nor the cause to harm.

The ouster of Saddam has indeed made the world, or at least Iraq, a better place. But when the United States commits tens of billions of dollars to any worthwhile project, that is the least it should be able to say. Even more vital is progress toward mobilizing the kind of multinational, multicultural, multifaceted, and multiyear initiative required to discredit, disrupt, and dismantle al Qaeda and whatever splinter factions it may one day spawn. That initiative will require a maximum degree of global coordination and the integration of force, diplomacy, intelligence, and law. It will require strong working relationships in regions where radical ideologies thrive and pro-Western sentiments are scant. And above all, it will require vigorous leadership from Islamic moderates, who must win the struggle for control of their own faith. Unfortunately, the Iraq war and the subsequent U.S. occupation of Baghdad—the capital of Islam during that faith's golden age—have made more difficult the choices Islamic moderates and others around the world must make.

The problem is that President Bush has reframed his initial question. Instead of simply asking others to oppose al Qaeda, he now asks them to oppose al Qaeda, support the invasion of an Arab country, and endorse the doctrine of preemption—all as part of a single package. Faced with this choice, many who staunchly oppose al Qaeda have nevertheless decided that they do not want to be "with" the United States, just as some Iraqis are now making clear their opposition both to Saddam and to those who freed them from him.

It is perhaps unsurprising to find attitudes of this sort widespread in the Arab world. But it is more remarkable to find them taking hold in much of Europe. President Bush ran for office pledging to be "a uniter, not a divider," but as the numbers suggest, he has proved highly divisive among the United States' closest friends. This was true even before September 11, thanks to his administration's scorn for international measures such as the Kyoto Protocol on climate change. But the divide deepened considerably in the run-up to the second Gulf War, and it has moderated only slightly since. Transatlantic friction, of course, is not new. But European unease with American pretensions, coupled with American doubts about European resolve, has created the potential for a long-term and dangerous rift.

Some commentators have tried to explain European opposition to the war as being based on a slavish allegiance to multilateral organizations, a sense of relative powerlessness, or simple jealousy of the United States. Such analyses, however, miss the possibility that the American arguments simply were not fully persuasive. I personally felt the war was justified on the basis of Saddam's decade-long refusal to comply with UN Security Council resolutions on WMD. But the administration's claim that Saddam posed an imminent threat was poorly supported, as was its claim of his alleged connections to al Qaeda. The war's opponents also raised a number of questions that were not very ably answered regarding American plans for postwar reconstruction and the possibility that the war would actually enhance al Qaeda's appeal to potential recruits. It should be no wonder, then, that there were disagreements about the wisdom of going to war. It was, after all, a war of choice, not of necessity. And it was initiated by Washington in a show of dominance prompted by a sense of vulnerability that most Europeans do not fully share.

The concerns raised by European critics of the war were neither trivial nor unanswerable. They should, however, have been answered not with exaggerated, unproven allegations, but with a combination of patience and ample evidence. By linking Baghdad to al Qaeda, the Bush administration sought to equate opposition to fighting Iraq with gutlessness in confronting bin Laden. This tactic, wildly unfair, contributed to a perception within the American public that the French and the Germans were not simply quarrelsome but traitorous. The real problem with the war critics, however, was not their timidity toward al Qaeda but their record of having cut Saddam too much slack in complying with UN Security Council resolutions over the last decade. The French and the Russians were especially culpable in this regard; their special pleading had, for years, given Saddam hope that he could divide the council and get sanctions lifted without coming clean about his weapons programs.

The best rebuttal Washington had to qualms about regime change was that military force was the only way (in the absence of effective UN inspections) to enforce the council's resolutions and thereby strengthen both the UN's credibility and international law. Unfortunately, the Bush administration made its eagerness to pull the plug on chief UN weapons inspector Hans Blix and his team transparent and billed its preemptive war doctrine as a replacement for international law. As a consequence, much of the world saw the invasion not as a way to put muscle into accepted rules, but rather as the inauguration of a new set of rules, written and applied solely by the United States.

It didn't have to be this way. After World War II, the United States was also at a pinnacle of power, and also faced new and unprecedented dangers. Yet the Truman administration still sat down and haggled with a flock of less powerful countries about what the rules of the new international game should be. The current administration, however, has created the impression that it does not care what others think, and it has thereby set the world's teeth on edge.

As I suggested above, responsibility for the transatlantic split does not rest on the shoulders of the Bush administration alone. The French certainly have not helped matters, by arguing, for example, that the very purpose of European integration should be to create a counterweight to American power. This constitutes de Villepin's choice "between two visions of the world," by which he means a choice between a unipolar world in which Washington acts as an unrestrained hegemon and a multipolar one in which American power is offset and balanced by other forces, most particularly a united Europe. But that argument is ludicrous. The idea that the power of the United States endangers the interests of European democracies, rather than strengthens and helps shield them, is utter nonsense. American power may harm French pride, but it also helped roll back Hitler, save a blockaded Berlin, defeat communism, and rid the Balkans of a rampaging Slobodan Milosevic.

The divisions that have arisen between the United States and many in Europe can and must be narrowed. The challenge for

Europe is to reject French hyperventilating about American hyper-power and keep its perspective. The United States has not lost its moorings, and the American people, with an assist from Secretary of State Colin Powell and other voices of reason, will not let the administration go too far.

The challenge for the United States, however, is to frame a choice for Europe that most of Europe can embrace with dignity (if not always with France). To help this mission along, NATO should be used in Afghanistan (where it has finally gained a role, two years after September 11) and in Iraq, where its umbrella might help relieve the pressure on hard-pressed U.S. troops. The Bush administration should enthusiastically welcome European efforts to develop an independent rapid reaction capability, especially to conduct peacekeeping operations and respond to humanitarian emergencies. When Europeans perform important jobs, as the Germans and the Turks have done over the past year in Afghanistan, they deserve congratulations, regardless of differences over less basic issues. Furthermore, the Europeans should be invited, not directed, to work closely with Washington on the toughest challenges, including that posed by Iran's nuclear program. Perhaps above all, the Europeans should be treated as adults. If they have differences with U.S. policy, those differences should be considered seriously, not dismissed as signs of weakness (or age) or tantamount to treason. Washington needs to recall that "allies" and "satellites" are distinctly different things.

JUDGING SUCCESS IN IRAQ

Perhaps one reason this administration does not feel the need to consult much with others is its surety of vision. President Bush proclaimed last March that the war in Iraq would prove a decisive first step toward the transformation of the entire Middle East. The demonstration of U.S. resolve, so his logic went, would cause terrorists and those who shelter and sponsor them to tremble. According to the president, "the terrorist threat to America and the world will be diminished the moment that Saddam Hussein is

Madeleine K. Albright

disarmed." The creation of a democratic Iraq, to be achieved with the assistance of a modest number of American troops for a relatively short period of time, would send an instructive message to undemocratic Arab regimes and provide a helpful model for a potential new Palestinian state. Deprived of Iraqi payments to the families of suicide bombers, anti-Israeli terrorists would soon close their bomb factories, and serious peace negotiations could begin. Saddam's fall would also provide a useful lesson to would-be WMD proliferators, both in faraway North Korea and in nearby Iran.

Whatever one might think of the likelihood that this vision will be realized, it certainly qualifies as sweeping and well intentioned. Those who suspect the war in Iraq was a grab for oil are mistaken; it was a grab for a place in history. It deserves time now to play itself out. No one expected every element to fall into place smoothly. Critics such as myself may carp about bumps in the road and setbacks, but the problems will matter little if momentum does build toward a truly democratic and stable Iraq, the weakening of al Qaeda, an end to anti-Israeli terrorism, a halt to Iran's nuclear ambitions, and movement toward accountable government within the Arab world. These are the standards for success the Bush administration set for itself in going to war with Iraq at the moment and under the circumstances it did. The administration merits the courtesy of a reasonable period of time to achieve those goals.

Whether time will in fact bring such successes depends on a series of choices the United States can help frame. The most basic concerns the legitimacy or illegitimacy of the use of terror as a means to achieve political change.

To most Americans, the choice is simple. As the president has said, the use of terror is something you are either for or against, and if you are against it, certain actions must follow. Americans may find it absurd that decent people could believe differently. But history shows that most people, not exceptionally villainous themselves, can nonetheless be persuaded that evil is not evil but rather something else. Romans saw glory in the pillage of the Parthians; pious Catholics saw purity of faith in the Spanish Inquisition; the United States' founding fathers saw economic necessity in slavery; Bosnian Serbs saw justice for past wrongs in ethnic cleansing. Even many Nazi collaborators and appeasers were sure they were doing the right thing; after all, what could be more moral than "peace in our time"? In 1940, the poet Archibald MacLeish wrote, "Murder is not absolved of immorality by committing murder. Murder is absolved of immorality by bringing men to think that murder is not evil. This only the perversion of the mind can bring about. And the perversion of the mind is only possible when those who should be heard in its defense are silent." The lesson for us now is that the longer the illusion of evil as somehow justified lasts—whether buttressed by propaganda, ignorance, convenience, or fear—the harder it is to dispel. That is why we must take nothing for granted. We must be relentless in shaping a global consensus that terrorism is fully, fundamentally, and always wrong. No exceptions, no excuses.

I made this argument to Arab leaders many times when I was secretary of state. Their responses, however, were rarely satisfactory. Most often, my interlocutors would condemn terror unconditionally before commenting parenthetically on the legitimacy of the struggle to free occupied Arab lands. In other words, terrorism was despicable—except where it was most regularly practiced, namely in and against Israel. To this day, it remains the majority Arab view that the militarily overmatched Palestinians are justified in fighting Israelis with whatever means they have. On the issue of terrorist financing, the answers I received were equally inadequate. When I confronted one Saudi leader about payments to Hamas, he said they were merited because Hamas, unlike Yasir Arafat and his government, actually delivered social services to the Palestinian people. As for payments to the families of suicide bombers, those were justified not as an enticement or a reward but as a humanitarian gesture.

The attitude of Arab conservatives toward the terrorism practiced by al Qaeda is another matter. Bin Laden is the cobra that turned on its master. The teaching of Wahhabi Islam in Saudi Arabia's mosques, generously supported by the royal family, has combined with a mix of other factors (globalization, rising unemployment, and the U.S. military presence) to create a global center for the dissemination of hatred. To the discomfort of Saudi leaders, that hatred is now directed not only at the United States and Israel, but also at them. The three explosions set off in Riyadh in May killed 34 people, and hopefully destroyed the last set of lingering Saudi illusions as well. The Saudis have since arrested more than a dozen suspects, fired hundreds of radical clerics, and suspended a thousand more. They also claim to have implemented new regulations designed to prevent the flow of charitable contributions from Saudis overseas to terrorist groups. At the same time, however, the country's leading liberal newspaper editor recently lost his job for seeming to suggest there was a connection between terror and what is being taught in radical mosques. As his firing suggests, the fight for the collective heart and mind of Saudi Arabia has barely begun. Crown Prince Abdullah and his successors must do more than simply condemn extremism and terror; they must rip them out by roots that have become deeply implanted in the kingdom's sandy soil.

Even if the Saudis succeed in such efforts, the roots of terror will continue to throw up shoots elsewhere. The Iraqi imam quoted at the beginning of this article did not explicitly advocate terror in his speech, but he did use the kind of clash-of-civilizations terminology that tends to make Samuel Huntington look retrospectively prescient. The "with us or against us" choice put forward by President Bush has been pulled apart and reassembled, with Islam taking the high ground and with alleged American evil substituted for the real evil: terror. This bit of sophistry illustrates the immense difficulty the United States will have trying to categorize Iraqis on the basis of whether they are willing to cooperate openly with the United States. Iraqis, and Arabs more generally, need the space to design their own choices free from the diktats of authoritarian leaders and notwithstanding the preferences of the United States (provided those choices exclude violence, include tolerance, and are fair to women). This will, I concede, be no simple matter to put into practice.

There are, however, grounds for hope. It is true that the Pew survey found widespread antipathy toward American policies, especially in the Middle East. But it also found widespread enthusiasm among Arab populations for values closely associated with the United States, such as freedom of expression, political pluralism, and equal treatment under the law. Solid majorities in places such as Jordan, Kuwait, and Morocco now believe that Western-style democracy would work well in their countries. And since democracy is built from the bottom up, one step at a time, U.S. leaders have an opportunity (risky as it is) to go around Arab governments to find values in common with the much-vaunted "Arab street." Washington might, for example, spend less time condemning what the Qatar-based independent al Jazeera television network chooses to broadcast and more time acknowledging the importance of its right to choose and encouraging other media outlets to start up.

Although I was proud of the Clinton administration's foreign policy, and I understand that democracy cannot be imposed from the outside, I regret not having done more to push for liberalization within the Arab world. We did nudge at times, supporting Kuwaiti leaders in their initiative to give women the vote and encouraging the creation of representative bodies in Bahrain and Jordan. But we did not make it a priority. Arab public opinion, after all, can be rather scary. The same Pew survey that detected Arab enthusiasm for democracy also found that the "world leader" in whom Palestinians have the most confidence is Osama bin Laden. Who wants to give people with such opinions the right to choose their own leaders? The answer is us: we should do everything possible to see that they are given that right.

For years, Arab populations have received a distorted message from Washington: that the United States stands for democracy, freedom, and human rights everywhere except in the Middle East and for everyone except the Arabs. The time has come to erase that perception and the reality that too often lies behind it. Democracy will not end terrorism in the Arab world, but neither will it nourish it, as despotism does. Bin Laden's appeal is based on what he symbolizes: defiance. In fact, he offers nothing except death and destruction, and Muslim majorities will reject this if they are offered real alternatives.

Indeed, democratization is the most intriguing part of the administration's gamble in Iraq. The creation of a stable and united Iraqi democracy would be a tremendous accomplishment, with beneficial repercussions in other Arab societies. But was invading Iraq the right way to start building democratic momentum in the Arab world? The answer will depend on how divided Iraq remains, and how dicey the security situation becomes. U.S. soldiers will have a hard time democratizing Iraq if they are forced to remain behind walls and inside tanks. And U.S. officials will lack credibility preaching the virtues of freedom if they feel compelled to censor broadcasts, search houses, ban political parties, and repeatedly reject Iraqi demands for more complete self-rule. The Bush administration was determined to retain for itself the authority to supervise every aspect of Iraq's postwar transition. History will judge whether that was a wise decision, but I am reminded in this context of one of "Rumsfeld's Rules," the Pentagon chief's guide for wise public policy: "It is easier to get into something than to get out of it."

CHANGING DIRECTION IN THE MIDDLE EAST

A second, concurrent test of Arab democratization is occurring within the Palestinian Authority, where the Bush administration deserves credit for pushing for reform of Palestinian institutions. The selection of Prime Minister Mahmoud Abbas and the appointment of Finance Minister Salam Fayyad are necessary steps toward democracy and sound governance. The creation of political freedom is essential to allow the emergence of a new generation of Palestinian leaders, comfortable with democratic ways. At the same time, democracy—if it does come—is unlikely to produce a Palestinian government willing to make peace on terms Israelis will accept, or at least not for many years. The Pew survey found that 80 percent of Palestinians do not believe they can realize their rights while coexisting with an Israeli state. That doubt is surely justified if Palestinian rights are thought to include the recovery of all lands taken during the 1967 war, full sovereignty over al-Haram al-Sharif (the Temple Mount), and the right of Palestinian refugees to return to their pre-1948 homes. Unless those demands are modified, or the issues somehow sidestepped, the journey to a Middle East peace will stretch far beyond the boundaries envisioned in the current road map.

Making progress will therefore require new thinking on both sides. The Israelis must help Abbas to succeed in a way they never did with Arafat. This will mean recognizing the elementary fact that Abbas is accountable to the Palestinians, not to Israeli Prime Minister Ariel Sharon or Bush. Unless the new Palestinian regime is able to show greater results than Arafat delivered, Abbas will soon find himself a footnote to history.

The Palestinians, meanwhile, must reject terror—not because the United States or other outsiders want them to, but because terror, far more than Israel, is the enemy of the Palestinian people. It is destructive not only of the Palestinian economy and Palestinian territorial hopes, but of the people's very soul. Terror is a choice, and when people have the power to choose, they have the power to change. The Bush administration, European governments, the Arab world, and Palestinian moderates must all work to create a Palestinian consensus that excludes and excoriates terror. As long as murderers are hailed as martyrs, there can be no real peace, nor any Palestinian state worthy of the name.

Making progress will therefore require new thinking on both sides. The Israelis must help Abbas to succeed in a way they never did with Arafat. This will mean recognizing the elementary fact that Abbas is accountable to the Palestinians, not to Israeli Prime Minister Ariel Sharon or Bush. Unless the new Palestinian regime is able to show greater results than Arafat delivered, Abbas will soon find himself a footnote to history.

The Palestinians, meanwhile, must reject terror—not because the United States or other outsiders want them to, but because terror, far more than Israel, is the enemy of the Palestinian people. It is destructive not only of the Palestinian economy and Palestinian territorial hopes, but of the people's very soul. Terror is a choice, and when people have the power to choose, they have the power to change. The Bush administration, European governments, the Arab world, and Palestinian moderates must all work to create a Palestinian consensus that excludes and excoriates terror. As long as murderers are hailed as martyrs, there can be no real peace, nor any Palestinian state worthy of the name.

The Israelis, too, must be wary of the impact of their own policies of aggressive self-defense. Former Israeli Prime Minister Golda Meir once said that she blamed Arabs less for killing Israelis than for making it necessary for Israelis to kill. Israel has a right to protect itself against terror and, at times, to take preemptive action. But it should never forget that it is destined to live next door to the Palestinians forever, sharing the same land. There is no military solution to that.

REFRAMING THE CHOICE

After September 11, President Bush asked the world to stand with the United States against the terrorists who had attacked the country. In the years since, however, he has broadened that request and altered its tone. No longer is Bush asking the world to join a common struggle; instead, he is demanding that it follow along as the United States wages its own battle against threats the president has defined. September 11 proved, Bush has said, that the institutions, alliances, and rules of the past are no longer adequate to protect the American people. Terrorists who cannot be deterred are on the loose. If they gain access to WMD, unspeakable horrors will ensue. And so the United States, Bush has warned, will act when and where it perceives an actual, possible, or potential connection between terrorists and dangerous technology. Those who join it will be rewarded. Those who do not will be scorned, and worse.

I credit Bush for his ambition and for taking political risks he did not have to take. I harbor no doubts about his sincerity. I agree with him that the United States cannot be complacent. I share his assessment of the need not simply to oppose but also to defeat the declared enemies of the country. For the good of the United States, I hope his policies succeed. But I am left with the feeling that he has needlessly placed obstacles in his own path.

After all, the attacks of September 11 were dramatic and shocking, but hardly the first time this country has realized the extreme danger it will face if it allows WMD to fall into the wrong hands. President Bill Clinton warned regularly of that very thing. One of his earliest accomplishments was to persuade Ukraine, Kazakhstan, and Belarus to give up their nuclear weapons. He promoted the Nunn-Lugar Cooperative Threat Reduction Program tirelessly, spending American money to secure nuclear materials and expertise throughout the former Soviet Union. Clinton made himself an expert on the threat of a biological weapons attack on U.S. soil. He reorganized the National Security Council to broaden and intensify the fight against terrorism months before the August 1998 bombings of the U.S. embassies in Kenya and Tanzania brought global notoriety to bin Laden. Year after year, Clinton traveled to the UN in New York to emphasize two themes: the importance of halting WMD proliferation and the need for nations to unite in eliminating terrorist sanctuaries and funding. But President Clinton differed from his successor in that he believed the United States' ability to beat the country's enemies would be strengthened if NATO were strong and united, UN agencies such as the International Atomic Energy Agency were enhanced, and America's friends around the world were consulted and respected. Clinton saw fighting terror as a team enterprise, not a solo act.

September 11 showed that what the United States had been doing to identify and defeat al Qaeda was not enough. It did not, however, discredit the premise that to defeat al Qaeda, Americans need the active help and cooperation of other countries.

The Bush administration has chosen to take the problem of al Qaeda and meld it with the challenge of halting WMD proliferation—two issues that overlap but are by no means identical in the military, political, and technical issues they raise.

Defeating al Qaeda would not end the problem of proliferation; al Qaeda is deadly even without nuclear, chemical, and biological arms. Meanwhile, the nuclear programs of North Korea and Iran are driven by nationalism, not terrorism, and must be dealt with primarily on that basis. September 11, the administration's eureka moment, caused it to lump together terrorists and rogue regimes and to come up with a prescription for fighting them—namely, preemption—that frightens and divides the world at precisely the moment U.S. security depends on bringing people together.

I believe a different approach, focused more sharply and insistently on al Qaeda, with the Middle East, Iraq, Iran, and North Korea treated vigorously but separately, might have yielded a better result. Such an approach would, I believe, have enabled Bush to formulate a much clearer choice on the core issue of terror for allies in Europe and for the most critical audience of all: the sometimes silent majority of Muslims in the Middle East and around the world. The seriousness of that choice would have been backed under this scenario by Washington's own seriousness in Afghanistan, which would have remained the focus of U.S. nation-building efforts. Rather than flaunting American power, the U.S. government would have stressed the collective power of a world united in asserting that terrorism is wrong, just as genocide, apartheid, and slavery are wrong. U.S. efforts would have been directed not simply at the apprehension of al Qaeda suspects, but also at stopping the teaching of hate, the glorification of murder, and the endless manufacture of lies about the West that continues to this day in much of the Middle East and South Asia. Reinforced by a united Europe, American officials would have pressed over time for the gradual opening of Arab political and economic systems and for support for the democratic changes that surveys suggest most Arabs want. Washington would also have shown its respect for the value of every human life by staying engaged on a daily basis in the uphill struggle to halt killing on both sides in the strife-torn Middle East.

By complicating its own choice, the administration has instead complicated the choices faced by others, divided Europe, and played into the hands of extremists who would like nothing better than to make the clash of civilizations the defining struggle of our age.

It is late, but not too late, for the Bush administration to adjust its course. It has already shed some of its more optimistic illusions about Iraq, pledged presidential involvement in the Middle East, mended some fences with Europe, and reduced the level of self-congratulation in its official pronouncements.

It would be helpful now if the doctrine of preemption were to disappear quietly from the U.S. national security lexicon and be returned to reserve status. It is imperative, as well, that the missions in Afghanistan and Iraq actually be completed before victory is once again declared. To that end, perhaps administration officials will recognize that although none of the existing international institutions can do everything, each can do something. Perhaps the United States' current leaders will even put aside their reflexive disdain for all things Clintonian and consider the model of Kosovo. There, a NATO-led peacekeeping force, with Russian participation and assisted by a new civilian police force, is providing security for administrators from the United Nations, the European Union, and the Organization for Security and Cooperation in Europe, who are working with local parties to prepare a democratic transition. Not only is this setup operating fairly well, it has also given everyone involved a sense of mission and a stake in success. It takes patience to work with allies and to bring out the best in international organizations. But doing so also delivers great benefits: costs are shared, burdens distributed, legitimacy enhanced, diverse talents engaged. And everyone joins in wanting success.

Finally, the administration should do more of what President Bush did during his recent, welcome trip to Africa—play to the United States' true strengths. The idea that Americans—residents of the most powerful land in history—are now truly living in fear of bin Laden has failed to impress the majority of people around the globe, whose concerns about terrorism are dwarfed by the challenge they face in simply staying alive despite the ever-present perils of poverty, hunger, and disease. The United States' cause would therefore be heard more clearly and listened to more closely if the administration substituted bridges for bluster and spoke more often of choices relevant to the day-to-day lives of more of the world's people. That means spelling out consistently not only what Americans are against, but also what they are for, and making clear that this includes helping people everywhere live richer, freer, and longer lives.

MADELEINE K. ALBRIGHT was U.S. Secretary of State from 1997 to 2001. She is the author of the forthcoming *Madam Secretary: A Memoir*.

A Strategy of Partnerships

Colin L. Powell   JANUARY/FEBRUARY 2004

U.S. Secretary of State Colin Powell adjusts his earphone at a news conference after a meeting with European Union foreign ministers in Brussels, November 18, 2003.

BROAD AND DEEP

When most people think about U.S. foreign policy these days, they think first and sometimes only about aspects of the war on terrorism: the reconstruction of Iraq and Afghanistan, the troubles of the Middle East, and the terror cells lurking in Southeast Asia, Europe, and even the United States. This preoccupation is natural. International terrorism literally hit home on September 11, 2001, and, for understandable reasons, an outraged American public wants those responsible brought to justice. The American people also want to understand why the attacks happened—and demand a foreign policy that makes sure such events will never happen again.

It is also natural that the war on terrorism has become the United States' number one foreign policy priority. It will remain so for as long as necessary, because terrorism—potentially linked to the proliferation of weapons of mass destruction (WMD)—now represents the greatest threat to American lives. Defeating terrorism is a priority that drives not only military action to subdue individual terrorists and deter their state supporters but also multilateral cooperation in law enforcement and intelligence sharing. It encompasses efforts both to stigmatize terrorism as a political instrument and to reduce the underlying sources of terrorist motivation and recruitment.

But the breadth of U.S. strategy transcends the war on terrorism. Indeed, a strategy limited to dealing with immediate threats would in the end fail to defeat them—just as bailing water out of a boat would not fix a leak. The sharp focus on the front lines of the war against terrorism, however, has made it harder than usual for people to grasp what American strategy is really all about. We all know the old aphorism that you can lead a horse to water but you can't make it drink. These days, it seems that an administration can develop a sound foreign policy strategy, but it can't get people to acknowledge or understand it.

PRESIDENT BUSH'S VISION

It is an unfailingly effective applause line for critics of any U.S. administration to charge that the president has no vision for the world, that he has no strategy. Every trouble is attributed to this failing, as though the world would otherwise be perfectly accommodating to U.S. purposes. Unfortunately, this criticism has come close to being true in some administrations. But it is not true in the present one. President George W. Bush does have a vision of a better world. And he also has a strategy for translating that vision into reality. I know—I was present at its creation.

The president's strategy was first laid out publicly in September 2002, in the National Security Strategy of the United States (NSS). A succinct document of fewer than 40 pages, the NSS defines U.S. policy priorities in eight substantive sections. Together, these parts add up to an integrated strategy that is broad and deep, far ranging and forward looking, attuned as much to opportunities for the United States as to the dangers it faces.

Of course, a public strategy document cannot be entirely frank about all the choices that U.S. leaders make; we do ourselves and our allies no favors by telling our adversaries everything that we think and plan. Nonetheless, this administration's public pronouncements have been remarkably candid. They reflect the personality of the president himself, a man who, with great consistency, says what he means and means what he says.

It is somewhat odd, therefore, to discover that our foreign policy strategy is so often misunderstood by both domestic and foreign observers. U.S. strategy is widely accused of being unilateralist by design. It isn't. It is often accused of being imbalanced in favor of military methods. It isn't. It is frequently described as being obsessed with terrorism and hence biased toward preemptive war on a global scale. It most certainly is not.

These distortions are partly explained by context. The NSS made the concept of preemption explicit in the heady aftermath of September 11, and it did so for obvious reasons. One reason was to reassure the American people that the government possessed common sense. As President Bush has said—and as any sensible person understands—if you recognize a clear and present threat that is undeterrable by the means you have at hand, then you must deal with it. You do not wait for it to strike; you do not allow future attacks to happen before you take action.

A second reason for including the notion of preemption in the NSS was to convey to our adversaries that they were in big trouble. Instilling a certain amount of anxiety in terrorist groups increases the likelihood they will cease activity or make mistakes and be caught. Moreover, some states have been complicit in terrorism not for ideological reasons but for opportunistic ones. It was worth putting the leaders of such countries on notice that the potential costs of their opportunism had just gone way up.

Sensible as these reasons are, some observers have exaggerated both the scope of preemption in foreign policy and the centrality

Colin L. Powell

of preemption in U.S. strategy as a whole. As to preemption's scope, it applies only to the undeterrable threats that come from nonstate actors such as terrorist groups. It was never meant to displace deterrence, only to supplement it. As to its being central, it isn't. The discussion of preemption in the NSS takes up just two sentences in one of the document's eight sections.

Some at home have distorted the NSS for partisan reasons, attempting to make the Bush administration look bad by turning fear of preemption into an early twenty-first-century equivalent of the Cold War era's "rocket rattle." Some abroad, meanwhile, have distorted U.S. intentions through an apparent exercise in mirror imaging. Using their own mottled political histories as a reference point, they have asked what they would do with the power that the United States possesses and have mistakenly projected their own Hobbesian intentions onto our rather more Lockean sensibilities.

But however it has happened, the distortion of U.S. foreign policy strategy requires repair. This distortion does a disservice to honest observers trying to understand U.S. policy, and it contributes to irrational partisanship.

THE PRIMACY OF PARTNERSHIPS

The United States' National Security Strategy does commit us to preemption under certain limited circumstances. We stand by that judgment, the novelty of which lies less in its substance than in its explicitness. But our strategy is not defined by preemption. Above all, the president's strategy is one of partnerships that strongly affirms the vital role of NATO and other U.S. alliances—including the UN.

Don't believe it? Perhaps this is because the commentariat widely claimed that the president's recent decision to seek a new UN Security Council resolution on the postwar reconstruction of Iraq was a sharp break with policy. To think this, one would have to ignore the fact that President Bush went before the UN on September 12, 2002, to make his case for the UN's enforcing its own resolutions (16 of them in total); that Security Council Resolution

192 FOREIGN AFFAIRS

1441—which warned the Iraqi regime to comply with its own obligations under previous UN resolutions—passed unanimously in November 2002; that we tried for a further resolution to unite the international community in the months before Operation Iraqi Freedom began; that we went to the UN in May 2003 after Operation Iraqi Freedom to secure Resolution 1483, lifting sanctions against Iraq that had become obsolete; and that we sought and secured Resolution 1500 in August, recognizing the Iraqi Governing Council.

Had we not done all of these things, month after month, the president's decision to go to the UN Security Council in September 2003—and to persevere in his efforts until Resolution 1511 was approved by a 15–0 vote on October 16—would have been a significant departure from policy. But the administration did do all of these things. Indeed, it would have been a departure from policy not to go to the UN when, in our judgment, the next phase of Iraqi reconstruction was at hand. If there has been any departure here, it is the commentariat's departure from the basic rules of logic.

Partnership is the watchword of U.S. strategy in this administration. Partnership is not about deferring to others; it is about working with them. Beyond upholding the partnerships we have inherited, the president seeks new ones to deal with new challenges. Some are global in scope, such as the Global Fund for HIV/AIDS. Others are regional, such as the Middle East Partnership Initiative, which provides assistance for educational, economic, and political reform throughout the Arab world.

Beyond partnership comes principle. The president's strategy is rooted, above all, in the promotion of freedom and dignity worldwide. "America must stand firmly," the president wrote, "for the non-negotiable demands of human dignity: the rule of law; limits on the absolute power of the state; free speech; freedom of worship; equal justice; respect for women; religious and ethnic tolerance; and respect for private property." We stand by these values now and always. They are the values served by the partnerships that we build and nurture.

Free trade and new American initiatives for economic development also figure prominently in the president's strategy. The Free Trade Area of the Americas, the expanded Africa Growth and Opportunity Act, and especially the Millennium Challenge Account are our policy vanguards in this area. Our efforts to control the proliferation of WMD also form part of the president's strategy. These efforts led to the Proliferation Security Initiative in May 2003, an 11-nation effort to seize materials related to WMD in transit to countries of concern. In September 2003, signatories were able to agree on basic implementation guidelines, and in the president's address to the UN General Assembly on September 24, he called other nations to join. I hope they will heed his invitation.

President Bush's strategy also demands that we play a role in helping to solve regional conflicts. Not only do such conflicts cause much suffering, but they can also spread to envelop societies now at peace and can stoke the fires of terrorism. Nowhere is the U.S. role in helping to resolve regional conflicts more important than in bringing Israelis and Palestinians to a stable peace settlement. We are obviously not there yet, but this administration's policies have brought peace closer.

The Bush administration was widely criticized during its first two years in office for not being more active in solving the Arab-Israeli conflict. To many, "more active" meant spending presidential and secretarial capital on state visits and photo opportunities, as if nearly a decade of such activity had not already been tried without managing to resolve the conflict. But diplomacy can take other, more appropriate forms. In reality, we have worked hard on advancing peace, if often quietly, making the proper analysis of the situation and determining our tactics accordingly.

As a result, we created the Quartet—another partnership—made up of the United States, the European Union, Russia, and the UN. We developed the "road map" out of this partnership, and the president went to Aqaba, Jordan, in June 2003 to commit the parties to it.

Most important, we recognized that there needed to be fundamental reform inside the Palestinian Authority if the forces for peace among Palestinians were to prevail. After it became clear that the United States would not obstruct Israel's efforts to defend itself from Palestinian terrorism, pressures for genuine reform grew within the Palestinian community. This convergence produced the hopeful premiership of Mahmoud Abbas.

Unfortunately, Abbas' efforts were aborted by Chairman Yasir Arafat, and Abbas' successor, Ahmed Qurei, has been obstructed as well. Chairman Arafat has not been a genuine interlocutor for peace; he has been an obstacle to it. Although our hopes for progress have been temporarily disappointed, it is now clear to all where the real problem lies. One way or another, we are bound eventually to get past this problem. Moreover, there is now a solid and growing constituency in Israel that supports prominent Palestinian leaders who genuinely seek an honorable and stable peace. Bleak as things often seem in this conflict, this does represent progress.

Conflicts in other regions have also demanded our attention—and our compassion. The United States has not turned away from the suffering of the Liberian people, and we have been actively trying to end strife in Sudan and the Democratic Republic of the Congo. Nor have we forgotten the need for continued progress in the Balkans, in Northern Ireland, and in East Timor. We are making progress in most if not all of these areas, and we are often doing so by supporting other governments that are taking the lead. In other words, we are working as a partner.

AN AGE OF COOPERATION

Not least among the policy priorities laid out in the NSS is our determination to develop cooperative relations among the world's major powers. It is here, above all, that the key to a successful conclusion to the war against terrorism lies.

To say that the world has changed is a truism: the world, after all, is always changing. It is not so trivial, however, to specify just how it has changed. As I see it, the critical tipping point of recent years was the evening of November 9, 1989. That date is when the Berlin Wall was first breached, never to be repaired, marking the end of the Cold War and, before long, of the Soviet Union itself. These events, in turn, ended the epoch of intense struggle between liberty and totalitarianism that had shaped most of the twentieth century.

The president grasps the importance of these momentous events. As he wrote in the NSS, "today, the international community has the best chance since the rise of the nation-state in the seventeenth century to build a world where great powers compete in peace instead of continually prepare for war. Today, the world's great powers find ourselves on the same side."

This development is not just good news; it is revolutionary news. For too many years—too many centuries—the imperial habits of great powers squandered untold resources and talent by jousting for land, glory, and gold. The futility of such habits has become evident in the twenty-first century. The possession of vast territory, raw physical resources, and brute power guarantees neither prosperity nor peace. Investment in human capital, social trust, trade, and cooperation within and among nations does.

The sources of national strength and security for one nation thus need no longer threaten the security of others. An insight of the Enlightenment and a deep belief of the American founders— that politics need not always be a zero-sum competition—has at last been adopted by enough people worldwide to promise a qualitative difference in the character of international relations. If, instead of wasting lives and treasure by opposing each other as in the past, today's powers can pull in the same direction to solve problems common to all, we will begin to redeem history from much human folly.

One of these common problems is, of course, terrorism, and American strategy endeavors to solve it by integrating it into the management of our key international relationships. We do not see the war against terrorism and the nurturing of constructive relationships among the major powers as mutually exclusive tasks. We conduct the war on terrorism with an eye toward great-power cooperation, and we seek enhanced great-power cooperation with an eye toward success in the war on terrorism.

The logic of this dual approach rests on the fact that terrorism threatens the world order itself—and thus creates a common interest among all powers that value peace, prosperity, and the rule of law. The civilized world has spent more than a thousand years trying to limit the destructiveness of war. Drawing a distinction between civilians and combatants has been an essential part of this process. But terrorism aims to erase that distinction. We cannot allow this to happen, not because we want to "make the world safe" again for major conventional war, but because we must reassure people everywhere that the world has not just traded one kind of danger for another with the end of the Cold War. The victory of freedom will turn hollow if new fears replace old ones.

The common interest of all major powers in defeating terrorism is one source of a rare and remarkable opportunity: the United States' chance to enjoy excellent relations with all the world's major powers simultaneously. Of course, we have a head start in this, because we are blessed with many enduring friendships. None is more important than those enshrined in NATO.

Some observers predicted that NATO would wither away after the Cold War, others that the United States and the European Union would even end up on a collision course. Neither prediction has, or will, come true. Not only has NATO survived, but both its membership and its mission have expanded. As for our relations with the EU, never has our common agenda been so large and mutually significant—from advancing free trade to joint efforts in counterproliferation.

It is true that we have had differences with some of our oldest and most valued NATO allies. But these are differences among friends. The transatlantic partnership is based so firmly on common interests and values that neither feuding personalities nor occasional divergent perceptions can derail it. We have new friends and old friends alike in Europe. They are all, in the end, best friends, which is why the president continues to talk about partnerships, not polarities, when he speaks about Europe. Some authorities say that we must move to a multipolar world. We do not agree—not because we do not value competition and diversity, but because there need be no poles among a family of nations that shares basic values. We believe that it is wiser to work at overcoming differences than to polarize them further.

EMBRACING MAJOR POWERS

We work hard to have the best relations we can with nations large and small, old and new. But for practical purposes we concentrate on relations with major powers, especially those with whom we have had difficult relationships in the past, notably Russia, India, and China.

Our relationship with Russia has been dramatically transformed since that November evening in 1989. Americans and Russians no longer point growing arsenals of missiles at each other. Thanks to the leadership of President Bush and President Vladimir Putin, we are now radically reducing our strategic weapons arsenals. Moscow is also a committed partner in fighting terrorism and in combating the global spread of WMD.

U.S.-Russia commercial relations have also expanded and will expand further to mutual benefit—not least, we trust, in the energy sector. The new relationship that is developing between Russia and NATO has real substance as well. From sharing intelligence on terrorism to working together to deal with humanitarian crises and peacekeeping, the NATO-Russia Council is operational. That relationship can expand as far as our creativity and mutual effort will let it. We are closer than ever to a Europe whole, free, and at peace. Such a Europe definitely includes Russia, as well as the other new and reborn republics that emerged from the Soviet Union.

Perhaps most important, U.S. and Russian political and economic philosophies are converging. Today, Russia is more democratic than not. It is also more of a market economy than not. We should be patient as Russia develops its democratic institutions and as the remnants of Soviet-era corruption are rooted out and the rule of law firmly established.

We do not agree on everything, of course. We had hoped for more Russian support for our Iraq policy, and we still hope Russia will change its attitude toward the Iranian nuclear program. We also differ over aspects of Russian policy in Chechnya. But the relationship as a whole is no longer locked in knee-jerk antagonism. We now have the necessary level of trust to resolve even the most difficult issues between us.

Whereas Russia is still developing its democracy, India's democracy dates from its independence in 1947. With recent economic reforms setting institutional roots, India is developing into a mature market economy. As Indians themselves are the first to admit, however, their country still faces many challenges. Illiteracy, poverty, environmental degradation, and inadequate infrastructure all hamper progress. We want to help India overcome these challenges, and we want to help ourselves through a closer association with one of the world's venerable cultures. We have therefore worked to deepen our relationship with India. The two largest democracies on earth are no longer estranged. At the same time, we have also been able to advance our relations with Pakistan—a country with domestic challenges of its own.

India and Pakistan still dispute who should control Kashmir. During 2002, a major war between them—perhaps involving nuclear weapons—seemed distinctly possible. So, working with partners in Europe and Asia, we mobilized to help end the crisis. We have since been trying to turn our parallel improvement of relations with India and Pakistan into a triangle of conflict resolution. We do not impose ourselves as a mediator. But we do try to use the trust we have established with both sides to urge them toward conciliation by peaceful means.

What the United States has done in South Asia is an example of "turning adversity into opportunity," to quote President Bush. In a different way, we have done the same with China.

Sino-American relations got off to a bad start in this administration when a certain American airplane made an unscheduled visit to Hainan Island in April 2001. Today, however, U.S. relations with China are the best they have been since President Richard Nixon first visited Beijing more than 30 years ago. This is not just because the September 11 attacks led us to shuffle priorities, nor only because we championed Chinese accession to the World Trade Organization; nor is it the result of the accession of a new generation of Chinese leaders. It is certainly not because we have ignored Chinese human rights abuses, China's still unacceptable weapons proliferation activities, or the reluctance of China's leadership to match political to economic reform. We have never downplayed these difficulties.

The Sino-American relationship has nonetheless improved for a reason that transcends all these particulars: neither we nor the Chinese believe that there is anything inevitable about our relationship any longer—either inevitably bad or inevitably good. Instead, we now believe that it is up to us, together, to take responsibility for our common future. The NSS put it directly: "We welcome the emergence of a strong, peaceful, and prosperous China." We also seek a constructive relationship. Indeed, we welcome a global role for China, so long as China assumes responsibilities commensurate with that role. China's leaders know all this. Neither false fear about the future nor the overhang of Cold War enmity prevents us from cooperating where our interests coincide.

A case in point is North Korea. American and Chinese interests on the Korean Peninsula may not overlap completely, but they do so considerably. Neither side wishes to see nuclear weapons developed and deployed there. Neither side enjoys the spectacle of the dilapidated North Korean economy. Neither side wants the refugee crisis on China's border to worsen nor relishes a North Korean regime that smuggles drugs and weapons, counterfeits currencies, and engages in the periodic extortion of its neighbors through brinkmanship. And neither side, to be sure, has any interest in another Korean war.

Thus we have worked to transform our common interests with China into solid and productive cooperation over the challenges posed by Pyongyang. We are also cooperating with Japan, Russia, and South Korea on the issue. Our agenda is ambitious, but it is succeeding, as attested to by the six-party framework for talks over North Korea's nuclear program. We employed this framework in September 2003, and we will do so again soon. Beijing, as well as Washington, deserves credit for this achievement.

We still have a long way to go in dealing with North Korea's dangerous nuclear weapons program. As we have told the North Koreans, we have no intention of invading or attacking North Korea. During his trip to Asia in October 2003, President Bush suggested that he was even open to putting this intention in writing. We have stated our policy openly and honestly: we want peace, not war, and we want security, not fear, to envelop the Korean Peninsula and its neighbors. But we will not yield to threats and blackmail; if we did, we would only guarantee more threats and more attempts at blackmail. Nor will we take any options off the table.

It is now well past time for North Korea to alter its behavior, cease its threats, and end its nuclear weapons program in a verifiable manner. That is what all of North Korea's neighbors desire, which is why, in the end, a diplomatic solution to the problem can be achieved. When this happens, we will have demonstrated that American diplomacy is designed to satisfy not only our own national interests, but also those of international security as a whole. We will show that the equities of other powers can be best advanced along with American ones, not in opposition to them.

INTERESTS AND RESPONSIBILITIES

We must not take the present peace among the world's nations for granted. Today's peace will not just take care of itself. We have to work at it with patience, mindful that major war has broken out in the past despite a widespread conviction that it simply could not happen again.

Of course, we want to promote human dignity and democracy in the world, to help people raise themselves from poverty, and to transform the inadequate system of global public health. We are pursuing these goals right now. But only if the deep peace of our era can be "preserved, defended, and expanded"—to use the president's words—can we pursue these goals for as long as it will take to achieve them.

And make no mistake, these are the central goals of American policy in the twenty-first century. We fight terrorism because we must, but we seek a better world because we can—because it is our desire, and our destiny, to do so. This is why we commit ourselves to democracy, development, global public health, and human rights, as well as to the prerequisite of a solid structure for global peace. These are not high-sounding decorations for our interests. They are our interests, the purposes our power serves.

Because this is so, the United States' reputation for honesty and compassion will endure. Today, U.S. motives are impugned in some lands. But as we preserve, defend, and expand the peace that free peoples won in the twentieth century, we will see the United States vindicated in the eyes of the world in the twenty-first.

It would be churlish to claim that the Bush administration's foreign policy has been error-free from the start. We are human beings; we all make mistakes. But we have always pursued the enlightened self-interest of the American people, and in our purposes and our principles there are no mistakes.

Our enlightened self-interest puts us at odds with terrorists, tyrants, and others who wish us ill. From them we seek no advice or comity, and to them we will give no quarter. But our enlightened self-interest makes us partners with all those who cherish freedom, human dignity, and peace. We know the side on which the human spirit truly abides, and we take encouragement from this as our strategy unfolds. In the end, it is the only encouragement we really need.

COLIN L. POWELL is the U.S. Secretary of State.

Foreign Policy for a Democratic President

Samuel R. Berger   MAY/JUNE 2004

U.S. Marine Corp Assaultman Kirk Dalrymple watches as a statue of Iraq's President Saddam Hussein falls in central Baghdad in this April 9, 2003 file photo.

Editor's note: This is the second in a series of commissioned essays on foreign policy concerns for the next president. A Republican view is scheduled for the July/August issue.

FALL FROM GRACE

Speaking before the National Endowment for Democracy last fall, President George W. Bush delivered an important statement of American purpose. He rightly argued that the United States has an interest in political freedom in Muslim countries, because the absence of freedom denies people peaceful avenues for expressing dissent and thus drives them toward shadowy, violent alternatives. He fairly criticized past administrations for having been too tolerant of authoritarian Arab regimes. And he committed the United

States to the difficult but vital task of supporting more open and democratic societies in the Middle East.

But with few exceptions, the democratic activists, politicians, journalists, and intellectuals in the Muslim world—our natural partners in this effort—met President Bush's speech with skepticism, even disdain. Across the Middle East, his words did little to improve popular perceptions of the United States and its intentions.

The problem is not that Arabs reject the president's message. According to recent surveys of the region by the Pew Research Center for the People and the Press, significant majorities of people from Morocco to Jordan to Pakistan are democrats: they say they want to live in societies where leaders are freely elected, where free speech is protected, and where the rule of law is respected. Yet paradoxically, equally large majorities in the very same countries now insist that they do not "like American ideas about democracy."

Similar contradictions abound in other parts of the world. Washington is committed to defending South Korea if war breaks out on the Korean Peninsula, yet growing numbers of young South Koreans see the United States as a greater threat to security than North Korea. We are waging a war on terrorism that is as vital to Europe's security as to our own, yet increasing numbers of Europeans associate it with self-interested American power and therefore press their leaders to reject it.

Such negative feelings result in part from a natural resentment of U.S. military, economic, and cultural might, about which we can do little and for which we need not apologize. But they have been accentuated by the manner in which the Bush administration has pursued its goals. The administration's high-handed style and its gratuitous unilateralism have embittered even those most likely to embrace American values and invited opposition even from those with most to gain from American successes. All around the world, fewer and fewer people accept that any connection exists between their aspirations and the principles Washington preaches.

As a result, although the United States has never enjoyed greater power than it does today, it has rarely possessed so little influence.

We can compel, but far too often we cannot persuade. Our most important global initiatives, from advancing reform in the Middle East to defeating terrorism, will likely fail, unless there is a change in approach—or a change in leadership.

MISPLACED MEANS

The foreign policy debate in this year's presidential election is as much about means as it is about ends. Most Democrats agree with President Bush that the fight against terrorism and the spread of weapons of mass destruction (WMD) must be top global priorities, that the war in Afghanistan was necessary and just, and that Saddam Hussein's Iraq posed a threat that needed to be dealt with in one form or another. Over time, moreover, the Bush administration has, at least rhetorically, embraced the Democrats' argument that to win the war on terrorism the United States must do more than destroy something bad; it must also construct something good, supporting other peoples' aspirations to live in freedom and peace and to conquer poverty and disease.

But the manner in which the Bush administration has advanced these goals has been driven by a radical set of convictions about how the United States should act on the world stage. Key strategists inside the administration appear to believe that in a chaotic world, U.S. power—particularly military power—is the only real force for advancing U.S. interests, that as long as the United States is feared it does not matter much if we are admired. These same people believe it is best to recruit temporary "coalitions of the willing" to back our foreign actions, because permanent alliances require too many compromises. They believe the United States is perforce a benign power with good intentions and therefore does not need to seek legitimacy from the approval of others. And they believe that international institutions and international law are nothing more than a trap set by weaker nations to constrain us.

These are not new ideas. During the Truman and Eisenhower administrations, a hard-line faction of congressional Republicans, led by Senate Majority Leader Robert Taft, fought virtually every measure to build the postwar international order. They opposed NATO and the permanent deployment of U.S. troops in Europe, believing we should rely on the unilateral exercise of military power to defeat Soviet designs. They fought the creation of the World Bank and the International Monetary Fund and turned against the UN. And they disdained "one worlders" such as Eleanor Roosevelt for their support of international law. Taft Republicans were briefly dominant in the U.S. Congress (until the combined efforts of Democrats and internationalist Republicans such as Dwight Eisenhower relegated them to the sidelines). But their radical world-view never drove policy in the executive branch—until today.

The real "clash of civilizations" is taking place within Washington. Considering the open differences between Secretary of State Colin Powell and Secretary of Defense Donald Rumsfeld, it is even playing out within the Bush administration itself. It is not really a clash over discrete policy issues—the merits of the war in Iraq, the costs of the Kyoto Protocol, or the level of spending on foreign aid, for example—but between diametrically opposed conceptions of America's role in the world. It is a battle fought between liberal internationalists in both parties who believe that our strength is usually greatest when we work in concert with allies in defense of shared values and interests, versus those who seem to believe that the United States should go it alone—or not go it at all.

Bush administration hard-liners have not been bashful about defining and defending their vision. In an election year, Democrats must also be clear about what they believe and about what they would do to advance U.S. security, prosperity, and democratic ideals, to restore our influence, standing, and ability to lead. Democrats must outline a foreign policy that not only sets the right goals, but also rebuilds America's capacity to achieve them.

WITH US, NOT AGAINST US

Every postwar administration, Republican and Democratic, has believed that there are things in this world worth fighting:

threatening regimes or individuals who deserve to be called evil and can be stopped only by force. And today, although we must try to change the political and economic conditions in which terrorist movements are spawned, we must recognize that simply addressing root causes will not stop committed terrorists from attacking the United States and our allies; such people must be apprehended or killed.

Likewise, we must reject the convenient fallacies that free markets inevitably give rise to free societies or that globalization by itself will lead to peace. Nations and leaders are not captive to abstract historical forces but act in accordance with their interests and ambitions. For the foreseeable future, the United States and its allies must be prepared to employ raw military and economic power to check the ambitions of those who threaten our interests.

A posture of strength and resolve and a willingness to define clear terms and to impose consequences are clearly the right approach for dealing with our adversaries. But where the Bush administration has gone badly wrong is in applying its "with us or against us" philosophy to friends as well as foes. Put simply, our natural allies are much more likely to be persuaded by the power of American arguments than by the argument of American power. Democratically elected leaders—whether in Germany, the United Kingdom, Mexico, or South Korea—must sustain popular support for joint endeavors with the United States. When we work to convince them that the United States is using its strength for the common good, we enable them to stand with us. But when we compel them to serve our ends, we make it politically necessary, even advantageous, for them to resist us. It would have been hard to imagine a decade ago that leaders of Germany and South Korea—two nations that owe their existence to the sacrifice of American blood—would win elections by appealing to anti-Americanism.

Going into Iraq, the Bush administration believed that most of our allies would get on board if we made it clear that the train would leave without them. It also believed that we did not need the legitimacy UN authorization and involvement would have

207

bestowed. Those theories did not stand up to reality. Washington's failure to gain the support of capable allies (France, Germany, and Turkey, rather than, say, the Marshall Islands) vastly increased the human, financial, and strategic costs of the war and has threatened the success of the occupation.

The administration continued to squander U.S. influence with its allies even after the war. Much has been said about the Pentagon's rash decision to deny Iraqi reconstruction contracts to companies from NATO allies such as Canada, France, and Germany, just as the United States was asking them to forgive Iraqi debt. But few people noticed the administration's even more bizarre decision to suspend millions in military aid to countries that supported the war because they refused to grant Americans full immunity from prosecution by the International Criminal Court (ICC). In the end, we treated "new Europe" as shabbily as we treated "old Europe."

As for the UN, a few months after the Iraq invasion the administration found that the leader of Iraq's dominant Shia community would not even talk to American officials, much less accept our plan for elections in Iraq. So Washington begged the UN to step in on our behalf: a belated recognition that our actions are seen as more legitimate when the international community embraces them.

A Democratic administration will need to reaffirm the United States' willingness to use military power—alone if necessary—in defense of its vital interests. But it will have no more urgent task than to restore America's global moral and political authority, so that when we decide to act we can persuade others to join us. Achieving this reversal will require forging a new strategic bargain with our closest allies, particularly in Europe. To this end, Washington should begin with a simple statement of policy: that the United States will act in concert with its allies in meeting global threats as a first, not last, resort. When we ask our allies to join us in military action, or in nation-building efforts in places such as Iraq and Afghanistan, we should be ready to share not just the risks but also the decision-making. That is what we did when NATO went to war in Bosnia and Kosovo, and what the administration irresponsibly failed to do when NATO invoked its collective defense clause to offer aid to the United States in Afghanistan. The U.S. side of the bargain must also include a disciplined focus on our true global priorities, starting with the war on terrorism, undistracted by petty ideological disputes over issues such as Kyoto, the ICC, and the biological weapons convention.

The Democratic approach to resolving disputes with Europe over treaties should be pragmatic, focused on improving flawed agreements rather than ripping them up. International law is not self-enforcing. It does not, by itself, solve anything. But when our goals are embodied in binding agreements, we can gain international support in enforcing them when they are violated. By the same token, nothing undermines U.S. authority more than the perception that the United States considers itself too powerful to be bound by the norms we preach to others.

POWER TO PERSUADE

As part of a new bargain with our allies, the United States must re-engage in what the rest of the world rightly considers the cornerstone of a lasting transformation of the Middle East: ending the Israeli-Palestinian conflict. So long as that dispute continues, Arab rulers will use it as an excuse to avoid reform and to resist open cooperation with the United States in the war on terrorism.

A point may have been reached where unilateral steps by Israel to protect its security are inevitable. For more than three years now, the people of Israel have been subjected to a brutal, unprecedented assault. But the Israeli government's moves must be a way station, rather than an illusory end point, advancing changes in Palestinian leadership that could help foster a negotiated settlement. If Israeli withdrawals from Gaza and the West Bank are coordinated with the Palestinians, and if an Israeli fence is seen as a temporary measure shaped by security and demographic concerns (as opposed to a land grab), hope for a real solution will be preserved. If not, the vacuum left by the withdrawals could result in a failed terrorist haven dominated by Hamas radicals. In this night-mare scenario, the suicidal Palestinian strategy of terror would continue, pushing Israel not to the sea but to the right. A long-term war of attrition would leave Israelis even more divided and disillusioned, and a whole new generation of children in the region would grow up seeing the United States as the problem, not the solution.

U.S. policy toward the Israeli-Palestinian conflict has tradition-ally rested on two pillars. We are Israel's staunchest ally. And we are an honest broker between the two sides, which has made us not impartial, but, rather, partial to an agreement that both assures Is-rael's security and guarantees a dignified life for Palestinians. A Democratic administration must return with energy and urgency to these principles. It should stand solidly behind Israel in its fight against terrorism and help ordinary Palestinians to liberate them-selves from a leadership concerned with little more than its own survival. It should also lead the international community in offer-ing a realistic vision of how life would look for Palestinians if they were to accept and respect the security and existence of the Jewish state of Israel. And it should offer the outlines of a two-state solution—giving Palestinians something to gain and something to lose. The stakes are enormous and there is no way forward without active American engagement.

As we re-engage in the peace process and rebuild frayed ties with our allies, what should a Democratic president ask of our al-lies in return? First and foremost, we should ask for a real commit-ment of troops and money to Afghanistan and Iraq. Now that NATO has finally agreed to lead an expanded peacekeeping mis-sion in Afghanistan, there is a desperate need for European forces to augment the existing U.S. military presence in the country, to ensure that it does not return to a state of chaos that threatens our interests. Afghanistan, with Pakistan, remains a frontline battle-ground in the war on terrorism. But given the state of transatlantic relations, there is little support in Europe for sending troops on dangerous missions there. A new administration will have to overcome this challenge if it is to restore security to Afghanistan and relieve the burden on U.S. forces.

Iraq, too, will require a generational commitment by the international community. Regardless of whether the war was justified, everyone now has a profound stake in Iraq's success. The disintegration of that country along ethnic and religious fault lines would destabilize the Middle East and energize radical movements that threaten the world. A stable and democratic Iraq, on the other hand, would stimulate reform throughout the region. Attaining the latter outcome will require continuous involvement in Iraq's reconstruction and political development, as well as a proactive military posture that does not leave foreign troops hunkered down in bases and barracks, delegating security to an ill-prepared Iraqi security force. But that level of involvement will be unsustainable—and will be considered illegitimate by ordinary Iraqis—unless it is viewed as a truly international, rather than exclusively American, effort.

The irony is that the Bush administration's unilateralist approach has let our allies off the hook: it has given them an excuse to shirk these and other global responsibilities. A Democratic administration would not be so dismissive of our allies on the issues that matter to them. In turn, it would have authority to demand far more of them on the issues that matter to us—whether stabilizing Iraq and Afghanistan, democratizing the Middle East, or combating the spread and potential use of WMD.

PREVENTION, NOT JUST PREEMPTION
The Bush administration's argument for invading Iraq rested, in part, on the belief that the United States cannot wait until a WMD threat is imminent before taking action. Yet its overall approach to combating WMD proliferation defies the logic of this position.

A Democratic administration should use every tool at its disposal to prevent WMD threats from arising before force becomes the only option. The most obvious early measure Washington can take to keep deadly weapons materials from falling into the hands of terrorists or rogue regimes is to secure them at source. Yet the current administration has shown little interest in accelerating or expanding programs to do this. Indeed, President Bush tried to cut back the Nunn-Lugar Cooperative Threat Reduction Program for the former Soviet Union early in his term. At our current pace, it will take 13 years to complete security upgrades at every site containing plutonium and highly enriched uranium in Russia. With increased funding for Nunn-Lugar, this process could be accelerated to 4 years. Beyond Russia, dozens of research reactors contain the raw materials for making a radiological or nuclear weapon. We should lead a global effort to secure nuclear materials at all such sites.

The one country that we know has the capacity, and conceivably the inclination, actually to sell a working nuclear weapon to a terrorist group is North Korea. Yet the administration has reacted with inexplicable complacency as North Korea has crossed line after line on its way to becoming the world's first nuclear Wal-Mart. Pyongyang is now capable of producing, and potentially selling, up to 6 nuclear weapons at any time—possibly 20 a year by the end of this decade—something that even the most dire intelligence estimates did not predict in Iraq. We do not know how much plutonium North Korea has reprocessed into useable nuclear fuel over the past 18 months, since it expelled international monitors while we were busy negotiating the shape of the table.

A Democratic administration must clearly and promptly test whether Kim Jong Il intends North Korea to become a nuclear factory or whether he will negotiate his way into the international community. U.S. officials must put a serious proposition on the table—a nationwide, verifiable dismantlement of North Korea's nuclear programs in exchange for economic and political integration—and be prepared to sequence implementation in a reciprocal way once the ultimate objectives are accepted. We must be prepared to take yes for an answer. And if Pyongyang's answer is no, South Korea, Japan, and China will join us in coercive actions only if they are convinced that we made a serious, good-faith effort to avoid confrontation. The worst option is one in which cash-starved North Korea becomes a supplier of nuclear weapons to al Qaeda or Hamas or to radical Chechens, who then deliver them to Washington, London, or Moscow.

We need the same kind of "overt action" plan for Iran, offering—in full public view—normal relations in exchange for total renunciation of nuclear aspirations and terrorism by Tehran. Let the Iranian government say no to such an offer and be the obstacle to its people's aspirations, a decision that would create its own dynamic inside Iran. We have other problems with Iran and North Korea, including their appalling human rights abuses. But those can best be addressed if we first bring them out of isolation.

A Democratic administration should seek to strengthen global rules against proliferation more generally. The existing Non-Proliferation Treaty (NPT) established an important norm. Since 1975, South Korea, Argentina, Brazil, Taiwan, South Africa, Kazakhstan, Belarus, Ukraine, and now Libya have reversed course and given up their nuclear weapons programs under its auspices. But the NPT remains flawed, because it permits countries to develop all the building blocks of a nuclear weapons program and then to withdraw from the treaty without penalty once they are ready to enrich uranium or produce plutonium for nuclear weapons.

We should press for a new bargain. Nuclear powers such as the United States should help non-nuclear countries develop nuclear energy and provide them with uranium. But they should maintain control of the fuel cycle, taking back spent nuclear material and storing it securely so it cannot be used to build weapons. (Clearly, there are risks associated with how and where fuel is stored, but there is no risk-free alternative.) Any country that seeks to escape this strict system of controls should be subject to automatic UN sanctions. To hope to convince non-nuclear powers to agree to this arrangement, the United States should lead by example. That means giving up the Bush administration's irresponsible plan to develop a new generation of low-yield nuclear weapons (which sends the message that nuclear weapons are a useful instrument of war) and joining the Comprehensive Test Ban Treaty.

NEW MISSIONS, NEW CAPABILITIES

Most Democrats agree with President Bush that terrorists, and even recalcitrant regimes on occasion, must be confronted with force. The question should be how, not whether, our military and intelligence assets are employed, and whether we are adapting them rapidly enough to the challenges the United States faces today.

Since the Cold War ended, we have witnessed two generations of military reform: from amassing huge armored units to an emphasis on deploying light forces anywhere in the world, and from analog-based technology to the digital information age. The war on terrorism will require a third military transformation. Although we still need the capacity to fight conventional wars, we now must seek out and destroy enemies that hide in the shadows, often among civilians, without tanks or fighter planes. At heart, this effort will be an intelligence challenge. A new administration should launch a major retooling of our intelligence agencies, including appointing a director of national intelligence with authority over our entire intelligence budget, rather than the 20 cents on the dollar that the current CIA director controls.

Of course, there will also be times when the war on terrorism tests our military, as in Afghanistan and Pakistan, in Yemen, and in the Philippines. What will the war on terrorism require in terms of new doctrines, tactics, equipment, and training? How will it change our military organization? How can we defeat this new enemy while upholding the values that protect our own troops in wartime and that define who we are? The Bush administration has not addressed these questions. A Democratic administration must answer them.

The Bush administration believes that our military should be reserved for war fighting; it came to office averse to peacekeeping and nation building and deeply suspicious of long-term U.S. military deployments overseas. This prejudice drove strategy in Afghanistan and Iraq—with disastrous consequences. After driving the Taliban from power in Afghanistan, the administration delegated the building of a nation to the same warlords who destroyed the Afghan nation in the early 1990s. As for Iraq, it sent the minimum number of troops needed to defeat the enemy, without simultaneously deploying forces to occupy and secure the ground those troops were liberating. The result was postwar chaos that emboldened terrorists and soured the coalition's relationship with Iraqis.

What Democrats must offer is a sense of realism: when the United States goes to war it had better be prepared to stay where it has fought, to fix what it has broken, and to work with allies for years, if necessary, to consolidate its victories. We must demonstrate staying power, not just firepower, whether in the Balkans or Afghanistan or Iraq.

Part of the problem has been reluctance in certain military quarters to adapt our armed forces to these kinds of missions. Some military leaders fear that if the army develops peacekeeping capacity, civilian leaders will be too tempted to use it. But the fact remains that presidents of both parties have sent our forces on at least seven major postconflict peacekeeping or "stability" operations in the last decade. Denial is not a strategy for preparedness. Like it or not, such operations will inevitably be a large part of the military's role for the foreseeable future. A Democratic administration will need to ensure that our army has the force structure, training, and appropriate weaponry to do what we ask of it, including fighting enemies, combating insurgencies, safeguarding public security, and protecting civilians. And it must ensure that we have civilian institutions—domestic and international—that are prepared to act so that our military is not asked to do more than is necessary.

If the Bush administration were more committed to collective action, it would have greater authority to press NATO allies to improve their military capabilities. We cannot accept a division of labor in which we fight and they talk. We will be confronted with the need to rebuild failed and postconflict societies, yet we should not be compelled to do so alone. We need international institutions with ready-to-move capability. Ensuring such capability is imperative for the UN if it is to maintain its relevance. A Democratic administration should lead an effort to turn the UN into the NATO of civilian peacekeeping, giving it the capacity to call upon member countries' dedicated capabilities—from police to civil servants—and deploy them rapidly to hot spots around the world.

MAKING THE WORLD'S FIGHT OUR OWN

The primary objective of U.S. foreign policy should be to make the United States more secure, which means applying our power to the fight against terrorism and the spread of deadly weapons. But if there is one lesson we should have learned in the last three years, it is that American power will be resisted—even by our friends—if it is applied solely for self-protection and not for purposes that are more broadly shared.

With precious few exceptions (including President Bush's Middle East democracy initiative and his realization that the United States must help combat AIDS), we have witnessed a narrowing of purpose and vision since September 11, 2001. Before that date, the administration had a national missile defense policy. It now has a terrorism policy and an Iraq policy. But the Bush administration still does not have a true foreign policy suited to the demands of a global power with global responsibilities. We must start leading again across a broader agenda, in more places, and with a wider definition of our national interest.

The next president must end our neglect of Latin America and restore the United States' reputation as a defender of democracy, which has been frayed by the Bush administration's approaches to Venezuela and Haiti. He must treat Africa as more than a backwater in the war on terrorism. President Bush's promise to send U.S. troops to Liberia, only to pull them back after ten days ashore, did enormous damage to our reputation on that continent.

In Asia, home to more than half of the world's people, a tectonic geopolitical and economic shift is taking place. But the United States remains strangely disengaged. Not long ago, the nations of the region feared China and saw their future tied to ours. Today, the reverse is happening. China has skillfully turned most of the countries of Southeast Asia, including Australia, into allies. Its economy is growing by leaps and bounds, it has stepped up to diplomatic challenges such as that posed by North Korea, and it is increasingly seen as a dominant power in the region. Russia, flush with oil, is emerging as a stable and growing power and asserting itself in Asia. India is emerging from generations of insularity and self-absorption, opening itself up to the world. A Democratic administration will have to ensure that the United States stays in the game in Asia. It must encourage emerging regional powers to channel their energies in the right directions and restore our leadership in responding to regional crises.

The new president will also need to reassert U.S. interest in what happens inside the borders of China and Russia. The stakes are enormous: without political reform, China will stagnate economically, unable to meet the demands of hundreds of millions dislocated by change. And without more widespread respect for the rule of law, or for its neighbors' sovereignty, Russia will neither attract investment nor energize its people. True realists understand the linkage between the way countries are governed and their external behavior. Yet the Bush administration has largely ignored questions of internal development in these countries. President Bush has not once articulated a comprehensive strategy for dealing with China or Russia, instead concerning himself narrowly with their actions on the global stage.

A Democratic president will face the challenge of restoring the substantive as well as the geographical reach of our foreign policy, showing the world that we understand a simple truth: all terrorism is evil, but not all evil is terrorism. For the vast majority of people in the world, the greatest danger is not al Qaeda. It is localized armed conflict over political power, resources, and ethnicity. It is poverty, disease, and environmental destruction. These scourges claim exponentially more lives each year than terrorism does. They should matter to us as much as we expect our concerns to matter to others.

To this end, the United States should be seen as a peacemaker again, actively engaged in the resolution of conflicts from the Middle East to Southeast Asia to Central and West Africa, helping to build the peacekeeping capabilities of other nations, and willing to contribute money and troops, alongside our allies, when our interests and values are at stake. Even when the chances of success are small, such efforts help reveal that American power can serve the common good.

A Democratic administration should also fund a greater U.S. commitment to combating infectious disease. For all the headlines and paper promises of action, fewer than 1 in 5 people in the world at risk of AIDS have access to preventive services. Fewer than 1 in 50 infected people receive the drugs they need; in Africa, the number is only 1 in 1,000. The Global Fund to Fight AIDS, Tuberculosis, and Malaria has asked rich countries to contribute just $10 billion a year to save millions of lives. The United States can and should give more than its fair share of this amount, so we can prod other countries to do the same.

A Democratic administration should launch a major global initiative to bring clean water to the hundreds of millions of people in poor countries who do not have it. It must do more to enable children, especially girls, to go to school. And it must seek to close the "digital divide"—the increasing gap between rich and poor in technology availability. A Democratic president must treat these issues as part of a personal crusade again, including them in every foreign summit and speech, and challenging leaders around the world and in the private sector to do more.

A Democratic administration should champion expanding trade as the best long-term hope for gaining prosperity in rich and poor countries alike. It should urge Europeans to end their farm subsidies, which impoverish farmers in the developing world (the average cow in the European Union gets more than $2 a day in state support, more than most people in Africa have to live on), while having the courage to cut U.S. farm subsidies as well. The next president must also recognize that an agenda that pursues growth without equity is destined to achieve neither goal. Gene Sperling, President Bill Clinton's former national economic adviser, has proposed a "new consensus on free trade," one that expands open markets while addressing the legitimate concerns of workers. His proposal prioritizes investing in education and retraining before jobs are lost, providing comprehensive services to dislocated workers, adjusting tax and health care policies that make job creation in the United States less attractive, and fighting abuses of labor rights overseas.

Finally, it is time for the United States to confront climate change. Unchecked global warming could devastate the global economy and global agriculture, lead to massive population movements, and literally wipe some nations off the face of the earth. This rising tide will sink all boats. A Democratic president will need to meet this threat with courage and alacrity, strengthening bipartisan efforts, such as the McCain-Lieberman Climate Stewardship Act (which was narrowly defeated in the Senate last year), to cut greenhouse gas emissions, re-engaging with our allies either to rescue or to revise the Kyoto Protocol, and launching initiatives to address life-and-death concerns such as expanding deserts and shrinking forests.

WHO WE ARE MATTERS

President Bush says that the front line of the war on terrorism is in Iraq and that it is better to fight our enemies in Baghdad than in Baltimore. That formulation is fundamentally flawed. The front line today is wherever we are, particularly in those places where people don't want us to be. Because of this reality, it is essential that we define who we are in a way that isolates our enemies, rather than ourselves. That notion was something well understood by American leaders during the Cold War. Of course, the United States was not universally loved, but we did at least build an enduring set of alliances, rooted in a genuine sense of shared interests and based on ties among peoples, not just governments. During those years, America was admired where it counted most: in the nations behind the Iron Curtain, the chief battleground of the Cold War. Poles, Hungarians, and ordinary Russians saw us as credible champions of their democratic aspirations. There was no anti-Americanism in Eastern Europe that communist governments could stoke to deflect U.S. pressure for change or that extremists could exploit to win support for their aims. Imagine if there had been. Would the Cold War have ended as it did? Would the Soviet empire have collapsed when it did? If it had, what would have replaced it?

These are precisely the kinds of questions we face now in the greater Middle East and more broadly around the world. We have the raw power to impose our will when we must, and far more often than not that power has been used for good, not ill. But whoever is president, we will need to rely most often on persuasion, not power, to achieve our goals. Who will be persuaded to stand with America if we do not stand for something larger than ourselves? Who will voluntarily work with us if we demand cooperation entirely on our terms? And if we do succeed in challenging the status quo in the Islamic world, as we did in Eastern Europe a generation ago, what will take its place, if U.S. leadership is rejected by those people who wish to bring about change?

The good news is that the world is eager for the United States to return to its tradition of leadership. Most countries would still be far more worried by the prospect of American isolationism than by American unilateralism. We can seize on these sentiments to forge new coalitions against terrorism and WMD and to build a freer, safer world.

But having the right aims is not enough. The United States needs leaders who ensure that our means do not undermine our ends. We need a forward-looking realism, without the ideological rigidity that has alienated our natural allies around the world. We need, in short, to reunite our power with moral authority. Only that combination will weaken our enemies and inspire our friends.

SAMUEL R. BERGER served as National Security Adviser to President Bill Clinton from 1997 to 2001 and is Chairman of Stonebridge International, LLC.

Campaign 2000: Promoting the National Interest

Condoleezza Rice   JANUARY/FEBRUARY 2000

U.S. President George W. Bush listens to National Security Advisor
Condoleezza Rice speak after he nominated her to replace Colin Powell as
Secretary of State, November 16, 2004.

LIFE AFTER THE COLD WAR

The United States has found it exceedingly difficult to define its
"national interest" in the absence of Soviet power. That we do not
know how to think about what follows the U.S.-Soviet confrontation is clear from the continued references to the "post-Cold War
period." Yet such periods of transition are important, because they
offer strategic opportunities. During these fluid times, one can affect the shape of the world to come.

The enormity of the moment is obvious. The Soviet Union was
more than just a traditional global competitor; it strove to lead a
universal socialist alternative to markets and democracy. The

Soviet Union quarantined itself and many often-unwitting captives and clients from the rigors of international capitalism. In the end, it sowed the seeds of its own destruction, becoming in isolation an economic and technological dinosaur.

But this is only part of the story. The Soviet Union's collapse coincided with another great revolution. Dramatic changes in information technology and the growth of "knowledge-based" industries altered the very basis of economic dynamism, accelerating already noticeable trends in economic interaction that often circumvented and ignored state boundaries. As competition for capital investment has intensified, states have faced difficult choices about their internal economic, political, and social structures. As the prototype of this "new economy," the United States has seen its economic influence grow—and with it, its diplomatic influence. America has emerged as both the principal benefactor of these simultaneous revolutions and their beneficiary.

The process of outlining a new foreign policy must begin by recognizing that the United States is in a remarkable position. Powerful secular trends are moving the world toward economic openness and—more unevenly—democracy and individual liberty. Some states have one foot on the train and the other off. Some states still hope to find a way to decouple democracy and economic progress. Some hold on to old hatreds as diversions from the modernizing task at hand. But the United States and its allies are on the right side of history.

In such an environment, American policies must help further these favorable trends by maintaining a disciplined and consistent foreign policy that separates the important from the trivial. The Clinton administration has assiduously avoided implementing such an agenda. Instead, every issue has been taken on its own terms—crisis by crisis, day by day. It takes courage to set priorities because doing so is an admission that American foreign policy cannot be all things to all people—or rather, to all interest groups. The Clinton administration's approach has its advantages: If priorities and intent are not clear, they cannot be criticized. But there is a high price to pay for this approach. In a democracy as pluralistic as ours, the absence of an articulated "national interest" either produces a fertile ground for those wishing to withdraw from the world or creates a vacuum to be filled by parochial groups and transitory pressures.

THE ALTERNATIVE

American foreign policy in a Republican administration should refocus the United States on the national interest and the pursuit of key priorities. These tasks are

- to ensure that America's military can deter war, project power, and fight in defense of its interests if deterrence fails;
- to promote economic growth and political openness by extending free trade and a stable international monetary system to all committed to these principles, including in the western hemisphere, which has too often been neglected as a vital area of U.S. national interest;
- to renew strong and intimate relationships with allies who share American values and can thus share the burden of promoting peace, prosperity, and freedom;
- to focus U.S. energies on comprehensive relationships with the big powers, particularly Russia and China, that can and will mold the character of the international political system; and
- to deal decisively with the threat of rogue regimes and hostile powers, which is increasingly taking the forms of the potential for terrorism and the development of weapons of mass destruction (WMD).

INTERESTS AND IDEALS

Power matters, both the exercise of power by the United States and the ability of others to exercise it. Yet many in the United States are (and have always been) uncomfortable with the notions of power politics, great powers, and power balances. In an extreme form, this discomfort leads to a reflexive appeal instead to notions of international law and norms, and the belief that the support of many states—or even better, of institutions like the United Nations—is essential to the legitimate exercise of power. The "national interest" is replaced with "humanitarian interests" or the interests of "the international community." The belief that the United States is exercising power legitimately only when it is doing so on behalf of someone or something else was deeply rooted in Wilsonian thought, and there are strong echoes of it in the Clinton administration. To be sure, there is nothing wrong with doing something that benefits all humanity, but that is, in a sense, a second-order effect. America's pursuit of the national interest will create conditions that promote freedom, markets, and peace. Its pursuit of national interests after World War II led to a more prosperous and democratic world. This can happen again.

So multilateral agreements and institutions should not be ends in themselves. U.S. interests are served by having strong alliances and can be promoted within the U.N. and other multilateral organizations, as well as through well-crafted international agreements. But the Clinton administration has often been so anxious to find multilateral solutions to problems that it has signed agreements that are not in America's interest. The Kyoto treaty is a case in point: whatever the facts on global warming, a treaty that does not include China and exempts "developing" countries from tough standards while penalizing American industry cannot possibly be in America's national interest.

Similarly, the arguments about U.S. ratification of the Comprehensive Test Ban Treaty are instructive. Since 1992, the United States has refrained unilaterally from testing nuclear weapons. It is an example to the rest of the world yet does not tie its own hands "in perpetuity" if testing becomes necessary again. But in pursuit of a "norm" against the acquisition of nuclear weapons, the United States signed a treaty that was not verifiable, did not deal with the threat of the development of nuclear weapons by rogue states, and threatened the reliability of the nuclear stockpile. Legitimate congressional concerns about the substance of the treaty were ignored during negotiations. When faced with the defeat of a bad treaty, the administration attacked the motives of its opponents—incredibly branding long-standing internationalists like Senators Richard Lugar (R-Ind.) and John Warner (R-Va.) as isolationists.

Certainly, Republican presidents have not been immune to the practice of pursuing symbolic agreements of questionable value. According to the Senate Foreign Relations Committee, some 52 conventions, agreements, and treaties still await ratification; some even date back to 1949. But the Clinton administration's attachment to largely symbolic agreements and its pursuit of, at best, illusory "norms" of international behavior have become an epidemic. That is not leadership. Neither is it isolationist to suggest that the United States has a special role in the world and should not adhere to every international convention and agreement that someone thinks to propose.

Even those comfortable with notions of the "national interest" are still queasy with a focus on power relationships and great-power politics. The reality is that a few big powers can radically affect international peace, stability, and prosperity. These states are capable of disruption on a grand scale, and their fits of anger or acts of beneficence affect hundreds of millions of people. By reason of size, geographic position, economic potential, and military strength, they are capable of influencing American welfare for good or ill. Moreover, that kind of power is usually accompanied by a sense of entitlement to play a decisive role in international politics. Great powers do not just mind their own business.

Some worry that this view of the world ignores the role of values, particularly human rights and the promotion of democracy. In fact, there are those who would draw a sharp line between power politics and a principled foreign policy based on values. This polarized view—you are either a realist or devoted to norms and values—may be just fine in academic debate, but it is a disaster for American foreign policy. American values are universal. People want to say what they think, worship as they wish, and elect those who govern them; the triumph of these values is most assuredly easier when the international balance of power favors those who believe in them. But sometimes that favorable balance of power takes time to achieve, both internationally and within a society. And in the meantime, it is simply not possible to ignore and isolate other powerful states that do not share those values.

The Cold War is a good example. Few would deny that the collapse of the Soviet Union profoundly transformed the picture of democracy and human rights in eastern and central Europe and the former Soviet territories. Nothing improved human rights as much as the collapse of Soviet power. Throughout the Cold War, the United States pursued a policy that promoted political liberty, using every instrument from the Voice of America to direct presidential intervention on behalf of dissidents. But it lost sight neither of the importance of the geopolitical relationship with Moscow nor of the absolute necessity of retaining robust American military power to deter an all-out military confrontation.

In the 1970s, the Soviet Union was at the height of its power—which it was more than willing to use. Given its weak economic and technological base, the victories of that period turned out to be Pyrrhic. President Reagan's challenge to Soviet power was both resolute and well timed. It included intense substantive engagements with Moscow across the entire range of issues captured in the "four-part agenda" (arms control, human rights, economic issues, and regional conflicts). The Bush administration then focused greater attention on rolling back Soviet power in central and eastern Europe. As the Soviet Union's might waned, it could no longer defend its interests and gave up peacefully (thankfully) to the West—a tremendous victory for Western power and also for human liberty.

SETTING PRIORITIES

The United States has many sources of power in the pursuit of its goals. The global economy demands economic liberalization, greater openness and transparency, and at the very least, access to information technology. International economic policies that leverage the advantages of the American economy and expand free trade are the decisive tools in shaping international politics. They permit us to reach out to states as varied as South Africa and India and to engage our neighbors in the western hemisphere in a shared interest in economic prosperity. The growth of entrepreneurial classes throughout the world is an asset in the promotion of human rights and individual liberty, and it should be understood and used as such. Yet peace is the first and most important condition for continued prosperity and freedom. America's military power must be secure because the United States is the only guarantor of global peace and stability. The current neglect of America's armed forces threatens its ability to maintain peace.

The Bush administration had been able to reduce defense spending somewhat at the end of the Cold War in 1991. But the Clinton administration witlessly accelerated and deepened these cuts. The results were devastating: military readiness declined, training suffered, military pay slipped 15 percent below civilian equivalents, morale plummeted, and the services cannibalized existing equipment to keep airplanes flying, ships afloat, and tanks moving. The increased difficulty in recruiting people to the armed forces or retaining them is hardly surprising.

Moreover, the administration began deploying American forces abroad at a furious pace—an average of once every nine weeks. As it cut defense spending to its lowest point as a percentage of GDP since Pearl Harbor, the administration deployed the armed forces more often than at any time in the last 50 years. Some of the deployments themselves were questionable, such as in Haiti. But more than anything it was simply unwise to multiply missions in the face of a continuing budget reduction. Means and mission were not matched, and (predictably) the already thinly stretched armed forces came close to a breaking point. When all these trends became so obvious and embarrassing that they could no longer be ignored, the administration finally requested increased defense spending. But the "death spiral," as the administration's own undersecretary of defense called it—robbing procurement and research and development simply to operate the armed forces—was already well under way. That the administration did nothing, choosing instead to live off the fruits of Reagan's military buildup, constitutes an extraordinary neglect of the fiduciary responsibilities of the commander in chief.

Now the next president will be confronted with a prolonged job of repair. Military readiness will have to take center stage, particularly those aspects that affect the living conditions of the troops—military pay, housing—and also training. New weapons will have to be procured in order to give the military the capacity to carry out today's missions. But even in its current state, the American military still enjoys a commanding technological lead and therefore has a battlefield advantage over any competitor. Thus the next president should refocus the Pentagon's priorities on building the military of the 21st century rather than continuing to build on the structure of the Cold War. U.S. technological advantages should be leveraged to build forces that are lighter and more lethal, more mobile and agile, and capable of firing accurately from long distances. In order to do this, Washington must reallocate resources, perhaps in some cases skipping a generation of technology to make leaps rather than incremental improvements in its forces.

The other major concern is a loss of focus on the mission of the armed forces. What does it mean to deter, fight, and win wars and defend the national interest? First, the American military must be able to meet decisively the emergence of any hostile military power in the Asia-Pacific region, the Middle East, the Persian Gulf, and Europe—areas in which not only our interests but also those of our key allies are at stake. America's military is the only one capable of this deterrence function, and it must not be stretched or diverted into areas that weaken these broader responsibilities. It is the role that the United States played when Saddam Hussein threatened the Persian Gulf, and it is the power needed to deter trouble on the Korean Peninsula or across the Taiwan Strait. In the latter cases, the goal is to make it inconceivable for North Korea or China to use force because American military power is a compelling factor in their equations.

Some small-scale conflicts clearly have an impact on American strategic interests. Such was the case with Kosovo, which was in the backyard of America's most important strategic alliance: NATO. In fact, Yugoslav President Slobodan Miloševic's rejection of peaceful coexistence with the Kosovar Albanians threatened to rock the area's fragile ethnic balance. Eastern Europe is a patchwork of ethnic minorities. For the most part, Hungarians and Romanians, Bulgarians and Turks, and even Ukrainians and Russians have found a way since 1991 of preventing their differences from exploding. Miloševic has been the exception, and the United States had an overriding strategic interest in stopping him. There was, of course, a humanitarian disaster looming as well, but in the absence of concerns based on the interests of the alliance, the case for intervention would have been more tenuous.

The Kosovo war was conducted incompetently, in part because the administration's political goals kept shifting and in part because it was not, at the start, committed to the decisive use of military force. That President Clinton was surprised at Miloševic's tenacity is, well, surprising. If there is any lesson from history, it is that small powers with everything to lose are often more stubborn than big powers, for whom the conflict is merely one among many problems. The lesson, too, is that if it is worth fighting for, you had better be prepared to win. Also, there must be a political game plan that will permit the withdrawal of our forces—something that is still completely absent in Kosovo.

But what if our values are attacked in areas that are not arguably of strategic concern? Should the United States not try to save lives in the absence of an overriding strategic rationale? The next American president should be in a position to intervene when he believes, and can make the case, that the United States is duty-bound to do so. "Humanitarian intervention" cannot be ruled out a priori. But a decision to intervene in the absence of strategic concerns should be understood for what it is. Humanitarian problems are rarely only humanitarian problems; the taking of life or withholding of food is almost always a political act. If the United States is not prepared to address the underlying political conflict and to know whose side it is on, the military may end up separating warring parties for an indefinite period. Sometimes one party (or both) can come to see the United States as the enemy. Because the military cannot, by definition, do anything decisive in these "humanitarian" crises, the chances of misreading the situation and ending up in very different circumstances are very high. This was essentially the problem of "mission creep" in Somalia.

The president must remember that the military is a special instrument. It is lethal, and it is meant to be. It is not a civilian police force. It is not a political referee. And it is most certainly not designed to build a civilian society. Military force is best used to support clear political goals, whether limited, such as expelling Saddam from Kuwait, or comprehensive, such as demanding the unconditional surrender of Japan and Germany during World War II. It is one thing to have a limited political goal and to fight decisively for it; it is quite another to apply military force incrementally, hoping to find a political solution somewhere along the way. A president entering these situations must ask whether decisive force is possible and is likely to be effective and must know how and when to get out. These are difficult criteria to meet, so U.S. intervention in these "humanitarian" crises should be, at best, exceedingly rare.

This does not mean that the United States must ignore humanitarian and civil conflicts around the world. But the military cannot be involved everywhere. Often, these tasks might be better carried out by regional actors, as modeled by the Australian-led intervention in East Timor. The U.S. might be able to lend financial, logistical, and intelligence support. Sometimes tough, competent diplomacy in the beginning can prevent the need for military force later. Using the American armed forces as the world's "911" will degrade capabilities, bog soldiers down in peacekeeping roles, and fuel concern among other great powers that the United States has decided to enforce notions of "limited sovereignty" worldwide in the name of humanitarianism. This overly broad definition of

America's national interest is bound to backfire as others arrogate the same authority to themselves. Or we will find ourselves looking to the United Nations to sanction the use of American military power in these cases, implying that we will do so even when our vital interests are involved, which would also be a mistake.

DEALING WITH THE POWERFUL

Another crucial task for the United States is to focus on relations with other powerful states. Although the United States is fortunate to count among its friends several great powers, it is important not to take them for granted—so that there is a firm foundation when it comes time to rely on them. The challenges of China and North Korea require coordination and cooperation with Japan and South Korea. The signals that we send to our real partners are important. Never again should an American president go to Beijing for nine days and refuse to stop in Tokyo or Seoul.

There is work to do with the Europeans, too, on defining what holds the transatlantic alliance together in the absence of the Soviet threat. NATO is badly in need of attention in the wake of Kosovo and with the looming question of its further enlargement in 2002 and beyond. The door to NATO for the remaining states of eastern and central Europe should remain open, as many are actively preparing to meet the criteria for membership. But the parallel track of NATO's own evolution, its attention to the definition of its mission, and its ability to digest and then defend new members has been neglected. Moreover, the United States has an interest in shaping the European defense identity—welcoming a greater European military capability as long as it is within the context of NATO. NATO has a very full agenda. Membership in NATO will mean nothing to anyone if the organization is no longer militarily capable and if it is unclear about its mission.

For America and our allies, the most daunting task is to find the right balance in our policy toward Russia and China. Both are equally important to the future of international peace, but the challenges they pose are very different. China is a rising power; in economic terms, that should be good news, because in order to maintain its economic dynamism, China must be more integrated into the international economy. This will require increased openness and transparency and the growth of private industry. The political struggle in Beijing is over how to maintain the Communist Party's monopoly on power. Some see economic reform, growth, and a better life for the Chinese people as the key. Others see the inherent contradiction in loosening economic control and maintaining the party's political dominance. As China's economic problems multiply due to slowing growth rates, failing banks, inert state enterprises, and rising unemployment, this struggle will intensify.

It is in America's interest to strengthen the hands of those who seek economic integration because this will probably lead to sustained and organized pressures for political liberalization. There are no guarantees, but in scores of cases from Chile to Spain to Taiwan, the link between democracy and economic liberalization has proven powerful over the long run. Trade and economic interaction are, in fact, good—not only for America's economic growth but for its political aims as well. Human rights concerns should not move to the sidelines in the meantime. Rather, the American president should press the Chinese leadership for change. But it is wise to remember that our influence through moral arguments and commitment is still limited in the face of Beijing's pervasive political control. The big trends toward the spread of information, the access of young Chinese to American values through educational exchanges and training, and the growth of an entrepreneurial class that does not owe its livelihood to the state are, in the end, likely to have a more powerful effect on life in China.

Although some argue that the way to support human rights is to refuse trade with China, this punishes precisely those who are most likely to change the system. Put bluntly, Li Peng and the Chinese conservatives want to continue to run the economy by state fiat. Of course, there should be tight export controls on the transfer of militarily sensitive technology to China. But trade in general can open up the Chinese economy and, ultimately, its politics too. This view requires faith in the power of markets and economic freedom to drive political change, but it is a faith confirmed by experiences around the globe.

Even if there is an argument for economic interaction with Beijing, China is still a potential threat to stability in the Asia-Pacific region. Its military power is currently no match for that of the United States. But that condition is not necessarily permanent. What we do know is that China is a great power with unresolved vital interests, particularly concerning Taiwan and the South China Sea. China resents the role of the United States in the Asia-Pacific region. This means that China is not a "status quo" power but one that would like to alter Asia's balance of power in its own favor. That alone makes it a strategic competitor, not the "strategic partner" the Clinton administration once called it. Add to this China's record of cooperation with Iran and Pakistan in the proliferation of ballistic-missile technology, and the security problem is obvious. China will do what it can to enhance its position, whether by stealing nuclear secrets or by trying to intimidate Taiwan.

China's success in controlling the balance of power depends in large part on America's reaction to the challenge. The United States must deepen its cooperation with Japan and South Korea and maintain its commitment to a robust military presence in the region. It should pay closer attention to India's role in the regional balance. There is a strong tendency conceptually to connect India with Pakistan and to think only of Kashmir or the nuclear competition between the two states. But India is an element in China's calculation, and it should be in America's, too. India is not a great power yet, but it has the potential to emerge as one.

The United States also has a deep interest in the security of Taiwan. It is a model of democratic and market-oriented development, and it invests significantly in the mainland's economy. The longstanding U.S. commitment to a "one-China" policy that leaves to a future date the resolution of the relationship between Taipei and Beijing is wise. But that policy requires that neither side challenge the status quo and that Beijing, as the more powerful actor, renounce the use of force. U.S. resolve anchors this policy. The Clinton administration tilted toward Beijing, when, for instance, it used China's formulation of the "three no's" during the president's trip there. Taiwan has been looking for attention and reassurance ever since. If the United States is resolute, peace can be maintained in the Taiwan Strait until a political settlement on democratic terms is available.

Some things take time. U.S. policy toward China requires nuance and balance. It is important to promote China's internal transition through economic interaction while containing Chinese power and security ambitions. Cooperation should be pursued, but we should never be afraid to confront Beijing when our interests collide.

RUSSIAN WEAKNESS

Russia presents a different challenge. It still has many of the attributes of a great power: a large population, vast territory, and military potential. But its economic weakness and problems of national identity threaten to overwhelm it. Moscow is determined to assert itself in the world and often does so in ways that are at once haphazard and threatening to American interests. The picture is complicated by Russia's own internal transition—one that the United States wants to see succeed. The old Soviet system has broken down, and some of the basic elements of democratic development are in place. People are free to say what they think, vote for whom they please, and (for the most part) worship freely. But the democratic fragments are not institutionalized—with the exception of the Communist Party, political parties are weak—and the balance of political power is so strongly in favor of the president that he often rules simply by decree. Of course, few pay attention to Boris Yelstin's decrees, and the Russian government has been mired in inaction and stagnation for at least three years. Russia's economic troubles and its high-level corruption have been widely discussed in recent months; Russia's economy is not becoming a market but is mutating into something else. Widespread barter, banks that are not banks, billions of rubles stashed abroad and in mattresses at home, and bizarre privatization schemes that have enriched the so-called reformers give Moscow's economy a medieval tinge.

The problem for U.S. policy is that the Clinton administration's embrace of Yeltsin and those who were thought to be reformers around him has failed. Yeltsin is Russia's president and clearly the United States had to deal with the head of state. But support for democracy and economic reform became support for Yeltsin. His agenda became the American agenda. The United States certified that reform was taking place where it was not, continuing to disburse money from the International Monetary Fund in the absence of any evidence of serious change. The curious privatization methods were hailed as economic liberalization; the looting of the country's assets by powerful people either went unnoticed or was ignored. The realities in Russia simply did not accord with the administration's script about Russian economic reform. The United States should not be faulted for trying to help. But, as the Russian reformer Grigori Yavlinsky has said, the United States should have "told the truth" about what was happening.

Now we have a dual credibility problem—with Russians and with Americans. There are signs of life in the Russian economy. The financial crash of August 1998 forced import substitution, and domestic production has increased as the resilient Russian people have taken matters into their own hands. Rising oil prices have helped as well. But these are short-term fixes. There is no longer a consensus in America or Europe on what to do next with Russia. Frustrated expectations and "Russia fatigue" are direct consequences of the "happy talk" in which the Clinton administration engaged.

Russia's economic future is now in the hands of the Russians. The country is not without assets, including its natural resources and an educated population. It is up to Russia to make structural reforms, particularly concerning the rule of law and the tax codes, so that investors—foreign and domestic—will provide the capital needed for economic growth. That opportunity will arise once there is a new government in Moscow after last December's Duma elections and next June's presidential election. But the cultural changes ultimately needed to sustain a functioning civil society and a market-based economy may take a generation. Western openness to Russia's people, particularly its youth, in exchange programs and contact with the private sector and educational opportunities can help that process. It is also important to engage the leadership of Russia's diverse regions, where economic and social policies are increasingly pursued independently of Moscow.

In the meantime, U.S. policy must concentrate on the important security agenda with Russia. First, it must recognize that American security is threatened less by Russia's strength than by its weakness and incoherence. This suggests immediate attention to the safety and security of Moscow's nuclear forces and stockpile. The Nunn-Lugar program should be funded fully and pursued aggressively. (Because American contractors do most of the work, the risk of the diversion of funds is low.) Second, Washington must begin a comprehensive discussion with Moscow on the changing nuclear threat. Much has been made by Russian military officials about their increased reliance on nuclear weapons in the face of their declining conventional readiness. The Russian deterrent is more than adequate against the U.S. nuclear arsenal, and vice versa. But that fact need no longer be enshrined in a treaty that is almost 30 years old and is a relic of a profoundly adversarial relationship between the United States and the Soviet Union. The Anti-Ballistic Missile Treaty was intended to prevent the development of national missile defenses in the Cold War security environment. Today, the principal concerns are nuclear threats from the Iraqs and North Koreas of the world and the possibility of unauthorized releases as nuclear weapons spread.

Moscow, in fact, lives closer to those threats than Washington does. It ought to be possible to engage the Russians in a discussion of the changed threat environment, their possible responses, and the relationship of strategic offensive-force reductions to the deployment of defenses. The United States should make clear that it prefers to move cooperatively toward a new offense-defense mix, but that it is prepared to do so unilaterally. Moscow should understand, too, that any possibilities for sharing technology or information in these areas would depend heavily on its record—problematic to date—on the proliferation of ballistic-missile and other technologies related to WMD. It would be foolish in the extreme to share defenses with Moscow if it either leaks or deliberately transfers weapons technologies to the very states against which America is defending.

Finally, the United States needs to recognize that Russia is a great power, and that we will always have interests that conflict as well as coincide. The war in Chechnya, located in the oil-rich Caucasus, is particularly dangerous. Prime Minister Vladimir Putin has used the war to stir nationalism at home while fueling his own political fortunes. The Russian military has been uncharacteristically blunt and vocal in asserting its duty to defend the integrity of the Russian Federation—an unwelcome development in civil-military relations. The long-term effect on Russia's political culture should not be underestimated. And the war has affected relations between Russia and its neighbors in the Caucasus, as the Kremlin hurls charges of harboring and abetting Chechen terrorists against states as diverse as Saudi Arabia, Georgia, and Azerbaijan. The war is a reminder of the vulnerability of the small, new states around Russia and of America's interest in their independence. If they can become stronger, they will be less tempting to Russia. But much depends on the ability of these states to reform their economies and political systems—a process, to date, whose success is mixed at best.

COPING WITH ROGUE REGIMES

As history marches toward markets and democracy, some states have been left by the side of the road. Iraq is the prototype. Saddam Hussein's regime is isolated, his conventional military power has been severely weakened, his people live in poverty and terror, and he has no useful place in international politics. He is therefore determined to develop WMD. Nothing will change until Saddam is gone, so the United States must mobilize whatever resources it can, including support from his opposition, to remove him.

The regime of Kim Jong Il is so opaque that it is difficult to know its motivations, other than that they are malign. But North Korea also lives outside of the international system. Like East Germany, North Korea is the evil twin of a successful regime just across its border. It must fear its eventual demise from the sheer power and pull of South Korea. Pyongyang, too, has little to gain and everything to lose from engagement in the international economy. The development of WMD thus provides the destructive way out for Kim Jong Il.

President Kim Dae Jung of South Korea is attempting to find a peaceful resolution with the north through engagement. Any U.S. policy toward the north should depend heavily on coordination with Seoul and Tokyo. In that context, the 1994 framework agreement that attempted to bribe North Korea into forsaking nuclear weapons cannot easily be set aside. Still, there is a trap inherent in this approach: sooner or later Pyongyang will threaten to test a missile one too many times, and the United States will not respond with further benefits. Then what will Kim Jong Il do? The possibility for miscalculation is very high.

One thing is clear: the United States must approach regimes like North Korea resolutely and decisively. The Clinton administration has failed here, sometimes threatening to use force and then backing down, as it often has with Iraq. These regimes are living on borrowed time, so there need be no sense of panic about them. Rather, the first line of defense should be a clear and classical statement of deterrence—if they do acquire WMD, their weapons will be unusable because any attempt to use them will bring national obliteration. Second, we should accelerate efforts to defend against these weapons. This is the most important reason to deploy national and theater missile defenses as soon as possible, to focus attention on U.S. homeland defenses against chemical and biological agents, and to expand intelligence capabilities against terrorism of all kinds.

Finally, there is the Iranian regime. Iran's motivation is not to disrupt simply the development of an international system based on markets and democracy, but to replace it with an alternative: fundamentalist Islam. Fortunately, the Iranians do not have the kind of reach and power that the Soviet Union enjoyed in trying to promote its socialist alternative. But Iran's tactics have posed real problems for U.S. security. It has tried to destabilize moderate Arab states such as Saudi Arabia, though its relations with the Saudis have improved recently. Iran has also supported terrorism against America and Western interests and attempted to develop and transfer sensitive military technologies.

Iran presents special difficulties in the Middle East, a region of core interest to the United States and to our key ally Israel. Iranian weaponry increasingly threatens Israel directly. As important as Israel's efforts to reach peace with its Arab neighbors are to the future of the Middle East, they are not the whole story of stability in the region. Israel has a real security problem, so defense cooperation with the United States—particularly in the area of ballistic missile defense—is critical. That in turn will help Israel protect itself both through agreements and through enhanced military power.

Still, it is important to note that there are trends in Iran that bear watching. Mohammad Khatami's election as president has given some hope of a new course for a country that once hosted a great and thriving civilization—though there are questions about how much authority he exercises. Moreover, Khatami's more moderate domestic views may not translate into more acceptable behavior abroad. All in all, changes in U.S. policy toward Iran would require changes in Iranian behavior.

BUILDING A CONSENSUS FOR THE NATIONAL INTEREST

America is blessed with an extraordinary opportunity. It has had no territorial ambitions for nearly a century. Its national interest has been defined instead by a desire to foster the spread of freedom, prosperity, and peace. Both the will of the people and the demands of modern economies accord with that vision of the future. But even America's advantages offer no guarantees of success. It is up to America's presidential leadership and policy to bridge the gap between tomorrow's possibilities and today's realities.

The president must speak to the American people about national priorities and intentions and work with Congress to focus foreign policy around the national interest. The problem today is not an absence of bipartisan spirit in Congress or the American people's disinterest. It is the existence of a vacuum. In the absence of a compelling vision, parochial interests are filling the void.

Foreign policy in a Republican administration will most certainly be internationalist; the leading contenders in the party's presidential race have strong credentials in that regard. But it will also proceed from the firm ground of the national interest, not from the interests of an illusory international community. America can exercise power without arrogance and pursue its interests without hectoring and bluster. When it does so in concert with those who share its core values, the world becomes more prosperous, democratic, and peaceful. That has been America's special role in the past, and it should be again as we enter the next century.

Editors' Note: Democratic views will be published in forthcoming issues.

CONDOLEEZZA RICE is Senior Fellow at the Hoover Institution and Professor of Political Science at Stanford University. She is also foreign policy adviser to Republican presidential candidate George W. Bush.

Campaign 2000: A Republican Foreign Policy

Robert B. Zoellick JANUARY/FEBRUARY 2000

U.S. President George W. Bush speaks under a U.S. flag at a Tennessee welcome ceremony upon his arrival in Knoxville, October 8, 2002.

AN ERA OF CHANGE

At the opening of the twentieth century, the United States began a quest similar to today's. The rise of American power, revolutions in technology, and great clashes abroad set the stage for a historic transformation. Theodore Roosevelt and Woodrow Wilson dominated the age, as they debated and labored to promote their visions of America's role in a new international system. In 2000, the world is again in an era of rapid change, reminiscent of a century ago. The vitality of America's private economy, the preeminence of its military power, and the appeal of the country's ideas are unparalleled. But as former British Prime Minister Margaret Thatcher cautioned her colleagues, we must "expect the unexpected." A primary task for the next president of the United States is to build public support for a strategy that will shape the world so as to protect and promote American interests and values for the next 50 years.

At the end of the Cold War, President George Bush built on Ronald Reagan's legacy by beginning to adapt American foreign policy to the challenges of changed circumstances. Recognizing the importance of economic ties, his administration negotiated the North American Free Trade Agreement (NAFTA), supported a free-trade agreement with Chile as a step toward free trade throughout the western hemisphere, and promoted the Asia-Pacific Economic Cooperation (APEC) group to bind U.S. economic interests across the Pacific. The United States then employed these regional initiatives to bring the global trade talks of the Uruguay Round to the edge of conclusion. Those initiatives have created the most powerful movement toward free trade in history.

The United States also took advantage of its preeminent position to push hard for peace in a number of vital areas. In the Middle East, the United States used its standing after the Cold War and the Gulf War to break old deadlocks at the Madrid Conference and to push the Arab-Israeli peace process to a totally new plane. The Bush administration sought to reshape the strategic landscape across Europe and Russia by uniting Germany within NATO in 1990, defining a new strategic concept for NATO in 1991, opening the alliance to former enemies in 1990 and 1991, and negotiating landmark conventional and nuclear arms reduction agreements to underpin the new security framework. U.S. ties with Russia reached an impressive level of effectiveness, as demonstrated by their cooperation in the Gulf War. U.S. links with China were also slowly improving after the Tiananmen Square tragedy, as the Bush administration handled sharp differences in a way that still enabled it to foster positive change. By the end of its term, the administration had created a climate of cooperation among the world's major powers.

CLINTON'S FLAWED APPROACH

President Bill Clinton's intelligence and his ability to synthesize policy and politics at home held out the prospect that he could build on Bush's initial efforts to redefine America's position in the world. Unfortunately, the Clinton administration never adopted a guiding strategy or even demonstrated a sustained commitment to foreign policy. As a result, Clinton has failed to define a new internationalism for the United States, thus letting historic opportunities slip away.

Clinton's foreign policies have been stymied by five flaws. The first, an unwillingness to remain committed to his own priorities, has been demonstrated by his drift on international trade. Clinton started with an encouraging emphasis on trade, perhaps because he inherited a signed NAFTA deal and a partial Uruguay Round agreement that he could not abandon easily. But after 1994, the Clinton administration changed its course: it made pledges for free trade, but the reality of its policies did not match the rhetoric. Instead, the United States demanded managed-trade quotas with Japan—precisely the wrong remedy for a country needing deregulation—until it was compelled to retreat. Fearful of alienating protectionist political constituencies, Clinton was unwilling to build on NAFTA or even to defend it. After deferring to the new economic isolationists, Clinton seemed surprised in 1997 when he could muster only about 40 out of 200 members of his own party in the House of Representatives to support his forlorn search for the authority necessary to negotiate additional trade agreements.

These mistakes have had lasting consequences. In the early 1990s, countries throughout Latin America were competing to negotiate free-trade agreements with the United States. Recognizing the strategic value of NAFTA, they wanted to connect their economies, societies, security, and even political systems to America. Today, no one in Latin America or elsewhere expects the current administration to follow through on its statements. Latin Americans proceeded with their own customs union, which has been negotiating new trade ventures with the European Union (EU) and

Robert B. Zoellick

Japan. When East Asian economies faced their greatest financial shock in generations—creating possibilities for structural reforms but also a need to fight protectionism with mutual liberalization—-U.S. trade negotiators stood on the sidelines. Without the initiative and leadership of the United States, all participants involved in launching the global trade talks in Seattle last November approached the meeting defensively. So the new trade round was stymied by stalemate. Washington has the power to shape global economic relations for the next 50 years, but it has marginalized itself in this crucial area.

The White House's second flaw has been to erode its credibility by offering words that are not backed by actions; this has taken a special toll with U.S. allies. It is ironic that an administration that came into office proclaiming "assertive multilateralism" has dissipated America's energies as a coalition leader. The Gulf War coalition is in tatters, not surprisingly, after years of strong language about the dangers of Saddam Hussein's machinations, followed by only tepid and reflexive actions. Despite the American military's overwhelming superiority in Kosovo, at the end of the bombing its European allies concluded that they needed to create their own alternative to U.S. political and security leadership. After China harshly criticized Japan for agreeing to new defense guidelines with the United States, Clinton could not find one minute during his nine-day trip to China to stand by his struggling Japanese ally. The administration managed to boot out a U.N. secretary-general, but it has never developed a sustained, consistent strategy toward the organization that would serve U.S. ends. (Only a few years earlier, America had proved that a more constructive approach to the U.N. was possible when it built the Gulf War coalition and organized the repeal of the "Zionism is racism" resolution.)

The Clinton administration's third flaw is its inability to frame strategies supported by operations, which has particularly damaged its dealings with China and Russia. Neither one is the "strategic partner" that Clinton proclaimed. In fact, the distrust created by the administration has made it hard for the United

States to cooperate with either country on long-term mutual interests. Sadly, the Clinton legacy with both China and Russia—the two great powers whose future paths remain uncertain and potentially unstable—is one of tense and suspicious relations that have been getting worse.

In the case of China, at first the administration linked human rights to normal trading relations, but it later backed down—a clear sign of weakness. Clinton then mistakenly promised the Chinese that the United States would not grant a travel visa to the president of democratic Taiwan, Lee Teng-hui; his subsequent reversal of that decision generated distrust and counterreactions that have increased dangers between Beijing and Taipei. During Clinton's high-profile trip to China in 1998, he neglected to explain serious security differences, ultimately misleading China and failing to prepare the American public for China's missile buildup, its nuclear espionage, and its crackdowns on democracy. Next, Clinton prodded Chinese Prime Minister Zhu Rhongji to offer the United States concessions in exchange for Chinese membership in the World Trade Organization (WTO) but then inexplicably spurned Zhu's proposal during a high-profile visit, thereby weakening China's reform efforts. The agreement with China on the WTO in November 1999, although welcome, only underscores that Clinton could have cut a deal earlier that was as good or better—avoiding a crisis that left unnecessary scars.

Clinton's Russia policy has discredited free-market economics, squandered money from the International Monetary Fund (IMF), and generated widespread anti-Americanism. His "Monroeski doctrine" and his comparison of the battle in Chechnya to the U.S. Civil War have encouraged both a view of state power that conflicts with a modern, democratic Russia and a revival of Russian imperialistic attitudes. The administration's indifference to Yeltsin's shelling of the Russian legislature, among other autocratic measures, revealed a blind spot in the importance of Russia's rule of law and democratic process. Clinton has never seemed to grasp the costs of embracing an elected czar, one who oversaw a privatization drive that turned into massive theft and who now presides over pervasive corruption. Not surprisingly, this system has failed to improve the livelihood of average Russians, setting the stage for future trouble.

A fourth flaw has been Clinton's uncertainty on when and how to use American power—frequently hesitating, then overcommitting, and regularly failing to match means with ends. This weakness has shadowed his initiatives to resolve humanitarian and ethnic strife with military intervention. His "nation-building" failure in Somalia was costly in terms of lives, the reputation of the United States, and America's confidence that it can deal effectively with such problems. The U.S. invasion of Haiti and its multi-billion-dollar effort to bring "democracy" turned out to be an unhappy reminder that supposedly good intentions cannot save a flawed policy. The United States continued to be drawn into mini-wars in the Balkans without clarifying its goals or being honest about the ongoing commitment of human and material resources these U.N. "colonies" would require. The history of false starts and missteps was captured well by Clinton's own new "doctrine" on intervention in such conflicts: his words were at first stunning in their reach but were then quickly reinterpreted, leaving the world to conclude that America is confused, cynical, or both.

Finally, many of Clinton's ventures have the disquieting feature of being driven significantly by political polls and calculations; this perception has made it exceedingly hard for him to call credibly for bipartisan foreign policies. As Clinton's ad hoc foreign policies have frayed, the administration has lashed out at its critics, calling them isolationists. In fact, Clinton's inability to develop a foreign policy disciplined by sustained priorities, reliability, strategy, selectivity, and frankness has squandered opportunities. The president's mistakes have made it harder for him to complete work in areas—such as the Middle East and Northern Ireland—where he has invested considerable effort in bringing parties together for peace processes. The Clinton foreign policy style has also taken its toll abroad. The administration has caused too many countries to be weary, and even resentful, of the United States. The power of the United States is obvious to the world, but Clinton has failed to use that power wisely or diplomatically. His rhetoric has contained much hubris but little credibility. America is more influential if it speaks softly, but with firm conviction. If it asserts that it is committed to do everything, its commitments to everything are suspect.

REPUBLICAN PRINCIPLES

Five principles distinguish a modern Republican foreign policy. First, it is premised on a respect for power, being neither ashamed to pursue America's national interests nor too quick to use the country's might. By matching America's power to its interests, such a policy can achieve its objectives and build credibility both at home and abroad. U.S. policy should respect the histories, perspectives, and concerns of other nations, but it should not be paralyzed by intellectual penchants for moral relativism. All states do not play equally important roles. Given America's responsibilities in the world, it must retain its freedom to act against serious dangers.

Second, a modern Republican foreign policy emphasizes building and sustaining coalitions and alliances. Effective coalition leadership requires clear-eyed judgments about priorities, an appreciation of others' interests, constant consultations among partners, and a willingness to compromise on some points but to remain focused on core objectives. Allies and coalition partners should bear their fair share of the responsibilities; if they do, their views will be represented and respected. Similarly, to have an effective U.N., the key nations that compose it must recognize that their actions—not their speeches and posturing in an international forum—will determine whether problems can be solved.

Third, Republicans judge international agreements and institutions as means to achieve ends, not as forms of political therapy. Agreements and institutions can facilitate bargaining, recognize common interests, and resolve differences cooperatively. But international law, unlike domestic law, merely codifies an already agreed-upon cooperation. Even among democracies, international law not backed by enforcement mechanisms will need negotiations in order to work, and international law not backed by power cannot cope with dangerous people and states. Every issue need not be dealt with multilaterally.

Fourth, a modern Republican foreign policy must embrace the revolutionary changes in the information and communications, technology, commerce, and finance sectors that will shape the environment for global politics and security. Because of these changes, people's aspirations—to exercise their free will and transform their lives—are rising in all corners of the globe. Communities of private groups, whether organized for business or social ends, will achieve results far beyond the reach of governments and international bureaucracies. The United States can leverage this dynamism to open minds and markets. America's foreign policy must promote these global trends. It must take practical steps to move the world toward greater freedoms and human rights. It should link itself to the agents of change around the world through new networks of free trade, information, and investment.

Finally, a modern Republican foreign policy recognizes that there is still evil in the world—people who hate America and the ideas for which it stands. Today, we face enemies who are hard at work to develop nuclear, biological, and chemical weapons, along with the missiles to deliver them. The United States must remain vigilant and have the strength to defeat its enemies. People driven by enmity or by a need to dominate will not respond to reason or goodwill. They will manipulate civilized rules for uncivilized ends.

POWER AND ECONOMICS

A modern Republican foreign policy should apply these principles within a long-term strategy to promote peace, security, and liberty. America must capture the dynamism of the era and transform its new elements into the economic and security foundations for a future system. The United States and its partners need to link the world's continental regions within a global economic system that secures the benefits of integration while coping with the inevitable stresses of capitalism. Looking at the twentieth century, it is clear that peace is not ensured through closer economic ties alone; so the United States must navigate changing great-power relations, strengthen its alliances, and maintain unquestioned military superiority over dangerous regimes.

In the information age, America should promote an open architecture in order to capitalize on its greatest assets: a vibrant, innovative economy and a society that continually reinvents itself. American concepts of corporate governance, shareholder value, benchmarking, and the "value chain" are now discussed in executive offices around the globe. By incorporating advances in information and communications technologies into business processes, U.S. corporations have triggered gains in productivity similar to those achieved when companies learned how to reengineer their businesses using electrical power 100 years ago. The surge in e-commerce, already a $500 billion activity, is transforming business models again. Governments everywhere are turning to privatization and deregulation to help their countries keep pace. The American entrepreneur commands an awe that matches the respect accorded the American military.

The American private sector is a powerful, attractive magnet. But the U.S. government has not used this energetic force to transform others in ways that enable America to build on its successes. Instead, growth and market imbalances have led to the largest trade deficits in American history. Although U.S. markets are generally open to the world, too many others remain closed to the United States. Countries should embrace changes that will tap the vitality and genius of people around the world, improve their livelihood and health, and open doors to freedom. Government efforts to turn back the clock, even if well-meaning, will end up hurting people. Instead, governments and societies should help people adjust to and benefit from new possibilities. Therefore, a successful U.S. foreign policy must also be based on superior education at home, low taxes that reward work and risk-taking, and secure savings and pensions for retirees.

The United States needs a strategic economic-negotiating agenda that combines regional agreements with the development of global rules for an open economy. To link up with Latin America and the Asia-Pacific region, the United States should propose free-trade agreements, with either individual countries or regional groups. If India continues its reforms, the United States should offer it a new economic partnership beginning with those Indian sectors that are open to the world or can offer large public gains through deregulation. As a new generation of leaders gains authority in the Middle East, possible peace agreements can be buttressed by drawing these societies into information-age economics and integrating their economies into world markets. African countries seeking to abandon the old, failed state controls need the incentive of open U.S. and world markets for their emerging enterprises, as well as financial backing for serious reforms. The EU and the United States should follow the lead of their increasingly integrated businesses by opening even more sectors to cross-investment and greater competition, with the aim of achieving transatlantic free trade.

These agendas should be ambitious—ranging from farm products to e-commerce. Tariffs should be cut further. The United States should support innovative business ventures to streamline common standards. It should promote the deregulation and opening of vast new global markets for services—in areas such as energy, airlines, finance, and entertainment. The United States should apply successful regional precedents in economic and trade liberalization to other regions or to global negotiations through the WTO. By operating at the center of this changing network, the United States—the one economy with a truly global reach—should promote openness among regions.

If some regions are too slow to open their markets, the United States should move on to others. America should spur a competitive dynamic for openness and transparency. Competition can work wonders: when the United States pursued NAFTA and APEC, the EU finally felt the pressure to complete the global Uruguay Round trade negotiations. If others hold back in the new WTO round, the United States should repeat this strategy of regionalism with a global goal in order to break the logjam.

This modern Republican design recognizes the benefits of regional integration and seeks to harness it for global purposes; regional integration can help countries deal more effectively with transnational problems, such as the environment or narcotics trafficking. The practice of joint action within regions, especially by private-sector groups, can be expanded to deal with common political and even security issues. The history of U.S. foreign policy is full of examples of private parties—from missionaries to engineers—who forwarded America's belief in the future by helping others face the challenges of the day. The very nature of the "new economy"—with its rapidly adapting technologies, fast-paced change, and innovative spirit—will elevate the role of private parties; they will often surpass the government in their ability to resolve inevitable disputes. These parties are not zero-sum thinkers. The U.S. government should create a climate in which citizens can serve both the private and the public good. Prosperity with a purpose is an idea that reaches far beyond U.S. borders.

If America links its economy to those of key regions, it can also promote its geopolitical agenda. Deeper integration with Latin America, Europe, and East Asia will support U.S. security commitments as citizens of these regions recognize their common interests. At best, economic interdependence will be a new glue that draws partners close together. More modestly, creating common rules for open economies will connect private sectors and help manage a combination of cooperation and competition.

This blueprint expands on America's political and economic principles. It promotes open markets and open societies, the free flow of information and ideas, and the development of the private sector—all of which contribute to the growth of economies, middle classes, and liberties. If China, Russia, India, and others want to keep up, they will have to open up. This plan offers a positive program around which internationalists of both parties can rally to counter protectionists and isolationists. It also challenges America to sustain its openness, a feature that attracts great thinkers and doers from all over the world. It creates a dynamism that gives its diverse society cohesion and a shared purpose; and it safeguards liberty and freedom.

The public international financial institutions—especially the IMF and the World Bank—also need to be overhauled to match the demands of the information age and the globalization of financial markets. Considering how private-sector financial firms have changed in recent years, it is understandable that the Bretton Woods institutions of 1944 require major reengineering. First, the operations of the IMF and the World Bank must be more transparent, on-line, and real-time. They should fight corruption, which can drain both money and confidence. But they should not, out of technocratic hubris, usurp the proper roles of either creditor or debtor governments or of the private financial sector. A dependency on international bureaucracies for solutions to tough problems will dissuade national governments from taking responsibility for their countries' futures and will ultimately erode the legitimacy of both governments and international financial institutions.

The IMF still has a role to play in buffering national financial markets against shocks that threaten global stability, until self-help rebalances the capital movements. But the IMF must exercise this role in a fashion that does not add to long-term financial instability by encouraging risks for which investors are not willing to pay. Furthermore, since today's global economy (different from what it was 50 years ago) rests on private capital flows, the IMF must "bail-in" creditors, not bail them out. Private creditors must play a financial role in restructuring "national bankruptcies," just as when they have loaned money to companies in trouble; creditors can reschedule loans, take discounts, and extend more money during workouts. The World Bank should concentrate on helping people adjust to change. In poor countries, this agenda may involve improving basic health and subsistence needs while creating economic opportunities. In other low-income countries, the World Bank can assist in developing markets that will enable people to benefit from self-help.

ALLIES, ENEMIES, AND IN-BETWEENS
In pursuing a reinvigorated foreign policy, the United States first needs to overhaul ties with its partners and allies: its North American neighbors and its two primary partners abroad, Europe and Japan. Mexico, Canada, and the United States share an interest in building on their common democracy and prosperity by addressing problems that require greater regional cooperation—such as narcotics, the environment, and illegal immigration. To operate effectively overseas, the United States must ensure that it has a strong neighborhood at home. Transatlantic and transpacific alliances can go a long way toward ensuring security in the eastern and western parts of Eurasia, where in the past dangerous powers have threatened the United States. These partnerships can enhance America's ability to address the uncertain futures of China and Russia. The EU and Japan are also important colleagues in ensuring an international economy hospitable to growth, dynamism, and the creative spirit.

The United States should not be complacent about its allies' roles. Europeans say they want to shoulder a greater defense responsibility—and they should—especially when it comes to policing their own continent. But a wide gap still separates Europe's defense oratory and its actual spending on the necessary capabilities. The United States should encourage its NATO allies to face this reality and to recognize the mutual benefit in having European defense forces operating in close concert with the U.S. military through coalitions. Ultimately, an effective European defense arm will require serious participation by British, French, and German troops.

Japan should evolve gradually toward assuming more responsibility for East Asian security, in concert with America and its allies. Only the United States can help Japan's neighbors accept this historic adjustment, which is the key to transforming Japan's domestic opinion. As a start, Japan, the United States, Korea, and Australia should form closer defense ties. Over time, Japan's forces should be more closely integrated to support the U.S. military in Asia. These steps will strengthen the posture of the Pacific democracies toward North Korea, demonstrate to China that it should seek security cooperation (and not competition) with the Asia-Pacific democracies, and channel any increased Japanese capabilities into a reassuring framework.

Second, the United States and its partners face three great challenges in Eurasia: China, Russia, and India. China has been rising, Russia has been weakening, and India has been reassessing its outlook. These are the "big ones," and more mistakes with them could cost America dearly in the future. The United States must be realistic, not romantic, about the prospects for China and Russia. These states should be integrated into the economic, security, and political arrangements that America and its allies have sponsored, although we must be prepared to shield against these countries if integration is not possible. These countries are "works in progress"; they are not yet friends and are certainly not partners, but they need not be enemies. The United States and its allies should explain to both China and Russia the steps that can build on shared interests and lessen differences. Ultimately, America will evaluate its own ability to cooperate—and the world will assess America's willingness to do so—based on concrete actions, not photo opportunities.

India, the world's largest democracy and before long its most populous nation, will play an increasingly important role in Asia. To grow and prosper, it will need to adjust to the global economy. To contribute to its prosperity and regional security, India will need to lower the risk of conflict with its neighbors. And to have influence with India, America must stop ignoring it. A more open India, possessing a broader understanding of its place in the world, could become a valuable partner of the United States in coping with Eurasia's uncertainties. In addition to proposing trade and investment liberalization, the United States should open a regular, high-level security dialogue with India on Eurasia and the challenges to stability.

Third, North America, the EU, and Japan need to reach out to the next group of potential partners. In varying degrees, moving at different paces, countries in central and eastern Europe, Latin America, and East Asia have been opening private markets, building middle classes, and developing representative democracies that respect individual liberties. But these countries have been subject to enormous stresses. With Latin America in particular, the United States has resumed its old, bad habit of overlooking its neighbors until problems compel it to pay attention. Resistance is slowing the momentum for democracy and free markets that Latin America kicked off a decade ago. More debt defaults, rising populism, frustrations with the lack of tangible results from economic reforms, and narcotics traffickers seeking to control governments all threaten to eclipse the movement toward what should be a historic and strategic achievement: a fully democratic and prosperous western hemisphere.

Fourth, the United States must counter those dangerous states that threaten its closest friends, such as Israel, or its vital interests, such as maintaining access to oil in the Persian Gulf. In dealing with the likes of Iraq and North Korea, the United States needs to offer consistent long-term directions to guide coalitions that will deter and even replace their brutal regimes. Concessions to blackmail and threats, even if they serve as temporary expedients, will exacerbate these problems. The United States must retain the initiative so that its opponents are so worried about what America is planning that they cannot plot attacks or new forms of blackmail. Theater and national missile defenses will let the United States counter missiles carrying weapons of mass destruction from those countries that might target U.S. conventional forces or paralyze the United States if it intervenes against their threats. Time is on America's side—not that of these decaying dictatorships—if the United States has the confidence and determination to stand up to, and if necessary defeat, its enemies.

MILITARY MIGHT

America's leadership in the next century requires a strong military, wisely used. The Clinton administration has too often relied on the U.S. military to bail out speculative diplomatic ventures that turned sour. Concurrently, America's military has been cut back some 40 percent. At some point, doing more with less just becomes doing less with less. Given the current demands on the U.S. military, the Pentagon has made the troublesome choice of trying to fund present needs at the expense of future capabilities. This spending improvisation is divorced from the administration's own plans. As the military equipment bought in the early 1980s ages, the armed services are spending more and more funds just to keep old planes, ships, and tanks operating. The administration's undersecretary of defense called this quandary a "death spiral." The chair of the joint chiefs of staff called it a "nosedive." These are strong words. The failure to prepare for the future will become sharply apparent during the next decade, when the wheels start to come off the weapons purchased some 25 years ago. As one Marine general said, "If parents are uncomfortable sending their sons and daughters to college in 25-year-old cars, what will they think about sending them into harm's way in 25-year-old helicopters?"

The challenge for the next president is not just to spend more on defense but to spend wisely. In transforming its defense strategy for the future, the United States should seek to align the military's strength with the nation's strengths: America's people and technology. U.S. companies that have not incorporated the revolutionary advances in information and communications technologies have been swept away by their competition with surprising rapidity. The Pentagon cannot afford to run a similar risk. The United States must invest in a combination of sophisticated sensors, information technology, real-time communications, and precision-guided weapons that will enable the individual services to fight together seamlessly in joint operations. Future networked forces should be smaller, quicker, easier to deploy, more dispersed, and able to destroy targets with fewer sorties and greater "standoff" capabilities. They must be able to act together when executing discrete missions—such as suppressing air defenses, achieving complete air dominance, and destroying small, mobile targets—that will be vital in the new security environment. They will need "more teeth and less tail." At the end of the day, gutsy soldiers in muddy boots will still have to hold ground, but they need to be the fastest to get to decisive points, with the most precise firepower to support them.

This transformation will take time. In many respects, technology is the easy part. The challenge is to integrate technology into new operational concepts, doctrines, and organizational structures—and then to practice them. (In June 1940, the French army had more and better tanks than the German army, but the panzer leaders knew how to use blitzkrieg operations to overwhelm France within weeks.) The experience of the private sector points the way toward a smart, modernized defense for the future. Like private business executives facing new challenges, the next generation of military officers needs clear goals to guide change—and strong support in making the country's forces achieve these goals. Only the president can establish these goals and provide the needed leadership.

The Pentagon can also learn from the private sector about cutting costs. Although the cost of civilian information-technology systems has fallen tremendously, the price of analogous military systems has not. Like other professional organizations, the Defense Department must focus on its core missions and outsource supporting activities. In leading this transformation, the next president must also challenge America's allies to keep up. In critical areas, U.S. allies in Europe and the Pacific can share significant burdens and make major contributions. In order to fight together, their forces must be interoperable. And allies should assume greater roles in peacekeeping operations, supported by unique U.S. capabilities and backed by the hammer of its robust force.

THE RIGHT TRACK

As Americans enter a new century, the history of the last one may inspire a sense of both caution and opportunity. The United States in 1900 seemed to have unbounded potential. But the first half of the twentieth century involved frightful costs. And although America achieved great accomplishments over the past 50 years, these came at a high price of lives, money, and national attention. Now a new generation must chart a course for America amid revolutionary changes in technologies, economies, societies, and weaponry. It is a mistake for the United States simply to react to events. America needs a strategy that blends traditional truths with the opportunities of a networked marketplace and a modernized army. It must be realistic about human nature and conflicting interests while being optimistic about the world's potential. America must deploy its power wisely, selectively, and consistently to mold an international system that will enhance its influence in future events. Drawing on this influence, modern Republicans believe they can work with like-minded Democrats so that America can advance both its interests and its ideals. America's potential is extraordinary, and so is the world's. It is time to get on the right track.

Editors' Note: Democratic views will be published in forthcoming issues.

ROBERT B. ZOELLICK served as Undersecretary of State, White House Deputy Chief of Staff, and Counselor to the Secretary of the Treasury during the Reagan and Bush administrations.

Campaign 2000: New World, New Deal

A Democratic Approach to Globalization

W. Bowman Cutter, Joan Spero,
and Laura D'Andrea Tyson   MARCH/APRIL 2000

Supporters of Vice President Al Gore demonstrate outside the U.S. Supreme
Court which was today set to intervene for the first time in an unresolved
presidential election, December 1, 2000.

AN ERA OF FUNDAMENTAL CHANGE

The United States enters the 21st century as the greatest beneficiary
of the global system it helped create after World War II. As a power
with unrivaled dominance, prosperity, and security, it must now lead
the peaceful evolution of this system through an era of significant
changes. Rapid shifts in technology and the embrace of markets by
developing and formerly communist countries are shifting the balance of power among nations, between nations and nonstate actors,

259

and between nations and global economic forces. New technologies are making the world much more interdependent. These technologies are accelerating the movement of goods, services, ideas, and capital across national boundaries. They are also displacing traditional security threats with nontraditional worries like international terrorism, organized crime, drug trafficking, and environmental degradation while strengthening the capacities of nongovernmental organizations (NGOs) to influence policy. Tension is mounting between the fixed geography of nation-states and the nonterritorial nature of global problems and their solutions.

The United States cannot shield itself from the effects of globalization. In today's interdependent capital markets, global perceptions of the stability of the American economy and the credibility of American economic policy can significantly affect the dollar's value and domestic interest rates. Despite its economic and military might, the United States cannot protect itself from global environmental problems like ozone depletion, climate change, and threats to biodiversity by acting alone.

The international economic challenges facing a new American president are twofold: first, to grasp the fundamental changes in the global economy, and second, to respond by fostering the conditions and institutions required for a world in which the United States can remain secure and prosperous. The central task of international economic policy is to help develop a new system of global economic relations—a task made essential, rather than simply desirable, by the enormous and irreversible changes now sweeping the world.

THE TRANSITIONAL 1990S

When the Clinton administration arrived in Washington in 1993, the changes engulfing the world economy were already under way, but their permanence, magnitude, and implications were still uncertain. In the absence of a reliable road map, the Clinton administration's approach to international economic policy was shaped by a few basic principles, which will also guide the next Democratic president. First, America's leadership is essential to developing and maintaining multilateral rules and institutions—not because they are ends in themselves, but because the health of the global economy depends on them. Second, America's credibility to lead on international economic issues depends first and foremost on the strength of the American economy. Third, the primary goal of American trade policy is improved market access abroad, not protected markets at home. More open markets and greater competition benefit both the United States and its trading partners. Fourth, those who might be harmed by economic change should have the tools to exploit the opportunities that it creates. Among the tools crafted by the Clinton administration are greater portability of health and pension coverage across jobs; individual training accounts and one-stop career centers for federal job-training programs; tax credits for postsecondary education; and substantial increases in the earned-income tax credit. Fifth, economic engagement with emerging countries, including China, serves America's interests because it enhances those countries' prospects for economic reform and political liberalization based on the rule of law.

Finally, national economic interests should not be considered "secondary" or subordinated to traditional security interests. National security must be broadly construed to include both economic and geopolitical concerns. And in many circumstances, economic policies may prove the best instrument for achieving geopolitical objectives.

During the last seven years, the basic principles motivating the international economic policies of the Clinton administration have not changed, but domestic and global circumstances have. The most important domestic change after 1995 was a Congress controlled by Republicans, many of whom are avowedly isolationist and prefer confrontation to cooperation with the Democratic White House. In addition, environmental, labor, and human rights groups have become increasingly well organized and vociferous in their efforts to block further trade liberalization. The result has been the continued erosion of presidential power over trade policy, culminating in successful congressional efforts to block passage of "fast-track" trade authority in 1997 and 1998. This hampered the administration's ability to move its ambitious trade agenda forward. Nonetheless, significant progress has been made during the last three years, including the completion of a global Information Technology Agreement, multilateral agreements on telecommunications and financial services, and an agreement with China on the terms of its accession to the World Trade Organization (WTO).

International economic policy during Clinton's second term has also been affected by the financial crises that erupted around the world in 1997. Working together as they had previously to alleviate Mexico's financial difficulties in 1995, the administration and the Federal Reserve first responded with several ad hoc crisis-management measures, including large International Monetary Fund (IMF) loan packages, informal debt-rescheduling agreements, and interest-rate cuts. These measures brought the world back from the brink of a global credit crunch in late 1998. Since then, the Clinton administration has led multilateral efforts to design new methods for reducing the frequency and intensity of future crises. The next Democratic president will have to shepherd these efforts as the global community searches for more effective ways to contain recurrent financial crises in a world of highly mobile private capital.

The protests at the WTO meetings in Seattle last November have been interpreted by some as a sign that globalization is in retreat. But the response of emerging markets to the pain of the 1997–98 financial crises is a more powerful sign that globalization will continue. Rather than turning inward and reverting to state controls over economic activity, these countries have continued on the path of market reform and greater integration into the world economy—affirming the basic principles of President Clinton's international economic agenda. Still, these recent crises, along with symptoms of a populist backlash against globalization in the United States and elsewhere, provide compelling evidence of the need for better management of the world economy.

To meet the challenges posed by the dramatic changes in the global economy during the 1990s, the next Democratic president should focus on three broad objectives: nurturing strategic partnerships with old, new, and changing players; strengthening existing multilateral regimes; and creating new regimes for emerging transnational issues including the environment, labor rights, and the appropriate governance of the global information economy.

THE CORE

History indicates that a preeminent power cannot long maintain its global leadership without the support and cooperation of other nations in the pursuit of agreed-upon interests. Hence forging a consensus with other major powers on international economic objectives and how to share the costs of achieving them will be key tasks confronting the new president.

One of the new centers of power is a united Europe. On the economic front, the European Union (EU) is already a reality. A common currency, free trade, and more unified regulations are propelling cross-border flows of money, goods, services, and people. Cross-border mergers and restructuring are making European firms more competitive and European capital markets more flexible. With time, the EU will gain new members, including Poland, Hungary, the Czech Republic, Slovenia, Estonia, and Turkey. Other central European and Baltic countries will complete the transition from communism to capitalism and will either join the EU or establish close economic ties with it. Although Europe will not form a supranational state, policy coordination among member states will gradually increase. The EU already conducts trade negotiations as a single entity. With the creation of European economic and monetary union and the establishment of a common currency and central bank, Europe will increasingly act as one on financial and monetary issues.

The next Democratic president must define American economic relations with Europe in terms of the EU. As it has long done, the United States should encourage European unification, which is a stabilizing, modernizing force. But while Europeans share U.S. goals and values, they also increasingly resent American economic, political, and security hegemony. Thus the next president must work to ensure that Europe does not turn inward and that transatlantic economic, political, and security ties are strengthened. The Clinton administration has already laid the groundwork for ongoing high-level dialogue with the Europeans on economic cooperation and common global challenges through the New Transatlantic Agenda.

Russia is a thornier challenge. The West has a profound interest in Russia's transition to a market economy and has been trying to help. Although this transition has been marred by corruption, on-again, off-again reforms, and a dramatic 1998 financial collapse, progress has been made during the 1990s. Russian citizens enjoy more basic freedoms in speech, travel, and religion and are more connected to the rest of the world than at any time in the twentieth century. Russia has a functioning central bank and stock and foreign-exchange markets, and two-thirds of Russian property is no longer under state control. Moreover, the "meltdown" of the Russian economy predicted after its 1998 default has not occurred. In fact, over the last year, industrial production has increased, the trade balance has improved, and Russian firms show signs of restructuring. By exploding the myth in global capital markets that Russia is too big to fail, the 1998 financial crisis weakened Russia's corrupt oligarchs and forced the Russian economy toward greater efficiency in the face of more realistic budget constraints. Perhaps most important, those now vying for political leadership in Russia—even the Communists—agree that there is no real alternative to market reform.

The next Democratic president must continue America's constructive engagement with Russia, relying wherever possible on multilateral institutions like the IMF and on cooperation with other advanced industrial countries. American policy should continue to be multifaceted, including trade; financial and technical assistance; educational exchanges; and programs to help Russia develop its civic institutions to combat corruption and safeguard an independent media. But America's interactions with Russia should not be based on illusions. Even with the West's financial and technical assistance, economic progress in Russia will be slow, unsteady, and largely dependent on political decisions made there. And the primary reason for the West's engagement with Russia is not economic—the Russian economy is too small to have much influence on global economic conditions—but geopolitical. Under the Clinton administration's leadership, more than 1,500 Russian nuclear warheads have been deactivated, and more than 300 missile launchers have been destroyed. Through the Cooperative Threat Reduction Program, the United States is working with the Russian leadership to try to ensure that Russian weapons of mass destruction do not fall into the wrong hands. Despite these successes, however, Russia poses a continuing nuclear-proliferation and security threat that must remain the central focus of American policy.

Asia poses quite different challenges. After a decade of stagnation, Japan is taking the first steps toward fundamental changes in its economic system. These changes are undermining traditional ways of doing business in Japan, including its lifetime employment system, its keiretsu supplier system, and its cross-shareholding system of "insider" corporate governance. Last year witnessed a dramatic increase in mergers and acquisitions in Japan, and foreign financial institutions were the dominant players. Foreign direct investment (FDI) increased sharply, although from a very low base. In a break with its past behavior, Tokyo has been promoting FDI, and the structural barriers to Japan's market that were a major irritant in U.S.-Japanese relations throughout most of the last quarter-century are gradually falling. Moreover, greater FDI will encourage imports into Japan by multinational companies operating there. Japan's imports will probably rise substantially as a share of its economy over the next decade, and U.S. firms—with their strong competitive position in information technologies—will likely win a significant share of Japan's market. Even during the 1990s, when slow growth depressed Japan's overall demand for U.S.

imports, the U.S. surplus in services trade with Japan increased steadily, reflecting the strong competitive edge of American companies. Nonetheless, Japan's transition to a more open economic system will not make the substantial U.S.-Japan trade imbalance disappear, for two reasons. First, despite its economic difficulties, Japan has remained a formidable competitor in many global markets, and its painful restructuring will only increase its long-run competitiveness; and second, differences in aggregate growth rates and changes in the dollar-yen exchange rate will continue to be the major force behind changes in the bilateral trade balance.

During Clinton's first term, the United States engaged Japan in highly charged bilateral trade talks, relying on deadlines and threats. Both the goals of these negotiations and their sometimes combative tone reflected more than a decade of escalating trade deficits between the United States and Japan and frustration from American companies over structural barriers to Japan's markets. During Clinton's second term, trade tensions began to ease as Japan's macroeconomic crisis intensified and as the terms of previous trade agreements were implemented. Currently, Washington is pursuing a two-pronged series of negotiations with Tokyo on deregulation and investment. Unlike prior talks, these negotiations have neither deadlines nor specific targets—nor much rancor.

The next Democratic president should continue this approach and maintain a high-level bilateral dialogue on trade. Such a dialogue lets both countries air complaints and avoid confrontation, thereby shielding other aspects of their relationship from commercial tensions. Regular high-level conversations also let the two countries develop joint initiatives on shared global economic challenges and common objectives for multilateral organizations like the WTO. Increasingly, the United States must treat Japan not just as an ally but as a partner in safeguarding economic, political, and military security in the Asia-Pacific, strengthening existing multilateral institutions, and building new ones.

The next Democratic president should continue Clinton's policy of constructive engagement with China. China's gradual emergence as a great power is a central feature of the new global system, and America's long-run interests are best served by China's stable evolution toward a more open, democratic system based on the rule of law. Constructive engagement with China does not guarantee this outcome, but it is the best option for increasing its likelihood. China may not be America's ally or partner—but as a result of constructive engagement, it has acted responsibly on issues of mutual importance like Hong Kong, North Korea, and Asia's financial crisis.

Constructive engagement is not an endorsement of China's human rights behavior. But revoking normal trading relations with China or blocking its WTO membership will not improve such behavior. Indeed, the opposite is true. Commercial considerations may seem crass when compared with human rights, but impeding commercial relations with China would impede the flow of information about Western culture, ideas, and business practices to China's emerging middle class and weaken reformers in the state and party leadership.

What about China's trade behavior? Don't large U.S. deficits with China imply that it engages in unfair trading practices? Won't China violate the rules of the multilateral system once it gains admission to the WTO and its trading partners lose leverage? Probably not. China does not enjoy a persistent current-account surplus—a defining characteristic of a mercantilist state. Moreover, China has encouraged FDI as part of its development strategy. Indeed, foreign-funded companies in China accounted for more than half of the growth of its exports during the last decade. China's openness to FDI will mean increased imports in the future. In the final WTO deal announced last November, China made big concessions on trade in manufactured goods, agriculture, and services. It further yielded to America's insistence on special protections against unexpected import surges from China. The consensus among China experts is that the WTO deal is a bold—some would say desperate—move by China's leaders to forge ahead with market reforms despite substantial adjustment costs. Finally, China's performance in other multilateral institutions indicates that it will honor its end of the bargain. And should violations occur, the United States will be able to turn to the WTO dispute-settlement mechanism to enforce compliance.

Another controversial aspect of economic relations with China is whether and how to regulate American exports of dual-use technologies—those with substantial military and commercial applications—to China and other countries that may pose security risks. Banning the export of such technologies seems to some the simplest way to safeguard American national security. But this approach is both ineffective and counterproductive. The United States is not the sole source for such products, so a unilateral ban would merely drive would-be importers to other suppliers. And for many dual-use goods, America's national security hinges on the success of their American producers in the commercial marketplace. Unilateral export controls undermine this success and thereby endanger national security. This realization lies behind the gradual easing of export controls by the American government since the end of the Cold War, a trend that the next administration should continue.

Like China, many other emerging nations are restructuring their political and economic systems, pursuing market policies, and shifting their world-views. The United States must work to engage these new players, together with existing powers, in the processes and institutions on which governance of the global economy depends.

Two of these new players—India and Brazil—are virtually certain to develop significant regional, if not global, influence and are strategically important to the United States. India has the smaller economy of the two but seems closest to a sustained breakthrough in economic growth. More rapidly than is generally realized, India is likely to become an important factor in the strategic equation in Asia as a whole. And Brazil, as a result of its size, economic development, and leadership of the Mercosur trade bloc, has already become an important factor in Latin America. Over time, other nations like South Korea, Mexico, and South Africa will probably grow in influence and become part of the complex coalitions of nations required to address global economic problems.

PUTTING IT TOGETHER

The next Democratic president must strengthen America's alliance with the other major players—Europe and Japan—to reshape existing multilateral institutions and rules and create new ones as necessary. Emphasizing cooperation with these nations will also discourage them from turning inward or creating competing economic blocs. The United States, Europe, and Japan still account for about two-thirds of global GDP. They have similar levels of per capita GDP, effective legal and regulatory regimes, and highly developed capital markets. All trade and invest more with each other than with other regions of the world, and all are becoming information and network economies. The United States, Europe, and Japan should, therefore, be able to agree on many of the new challenges posed by globalization and the information revolution; negotiate free-trade areas in services, investment, and electronic commerce; adopt common guidelines for intellectual property and privacy; develop common regulatory standards in sectors such as biotechnology, the environment, health, and food safety; and agree on qualifications for professions and industries. New forms of cooperation and joint decision-making among these three great powers should be carefully designed to support the multilateral system, and agreements among them should be open to participation by other countries or adoption by other multilateral institutions.

Historically, the G-7 group of highly industrialized nations has promoted economic cooperation among the United States, Europe, and Japan by engaging their heads of state in annual discussions about mutual concerns and creating working groups in each nation to develop mutual solutions. In recent years, however, the G-7 process has begun to lose its relevance because it excludes other nations important to the global economy. Because an ongoing, high-level dialogue among the heads of the world's major economic powers is important to the United States, the next Democratic president should encourage the G-7 to broaden its membership to include Russia (which is already included in most discussions), Brazil, China, and India.

The recent failure of the WTO talks in Seattle demonstrates the foolishness of launching global trade talks before developing a consensus on the issues among the United States, Europe, and Japan—still the largest trading nations in the world. But the lessons of the Seattle debacle go deeper.

First, the low-hanging fruit in multilateral trade negotiations has already been picked. In previous rounds, tariffs were slashed and quotas eliminated for most trade in manufactured products. Future negotiations will focus on agriculture and services—sectors that are politically sensitive and highly regulated by individual countries, including the United States—and will involve such traditionally domestic issues as antitrust policy, consumer safety, and other regulatory questions. Crafting multilateral agreements on such issues will be a long, painful process. And enforcing compliance with such agreements, which require nations to change entire areas of domestic law, will prove much harder than enforcing compliance with previous agreements barring overt trade barriers. Establishing a permanent executive committee within the WTO to replace the loose ambassadorial mechanism that currently proposes new multilateral trade talks could help. And the pointless practice of holding biennial WTO meetings at the ministerial level, even when there is nothing substantive to discuss, should end.

Second, given the complicated nature of future issues and the unwieldy number of future participants, the "global round" approach to trade talks—involving all WTO participants in a comprehensive agenda requiring bargains across several sectors—may have outlived its usefulness. Since it will be so difficult to forge consensus on the agenda for another global round, negotiations focused on liberalizing trade in individual sectors are an attractive alternative. In recent years, such negotiations have produced significant agreements in the diverse areas of information technology, telecommunications, and financial services. Moreover, since there is still much to do to implement these agreements, consolidating their achievements may be the best way to strengthen the multilateral trading system and achieve real progress over the next few years.

Third, to fight the burgeoning backlash against globalization and build public trust, WTO operations must become more transparent. At the same time, new multilateral approaches must be developed to address global concerns in other areas such as the environment, labor rights, and human rights. The next Democratic president should encourage such efforts while making sure that the WTO maintains its focus on trade. The WTO exists to develop and enforce trade agreements, and such agreements exist to foster trade. The WTO is not the appropriate forum for other issues, although it could adjust over time to permit trade restrictions to enforce multilateral pacts on issues negotiated elsewhere.

In the meantime, the United States should eschew unilateral trade restrictions, including sanctions, to compel other nations to comply with American laws on the environment, labor practices, or human rights. During the last several years, America has imposed some form of unilateral economic sanctions against 26 countries, accounting for half the world's population. These sanctions have not achieved their goals; indeed, sanctions often harm exactly those they seek to help. And sanctions have cost the United States about $20 billion in lost exports, 200,000 jobs, and the goodwill and trust of its allies abroad.

Finally, the next Democratic president must continue to educate the American public about the ways the U.S. economy is helped by enforceable multilateral trading rules. As the largest exporting country and the one with the lowest trade barriers, the United States reaps the greatest benefits from trade liberalization. The more countries trade with one another, the better off they are. But the more they need multilateral rules to settle disputes, the more these rules influence domestic practices. Still, the WTO is not a world government that can override or proscribe its members' laws. If the United States loses a case before the WTO, it can either retain its domestic laws and accept trade sanctions from the complaining nation or adjust these laws to eliminate discrimination against foreign producers.

Regional economic integration can complement and spur multilateral liberalization. It can also contribute to political stability. For these reasons, the next Democratic president should build on the efforts of the Clinton administration to promote regional cooperation and liberalization in both Asia and Latin America. The Asia-Pacific Economic Cooperation forum is the basis for a sound economic strategy in the Pacific basin. Its membership boasts a number of important regional players (among them China, Japan, South Korea, Mexico, and the members of the Association of Southeast Asian Nations), it provides a useful forum for the region's heads of state, and it is committed to trade liberalization and cooperation in fields from telecommunications to basic infrastructure.

Building on the success of the North American Free Trade Agreement, the United States has convinced Latin American countries to agree on a broad economic agenda whose centerpiece is the creation of a Free Trade Agreement for the Americas (FTAA), with additional cooperation on the environment, human rights, crime, and other global issues. The next Democratic president should accelerate the FTAA process, which has been hampered by the absence of fast-track trade authority. Without such a process, American influence in the region will diminish, and the likelihood of competing economic zones will increase.

FOR RICHER, FOR POORER

As globalization has intensified, the gap between per capita incomes in rich and poor countries has widened. Although this trend has been around for the past two centuries, it has accelerated in recent years. For the many emerging countries that already have the institutions and income levels to attract private capital and the education levels to prosper in the new information age, the private sector will fuel continued economic development. Indeed, for most of these countries, the economic development problem—although substantial—is best understood as an internal poverty problem. But this is not so for the nations of Africa, many of which are being left behind.

What should the next Democratic president do to address human needs and spur economic development in the most impoverished nations? First, the White House should espouse complete debt forgiveness for the world's poorest nations. Second, the president should lobby to increase America's inadequate foreign-aid budget and redirect it toward programs to meet basic human needs—for example, a U.S.-led effort among the developed nations to counter the aids epidemic in Africa or to establish a special fund to help the poorest nations honor multilateral environmental agreements. Third, the president should work with other advanced nations to reduce tariffs, ease antidumping penalties, and lower quotas on trade with developing countries. Finally, the administration should foster cooperation with the NGOs that already deliver more development assistance than the entire U.N. system, including the World Bank and the IMF.

EARTH IN THE BALANCE

The next Democratic president should establish a bipartisan group of experts to assess the lessons learned from recent financial crises, evaluate the adjustments already under way, and recommend additional changes. At the same time, the president should pledge America's commitment to the World Bank and the IMF, emphasizing their importance while recognizing the need for further reform. Such reform should be guided by two considerations. First, these institutions must adjust to the vastly greater scope and scale of private cross-border capital flows. Second, they must find ways to engage more of the public in the countries to which they lend—both to use their resources more efficiently and to help promote the stable civil societies on which successful economic development depends.

A growing number of environmental problems—ozone depletion, global climate change, threats to biodiversity—are international in scope and require cross-border solutions. Industrial countries, including the United States, are disproportionately responsible for most of these environmental problems, but developing countries are also rapidly damaging common environmental resources. Solutions, therefore, require the participation of both developed and developing nations. But since the costs and benefits of addressing common environmental problems vary among countries, as do the available resources, global agreements must include effective transfer mechanisms and flexibility about the methods used by different countries to achieve environmental targets.

No vehicle exists for nations to negotiate new multilateral pacts on environmental issues. That is one big reason why environmentalists have focused on the WTO. But using the WTO as the forum for multilateral environmental negotiations both endangers further trade liberalization and raises the risk that trade will be restricted in the name of environmentalism but in the service of protectionism. To head off these risks, a new Democratic president should propose creating a new Global Environmental Organization to develop and enforce new international agreements on specific problems, using the successful Montreal protocol on slowing ozone depletion as a model.

In recent years, a growing number of NGOs at home and abroad have called for a set of internationally recognized and enforced labor standards that would ban child labor and sweatshops and support workers' rights to organize. Logically, labor rights and standards are development and political issues, not trade issues. There is no evidence that trade undermines labor standards and leads to an international "race to the bottom." In fact, the opposite is true. Most global trade still occurs between developed countries, which enjoy the highest wages, labor standards, and productivity levels. And as trade and integration in the global economy have helped poor countries develop, their wages, productivity, and labor standards have improved. Developing countries that have strengthened their labor standards have done so because of more trade and integration, not less.

Despite such evidence, labor standards will move up the agenda of international economic negotiations as global integration continues. And the next Democratic president will have to be sensitive to the desires of both NGOs and organized labor for global workers' standards. Given the opposition of most of the rest of the world, however, this will not be easy. So Clinton's heir should continue to promote his reasonable Seattle approach of establishing a multilateral discussion group to examine some labor rights issues, including child labor and sweatshop conditions. The group should include the International Labor Organization, the United Nations, and the World Bank, and it should be charged with reporting its findings to the WTO by a specified date. Second, the president should encourage the private sector to develop labeling systems and codes of conduct certifying compliance with core labor standards. One promising effort is a program called Social Accountability 8000, launched by the Council of Economic Priorities and a group of influential American companies to encourage firms to comply with labor and human rights standards. Another is the United Nations' proposed Global Compact with Business, under which the U.N. will help multinational companies meet internationally accepted principles of human rights, labor practices, and environmental standards.

Third, the president must continue to educate the American people about the way trade boosts labor standards by highlighting American firms that have improved working conditions in their foreign operations. Polls indicate that most Americans would rather buy from companies committed to ending worker abuses and that American consumers would be willing to pay somewhat more for products made in worker-friendly environments. In addition, a growing number of American multinationals recognize that bad publicity about working conditions in their foreign operations can damage their reputations and bottom lines. A new Democratic president can effectively use the bully pulpit to shine the spotlight on American firms that are doing well by doing good and encourage a "race to the top."

Nations must also begin to work with one another and the business community to define appropriate policies for the world of e-business. Without cooperation, different policy regimes will develop within different regions and nations, each attempting to govern phenomena that are inherently transnational. Different sets of rules will in turn generate unnecessary transaction costs and slow the diffusion of wealth and knowledge made possible by the new technologies.

To date, the Clinton administration has avoided regulation of the networked economy at home and made the case for a similar approach abroad. American officials had hoped to include digital issues on the agenda for the next global trade round, but that has been delayed by the failure of the Seattle talks. In addition, the Seattle discussions suggest that even when a new round begins, negotiations will focus on highly visible, politically contentious issues such as agriculture, textiles, and dumping that traditionally dominate trade debates, rather than on digital issues.

Therefore, it is time to develop a specific multilateral process focusing exclusively on such issues. This should be a principal objective of the next Democratic president. There are three logical steps: first, establishing a trade and investment round within the WTO focusing specifically on e-commerce; second, developing a set of basic principles for such talks, with a broad agenda including crime prevention, privacy, intellectual property, taxation (including the possible establishment of a multilateral tax clearing-house), and dispute settlement processes; and third, providing access to the networked economy for all nations and regions. The last step will require targeted lending programs funded by the World Bank, NGOs, and developed countries to help the poorest countries build the necessary infrastructure.

STAY ON TARGET

The United States has benefited from globalization. Throughout much of the 1990s, exports accounted for about a third of U.S. growth. Even when American exports slowed in response to recessions in emerging markets, the same financial crises causing these recessions also increased flows of capital into American financial markets and reduced import prices for American consumers, fueling America's continued economic expansion during the last three years. This expansion—now the longest in the nation's history—has produced the lowest unemployment rate in more than 30 years and raised incomes for all groups of American workers, including the least skilled. True, the nation's trade and current-account deficits have hit record levels, but these primarily reflect the relative strength of the American economy compared to its trading partners and the resulting strength of the dollar, not an increase in protectionist barriers abroad.

It is easy to understand why a populist backlash against globalization has taken hold in much of the world, plagued by an endemic poverty made worse by recent contractions. As hundreds of millions of people in emerging markets have seen their jobs and incomes decimated by global financial shocks, modern information technologies have shown them images of American prosperity—and of American officials and business leaders lecturing them about the necessity of painful sacrifice. Signs of an emerging backlash against globalization in the United States, although perhaps harder to justify, are inflamed by some of the same concerns: rising income inequality, job insecurity in a rapidly changing and harshly competitive environment, and a sense of powerlessness and uncertainty about the future.

Economic integration among nations, although beneficial overall, does create winners and losers. And even many winners fear that the next wave of change spawned by footloose capital and technological change will make them losers. To allay such concerns about globalization, the next American president must design policies to sustain America's expansion and give Americans the tools they need in the global marketplace. Among the most important of these are lifetime education and training opportunities, portable and fair pensions and health-care benefits, and a safety net to support incomes during periods of adjustment or recession.

At the same time, the next president must work with the leaders of other nations to develop multilateral agreements and institutions to ease the economic downsides of globalization and address new global issues. As President Clinton noted in his 1998 speech before the Council on Foreign Relations, the multilateral system must evolve toward a kind of "Global New Deal." The painful experiences of many transition economies and the unexpected financial crises of the 1990s have reminded the world that to work well, markets require a strong commitment to the rule of law, transparent financial institutions, legitimate corporate and political governance structures, and adequate social safety nets. As the new millennium begins, a new Democratic president will have the opportunity to lead the world in creating institutions and policies to sustain a more equitable process of globalization built on the marvels of the market and modern technologies.

W. BOWMAN CUTTER is Managing Director of Warburg, Pincus and served as Deputy Assistant to President Clinton for Economic Policy.

JOAN SPERO is President of the Doris Duke Charitable Foundation and served as Undersecretary of State for Economic, Business, and Agricultural Affairs from 1993 to 1997.

LAURA D'ANDREA TYSON is Dean of the Haas School of Business at the University of California at Berkeley and served as National Economic Adviser and Chair of the Council of Economic Advisers during President Clinton's first term. They advise Vice President Al Gore's presidential campaign on economic issues.

A Republican Looks at Foreign Policy

James A. Leach   SUMMER 1992

President George H.W. Bush at the White House, August 29, 1990.

erspective is always difficult to apply to events of the day.
Centuries hence, however, historians will surely conclude
that this generation of Americans stood poised on a hinge of
history. Beginning with the east European revolutions of 1989 the
world has witnessed an astounding cataract of events, the triumphant culmination of forty years of steadfast alliance diplomacy.

America's principal adversary, the once-formidable Soviet empire, has collapsed from without and within. Militarily the threat
of sudden Muscovite aggression and of nuclear Armageddon has
diminished to imperceptibility. Philosophically communism is in
retreat, pell-mell. Economically the liberating logic of the free
market has challenged the world's remaining Marxist governments
with contrasting models of such greater efficiency and opportunity

that the demise of centralized-planning regimes is heralded, with only the time frame in doubt.

Through a strategy of economic development and political containment the United States and the community of free nations have achieved a more decisive victory over Bolshevism than could ever have been gained through war.

Meanwhile only one short year ago in the Persian Gulf, President Bush assembled an unprecedented international coalition to uphold the rule of law. For the first time since Franklin Roosevelt's New Deal, an American president has defined his presidency with a theme—New World Order—developed in action (or more precisely, reaction) rather than as campaign sloganeering.

II

Absent stark Cold War contrasts, the challenge for American leadership in the decade ahead will be to chart a course that is inclusive, not exclusive, of perspectives developed beyond our shores. America must look to constructive internationalism; to Pacificism, rather than pacifism; to Atlanticism rather than mere alliance-ism; to leadership of the Americas, rather than insular America First-ism.

The politics of hard times at home, however, has led some in American public life to suggest myopically that Russian roulette be played with our economy and national security by retreating from larger world affairs. At a time when public frustration with Congress has never been higher, a legislative branch on trial has caused members to become overwrought with concern for political survival; courage and largeness of the human spirit are not hallmarks of a legislative body fighting to reestablish both public and self respect.

The consequence of the American people's dwindling confidence in Congress is the potential breakdown not just of bipartisan but bi-institutional foreign policy. The demoralization of Congress has led to another Dullesque reappraisal of U.S. foreign policy, which is potentially most troubling in the area of commerce, where the Constitution gives the legislative branch a larger role than in state-to-state political relations.

The combination of political institutions in disrepute and an economy without growth has resulted in a dispirited civil polity, increased partisanship and pressure from the extremes of the political spectrum to play ostrich politics, to construct a Fortress America, to revive lost causes and lost illusions. However seductive, the lure of neo-isolationism—the dream of returning to relative economic autarky and somnolent continental security—appeals to the nostalgic instincts of the American public, much as do Norman Rockwell's depictions of the American character.

The danger of this contemporary "America First" movement is neither its premise nor its romanticism, but its implications: that the United States has nothing left to gain from or contribute to international peace and prosperity; that America should be an observer rather than a leader of the world; that political ambition can best be advanced by manipulating parochial fears rather than enlarging the human horizon.

Key leaders in Congress, largely Democratic, continue to peddle a protectionist insularism that amounts to a gospel of retreat from progressive foreign policy values. Frustrated by a dozen years of Republican control of the White House, theirs is the easy wisdom of those without accountability, the irresponsibility of semi-permanent foreign policy opposition. Hence the vacillation implicit in the refusal to endorse the president's approach to the Gulf War, and exasperated opportunism reflected in vehement anti-foreign aid pronouncements coupled simultaneously with criticism of the president for lacking the vision to present a forthcoming Soviet aid package. Hence also the hypocrisy of claiming to desire warmer, more respectful relations with Latin America while placing a series of delaying roadblocks in the paths of President Bush's North American Free Trade Area proposal and of his debt forgiveness and debt-for-nature swap programs that, with his investment program, comprise the Enterprise for the Americas Initiative.

On the Republican right, protest candidate Patrick A. Buchanan defines himself more in the tradition of Father Coughlin than Robert Taft. Repudiating core tenets of Nixonian and Reaganite foreign policy, Buchanan mixes diplomatic disengagement, economic protection and appeals to a new American nativism into a political apostasy rooted more in the nineteenth-century anti-immigrant biases of the Know-Nothings than the Lincolnian model of societal sacrifice to broaden the scope of individual rights and social tolerance.

In foreign policy the twentieth-century Republican tradition includes Theodore Roosevelt's brand of principled brigandage, Harding's coolness to the League of Nations and Wendell Willkie's "one worldism." In its history the G.O.P. has been isolationist and interventionist, unilateral and multilateral. Out of power, or at least outside the executive branch, it tends to intemperance. In power, in the last half century, with the possible exception of Reagan's first term, it has been professional, prepared and progressive.

President Bush has had the good fortune to oversee and lead a world in transition. The thaw in East-West relations has precipitated the winding down or conclusion of a number of bloody regional conflicts—from Afghanistan to Angola to Cambodia to Nicaragua and, at long last, war-torn El Salvador. And, in the cauldron that is the Middle East, the United States has embarked on a high-risk strategy to facilitate a process that could lead to a comprehensive peace.

Writing in 1950, Reinhold Niebuhr noted that the price of survival was our ability to give leadership to the free world. Today the price of the prosperity of the free world still depends on our ability and willingness to lead. No other society has the capacity or inclination to light freedom's lamp in quite the same way; nor is any other as capable of combining self-interest with a genuine historically rooted concern for others. For the United States to deny its transnational responsibilities and thwart the development of internationalist approaches to problem-solving is to jeopardize a future of peace and greater prosperity.

No principle of American foreign policy, no understanding of American history or the American people, no sober appreciation of the limits of our power or moral authority commends a Pax

Americana. By the same token no prudent statesman, surveying the breadth of our international interests and responsibilities, could find security or virtue in a new isolationism.

III

Few issues are more important to our long-term national interest than the future of democracy and free enterprise in the former Soviet Union and former Soviet bloc. President Nixon was correct when he observed in March 1992 that concern for the fate of the political and economic reforms in Russia had been a casualty of the early presidential primaries.

It may be ironic that it was Nixon who staked out the moral high ground on such a crucial strategic issue (and doubly so that it was a former manipulator of wage and price controls who expressed such telling criticism of politicians in both parties for pandering to voters in an election year). Nevertheless, while the greatest unfought war in history may be won, peace remains elusive. Failure of the West to engage in helping alleviate the problems in the wake of communism's demise carries as many liabilities today as failure to contain communist expansionism would have forty years ago.

Establishment thinking in Washington for much of the last decade centered on the dubious assumption that American interests were intertwined with those of Gorbachev and his commitment to preserve the Soviet Union. Gorbachev's claim to historical significance cannot be denied—primarily because like Tokugawa Keiki, the last shogun of Japan, he chose to yield rather than confront popular sentiment with the force of arms. Yet the weakness of Gorbachev's political mandate was revealed by the speed with which he, titular head of the world's largest army and internal security force, went from being a leader without a constituency to almost irrelevant status as the former chief of state of a nonexistent country.

While startling and unexpected in its swiftness, the collapse of the Soviet empire is a historical turning point that Americans should understand more profoundly than any other society, because the self-determination asserted by the newly independent states is rooted in the principles of our Declaration of Independence.

Seldom has there been a more profound conjunction of American philosophy and American national interest than in the self-determination issues involved in the splintering of the Soviet state. Despite the fact that nuclear weapons management has become more complex and that irredentism and violent ethnic prejudices, repressed for almost three-quarters of a century, have resurfaced as if merely buried in a time capsule, the threat of dealing with 15 democratizing republics has to be considered less challenging to American national interests than that emanating from a single united despotic state. There simply could be no better safeguard for our national security than the development of a multiplicity of independent Eurasian governments accountable to free peoples.

Marx notwithstanding, the real opiate of the twentieth century is intolerance, the instinct for hatred that becomes manifest in the individual and is unleashed in society when governments fail to provide safeguards for human rights and fail to erect civilizing institutions adaptable to change and accountable to the people. As the old world order passes and a new one is experimented with, policymakers have an obligation to look beyond the balance-of-power politics to a new civil community. The wolf is still at the door in relations between states, between peoples of differing ethnic and religious composition, and among the economic have-nots of the globe.

The immediate challenge for America is to craft techniques that nurture democratic values and retard the prospect of regression to police-state controls and aggressive foreign policies on the Eurasian land mass. Winning peace is always less costly than waging war, but it is not cheap; nor in some instances is it easy to justify to political constituencies. Yet, as Washington well understands but not so well dares to explain to the public, little is more worrisome than punitive indifference, as the victors of World War I applied to Germany. Likewise, little in retrospect appears more successfully enlightened than the more generous approach taken toward the losers of World War II.

In the long run, free enterprise and trade are the only answers; in the short run, a modest amount of humanitarian, technical and international financial assistance to the former Soviet republics may be the cheapest national security insurance policy the United States can consider taking out. Direct U.S. aid ought to emphasize exchange programs, humanitarian assistance—principally food and medicine—and help in dismantlement of nuclear weapons systems. For economic development and financial assistance, the West should rely primarily on the three relevant multilateral institutions: the World Bank, the International Monetary Fund and the newly created European Bank for Reconstruction and Development.

The role of the multilateral institutions should be stressed for three reasons. First, reliance on international institutions implies shared rather than singular U.S. aid responsibility; our European allies and Japan will provide the majority of financial resources. Second, in addition to leveraging dollars, these institutions allow the West to leverage principles. Few governments are prone to bow to pressure for market-oriented reform coming from a single country. Many, however, will institute politically difficult reforms as prerequisites for IMF and World Bank support. Third, in most cases the international financial institutions make loans rather than grants and have a far better record of receiving repayment than any individual country. Indeed, in the 1980s the United States earned over $600 million a year through participation in IMF loans.

While Americans may differ on the role and composition of foreign aid, consensus should be obtainable on the notion that progressive change can most likely be institutionalized through expanded trade and investment ties. Aid without trade is a prescription for dependency, not self-sufficiency. Likewise aid without the development of a free-enterprise psychology and legal infrastructure will be of fleeting significance. Unless laws are developed that protect property and provide incentives for entrepreneurship, all of the newly established states of the former Soviet Union and erstwhile Soviet bloc will likely stagnate for decades with per capita GNP wallowing at the level of less developed countries. What the former socialist states need is a cultural reordering of attitudes toward the relation of the state and individual. This can only occur through the widest possible contact with the West, particularly America.

What the West must do is conjoin political and economic principles, emphasizing that democracy and free enterprise go hand in hand and that those states that move the most progressively in tandem are likely to be recipients of most public assistance as well as private investment. In this regard the non-Russian republics of the former Soviet Union should be singled out for sympathetic concern, with the new leaders of the Kremlin put on frank notice that efforts to thwart independence movements, whether in the Baltics, Ukraine or Georgia, will be looked on with political disfavor carrying negative trade and investment implications.

Social dislocation too often leads to scapegoats and easy solutions, to a search for a strong man, a Ukrainian Mussolini or a Russian Milošević. Likewise the pace of reform itself may lead to disillusionment, like that expressed by Russian nihilist Dimitri Pisarev, who suggested in the mid-nineteenth century that a pair of boots was of more intrinsic human value than all the plays of Shakespeare. If communism is not simply to give way to nihilism, hope must be provided in democracy, market economics and trade.

The United States should not shy away from offering free trade agreements to the countries of east-central Europe and the Baltic. Such agreements would assure market access to the United States, stand as a beckoning incentive for foreign investment, counterbalance potential German dominance of the region and serve to undercut from behind any exterior trade walls the west Europeans might consider erecting.

IV

Nationalism may be an instrument for liberty. It may also be a harbinger of intolerance that must be vigilantly guarded against, especially in the part of Europe that has given birth to the two epochal conflicts of this century.

In Europe George Kennan's historic policy of containment represented a near-war defined as a Cold War response to the aggressive tendencies of a powerful totalitarian adversary. Premised on that containment doctrine, NATO's strategic policy and deterrence posture successfully thwarted any expansionist ambitions in Europe that may have been entertained by the Kremlin.

The very success of NATO ironically jeopardizes its future. But as new doctrines are considered care must be taken that NATO be sustained with a structure and a mission that provide security for the preservation of liberty in central and eastern Europe. While progressive winds continue to blow from behind the collapsed iron curtain, NATO must be prepared to deal with contingencies that may develop from a shift in these winds, accidental escalations or political misjudgments.

Unity based on common threat is easier to obtain than one based on common aspirations. The immediate challenges to NATO are likely to come more from within than without, from ethnic and nationalist discord and emerging parochialism on trade, with the resultant danger that a global trading system may collapse at precisely the moment when the peoples of east-central Europe need open markets most.

In 1944 Walter Lippmann coined the term "Atlantic Community" to convey America's strategic interest in the successful postwar reconstruction of Europe. Almost fifty years later, and half a world away, it is time for the United States to help establish a "Pacific Community," to convey our political and economic interests in the Far East and in reawakening south Asia.

The linchpin of American policy in the Far East is our relationship with Japan. The good news in the relationship is that, despite a hiccup in 1991, the bilateral trade deficit continues to decline, and that at long last American business has begun to warm to the task of competing and winning in the difficult Japanese market. The bad news is that in tough economic times national moods take on an uglier, more pessimistic tone, manifested in Japan-bashing and, across the Pacific, in kenbei.

Yet despite the rising tension America and Japan continue to share a remarkable coincidence of interests. All the United States asked of Japan at the end of World War II was that it be democratic, oriented toward free enterprise and peaceful. The competitive concerns Americans evidence today stem from the Japanese heeding our advice too well rather than too little.

The United States and Japan represent 40 percent of the world economy; neither can allow trade disputes to poison this relationship. The best way to keep simmering tensions manageable is for the two countries to work together to defend and expand a free world trading system and for Japan, preferably of its own free will, without foreign pressure or gaiatsu, to become a model of free trade internally as well as an advocate of the same abroad.

If history is a guide protectionism belies its name. It provides job security for candidates, not workers. Just as, in Pogo's terms, the enemy too often is us, in trade policy the enemy is politicians, usually one's own. As the world moves from a half century of obsession with geopolitics to stress instead geoeconomics, the challenge for all peoples and all political systems is to avoid the easy trap of economic nationalism.

For America the trade issue for the last decade of the twentieth century is not so much figuring out what new arrows should be added to the bulging quiver of existing sanctions, it is in selecting the right marksman with the right judgment to understand when and where to aim, with the first concern being to avoid at all costs driving a shaft into the heart of the U.S. and world economy.

One of the lessons of the 1930s was that protectionist legislation, such as the Smoot-Hawley tariff, lengthened and deepened the Great Depression. By reverse logic, in recessionary times, promoting policies that impel the growth of international trade is likely to serve as an economic stimulant. Hence the importance of advancing the Uruguay Round of the General Agreement on Tariffs and Trade and the negotiation of free trade agreements, first with Mexico and other Latin and east European countries, but eventually with the European Community and selected south Pacific and Asian countries.

V

Historically the strength of American foreign policy has been most evident when we have stood solidly for advancing abroad the principles and ideals upon which our society is based. Principles should not be sacrificed for shortsighted objectives or shortsighted leaders. In reflecting societal values no country should be more confident. After all, the philosophical taproot of the changes taking place in the world—from central Europe to the Baltic states, from Afghanistan to Tiananmen Square, from Nicaragua to South Africa—is a happy recognition that it is Jeffersonian democracy that provides the boldest and most humane model for political and economic organization in recorded history.

Conservative Republican thinking has two philosophical bedrocks. The first is a Burkean emphasis on respect for existing social structures: the assumption that for change to be effective it must be gradualist. The second, a Lockean emphasis on definable rights, is more radical and uncompromising.

President Bush in general is Burkean in temperament, emphasizing dialogue with the leadership in Moscow, Beijing and Pretoria, even when, for instance, a case might be made that in his Kiev speech of August 1991 he embraced Gorbachev beyond his due and his time.

Tiananmen produced stark challenges to conservative sensibilities about the rights of individuals. The president, however, has concluded that the maintenance of communication and trade not only advances short-term American interests on issues such as the Gulf War and peacekeeping in Cambodia, but in the long run bolsters the position in China of a Western-oriented entrepreneurial class that holds the best chance of promoting a regime more attuned to human rights concerns.

South Africa presents a similarly troubling philosophical dilemma for any conservative administration in Washington. While the first Republican presidency chose to risk war rather than compromise principles to end extremist apartheid—slavery—the last two Republican administrations have preferred to work with rather than against the government in Pretoria in an effort to help abolish apartheid in as civil and bloodless a way as possible. Fortunately, Washington has found in F. W. de Klerk an establishment leader heroically inclined to change and in Nelson Mandela a uniquely martyred aspirant. In competitive combination they give promise of an unusually civilized political phenomenon—evolutionary revolution.

VI

President Bush's critics have frequently gibed at him for problems with "the vision thing." Episcopalian in attitude as well as religious conviction, Bush eschews philosophical and even policy articulation, emphasizing reasoned decision-making and good judgment as contrasted with philosophical explication.

The Dutch architect Mies van der Rohe developed a theory of architecture around simplicity of design and the observation that "less is more," that is, the cluttering of design with fixtures and flourishes too often represents imperfection. Likewise, less can sometimes be more in public policy. In a variant of Teddy Roosevelt's "speak softly but carry a big stick" theme, President Bush's approach appears to be to speak little, sometimes in a convoluted fashion—with the manner more than the substance of his comments inducing confidence that he leads an administration capable of crafting reasoned responses to challenges of the day.

Instinctively, Bush at his low-key best appears to be attempting to follow the advice of Thomas Paine that "moderation in temper is always a virtue; moderation in principle is always a vice." To the extent the president attempts to appeal in public pronouncements to wider constituencies, his higher charged patriotic rhetoric often shields a deep-seated internationalism.

If one American political party has been historically identified with the advocacy of collective security and the multilateral diplomacy it implies, it is the Democratic Party. Collective security was the watchword of Woodrow Wilson, who literally drove himself to death defending the principle against strident critics. Franklin Roosevelt, arguably the greatest president of this century, insisted that collective security principles be espoused in the Atlantic Charter, in authoritative statements of American war aims in World War II and ultimately in the Charter of the United Nations.

Yet today it is a Republican president who, in opposition to both the isolationist and go-it-alone interventionist themes that have ambivalently represented much of this century's conservative tradition, is in the vanguard of constructive internationalism and credible collective security endeavors. Such is the implication of the extraordinary international coalition that Washington led in the Gulf War. Such is also the meaning of U.N.-sanctioned peacekeeping initiatives in Cambodia and Yugoslavia.

In a strategic sense, there have been three defining events in this century: World War I, World War II and the Cold War. The role of American soldiers and American military preparedness was crucial in winning each. Were it not for the American G.I., there would be no collective security. The only competition in the world today would be between the totalitarianism of the left and totalitarianism of the right. Europe would be freedom's toxic dump. Either the Nazi or the Soviet jackboot would be the symbol of order. The land mass that produced Montesquieu and Locke, Beethoven and Descartes would find its libraries filled with the class conflict implications of Das Kapital and the hate-ridden dogma of Mein Kampf.

While it would be overly optimistic to conclude that the wars of this century were wars to end all wars, it would be overly pessimistic to fail to recognize the extraordinary opportunity presented to the United States to advance verifiable arms control and strengthen collective security arrangements.

Seldom has a benchmark policy been less theoretically defined, but it would appear that what President Bush is attempting to develop in his New World Order theme is the precedent that aggression will not be rewarded; that countries should be expected to follow core precepts of international law; that countries distant from areas of conflict should be prepared to contribute to the preservation of worldwide norms; that international institutions and multilateral arrangements will be used to the maximum in developing collective approaches to common concerns.

Some 39 years ago President Eisenhower proposed an initiative called Atoms for Peace, a plan for the United States and the Soviet Union to dedicate fissionable materials from dismantled nuclear warheads for peaceful uses. Given the current momentum on arms control, the timing could not be more propitious for Russia and the other Soviet successor states to work with the United States to ensure that weapons-grade materials will not become "loose nukes" or recycled back into other deadly warheads, but instead that their awesome destructive potential will be converted to humanitarian purposes.

The 21st century can be looked to with an understanding that what distinguishes this generation of citizens from all others is that we are the first to have the capacity not just to wage war, but to destroy civilization. As Einstein once noted, "The unleashed power of the atom has changed everything save our modes of thinking." If war is a constant of history, the greatest political science quandary of all time is how to develop techniques to make it obsolete.

Avoiding a nuclear exchange implies the need to pay greater attention to the causes of war, such as impoverishment, as well as to the development of instruments of war. To halt the scourge of nuclear proliferation, arms control on a global as well as regional basis is a self-evident societal imperative.

Erecting effective barriers to the spread of nuclear and other weapons of mass destruction demands that restraint be accepted by the United States as well as developing countries. The first business of a new world order should be negotiation of a comprehensive test ban. In addition the United Nations ought to be mandated to develop a more rigorous International Atomic Energy Agency inspection regime than has heretofore been contemplated, and to authorize appropriate sanctions for regimes like that of North Korea.

The time is also ripe for the United States and the world community to consider creating within the U.N. system an international criminal court or courts, to hold accountable international criminals who violate specific international conventions such as those related to terrorism, drug trafficking and crimes against the peace. Such a court system would be complementary to the International Court of Justice at the Hague, which exclusively adjudicates disputes between states. There could be no more appropriate potential defendants to proceedings of this nature than Pol Pot, Saddam Hussein and Abu Nidal.

Since one of the most effective antidotes to the irrationality of ancient enmity is the swift justice of the law, a turn (or in the case of the United States, return) to the compulsory jurisdiction of the World Court would appear to be one of the most appropriate and achievable objectives of the decades ahead.

Any credible post-Gulf War scenario for encouraging peace and stability in the Middle East must include unprecedented multilateral restraints on the transfer of advanced conventional arms. If there is any lesson of the gulf conflict it is that the West was responsible for the creation of the armed camp known as Iraq.

Nevertheless the triumph of collective security in the Persian Gulf gives hope that a new international order will be established, with the understanding that peacekeeping is peacemaking. As Winston Churchill observed in his famous Iron Curtain speech some 46 years ago, U.N. peacekeeping efforts to be effective require "sheriffs and constables."

With the United Nations finally beginning to function as its framers intended, it is time for the United States to lead in the creation of a modest U.N. rapid-deployment force. Logistical and certain intelligence capabilities could be shared with the United Nations by the member states, as Congress originally contemplated in the 1945 U.N. Participation Act, and by U.N. members as a whole by "special agreements" under Article 43 of the charter. Likewise either the moribund Military Staff Committee needs to be revived or a new system established.

There is an ambivalence, if not tension, in the American psyche between isolationism and internationalism, between hubristic leadership and team playing. Given the traumas of post-World War II interventions, the American people are reluctant to assume the lonely and costly role of policeman for the world. On the other hand, they accept as a credible obligation that the United States should play a significant part with others as international highway patrolman.

Continued expansion of U.N. responsibilities, however, cannot be contemplated without adequate financing. It is ironic that as American policy and American interests are progressively being advanced by the United Nations, the United States has become the institution's single biggest deadbeat, with arrears in excess of $400 million. For Congress, it is not a proud moment that legislators are so stumped by a stultified appropriations process that peacekeeping in areas of the world as explosive as Cambodia, Yugoslavia and the Golan Heights does not receive the highest priority. Likewise, for the executive branch, it is not a proud moment that policymakers are so stymied by the domestic abortion debate that traditional American leadership in international family planning has ignominiously collapsed.

VII

Finally, a note about this century as it is beginning to unfold into the next. The twentieth century, like those of all recorded history, has been marked by war. For the first time, however, mankind has come to contemplate reasons why war should become obsolete and rational approaches to ensuring that such a prospect becomes possible. The existence of weapons of mass destruction gives unprecedented and compelling reason to work to ensure that they not be employed. The creation of international institutions—most importantly the United Nations—the expansion of international law and the demonstrated will of the international community to participate in collective security arrangements give hope that the next century will be marked by a dramatic diminution of cross-boundary conflict.

The simplest, although most dangerous, part of the Cold War is over. Now the complicated work begins. If the nascent experiments in democracy and free enterprise collapse in the former Soviet Union and central Europe, the potential ramifications for the national security of the United States—in dollar costs for military preparedness and human costs due to unanticipated threats and conflicts—could be staggering.

The challenge of our time is to grasp the opportunity created by the end of the Cold War. If America leads wisely, new wells of creative energy can be opened up and mankind's untapped productive potential released. The world can be enriched with a renaissance of the human spirit. If, on the other hand, America fails to secure the peace so many citizens have sacrificed so much to achieve, the mantle of 21st century leadership will pass to other less charitable societies and less liberal philosophies.

The weight of historical judgment is on our shoulders. As Dwight Eisenhower declared in his first inaugural address, "the faith we hold belongs not to us alone, but to the free of all the world."

JAMES A. LEACH, Representative from Iowa, is a member of the House Committee on Foreign Affairs.

A Democrat Looks at Foreign Policy

Lee H. Hamilton   SUMMER 1992

Democratic presidential candidate Bill Clinton reaches out to shake hands during an airport rally in Wilkes-Barre, November 1, 1992.

The world has turned upside down, but U.S. foreign policy has been slow to change. We have failed to develop a coherent strategy for the future—a successor to containment. A Republican sits in the White House, but Democrats also bear responsibility for foreign policy inertia. Democrats have ceded the field of foreign affairs to the president, let him set the agenda and not challenged him often enough on the specifics of policy. The result has been drift.

It is now up to Democrats to articulate a more compelling American foreign policy. Democrats have the opportunity to redefine the concept of national security and to strike a better balance between domestic and foreign affairs, and between leadership and partnership. The issues are no longer communist expansion and nuclear survival, but economic competitiveness, weapons proliferation, support for democracy, protection of the environment and the fight against human misery. The task is one of redefining America's role in the world.

II

America is the preeminent power today. Its economy is still the world's most productive. Militarily it is the world's only superpower. Countries and peoples around the world still admire its democratic political system and free-market economy.

Nevertheless, while we find reasons to celebrate our foreign policy successes, we find ourselves threatened at home: by recession, crises in our cities, in our education and health care systems, persistent budget and trade deficits, and a growing sense of political paralysis.

Domestic problems have made the American public ambivalent about the U.S. role in the world. Americans are proud of their country's international leadership, but they worry about its burdens. They want to see greater contributions from our allies. They are convinced that we could better solve domestic problems if we scaled back commitments overseas. Public opposition to foreign assistance is strong. Calls for deep cuts in defense spending are growing. Yet, when asked, Americans say they do not want the United States to relinquish its special place in the world.

How can these views be reconciled? My sense is that the American people intuitively understand what the present administration does not: the link between domestic well-being and America's role in the world. Americans recognize that the fundamental purpose of our foreign policy is to promote conditions abroad that protect and improve the quality of life at home. In turn they understand that our ability to solve problems abroad depends on our domestic vitality.

Many Americans sense that President Bush has had his priorities wrong. The first claim on his time, energy and skill has been foreign affairs. He has neglected the economy and domestic policy. Americans are hard-pressed to identify the president, now in his fourth year of office, with any successful domestic or economic initiative. He has failed to understand the linkage between the economy and American leadership.

What we are hearing from Americans today is first and foremost a demand to address problems at home. They are not calling on the United States to bring home all its troops or sever diplomatic and economic ties with the world. Rather, their plea—and the plea of Democrats—is for a better balance.

Disengagement is not possible in a world of instantaneous communication and economic interdependence. Neither isolation nor withdrawal is an option for the United States. If we forget about the world and focus only on our domestic problems, they would grow worse. The question is not whether we should participate in world affairs, but how.

The president so far has failed to instill a new sense of mission in American foreign policy. He maneuvered well in the waning days of the Cold War, but he is now without a new organizing principle. The administration's main effort to put together a blueprint for the post-Cold War era has come from the Pentagon, which argues for a one-superpower world. The president has yet to state his position on the Pentagon proposal. He has not articulated an answer to the real foreign policy question: What are the new threats to U.S. interests, and how should our foreign policy be reconfigured to defend those interests-

III

Our interests may be permanent, but the threats to them have changed. The demise of communism means we need to focus on new challenges and priorities. We must continue to be prepared to defend our vital economic and security interests—in Europe, east Asia, the Persian Gulf and areas directly adjacent to our borders. Now that the Soviet threat has vanished the dominant security threat comes from the breakup of states and the proliferation of deadly weapons and technologies. The United States needs a more effective policy in the 1990s to deal with both regional instability and aggression, as well as renegade states and groups that seek to acquire weapons of mass destruction.

The draft Pentagon planning paper leaked to the press in February is dead wrong in promoting the notion of a sole superpower dominating the rest of the world. The key to U.S. security is sustaining the democratic alliances that have been shaped over the last half century. We cannot build a new world order if our allies believe our foreign policy is designed to turn back any power that challenges our leadership. We will need to remain the world's strongest military power, but there is no contradiction between collective security and military preeminence—as the Gulf War illustrated.

Economic power is the new determinant of international stature. The restoration of U.S. competitiveness is critical not only to our domestic economy but to our foreign policy as well. Our economic problems are limiting the reach of our foreign policy at a time when the rest of the world is looking to the United States for leadership.

We need domestic policies that restore the foundation for U.S. competitiveness and economic growth—more private and public investment, better education, job training and health care—and a foreign policy that promotes open markets for U.S. goods and services. American voters have consistently rejected protectionist trade policies, but they insist on a level playing field.

We have a golden opportunity to foster the spread of democracy and free markets. But President Bush has been too selective in his application of democratic principles, forgetting them when it comes to China or the Middle East. He has been too focused on stability instead of the pursuit of freedom, self-determination and justice. There is no conflict between these values: promoting democracy builds long-term security. We should provide concrete political and economic advice and across-the-board assistance to struggling democracies. We need to keep American values where they belong—at the heart of our foreign policy.

Finally, we must address issues that pose a direct threat to our prosperity and quality of life. The president speaks expansively about the role of the United States in the world, but he has defined that role too narrowly. We are deeply involved in issues such as aggression in the gulf, but great problems such as the environment, energy use, population growth, hunger and health have been neglected. We also need to pay greater attention to the growing gap between rich and poor. Democracy cannot flourish in human misery. Economic growth in the world's poorest countries will have a direct, beneficial impact on our long-term national security. The end of the Cold War gives us an opportunity to focus on these neglected and vexing problems.

The new challenges to U.S. interests will require two adjustments in U.S. foreign policy. First, we need to achieve a better balance between leadership and partnership in our foreign policy. American leadership is necessary but no longer sufficient to solve many international problems. We are first among democratic equals and must recognize the limitations of unilateral action. Addressing new threats to peace and prosperity—nationalist conflict, arms proliferation, the consolidation of democracy and free markets, and environmental, health and population problems—will require unprecedented levels of international cooperation.

Second, we need a better balance between our domestic and foreign policies. The former affects the latter. If we do not provide Americans with quality education, health care and jobs, we will soon find that we lack the human and material resources required to fulfill our still necessary role as world leader. If we wish to lead abroad tomorrow, we must focus on our domestic problems today.

IV

U.S. economic performance is troubling. Economics can no longer take second place to national security in setting U.S. government policy. Under President Bush, U.S. gross domestic product has grown less than one percent annually. This is the worst economic performance under any president since Herbert Hoover. During the 1950s and 1960s America's economic growth was vigorous—averaging 3.9 percent in the 1950s and 4.1 percent in the 1960s. Growth slowed in the 1970s to 2.8 percent, and slowed further in the 1980s to 2.6 percent. In the 1990s growth all but stopped.

Due to sustained high rates of productivity growth, Japan and the European Community are rapidly closing the economic gap with the United States. Some experts predict that one or both will replace the United States as the world's leading economy. Both Japan and Europe have high savings rates and are making the investments in people and infrastructure that will help them ensure sustained improvements in living standards in the 1990s and beyond. Their foreign economic policies are just as effective. By 1993 the EC will be the world's largest trading bloc. Japan is weaving a web of trade and investment ties throughout the Pacific Rim, the world's most dynamic economic region. These ties will strengthen its economic position for years to come.

Economic weakness undermines the ability of the United States to achieve its foreign policy goals:

- We supplied the bulk of the military forces in the Persian Gulf, but the war was financed by payments of $54 billion from friends and allies. There is no guarantee that these partners will be so generous in future crises. When we rely on others to finance our foreign policy, we put it at risk.
- Sophisticated electronic components in weapons that performed so well during the Gulf War were manufactured abroad. A failure to maintain competitive high-technology industries will erode future U.S. military strength.
- U.S. inaction on the International Monetary Fund quota increase undercuts the ability of the IMF to support market economic reforms in eastern Europe and the former Soviet republics.
- Persistent arrears in our share of financing the United Nations harms the ability of that organization to carry out vital peacekeeping missions.

Strong and balanced economic growth would make it easier for Americans to deal with both domestic and international problems. In the 1950s and 1960s the United States was the engine of growth for the world economy and a force for promoting both democracy and more open international markets. German Chancellor Helmut Kohl boasts that the 1990s will be the "Decade of Europe," and it is commonplace now for Japanese politicians to speak of U.S. economic decline. If we do not deal with our domestic economic problems, they will be right.

Americans understand that an economy that performs below its potential will, over the long run, fail to provide quality jobs and high living standards. As a result, worries about foreign economic competition are growing. The lack of an effective strategy to improve the performance of the economy is stimulating protectionist sentiment.

No foreign competitor provokes greater concern than Japan. To be sure, Japanese policies and business practices have limited our business opportunities and hurt some U.S. industries. Many of these policies and practices are unfair, and other nations share our concern about them. International pressure remains necessary to end these practices and further open Japan's lucrative domestic market. Indeed, exports have been a major source of U.S. economic growth in recent years, which underscores the value of an aggressive trade strategy.

Yet our bilateral trade deficit with Japan was about $44 billion in 1991, less than one percent of our total output of $5.7 trillion. We exported $591 billion of this output, just over ten percent. These figures suggest that it would be a mistake to overstate the adverse impact of foreign trade restrictions on our economy, or the favorable impact of loosening those restrictions. Our current recession and competitiveness problems were not made in Japan or anywhere else. Primary responsibility for our economic problems—and for their solutions—rests with the policies of the U.S. government and the performance of U.S. firms. Scapegoating Japan or other countries is counterproductive: it increases trade tensions and diverts precious attention from the domestic sources of our economic problems.

Japan's economic challenge is, at root, a domestic challenge. It requires a strong domestic response. Too much of our national output is devoted to consumption and too little to investment, both public and private. To boost productivity, we need more saving and more investment—in better educated and healthier workers, in improved plant and equipment, and in science and technology. Government policies should encourage lifelong opportunities for education, job training and retraining to provide for a highly skilled work force. Without compromising free-market principles we can strengthen existing mechanisms for cooperation among universities, laboratories, industry and government.

Our economic performance would also be improved by a more aggressive response to foreign competition. With additional staff and resources U.S. embassies could do a far better job of promoting U.S. business abroad. Government and industry need to work more closely to identify and cultivate potentially significant technologies. U.S. trade negotiators should be given additional clout, which they need to pry open closed markets. We should insist on reciprocal treatment for U.S. exports.

The president needs to educate Americans about the nature of our international economic predicament. He should describe the extent of U.S.-Japan economic interdependence and the costs of a rupture in the relationship. He should try to persuade Americans that many foreign economic policies and practices, while different from ours, are not necessarily wrong or unfair. We could usefully adopt some of these policies and practices, and the president should help us identify them. Finally, the president needs to explain the structural features of the American and Japanese economies that will make it difficult in the near term to balance our bilateral trade.

The condition of American society also influences our role in the world. The example of America as a successful society has been a traditional source of U.S. influence abroad. Over the past two centuries many countries have tried to emulate our democracy, economy and society. But persistent poverty, the world's highest levels of violent crime and drug abuse, resurgent racial tensions and other problems suggest that the quality of American life today leaves much to be desired. The riots in Los Angeles have tarnished

America's image. The president speaks of domestic problems, but the record of his administration in solving them is unimpressive. The deterioration of American society handicaps our ability to lead by example.

The president has a unique ability to focus public attention and to set the nation's priorities. Throughout the Cold War fighting communism invariably prevailed over domestic needs. Now this president—or the next—must shift the balance back to the home front if America is to rebuild its strength and continue to play an important role in the world.

V

The choice before the United States is not whether it should repudiate international commitments and responsibilities. It is, again, a question of balance: between domestic and international priorities, and between U.S. leadership and partnership.

U.S. participation is still necessary to solve international problems. Yet the United States alone is no longer sufficient to get things done. Achieving our foreign policy objectives will require new forms of leadership and cooperation. This becomes clear when we look at several of the key challenges on the international agenda.

The United States should retain the capability to assure its security, but not every threat to international peace or stability will require a U.S. military response. The United States cannot, and should not, act as a global policeman or mercenary. But it is in our interest to take the lead in organizing collective responses to threats to peace.

When possible, Washington should try to respond to threats to collective security through the United Nations. If that body is recalcitrant or unable to respond, then we should try to build a coalition outside it. We should act alone only if we cannot find friends and partners with whom to work.

The Gulf War is both instructive and deceptive as an example for the future international security role of the United States. It is instructive in that only the United States had the ability to assemble an international coalition to oppose, and then reverse, Iraqi aggression. It is deceptive in that few threats to the peace will be so clear-cut and will so galvanize the United States and the international community as a direct military threat to the world's supply of oil.

Future threats to security are likely to be more complex and ambiguous: the messy breakup of states (the former Yugoslavia and the former Soviet Union), internal conflict (Somalia) or massive violations of human rights (Iraq). Internal upheavals threaten to spill across borders and directly challenge international peace and stability.

When states break up, the United States and the United Nations should not work on behalf of the political status quo, but on behalf of democracy, human freedom and the peaceful resolution of disputes. The use of force for domestic repression, or to change boundaries in former multiethnic states, must be condemned by the international community. Washington should be in the forefront of efforts to involve the United Nations, the Conference on Security and Cooperation in Europe or other regional organizations to keep the peace. The question for the future is whether and when the international community should intervene in circumstances where internal policies or human rights violations threaten international peace and stability.

The enduring lesson from the Gulf War should not be the military campaign, but the unprecedented cooperation that occurred within the Security Council. At last the United Nations is beginning to fulfill the security mission its founders intended. In Afghanistan, Namibia, Central America and Cambodia it has played a central role in ending East-West confrontation and brokering regional peace settlements. The United States should strongly support efforts to expand the U.N. peacekeeping role. The president's statements on funding the United Nations are positive, but his leadership is weak. He has not fought for his two-year, $700 million peacekeeping funding request and has not produced the congressional votes from his own party. Unfortunately, the Democratic

Party has not been much better, and peacekeeping contributions this year are likely to fall short.

In order to assist peacekeeping activities, the United States and other permanent members could share intelligence with the U.N. secretariat. Peacekeeping efforts would benefit as well from increased financial and personnel contributions by Japan and Germany. The contribution of helicopters and aircraft by Germany to the work of the U.N. inspectors in Iraq is an important first step that should be replicated elsewhere.

VI

Arms control is also an area where U.S. leadership is necessary to promote international peace and stability.

The greatest security danger of the 1990s is weapons proliferation. The first step is to gain control over "loose nukes" in the former Soviet republics. Second, the United States, Russia and Ukraine should cut strategic nuclear forces to levels far below those agreed in the START treaty. What we do not need are Pentagon experts trying to find new targets and adversaries for existing nuclear weapons.

Washington should also move far more aggressively to use the $400 million appropriated by Congress for the disabling and dismantling of nuclear and chemical weapons in the former Soviet Union. Congress took this step five months ago, without any help from the president. The administration has yet to spend these funds. We should act now, while we have influence with Russia and the new republics. Delay increases the chances that these weapons will be used by renegade states or terrorists or in interrepublic disputes.

Washington should also revive efforts begun by Presidents Eisenhower and Kennedy to negotiate a comprehensive test ban treaty. Stopping nuclear testing is central to our efforts to counter nuclear proliferation and is a solemn obligation undertaken by the nuclear signatories to the Nonproliferation Treaty. We must ask ourselves whether we have anything to gain from continued testing, in contrast to the powerful political example of stopping nuclear tests. If we want to stop others from acquiring nuclear weapons, we must uphold our part of the bargain.

We need to strengthen the International Atomic Energy Agency. We should support the IAEA's right to unlimited inspection without advance notice when violations of the Nonproliferation Treaty are suspected. We should also push for an international agreement that requires full-scope safeguards on all nuclear facilities within a country before that country may obtain nuclear technology from any source.

America also needs to strengthen its intelligence capabilities to detect covert weapons programs. We and our allies should make sure the IAEA has early warning of suspect activities. Concerted international pressure will be needed to contain nuclear programs in countries that remain outside the non-proliferation and safeguards regime (North Korea, India, Pakistan and Israel) and those whose adherence to its requirements is suspect (Libya, Iraq and Iran).

The spread of nuclear weapons and technology, unfortunately, is only one part of the proliferation problem. Western suppliers provided Iraq with the bulk of the components and critical technology not only for its nuclear program but for its chemical, biological and ballistic missile programs. The United States must work to develop an effective international policy for controlling the export and re-export of all sensitive technologies and materials related to weapons of mass destruction. We need to tighten restrictions on these exports through the Nuclear Suppliers Group, the Missile Technology Control Regime and the Australia Chemical Weapons Suppliers Group.

The proliferation of conventional weapons is also a threat to peace and stability. The five permanent members of the Security Council are the world's five largest arms sellers. They account for 80 percent of all weapons sales to the Third World. If we are to curb conventional weapons transfers, the suppliers must act—and the United States, the biggest exporter, should lead.

The United States is missing a unique opportunity to encourage arms restraint where the problem is the greatest—the Middle East. With less than three percent of the world's population the Middle East accounted for 45 percent of Third World arms purchases in the 1980s, and $150 billion in sales by the "big five" arms suppliers.

The president's May 1991 decision to convene a conference of major Middle East arms suppliers is only a small step in the right direction. It is doubtful whether the U.S. proposal for prior notification and consultation on arms sales will restrain the arms trade. In fact the major thrust of U.S. policy is precisely in the wrong direction. Since September 1990 the United States has gone ahead with over $22 billion in government-to-government military sales to Middle Eastern states and issued licenses for up to another $6 billion in commercial sales. Other arms sellers are complaining that aggressive U.S. marketing is closing them out of Middle East markets. We will not foster arms restraint by leading the way with arms sales.

The United States should challenge other suppliers to join in a multilateral moratorium on Middle East arms sales. During such a moratorium Washington and other weapons suppliers should adopt tough, permanent limits on the quantity and quality of arms transfers to the Middle East. Without American leadership on arms restraint, arms suppliers and recipients will continue to conduct business as usual in the Middle East arms bazaar. That will set the stage for future Middle East wars.

VII

The dramatic events in the former Soviet Union last year, in eastern Europe three years ago and in Latin America over the past decade show that the values of political and economic freedom are ascendant. The key policy question for the United States and other nations is how to help consolidate democracy and free-market economic reforms.

With respect to eastern Europe and the former Soviet republics, the United States is an important player, but by no means the only one. To date, Europe has provided most of the economic assistance. Nonetheless the United States has an indispensable leadership role to play, and the president has been timid and slow. In eastern Europe, Congress pushed the president to act. With respect to Russia, Richard Nixon and Bill Clinton pressed the president and made the case for assistance. The purpose of such assistance is to ease the pain of transition, to buy time for democratic and economic reform.

Successful reform in eastern Europe and in the former Soviet republics would make an enormous contribution to U.S. security. It would reduce U.S. defense expenditures, the nuclear threat, arms exports and the risk of environmental disaster. It would give the United States access to vast natural resources through peaceful commerce. It would redirect human talent to peaceful pursuits, open new markets for U.S. exports and promote world economic growth.

The president has now renewed his call for funding an IMF capital quota increase and has expressed his support for a currency stabilization fund for Russia tied to implementation of an IMF reform program. The United States along with the other Group of Seven leading industrial nations are now planning to provide $18 billion in balance-of-payments support and $6 billion for a stabilization fund to assist Russia's reform program. The proposal is a good one. But it is unclear how Washington will be able to play a leadership role on aid to Russia when, as the president says in this election year, such assistance can be provided with no new appropriations.

America and the EC must open their markets and give these new democracies an opportunity to export and grow. A successful conclusion of the Uruguay Round of the General Agreement on Tariffs and Trade would be a big boost for reformers in eastern Europe and Latin America. A GATT agreement that cuts deeply into agricultural subsidies, starts to dismantle the EC's Common Agricultural Policy and opens up the world market for farm produce would go a long way toward getting these economies back on their feet. Poland, Romania and Ukraine were once the breadbasket of Europe, and they can become so once again. What is required of these nations are reforms of their own, matched by an opening of world markets, especially the EC market. What is best for eastern Europe, former Soviet republics and Latin America is what is best for the GATT membership as a whole: an open, liberal economic order. The talks have been dragging on for seven years, and the president must press for their successful conclusion.

Trade liberalization will also enhance the prospects for successful reform in Latin America, to the benefit of the United States. Open and growing economies in this hemisphere would provide exceptional opportunities for U.S. trade and investment. Sound, market-based economies will help reduce corruption and maintain political stability, which would reinforce U.S. security. The United States and other countries can make the reforms more tolerable and reinforce democracy by providing larger markets for Latin American exports and by further reducing debt burdens.

President Bush's 1990 Enterprise for the Americas Initiative was welcomed in Latin America as a sign of renewed interest in the region's economic future. The initiative, which has yet to be fully implemented, contains trade, debt and investment components. The debt component addresses only government-to-government debt, and more needs to be done to encourage reductions in commercial debt payments. The administration has also completed preliminary agreements providing for free-trade negotiations with most countries in Latin America, but all free-trade talks are on hold until the completion of negotiations on the proposed North American Free Trade Agreement among Mexico, Canada and the United States.

The NAFTA talks could provide a model for free-trade accords with other Latin American countries or the foundation for a hemispheric free-trade area. Freer trade would boost growth in countries that engage in it, but congressional concerns about specific economic and environmental consequences of free trade with Mexico will make final approval of a NAFTA agreement difficult. Much is riding on the success of the NAFTA talks, which increases pressure on the administration to produce an agreement Congress can support.

VIII

Elsewhere the United States has been too selective in encouraging democracy. We need a more balanced approach.

We have pressed for democratic change in former communist countries, but those countries seen to have strategic importance— including Saudi Arabia, Kuwait, China, Indonesia and Turkey— have escaped strong pressure on democracy and human rights. We have not even called for democratic change in Iraq; U.S. sanctions are tied only to Saddam Hussein's ouster.

Moreover our foreign policy has focused too much on governments, instead of on the consequences of our policies for people. We should not permit short-term considerations of order and stability to override long-term interests in expanding freedom, democracy and basic human rights. For example the Algerian army intervened to prevent an Islamic party from winning recent elections. Because the Bush administration had misgivings about the party, it did not speak out in favor of the democratic process. The United States thereby supported the army's moves to undercut democratic rule.

Democracy promotes, rather than undermines, long-term stability. Democratic governments are more peaceful than authoritarian ones. They make better allies and more reliable partners in international affairs. The denial of basic political rights often leads to violent upheaval. When we promote respect for human rights, civil liberties and the rule of law, we build a better foundation for long-term security and prosperity.

No country can make another democratic, but democracy can be cultivated where the desire for it exists. Established democracies such as the United States can help in this effort. Conversely, we should reduce—if not eliminate—assistance to governments that oppose democratic change or suppress human rights.

Countries in need of democratic assistance fall into three broad categories: those still under authoritarian rule, those in transition to democracy and those with new democratic governments.

In countries still under authoritarian rule, such as China and Cuba, we should try to sustain and strengthen democratic forces. Our policies should seek to increase the likelihood of a leadership succession that produces a more democratic government. We should increase personal and professional exchanges, step up radio news broadcasts and help democratic activists—openly if possible, secretly if necessary.

Countries making the transition to democracy need several kinds of assistance. Initially they may need help monitoring internal settlements and organizing elections. They often need help providing basic services—food, health care, law and order—until elected leaders are in place. Multinational efforts are necessary. Wealthy Asian nations such as Japan should provide the major share of funding for the U.N.-sponsored transition in Cambodia. As civil wars in El Salvador, Mozambique, Angola and Liberia wind down, these countries will also need help. Too often assistance has been ad hoc, uncoordinated and inadequately funded. The United Nations, the United States, Europe and Japan should sort out and share responsibilities.

One important area is in public administration. The United States can provide excellent assistance to new officials with no experience in democratic governance. In eastern Europe, U.S.-funded nongovernmental organizations are advising parliaments and municipal and regional governments. These programs should be expanded elsewhere. Expatriate communities in the United States and other countries are another source of valuable assistance to new governments.

IX

International environmental problems demand complex multilateral negotiations and a willingness to make short-term sacrifices. Both require active U.S. leadership. In recent years the United States has too often served as an obstacle to, rather than a catalyst for, effective international action. Scientific research and citizen action have expanded the international environmental agenda:

Global warming. The production of carbon dioxide and other "greenhouse gases," primarily through the burning of fossil fuels, is causing world temperatures to rise. This warming trend could swamp coastal areas, destroy fragile ecosystems and harm agriculture.

The ozone layer. Chlorofluorocarbons (CFCs), chemicals used as coolants and in industrial processes, are depleting the stratospheric ozone layer that shields the earth from ultraviolet radiation. Increased exposure to ultraviolet radiation could increase skin cancer, damage eyesight, degrade human immune systems and disrupt food production.

Deforestation. The clearing of forests for timber, pasture and dwellings is causing soil erosion and destroying plants that soak up carbon dioxide. The burning of tropical forests also accounts for 25 percent of world carbon dioxide production.

Biological diversity. Human activity is destroying thousands of plant and animal species annually. One-fourth of current species could be extinct by 2020. The loss of plant species will harm crops and deprive the world of future medicinal advances.

International action on the environment is likely to succeed when the United States strongly backs it, and founder when we oppose it or sit on the sidelines. Active U.S. diplomacy was pivotal to the completion of the 1987 Montreal Protocol and subsequent agreements setting targets for reduced emissions of CFCs. In contrast, U.S. opposition prevented agreement last year on a permanent moratorium on mining in the Antarctic. The U.S. leadership deficit has been most glaring, and potentially most costly, in preparations for the June 1992 U.N. Conference on Environment and Development in Brazil.

Preparations for the UNCED in Rio de Janeiro highlight the growing rift between the world's industrialized and developing nations on the costs of environmental cleanup. Many developing countries say industrialized countries must provide financial aid and advanced technologies if they are to implement UNCED commitments. Aid pledges by industrialized nations for environmental cleanup are far short of what developing countries say is needed.

U.S. intransigence has weakened what was intended to be the UNCED summit's most important achievement: the treaty on global warming. For several years Washington's resistance to formal targets on reducing carbon dioxide emissions has slowed efforts to negotiate a climate treaty. Officials defended U.S. policy by citing conflicting scientific data and the cost of limiting emissions. Yet on this the administration is isolated. Every major industrial country except the United States has now pledged to limit emissions of carbon dioxide to 1990 levels by the year 2000.

Developing countries may not be persuaded to use alternative fuels or costly technologies if industrialized countries are unwilling to take tough steps to control their own greenhouse emissions. Some developing countries have also said they will withhold cooperation on forest protection efforts until the United States agrees to formal limits on carbon dioxide emissions. U.S. foot-dragging on carbon dioxide restrictions is thus impeding international action on global warming and deforestation.

The global warming issue underscores the linkage between domestic and foreign policy. Since Europe and Japan use energy more efficiently than we do, they find it easier to commit to reductions in carbon dioxide emissions. Our lack of effective energy conservation policies not only increases U.S. energy dependency, it also undercuts our ability to lead on an environmental issue in which we have a substantial long-term interest.

U.S. policy on world population growth also has been disappointing. We have slighted international population issues and allowed domestic politics and ideological issues to stand in the way of consistent funding for key family planning organizations, including the U.N. Fund for Population Activities. This will have harmful consequences for the international environment and for our own long-term quality of life.

In sum the United States has failed to lead—through diplomacy or by example—on multilateral efforts to address new threats to the international quality of life. Policy prescriptions for the government are clear. We should commit ourselves to specific targets and timetables for reductions in U.S. carbon dioxide emissions. We should work with other nations to devise promising approaches to the funding of environmental programs. We should seek to strengthen multilateral institutions that coordinate environmental research and programs. Funding for population programs should be increased and directed to organizations with demonstrated effectiveness. Funds for these initiatives should be drawn, in part, from money made available from defense spending cuts around the world.

X

The gulf crisis showed the president's weaknesses, as well as strengths, in making foreign policy. His performance during the war was impressive. But his policies prior to the war failed, and his follow-through afterward has been disappointing.

The president did not focus on the problem of Iraq soon enough. Iraqi policy became increasingly bellicose in the late 1980s, and the United States did not react. Indeed, U.S. policy may have emboldened Saddam. Washington continued to share intelligence with Baghdad, allow the export of goods with potential military use and provide Iraq with export credit guarantees. Until August 2, 1990, it was official U.S. policy to pursue good relations with Iraq. War might have been avoided if Washington had made crystal clear that it would oppose with military force an Iraqi invasion of Kuwait. Yet only two days before the invasion U.S. officials stressed publicly that we had no commitment to defend Kuwait.

The president deserves credit for assembling an anti-Iraq coalition and for leading a military victory, but we now risk losing the peace. Saddam remained in power long after his defeat in war. Iraqi compliance with U.N. resolutions is minimal. Political reform in Kuwait and Saudi Arabia is unimpressive. Gulf states are failing to build new security structures. Arms sales to the region are escalating. President Bush and Secretary Baker have started direct Arab-Israeli peace talks—for which they deserve praise—but those talks lack momentum.

The Gulf War shows that the president often reacts well to crises. He also gets high marks for his deft handling of German unification. But he and his inner circle hold the policy reins too tightly. They seek little advice from the Foreign Service or the rest of the government. As a result they often do not see problems coming and, subsequently, do not pay enough attention to them once they are off center stage. Iraq is only one example; the breakup of Yugoslavia and the Soviet Union did not draw attention from senior policymakers until it was too late. Issues no longer in the spotlight, such as Panama, suffer from inattention: drug trafficking in Panama remains endemic. The president's preoccupation with crises means that long-term issues—the Uruguay Round, energy security, the environment, the implications of EC-1992 and the Maastricht summit—are neglected at the top.

The overcentralized, crisis-oriented approach has also meant the neglect of special relationships that need constant care and attention. Frictions with Israel—some minor, some not—have been allowed to fester. Also at risk are U.S.-Japan ties. No relationship is more important to either country, yet the president has done little to arrest deterioration.

XI

President Bush has yet to reshape the institutions and programs that carry out U.S. foreign policy. They need an overhaul. The intelligence community is oriented to a world that no longer exists. Foreign aid reflects Cold War priorities and domestic political concerns. The defense budget does not correspond to current international threats.

If the U.S. intelligence community is to serve U.S. interests in the 1990s, it must be reformed. The intelligence community must focus on new challenges, including proliferation, economic and environmental issues. Better assessments will require improved information from human sources. Duplication of effort within and between military and intelligence agencies must end. The president has opposed a broad organizational overhaul of the intelligence community. He should tap more outside expertise to help with reform.

The foreign aid program's guiding principle is inertia. The president has been unwilling either to lead, or to support with enthusiasm, efforts to reform foreign aid. In fiscal year 1992 we are spending over $7.4 billion—more than three-fifths of all bilateral foreign aid—on military and economic assistance to countries deemed to be of strategic importance. The top three recipients of aid—Israel, Egypt and Turkey—receive nearly half of all U.S. bilateral assistance. Developmental assistance totals $2.15 billion, or less than one-fifth of all bilateral aid.

A bias toward security assistance and a skewed distribution make the U.S. foreign aid program look increasingly irrelevant. New transnational population, health and environmental problems threaten long-term stability and prosperity, but the focus of U.S. foreign aid continues to be Cold War security concerns. The poorest nations, which need help most, are getting least.

U.S. defense programs have also lagged behind political change. The central rationale for a $300 billion defense budget—the defense of western Europe against a Soviet invasion—has vanished. Steep spending cuts beyond the 25 percent reduction outlined in the Pentagon's five-year plan are possible and necessary. We may be able to cut defense spending by 50 percent over the next decade without harming U.S. security.

The Pentagon keeps searching for threats to justify its budget. A recent Pentagon document outlines seven war scenarios, including a Russian invasion of Lithuania that NATO would rush to reverse. It is hard to take such scenarios seriously when the White House has not bothered to coordinate them with either the State Department or the CIA. These are unconvincing exercises to justify the defense budget.

The United States also continues to bear a disproportionate share of common defense burdens. There is no longer any reason why the United States should devote a larger portion of its gross domestic product to defense spending than its wealthy European and Asian allies. These countries are capable of paying more for their own defense and supplying their own troops to replace U.S. forces.

Defense reform will require strong presidential leadership. It will require shutting down weapons production lines, closing military bases and cutting manpower. It will require worker-retraining and base-conversion programs. Budget cuts will impose pain in every state and congressional district. Only the president is in a position to rise above local interests to restructure the defense budget. But his approach has been to trim budgets, not to rethink manpower and weapons needs from the bottom up.

XII

The Cold War is over, but the United States has been slow to react. We now have a unique opportunity to redefine the purposes of American power.

We need a better balance in the making of foreign policy. Policy under President Bush has been too reactive, centralized and personalized. We need less emphasis on crisis management and more on long-term U.S. interests and American values. All institutions that carry out U.S. foreign policy need reform and overhaul.

Finally, we need a better understanding of the purposes of American foreign policy. It is to improve life at home, to build a stronger American society and economy, and to build a safer and more stable world. To serve these ends we need a foreign policy that recasts old notions of national security, retools outdated institutions and establishes new patterns of international partnership. We need to redefine America's role in the world.

LEE H. HAMILTON, **Representative from Indiana, is a member of the House Committee on Foreign Affairs.**

America's First Post-Cold War President

Theodore C. Sorensen   FALL 1992

East German citizens climb the Berlin Wall at the Brandenburg Gate after the opening of the border was announced early November 9, 1989.

O n the morning of November 4, 1992, the first person to be elected president of the United States since the end of the Cold War will awaken to a world remarkably un-like that following any presidential election in the last half century or more.

He will be the first president to start a four-year term without any need to worry seriously about this nation facing nuclear or even armed attack, the existence of another military superpower or a challenge from a hostile global ideology. He will be the first who can rely on a virtually veto-free Security Council in a more effective, respected United Nations. For the first time a worldwide community of nations under law will appear to be within our reach. He will be truly free, in short, to use his inaugural address to outline a new course in world affairs for America.

It will be a historic opportunity.

But along with that opportunity he will face challenges that his predecessors did not face—from the integration of western Europe and the disintegration of eastern Europe; from the spread of ethnic, tribal, religious and other micronationalist clashes that are undeterred by nuclear might and unresolved by free-market and free-election doctrines; and from the difficulties of converting to a less military-oriented economy without unacceptable dislocation.

With the Cold War out of the way the next president will be obliged to face long-deferred global problems, including population growth, food and water shortages and environmental hazards that in combination could create for the next generation of Americans a very ugly and perilous way of life. To an extent not shared by his modern predecessors he will face an anxious and inward-looking American public that generally feels neither generosity nor responsibility toward the plight of other peoples. He will find it more difficult to distinguish between friend and foe, now that the clear ideological colors of the Cold War are gone; to distinguish between real dangers and mere problems, now that all kinds of nonmilitary concerns have replaced one clear overriding threat to the nation's survival; and to distinguish between foreign and domestic issues, now that international influence depends less on military supremacy and more on market competitiveness.

In short America's first post-Cold War president will face a world of both unmatched opportunity and unprecedented opacity. Under pressure to choose a new course for the country, with the gravest consequences attendant upon that choice, he will be standing at a crossroads, looking at conflicting signposts and holding outdated maps.

II

He will not be the first president this century to stand at such a crossroads. Presidents Warren G. Harding, after the election of

1920, and Harry Truman, after the election of 1948, stood at comparable intersections. In each case the United States and its military allies, during the period following the previous presidential election, had won a stirring global victory and commenced demobilization. In each case the American people were weary of crisis and eager to resume a course of domestic tranquility and prosperity. In each case the newly elected president had unusual freedom to forge a new national consensus in foreign affairs. Each of them chose very differently.

Harding, elected by a record margin, regarded his victory as a "referendum" rejecting "internationality," as a mandate for "the resumption of our onward, normal way." Europe and Asia were racked by debt, famine and regional disputes, by communism in Russia and by uprisings in scattered colonies. But this country, said Harding, needs "not nostrums but normalcy, . . . not submergence in internationality but sustainment in triumphant nationality."

He appointed a brilliant secretary of state, Charles Evans Hughes, whose focus on international law led to a series of arms and naval limitation conferences and treaties. In the absence of political will and enforcement measures in Washington and other world capitals, all proved ultimately worthless.

In his inaugural address Harding recognized "the new order in the world" (a familiar refrain) and the need for international law and understanding. But his primary emphasis was on "the wisdom . . . of non-involvement in Old World affairs."

Confident of our ability to work out our own destiny . . . we do not mean to be entangled. We will accept no responsibility, except as our own conscience and judgment in each instance may determine . . . no permanent military alliance . . . no political commitments which will subject our decisions to any other than our own authority.

America's return to isolationism in the 1920s was soon symbolized and aggravated by higher tariff and immigration barriers and by the virulent anti-foreigner sentiment that raged in some regions.

Truman, barely returned by the voters in 1948 to the Oval Office that he had inherited three years earlier upon the death of Franklin D. Roosevelt, took a distinctly different course. Even before the 1948 election he had launched the Marshall Plan, embraced the United Nations and commenced the Berlin airlift, making clear America's commitment to Western Europe's security and to a continuing global role. Despite a large contraction of the military budget, he guided the nation's relatively smooth conversion to a civilian base. Immediately after his election he instructed the Department of State to open negotiations for a new North Atlantic Treaty Organization. The NATO agreement, establishing this nation's first "peacetime" military alliance, was signed in Washington only four months later.

Unlike Harding, Truman devoted all of his only inaugural address to foreign affairs. "Today," he declared, "marks the beginning not only of a new administration, but of a period that will be eventful, perhaps decisive, for us and for the world." He stressed, in addition to the need to negate the rising menace in Moscow, four themes of international cooperation: support for the United Nations, continuation of the Marshall Plan, the establishment of NATO and "Point Four," a bold new program to make the benefits of American know-how available to underdeveloped countries.

Between his election and inauguration Truman had accepted the resignation of the ailing George C. Marshall as secretary of state and named a strong successor, Dean Acheson. In the four years that followed, Truman and Acheson successfully met the multiple challenges of Western postwar reconstruction, Cold War confrontation, Old World decolonization and international economic harmonization, setting the country on a course that lasted almost four decades and that would ultimately "win" the Cold War. To be sure, support from Congress and the public was enormously facilitated by the fear of a visible, powerful enemy; but the nation's basic long-term approach of vigilance, restraint and cooperation with friends and allies had been set by the president in the first few months after his election.

III

Truman, like most presidents, perceived a mandate in his narrow electoral victory. But it may be difficult to discern any foreign policy mandate in this year's election returns, regardless of who wins.

Unfortunately presidential election campaigns often have an unhealthy effect on American foreign policy. Political promises are commonly designed to appeal to local and short-term interests and to ethnic voter blocs. Foreign countries and foreign imports make handy targets for campaign oratory. The leaders of allied nations, however important in the long run, cannot carry a single U.S. district. Overseas problems, particularly if they are controversial, are often neglected or postponed until election pressures are over. In 1976, for example, Republican challenger Ronald Reagan's campaign against President Gerald Ford helped delay both the second Strategic Arms Limitation Talks and Panama Canal treaties.

This election year has been worse than most. Logically this November's voting should constitute another great "referendum" on new directions in American foreign policy. Instead, as of this writing, the campaign has dwelt almost entirely on domestic politics, the economy and personalities. The two presidential candidates have largely downplayed major international issues. With public opinion polls consistently showing strong support for President Bush's handling of foreign affairs, particularly his leadership in Operation Desert Storm—a strength on which he had hoped to capitalize in the election—voters complained in the same polls that the president had spent too much time on foreign affairs and too little time on the domestic issues that were of primary importance to the country. Foreign economic, environmental and other hazards continue to threaten the nation's well-being (less visibly than did Soviet nuclear weapons, to be sure), but only one percent of poll respondents declared foreign policy issues to be the most important matters facing the nation.

As a result President Bush curtailed some of his foreign travels and activities, for months averted his gaze from the slaughter in

Sarajevo, delayed and diluted the U.S. contribution to a Russian aid package and—like his Democratic Party challenger—devoted his campaign speeches principally to domestic issues.

With the U.S. economy sluggish, the budget deficit still increasing and America's physical survival no longer at stake, this focus on the domestic front in the country's first post-Cold War election is not particularly surprising or troublesome. But at times only a fine line separated the Democratic Party campaign appeal to "take care of our own first" from the isolationist "America First" philosophy favoring wholesale withdrawal of U.S. forces and commitments. The presidential primaries of both parties appeared to reject outright protectionism and isolationism, making at least that much of a mandate clear. But the meaning of the November election will be harder to read.

IV

If President Bush is reelected, one factor will in theory alter his position the day after that reelection. Under the twentys-econd amendment to the Constitution, he will be a "lame duck," ineligible to succeed himself in office after another four years.

Will this make a difference? No doubt, starting early in his term, there will be increased scrambling and angling among both Republicans and Democrats hoping to succeed him. That will make his relations with Congress, including some members of his own party, even more difficult than they already are. The reported interest of members of his own cabinet in gaining the next Republican nomination, unusual in modern politics, though once a common occurrence, could add a still sharper partisan cast to national security debates. Even without any added and early emphasis on presidential ambition Mr. Bush's reelection is unlikely to return bipartisanship in foreign affairs to the level that generally but not inevitably prevailed in the first two decades of the Cold War.

Whether a president in his final term actually loses some of his influence with Congress and other countries, and even some of his own determination to please the electorate, is difficult to prove. He still holds the presidency with all its powers. He still occupies the "bully pulpit." He still dispenses patronage, party funds and endorsements. He may not need to win popular or party votes ever again but he will want to win his place in history and to influence the choice of his successor.

Foreign governments occasionally try to play games with the end of a U.S. president's term. The South Vietnamese were apparently induced by Richard Nixon's team in 1968 to stall any peace negotiations until he took charge. Inquiries are now under way to determine whether the Iranians were induced by Ronald Reagan's advisers in 1980 to postpone the return of U.S. embassy hostages until he took charge. Soviet leader Nikita Khrushchev claimed that he had deliberately deferred the release of downed U-2 pilot Gary Powers in 1960 until President Dwight D. Eisenhower, with whom he was feuding, was gone.

In general the last years in the presidencies of Eisenhower and Reagan, the only two presidents to have served two full terms since adoption of the twenty-second amendment, do not prove either side in this debate. President Eisenhower had his share of disappointments in 1960. His trip to Japan was canceled by an angry mob in Tokyo, and his trip to the Soviet Union was canceled by an angry Khrushchev, whose outrage over the U-2 incursion, real or feigned, also sank a much-awaited summit meeting in Paris. Nevertheless Eisenhower was able to proceed with a number of lesser trips and agreements and remained personally popular at term's end.

President Reagan was also popular after two terms, although his last 18 months in office were marred by the Iran-contra scandal. Inasmuch as the final White House years of both Eisenhower and Reagan shattered the age record for that office, a decline in vigor rather than influence may explain their respective lack of foreign policy initiatives during those years. If President Bush is reelected, the fact that he will be commencing his last term foretells little or nothing about his effectiveness in foreign affairs during the next four years.

V

If Democrat Bill Clinton is elected on November 3 to replace Mr. Bush the nation will commence on November 4 that unique 11-week phenomenon known as the "presidential transition period." To the leaders of other nations, who will have impatiently waited at least a year for the United States to complete its unduly long presidential selection process and get back to foreign policy decision-making, a further delay of 77 days before they know with whom and what they will be dealing may well seem intolerable. Many policymakers in an outgoing administration return to private life even before the new president is sworn in, and the momentum and interest of those who remain begin to sag. Secretary Acheson complained of the "virtual interregnum" of more than a year that accompanied the 1952–53 change of government. The world does not stand still during our election campaign and transition, and a widespread sense that no one is minding the store in the United States during this prolonged period can be dangerous. The growing crises in Laos during the winter of 1960 and in El Salvador during the winter of 1980 did not wait for new U.S. policymakers to be briefed and take charge.

For a new president-elect, however, the transition period seems all too brief. Unlike a newly chosen prime minister of Britain he has no previously selected, already functioning shadow cabinet, ready at a moment's notice to assume responsibility with total confidence in the permanent career services, with automatic support from the legislative branch and with relatively few important positions to be filled. On the contrary, while still exhausted from a far longer political campaign than Britain has ever endured, a new president must select hundreds of new appointees—most of them strangers to him and to each other— and fight to secure their confirmation by the Senate. He must reexamine America's position in the world from the vantage point of the presidency, very different from that of the candidate, and review in a new and cooler context his campaign promises for early legislative and executive action. He must prepare for the decisions and deadlines that the calendar unavoidably forces upon him soon after he takes office. Next year's list includes new protocols to the international Global Warming and Ozone Layer agreements, the General Agreement on Tariffs and Trade, the North American Free Trade Agreement and renewal of most-favored-nation status for China.

A new president's team needs time, even after inauguration, to move in, learn the ropes and find out more about each other, the responsibilities, personnel and other resources at its command. The working relationship between the new president, secretary of state and national security adviser also needs time to evolve.

Outgoing presidents have occasionally sought to involve their successors in some controversial international move during the transition, and incoming presidents-elect have occasionally acted to discourage one last summit or send-off for their predecessors. A 1992 transition, should President Bush be defeated, will see no such impropriety. Mr. Bush and Mr. Clinton can both be presumed to be men of goodwill, devoted to the national interest. Neither will be unclear as to who has full responsibility until January 20, 1993. The Foreign Service and other career services will accept and assist the members of the new leadership team, and in turn be accepted by them. No career ambassador is likely to be penalized (as some were in 1980–81) for having served in a policy position under the outgoing administration. Briefings for the new team will be comprehensive and objective. To be sure, the departing president may well include in his final budget submission to Congress, as so many have before him, a few hidden land mines, unachievable goals or parting jabs at his successor; but that kind of charade is neither unprecedented nor unforgivable.

Nevertheless transition periods have their dangers, particularly for a president-elect who (like Clinton, and Reagan and Carter before) is a relative newcomer to Washington. Self-appointed spokesmen for the new administration will inevitably sow confusion and concern in foreign embassies and capitals. A few self-important nominees will disdain help from more knowledge-able career officers. (The 1952–53 transition emissary from the newly appointed secretary of state, John Foster Dulles, demanded from the appropriate desk officer "all the telegrams" covering a particular country then in crisis; when asked if the secretary also wanted any background material, he stiffly replied: "No, we will provide our own background.") Occasionally a confidential com-mitment is unintentionally omitted from the briefing, or a covert operation is inadequately explained (for example, the Bay of Pigs in 1960–61), thereby creating serious problems for the new admin-istration at a later date.

A particularly dangerous practice in recent transitions has been the president-elect's selection of his own large, aggressive transi-tion team for each department and agency. These teams, often filled with ideologues, disappointed job-seekers and eager congres-sional staffers, all jockeying for power, setting their own agenda and determined to score political points, set out not to smooth the transfer of power but to conduct investigations or collect confiden-tial documents that will confirm their worst suspicions about the departing administration. Both the president-elect and the nation would be better served if he named for each department a small, low-profile, issue-oriented, fact-finding task force whose members recognize that the election is over and wish simply to pave the way for the new secretary and then disband.

The president-elect will also need to shift gears, to remember that the political campaign is over and that he no longer needs to respond to every news media demand, criticize his predecessor or take pains to distinguish his position on every issue. Nor in world affairs would it be wise to do so.

VI

Both Bush and Clinton have promised "change" to a frustrated electorate, without exempting world affairs from that prescrip-tion. Both have termed themselves "agents of change." But they have been understandably vague about any specifics of change in

U.S. foreign policy. Even with all the altered conditions and new opportunities noted above, the new president will not be writing on a clean slate. Continuity avoids confusion and builds consensus. Change solely for the sake of change, or solely for the sake of political appearance, is unworthy. Sudden change can be destabilizing, unsettling to allies, inconsistent with commitments and deemed further evidence of unreliability. Overly ambitious change can lead to embarrassing rejection abroad and to disillusionment at home.

Nevertheless, taking all that into account, the president elected this November, whether incumbent or challenger, will find that his unprecedented freedom to move the country in new directions is not only an opportunity but an obligation. He cannot, even if he wishes, adhere to the old foreign policy agenda, for it is now largely obsolete. Change, more fundamental than either party or any branch of government has discussed to date, will be required in virtually every aspect of national security policy. Without attempting to spell out specific details and numbers that will depend upon the next president's personal and political predilections, it seems clear that, regardless of party, he must reexamine our nation's course in the world in at least six overlapping areas: the approach to military matters, multilateral agencies, economic development assistance, international trade, human rights and democracy, and nonmilitary threats to security.

What is needed in each of these areas is not so much the invention of new ideas as the adoption of old ideas whose time has come—measures that do not merely prolong the status quo but ultimately transform it.

No doubt many will regard what follows as presumptuous, partisan and partial; they are right. But any foreign policy agenda offered to a future president whose identity is still unknown would be subject to the same three criticisms. The following agenda is a potential first draft, both to prod the November 3 winner and to provide him with a base upon which to build his own long-term vision of the world as it should be.

Theodore C. Sorensen

VII

In military matters the next president will need to decide whether
America should remain a global hegemonic power ready to "pay
any price, bear any burden, fight any foe" or evolve into a pivotal,
residual power. He will need to decide whether America should
transfer to independent regional security groups the primary and
initial responsibility for containing those threats to security that
arise in their respective regions. This includes those organizations
in which the United States has legitimate membership (NATO, the
Conference on Security and Cooperation in Europe, the Organization of American States).

Under the latter scenario those regional groups, back-stopped
by U.N. forces, would be supplemented by American troops only
when necessary to their success and to America's own vital interests. Consistent with this approach other leading nations would be
encouraged to join and help strengthen those regional groupings in
which they have a legitimate interest; our traditional concern for
the stability and safety of western Europe would be extended to all
of Europe, east and west; the historic turnabout represented by
French-German military cooperation would be encouraged, not
discouraged; and the worldwide elimination of all short-range nuclear weapons would become a priority.

Shooting last instead of first would mean transforming America's Cold War posture of ready global intervention into one of
intervening militarily abroad only in concert with other nations,
only when the military personnel burden as well as the financial
burden (and genuine decision-making) is shared with others,
and only when the likely enduring effectiveness of such intervention makes that action worthwhile. America needs to become
as skilled in the organization and enforcement of international
economic and political sanctions against transgressors as it is in
the deployment of military force, thereby increasing its willingness to prefer the former and defer the latter. America needs to
devote as much energy to halting, through economic and political pressures and strengthened international machinery, the

present "horizontal" proliferation of nuclear, chemical, biological, high-tech conventional and other weapons of mass destruction and their delivery systems, along with the technology, equipment, personnel and matériel needed to obtain them, as this country previously devoted to halting the "vertical" proliferation of such weapons in the Soviet Union. Accepting a comprehensive ban on nuclear testing would be a good start.

The next president, regardless of party, will be called on to submit a defense budget that is substantially below present levels. This is likely to involve sharply cutting back those overseas forces and major strategic weapons systems that were established primarily to prevent or resist a massive Soviet attack. America would emphasize instead a smaller, mobile conventional force, trained, equipped and ready for rapid and relatively brief Desert Storm-like deployment to meet the kind of regional aggressors, separatists or terrorists that now constitute the most likely threats the nation will face.

Such a reorientation could help win battles on the home front as well. The next president could divert the bulk of federal high-tech research and development funds from the task of increasing our military superiority to the task of enhancing our economic competitiveness; facilitate the conversion to a civilian economy of those communities and work forces now heavily dependent upon anachronistic military industries and installations; and make use of redundant Defense Department personnel and facilities in tackling the nation's need for teachers, crime fighters, schools, housing, job training and places of detention.

VIII

The next president should take considerable comfort from the fact that the post-Cold War United Nations, in providing an essential legal umbrella for the Persian Gulf War, helping to free the hostages in Lebanon and to end the fighting in El Salvador, and moving forcefully to underpin the perilous transitions of Namibia and Cambodia, demonstrated that it can bring to the solution of global problems not only machinery and talent but also legitimacy and credibility.

During his term the United States has the opportunity to lead the way in strengthening the effectiveness and efficiency of the United Nations, particularly the Security Council (ultimately with the European Community and Japan each holding permanent seats) and the Secretariat, but also such specialized agencies as the International Atomic Energy Agency, the U.N. Development Program and UNICEF. He should be able to make more consistent use of those bodies, referring more issues to them and to the International Court of Justice, whose compulsory jurisdiction we should once again accept. The new global problems—transborder environmental, economic, health, population, refugee, drugs and human rights—can all best be tackled through these international agencies, where future costs and past experience can be shared.

America can also lead in strengthening and making better use of international financial institutions such as the World Bank, International Monetary Fund and regional development banks. The world having breathed a sigh of relief over the disappearance of Soviet vetoes blocking U.N. Security Council actions, the next president should go slow in using for political reasons his own effective veto in these international financial bodies.

IX

The new conventional wisdom invariably emphasizes the importance of economics. The next president will recognize that, whatever other goals may have motivated Truman's original Marshall Plan and Point Four, economic development assistance was largely a creature of the Cold War. Public and congressional support for such an economic assistance program in the shifting power patterns of the post-Cold War era is not likely to be sustained. But neither is the peace of a world community (like that of a local community) harshly divided between rich and poor likely to be sustained. Today African and other nations no longer considered useful as anti-Soviet pawns find themselves largely ignored by

Washington. But over the years the multilayered U.S. Agency for International Development (USAID) bureaucracy, eager to show its flag in every corner of the developing world, has scattered its remaining funds among a variety of economic development, free enterprise development and democratization development projects with largely disappointing results.

The next president must decide whether to scale back costly country-by-country aid operations and the agency that administers them, instead leaving small emergency and discretionary funds in the hands of each American ambassador. The monies now used to support humanitarian, disaster relief and other grass-roots programs could be channeled through the World Bank and other multilateral agencies and through nongovernmental foundations and similar organizations, thus sharply reducing both tax-supported overhead and associated political payola, but still attaching basic conditions of human rights, arms reduction and accountability. (Those recipient governments instituting genuine administrative, political and economic reforms should also be forgiven all debts to the U.S. government.)

If USAID is scaled back, the bulk of the money it now handles—the "strategic" funds—could be distributed in much larger amounts in multiyear commitments as direct balance-of-payments or budgetary support to a much shorter list of recipients. Under this approach, the president and secretary of state would carefully select the most dynamic developing nations, regardless of size, that are clearly ready and willing to undertake the rapid but long-term political, economic and social development to make them strong, stable and peaceful leaders, regional models and enduring trading and political partners. These funds, along with Overseas Private Investment Corporation (OPIC) and Export-Import Bank guarantees and credits, should also be used to leverage an increased flow of private investment to the same targeted countries.

To create a viable free economy out of chaos in Russia and the other former Soviet republics, the emerging demilitarized democracies of the Commonwealth of Independent States (and not all of them will meet that standard) clearly must receive from the West more economic assistance (in addition to humanitarian aid and agricultural surpluses) than the amounts belatedly offered thus far. In return those states clearly must provide more adequate assurances than they have thus far that necessary long-term political, fiscal, monetary, military and structural reforms will be made. Both America's security and economic interests make stability in this region a high priority.

Finally the next president must take dramatic and decisive steps—such as paying for the destruction of Russian and Ukrainian nuclear stockpiles or establishing with each nation a joint investment guarantee fund—to make sure that prolonged studies and negotiations do not in the meantime cost the Russians their newfound freedom from authoritarianism and cost the world this historic opportunity for peace. Taking care not to pay attention solely to Russia—or even solely to Moscow—providing technical assistance in building free institutions as well as factories, opening U.S. markets to their goods and sending Peace Corps volunteers to their villages, he must initiate a post-Cold War effort in the former Soviet Union that will match the post-World War II vision demonstrated by Harry Truman 44 years ago.

X

With regard to international trade the next president will have no choice but to formulate a coherent national strategy to make American industry competitive again in all key sectors of the world marketplace, basing that strategy on results and consequences, not on some doctrine or dogma of free or fair or managed trade.

No strategy will succeed unless the president, like his Japanese and European counterparts, can build behind it a consensus among American workers, business leaders and consumers sufficiently strong to support a new social compact—a legislated understanding under which each group shares in the costs and sacrifices of that national strategy as well as its benefits. Accepting the self-discipline necessary to improve the nation's rate of savings, investment, productivity, quality control and functional literacy sufficiently to match those of America's principal competitors will be far more effective than trying to discipline those competitors.

To obtain the necessary consensus the next president must ask Congress to emulate our major competitors also in providing an adequate level of job retraining, special unemployment benefits, community compensation and other forms of trade adjustment assistance for those displaced by a national trade policy.

Increasing the export of American goods instead of jobs will require new measures not only to pry open particular foreign markets aggressively but also to build demand in new potential markets, including Russia, the developing nations and newly robust economies like India, Korea and Brazil. It will require as well the restoration of the manufacturing base through the reorientation of national research laboratories to civilian purposes, the modernization of infrastructure, the encouragement of emerging technologies and the investment, educational and other measures of self-discipline noted above.

Just as Truman initiated the grand military alliance of NATO immediately after his election, to meet the overriding challenge of his time, so must the next president initiate a grand economic alliance with Japan and the European Community to meet an equally urgent challenge. Its task will be the preservation and coordination of an open, integrated global trading system facilitating the increased worldwide flow of goods, services, capital and intellectual property, free from both protectionist and predatory practices and enhancing the stability of major currencies and exchange rates. Regional trading blocs would be required to keep open markets and membership rolls; weaker economies, including the ex-Soviet states, would be assured access to the system; most important, all nations would be held to the same rules of trade, proscribing not only open and hidden barriers and distortions (including antitrust violations as well as subsidies) but also the practice of shortchanging labor, environmental, health, safety or consumer protection standards as a means of lowering costs and attracting investment.

It is in that context that the next president must complete the GATT and North American Free Trade Area negotiations, ultimately extending the latter to the entire western hemisphere. But time is short.

XI

With respect to human rights and democracy, the next president will need to increase the transparency, integrity and consistency of U.S. policy, avoiding the double standards and hypocrisy that characterized America's approach when the Cold War inhibited criticism of anticommunist dictators.

America no longer needs to subsidize the activities and stroke the egos of military usurpers and other despots. It can now encourage consumer boycotts of products from wayward countries; support increased U.N. fact-finding and monitoring of human rights; encourage regional organizations to isolate any member-nation failing to meet basic standards; expand programs of the U.S. Information Agency (USIA) and National Endowment for Democracy (NED) that build and promote the institutions of democracy and concern for human rights; undertake every effort to make America's own race relations, political procedures and economic opportunity a model for the rest of the world.

Once the campaign rhetoric on human rights and democracy has faded, the next president should not be under the illusion that more far-reaching measures will be easy or automatic.

He must decide how far the nation can go in invoking human rights considerations in determining relations with both friend and foe. Clearly they can only be one factor, not the sole determinant. Nor can there be any single, simple litmus test in deciding who meets our standards, if we are to avoid the kind of cynical manipulation and denial that such a test invites.

He will wish to encourage democratization and discourage military and other dictators through trade, aid and other preferences, through the maintenance or severance of diplomatic relations and through the educational and promotional efforts of the NED and

USIA. But this country cannot afford to deal only with democracies or attempt to remake the world in its own image.

He will no doubt support international economic sanctions and suspend OPIC, Export-Import and economic assistance programs when necessary to penalize those governments that engage in the worst human rights abuses. But as the cases of Haiti and Iraq remind us, he must also beware of starving people or otherwise increasing the suffering of innocent captives as punishment for the sins of their rulers.

He will be under pressure to criticize openly, and to join in U.N. Security Council resolutions condemning, any government, whether allied or adverse, that consistently mistreats legitimate protesters and ethnic minorities. But quiet diplomatic warnings may prove more effective with some governments.

He will wish to support forceful regional and U.N. actions to halt and correct wholesale deprivations of human rights. But legitimate calls for military intervention on humanitarian or democracy-saving grounds can, if caution is not used, easily evolve into another Vietnam-type conflict.

XII

Finally, with regard to other nonmilitary threats, the next president, whoever he is, will need to recognize four basic facts:

- that nonmilitary developments can pose genuine threats to the long-term security and quality of life of American citizens as surely as armed aggression—but cannot be repelled militarily;
- that traditional concepts of national sovereignty are unable to cope with torrential transborder flows of not only money and information but also environmental scourges, AIDS and other diseases, illegal drugs, arms and immigrants;
- that no one of these threats can be ended by the United States acting alone; and
- that new international rules and institutions will be required to combat these nonmilitary threats.

The threat of environmental degradation, for example, by destroying this planet's life support systems—air, ozone, water and natural resources—can blight entire regions and ultimately make the whole earth inhospitable for human as well as other species. America can try to make certain that new U.S.-financed technology and industrial development proceed only with adequate environmental safeguards; but America alone cannot halt the danger to its health and ecology from those noxious and toxic emissions, rain forest depredations and biodiverse species reductions that occur outside its borders.

The threat of energy dependence and depletion requires not only increased international efforts but also a firm national policy emphasizing conservation and greater attention to cheaper alternative and renewable fuels. Operation Desert Storm was only the latest chapter in the age-old story of shedding blood to control energy and other natural resources (including fresh water, which America also wastes and consumes beyond all rational proportions). Yet this country remains lax in the imposition of fuel efficiency standards and in deterring the excessive use of hydrocarbons and other nonrenewable resources.

Overpopulation with all its many offspring—large-scale unemployment, poverty, hunger, desperation, crime, environmental destruction and great waves of economic migration—is already the province of an international agency, the U.N. Population Fund; but its family planning and information programs have not been fully backed by the United States. Unless more women in the poor nations are fully educated and emancipated with regard to their reproductive systems and rights, our children will live in a world in which the industrialized countries, with most of the planet's wealth, will have less than one-fifth of its population—a recipe for disaster.

All of these sobering global trends are illustrated in Haiti. A desperately poor, oppressed but rapidly growing population exhausted the wood fuel, topsoil and drinking water needed for survival and sought in large numbers to enter the United States

illegally by means of sea voyages that proved fatal to a large proportion of those who chanced them.

Is this the future of the world?

This presentation of a presidential agenda does not imply that
these measures can be promulgated by the president alone. On the
contrary they require the cooperation and participation of other
nations, the United Nations and, most important, the Congress.
They require the support of the next president's State Department,
Defense Department and National Security Council team. Above
all they require the support of the American people. Electing a
president who promises change is only the first step. Americans
must then display the political will to break with the old, to institute the new and to accept the risks and burdens inherent in each
of these changes.

The next president, needless to say, cannot lead unless he has a
vision of where to go. But neither can he lead, nor should he try to
lead, unless the American people are willing to shoulder the responsibilities of leadership in the new post-Cold War world.

**THEODORE C. SORENSEN is a Senior Partner at Paul, Weiss, Rifkind, Whar-
ton and Garrison in New York.**

A Republican Looks at Foreign Policy

Richard G. Lugar   WINTER 1987/88

George HW Bush in 1988.

ecently it was suggested that presidential primaries drive
Republican and Democratic hopefuls into making a mess
of foreign policy: Republicans emphasize their suspicions
about arms control agreements with the Soviets; Democrats rail
against new weapons systems and any resort to the use of force to
back up diplomacy. This commentary—an editorial in The Washington Post—concluded that the process of the primaries exacts a
high cost in American foreign policy, and that it will not be easy for
the next president to reclaim a middle ground laid waste by excessive partisan rhetoric.

But the middle can be variously defined. What will matter is
how a new administration deals with the core issues of American
security policy: arms control and national defense, the use of force,

including U.S. military forces, abroad. Even these issues must first be addressed in the broad historical context of those enduring post-war commitments and responsibilities that both Republicans and Democrats have subscribed to since 1945.

If the new administration is to develop a cohesive and coherent foreign policy, it cannot escape the changes in our nation's strategic position. It must recognize three fundamental new conditions. First, there is a potentially dangerous disparity developing between those vital security interests that the American people are prepared to support with force, and the degree and kind of force we are willing and able to employ to protect these interests. In short, our aims may exceed our resources.

The extent of American commitments abroad has not declined; in some parts of the world our obligations have even increased. This new reality has led some to argue once again that we must reduce our commitments and thereby decrease the risks our country must face. But it is far easier to demand a reduction in commitments than to define with clarity those commitments that can, in fact, be safely reduced. In practice, we must decide whether the loss of prestige from abdicating responsibilities will reduce the effective use of American power more than the reduced claims on our resources might enhance our standing.

Our current commitments are likely to continue even if our military power remains more limited, when measured against those commitments, than it has in the past. This situation implies an increased degree of risk. Both Republicans and Democrats will have to acknowledge this change in our global position, for there is not likely to be any acceptable way to escape from either responsibilities or risks.

This security dilemma, the growing gap between our objectives and our capabilities—sometimes described as a decline of relative American power—has been recognized in both parties, but the diversity of proposed remedies has accelerated the breakdown of the national consensus. The simultaneous end of any semblance of a national or bipartisan consensus in the country on foreign policy is the second new factor that the next administration must face.

Republicans, led by Arthur Vandenberg and Henry Stimson in the 1940s, promoted bipartisanship in foreign policy that was sustained until its demise over Vietnam. Efforts to restore a consensus on security issues under the Reagan Administration have run afoul of deep differences over U.S. policy toward Nicaragua and an appropriate U.S. role in the Persian Gulf. It has thus become increasingly difficult to maintain a national consensus in support of the employment of U.S. force and forces abroad. And, of course, no administration is eager to incur the domestic political penalties and divisions inherent in engaging U.S. military forces in combat situations.

It is clear that, as some of our strategic advantages have declined, a national consensus is all the more necessary in order to maximize the effective use of our residual power. But such a consensus cannot simply be wished into being. It can be restored only gradually over time, through the development of mutual trust and sustained credibility on the part of both the president and the Congress.

Reestablishing such trust, however, is all the more difficult in light of the third new factor: the revival of the struggle between the executive and legislative branches over foreign policy. This tension is inherent in the constitutional separation of powers but it has been exacerbated by new concerns over both the formulation as well as the implementation of policies—again, evident most recently in the debates over aid to the contras as well as the War Powers Act and its applicability in the Persian Gulf crisis.

Our nation must guarantee our essential interests at a reasonable risk through a judicious balancing of commitments and power: this means maintaining a credible deterrence and national defense as well as an ability and a willingness to use armed force, directly and indirectly. If we cannot achieve this, then a more restrictive interpretation of vital security interests must necessarily follow, at a cost to our national security that cannot be predicted. I believe that the Reagan Administration has succeeded in bringing our interests and power more into line, to the point that the inherent risks are approaching an acceptable level. The next Republican administration can build on this achievement.

II

The issue of military security has confronted every administration since the bombing of Pearl Harbor. How much is enough, and at what price, have been perennial questions. All presidential aspirants claim to favor a strong defense. Little agreement exists on the price of such a posture. It is already clear that opinions are divided on matters such as cutting the defense budget, spending levels for strategic defense, the timing of new conventional weapons programs and the pace of naval modernization. Consequently, much of the foreign policy debate leading up to the next national election will likely revolve around the role that arms control, and perhaps superpower cooperation in limiting regional conflicts, might play in the balancing of America's foreign interests and commitments with appropriate power, resources and the political will to support them.

The Reagan Administration focused its attention on enhancing the military strength of the country, as a central priority. Mr. Reagan's promise to do just that certainly contributed to his election in 1980, and his success in realizing this objective surely contributed to his reelection four years later. Critics may argue about the effectiveness of the allocation of funds to one or another specific defense program, and they may even debate the utility of the military strength achieved in the past years. But the perception of restored American military strength made it possible to negotiate with Moscow, and has given the Soviet Union an incentive to negotiate over outstanding issues in the Soviet-American relationship.

The new Soviet leader apparently recognized the new situation confronting the U.S.S.R. The Reagan Administration's enhancement of our country's military posture threatened not only Soviet gains in relative strategic offensive strength acquired in an earlier period but promised to mobilize our technological advantages in the furtherance of the Strategic Defense Initiative (SDI). This presented General Secretary Mikhail Gorbachev with a choice. He recognized that the Soviet industrial-technological base could not be used both to reform a stagnant and backward economy and, simultaneously, to sustain an arms competition with the United States. Thus he resumed arms control negotiations, met with President Reagan at the Geneva summit and, finally, accepted the American position on eliminating medium-range missiles.

The Administration was attacked for its strategy of building strength in part as one means of achieving a more advantageous negotiating position. That strategy has paid off. It has revived genuine arms control negotiations; indeed, it established arms control as a centerpiece of East-West relations and very likely West-West relations for some time to come. It is not at all clear whether strategic arms agreements, comprehensive or otherwise, will actually enable the United States to safeguard deterrence at less cost and risk. But we seem to be entering a more or less continuous round of negotiations on controlling strategic and nuclear arms—and doing so from a stronger position than when the talks began in 1981–82.

Some critics, Democrats and Republicans, contend that an agreement on intermediate-range nuclear forces creates a slippery slope toward the "denuclearization" of Europe. It is prudent to look into the risks and opportunities of a post-INF environment. But this long-term concern should not paralyze our consideration of the immediate unfinished business. An INF agreement along the lines presently contemplated should and is likely to be ratified in early to mid-1988.

Some people have genuine doubts about the political or military efficacy of such a treaty, but I suspect that much of the debate surrounding ratification will have little to do with the actual contents of such a treaty. On the one hand, any major controversy in the Senate's review of an INF treaty and the larger public debate could transform the consideration of the treaty into a referendum on nuclear and conventional force modernization, or the value of the 1972 Anti-Ballistic Missile Treaty, or even the future of SDI. On the other hand, concerns that an INF treaty might weaken our position in Europe could lead to demands or promises of undiminished or increased spending on various defense programs relative to NATO Europe.

The next stage may well be crucial. A general agreement exists between the Soviet Union and the United States to seek to negotiate a 50-percent reduction of strategic offensive forces. An agreement significantly reducing strategic nuclear offensive forces might be achievable even before the end of the Reagan Administration. But relating strategic offense and strategic defense, and most particularly dealing with the Soviet insistence on linking SDI to any START (Strategic Arms Reduction Talks) accord militates against optimism, both in the negotiations and in the Congress. Unfortunately, it is not at the negotiating table in Geneva but in the Congress that the most significant arguments could take place regarding the START-SDI linkage, as well as the link between arms control and strategic modernization programs.

A major issue in the Congress is the proper legal interpretation of the ABM treaty. The debate is between a "narrow" or a "broad" interpretation of that treaty. Unfortunately, the players in the debate are all on the American side of the table. The Soviet Union, by adopting a position at Reykjavik that can only be described as "super-narrow," has little incentive to deal with the issue seriously as long as it believes that it may be decided in its favor by American legislators. The Soviets are eager to maintain selected portions of the ABM treaty in order to constrain the SDI program.

In this light, I believe that a consensus on the nature of the country's commitments under the ABM treaty and a parallel commitment to a strong SDI program are essential. If there is no bipartisan consensus on these issues, we may never know whether areas of compromise are possible between the general Soviet determination to kill SDI and the Reagan Administration's commitment to advance it. Thus far, the Administration has successfully resisted crippling restrictions on SDI research permitted by the ABM treaty. Moreover, I think that the Soviets may settle for an outcome that provides a degree of predictability in the strategic defense area, while the United States moves forward with a robust program that includes research, testing and development.

Many Democrats, however, regard SDI only as a "bargaining chip," to be traded away for substantial Soviet reductions of offensive nuclear forces. On the other hand, some Republicans advocate the near-term deployment of a basic defensive system. While abandonment of research, testing and development would be dangerous, no favors would be done to the SDI program by rushing to a deployment based primarily on political calculations rather than technical feasibility.

Despite much Democratic opposition to it, the notion of strategic defense has become a permanent feature of the American strategic landscape. Strategic defense programs will outlast the SDI acronym, even though no administration can commit its successor to its policies and programs. But the next president will have to go back to the drawing board, not so much with respect to SDI research and testing programs, but because he will have to develop sustained domestic political support for the program. And to do so the next administration will have to put its case forward in a larger national security context.

The Strategic Defense Initiative stems from both a dissatisfaction with our existing nuclear strategy and a belief that changes in strategy might be technically feasible for us and the Soviets. The next administration will have to recast the SDI issue. The issue of what is technologically possible must be embedded in a debate over what is strategically desirable and practical. I hope that the next president and a majority of the Congress will permit full exploration of the contribution that strategic defense might make to our overall national security. It is to those security interests that SDI funding levels ought to be linked, not to transient arms control strategies.

Arms control cannot serve as a substitute for an adequate defense posture, any more than it can exist separately from national security policy. Too often, Western negotiating strategies have assumed it can. But it will be too easy to blame arms control alone for the problems the next administration will encounter in adjusting to a changing strategic environment. If arms control is to serve as a flexible instrument of military strategy and further the prospect of achieving greater compatibility between negotiating policies and military strategy, then military and foreign policy objectives will need to be spelled out with greater clarity.

III

Managing the Soviet-American relationship is the core issue. But it is integrally related to a second major issue: redistributing military and nonmilitary burdens around the world. Both the U.S. involvement in the Persian Gulf and the prospect of an INF agreement have stimulated congressional demands for greater burden-sharing by our allies. The demands have, in turn, generated reluctance and skepticism within the alliance regarding American motives and the wisdom of American policies.

The task of strengthening conventional forces in NATO Europe has always been urgent, expensive and politically sensitive. Despite the important link between Europe's security and our own, and despite concern in the Congress that an INF agreement will highlight the conventional force imbalance in Europe, political sentiment in the United States has been running in the direction of reducing our NATO expenditures. Such sentiments will be all the more difficult to resist if the Congress cannot be convinced that the NATO allies are assuming a larger share of the burden in strengthening the alliance's conventional forces in a post-INF environment. But even assuming a political willingness on the part of the European allies to do more, there will continue to exist some sentiment in the United States to reallocate military resources away from NATO and in the direction of the Middle East and the Third World in general, where American commitments outpace capabilities.

In the early 1970s, Democratic leaders in the Senate demanded a unilateral reduction in American forces. This was resisted by a Republican White House. Now the pattern is reemerging. I believe the national interest dictates that it should not be a partisan issue, and I hope that a viable consensus can be created in order to meet our obligations and responsibilities.

Any debate over a redistribution of responsibilities around the world will not be limited to defense budgets and commitments alone. A third major issue is also related: how to deal, in an explicit and comprehensive fashion, with the enormous changes in our relative economic strength. During the last four decades our nation has countered the Soviet military threat and provided a strategic safety net for the free world, but at staggering costs. Previous administrations have demanded persistently that wealthy friends in Europe and Japan do their duty in the furtherance of common aspirations of mutual defense and maintenance of world economic prosperity. But our friends have acted on the assumption that the United States remains the world's greatest power and that it will continue to act responsibly whether or not others follow suit and pay their share.

One of the most crucial tasks for the next president will be to negotiate much more successfully a redefinition of the roles that we and our allies must play and the accompanying allocation of resources to pay for those roles. Without such negotiation, the United States will fall victim to a piecemeal reordering of domestic spending priorities among legitimate demands for defense, for investment to modernize our competitive industries and social infrastructure, and for expenditures vital to the health, education, safety and economic security of American citizens. The gap between missions and means will become larger and the risks to collective Western security will increase substantially.

Similar budget and resource debates occur in every vital democracy, and the larger industrialized democracies are becoming more adept in advising each other on desired outcomes. Moreover, it is important to understand that greater burden-sharing is not confined to the defense sector. Failure to end disastrous agricultural subsidization and dumping policies, for example, can affect the political will of one ally to defend another. There is a subtle relationship between nuclear arms control and a commercial trade tax proposal on soybean exports and farmer subsidies in the European Community. Agricultural subsidies and dumping conflicts undermine not only our economic efficiency but the grass-roots sentiments in the United States that are so vital to our defense commitments. To the extent that American exporters believe they are being treated unfairly while European allies run large balance-of-payments surpluses with the United States, a sense of alienation will erode popular support for meeting defense commitments in Europe.

Over the next several years, during the implementation of an INF agreement, the priority task in NATO Europe will be to strengthen our mutual conventional force posture. This will require expenditures to correct critical deficiencies and integration of new conventional technologies with tactical military innovations. It is also likely that alliance members will insist that such efforts be supplemented by arms control negotiations to reduce conventional force disparities between NATO and the Warsaw Pact. In short, another "dual-track" approach.

But this time around, it may not work. It will certainly be argued, once again, that the time is not propitious for the United States to seek a major redistribution of security burdens with its allies, at least in Europe. But given that a reduction in our national budget deficit is so critical to America's economic well-being, it is unlikely that our global defense burdens can be maintained solely on the promise of anticipated arms control outcomes.

IV

The Reagan Administration will leave to its successor several innovations in Third World policy. The Vietnam experience not only still influences our willingness to intervene in any Third World conflict; it still inhibits the prospect of any direct U.S. military intervention. The Soviet invasion of Afghanistan, however, lessened popular opposition to indirect military involvement, and the Reagan Administration has been able to regain some freedom of action to permit assistance, or military advice and training, or covert aid, for groups like the Afghan freedom fighters, Jonas Savimbi's rebel forces in Angola, and, of course, the Nicaraguan contras. One reason is unaltered national opposition to the establishment of Soviet bases and/or Cuban dependencies, especially in the western hemisphere. Yet there remain strong inhibitions against intervention and the use of force, directly or indirectly, to accomplish such aims, not only in Latin America but in the Third World at large.

Reinforcing inhibitions against either the direct or indirect use of military force to promote America's interests in the Third World is congressional reassertion of its role in the war-making process, as vividly demonstrated in connection with events in the Persian Gulf. The jury is still out on the impact of U.S. involvement in that region. At issue is the gap between a commitment to an objective and the political will to support it in practice. The next administration will discover that there is no logical solution to the disparity.

With regard to our Latin American policy, for the moment, both the Administration and the Democratic leadership in Congress provide verbal support for the Arias "peace" plan while continuing their guerrilla warfare over aid to the contras. To be sure, the Administration is rightly skeptical about Sandinista willingness to comply with the terms of the plan, and seeks to use that as leverage to gain renewed military aid to the contras. For its part, the Democratic leadership, which applauded the Arias plan as a pretext for cutting off such aid, grows concerned as Latin leaders themselves insist on full Sandinista compliance and denounce cosmetic or half-measures. The Democratic leadership in the Congress at times seems more interested in halting aid to the contras than in promoting democracy through full implementation of the Arias plan.

Debate continues over the direction of American policy in the Third World. Under the so-called Reagan Doctrine, we have supported anti-communist forces in countries currently dominated by Marxist regimes or clients of the Soviet Union. Viewed as the conscious promotion of such Western values as individual freedom and democracy in places where these values are denied (and where such a pursuit is not deemed dangerously explosive or excessively expensive in military terms), the Reagan Doctrine appears to fit comfortably into the objective of containing Soviet influence and power. But much of the political attractiveness of the doctrine flows from the effort to go beyond the defensive terms of limiting Soviet expansionism to the offensive in positively promoting liberation and seeking to reverse communist or Marxist control over various countries and their internal institutions.

There is a relationship between the Reagan Doctrine and the objective of improved superpower cooperation in nuclear arms control. In the 1970s efforts to reconcile conflicting objectives in these two areas involved codes of conduct or rules of the game. These efforts foundered when the Soviets sought to take advantage of new targets of opportunity in the Third World (e.g., Angola).

Some will counsel the next president to resume that effort with the argument that the wide-ranging reassessment, under Gorbachev, of Soviet involvement in the Third World has led to a decision in Moscow to reduce sharply Soviet "interests" and material support for marginal Marxist-Leninist states. I am skeptical. There are no indications that the Soviet leadership will countenance a retreat from established positions in the Third World. Moscow may be engaged in a "breathing period," a reassessment of the risks it is willing to run on behalf of prospective clients and the military and economic resources it will or can devote to such commitments. Mr. Gorbachev may even be disinclined to take on costly new commitments while simultaneously seeking to lessen the costs of existing ones over the long haul. But there are few signs of a conscious policy decision to diminish support for existing clients in the near term.

The next administration can adapt the Reagan Doctrine to the changing relationships between the superpowers and their respective policies toward the Third World. Thus far the Reagan Doctrine has emphasized military pressure as a means of raising the costs of Soviet involvement in the Third World. That emphasis alone is unlikely to achieve a major reduction in Soviet influence. It is time to ask what the American strategy ought to be during any Soviet "breathing period." If the Soviet Union should feel more vulnerable in the Third World, this will present new opportunities for American policy. What can American strategy build on the successes of the Reagan Doctrine? To the extent that an American policy of supporting struggles against tyranny of the left or the right is successful, what then?

We should move beyond the current version of the Reagan Doctrine by combining military and economic inducements in a political framework reflecting our estimates of the optimum possibilities in each region. The President and Congress must find a new consensus on appropriate funding of an imaginative and comprehensive economic and political program.

Currently, funds are virtually nonexistent for ongoing efforts in most countries and for new initiatives. We must enlist the vast economic resources of Japan and our NATO allies to work with us in encouraging the foundation of market-oriented democracies. Our collective plans to do so must be bold and broad. The Reagan Doctrine ought not to be viewed only in the context of Soviet-American competition; it provides policy guidance as well to U.S. bilateral relations with a number of Third World countries. Aid to anti-communist forces must be taken beyond the notion of a proper and not necessarily proportionate response to Soviet assistance to Marxist regimes or insurgencies: the commitment flowing from the doctrine should not cease abruptly because of successes earned through various pressures.

The defensive-deterrent shield provided by the United States for the promotion of its national security interests and those of its allies is also the shield that makes possible the promotion and maintenance by the United States and its allies of democratic ideals and institutions throughout the world. As we promote the building of democratic institutions abroad we may find that this policy is sometimes at odds with our commitment to provide for a common defense, in which case security measures often are given precedence over democratic aspirations.

But consider our recent experience with the Philippines. Events in 1986 suggest how American ideals of promoting legitimate security interests are mutually reinforcing. Former President Ferdinand Marcos won the support of successive American administrations because our officials were confident that he would ensure continued joint use of Subic Bay and Clark military facilities. Eventually, his position eroded because of his incompetence in prosecuting resistance against an internal Marxist insurgency and in protecting our base facilities, quite apart from growing perceptions of his political corruption. The Administration came to the view that the survival of the U.S. bases in the Philippines was "ancillary" to the issue of encouraging democratic reform in the government, and that the failure to undertake such reforms would inevitably result in the loss of the bases in the intermediate future. In the process of noting the growing failure of Marcos, the United States rediscovered that only by focusing on the policy objective of restoring democracy in the Philippines could we hope to retain a stable alliance and preserve mutual use of valuable military facilities on the soil of that sovereign country over the longer term.

There is a valuable lesson in this experience. Support for democratic progress can be compatible with maintenance of our security interests. We must seek to make this the rule rather than the exception.

V

Since 1940, when the Republican statesman Henry Stimson joined President Roosevelt's cabinet, Republicans have considered bipartisanship an essential feature of our party's approach to foreign affairs. Republicans, for the most part, supported the Truman

Doctrine, the Marshall Plan, NATO and the Korean War. The Truman foreign policy could not have succeeded without the initiatives and cooperation of Senator Arthur Vandenberg in forging bipartisan support in Congress. In those years, Republicans took long steps to move away from a heritage of isolationism.

In doing so, however, Republicans preserved some ideas and attitudes—principles if you will—that have evolved over time even while differentiating them from many Democrats in foreign policy.

The Democratic Party has had great difficulty in reconciling its recent noninterventionist goal—"no more Vietnams"—with the need for a strong, confident and globally engaged United States. The Republican Party has sought to combine the twin imperatives of strength and prudence. A globally engaged great power is unlikely to be able to avoid involvements in peripheral conflicts.

Some Democrats continue to revert to moralistic arguments with a human rights content to criticize the foreign policy initiatives of the Reagan Administration. Still others adopt the language of "national interests" and "political realism" as a short-term political tactic to attack the Reagan Doctrine. For example, many Democrats continue to make largely moralistic arguments against the Administration's policy toward Nicaragua. Instead of directly addressing the Sandinista threat to U.S. interests in Central America, many Democrats concentrate on the Administration's tactics while simultaneously seeking to rebut the ideological rationale underlying the current policy.

Too many Democrats have focused their attention and criticisms on how the Administration has involved the country in Central American politics, and eschewed debate on how U.S. interests in effectively promoting peace and security in the region can be furthered. Too often, Democratic inputs to the debate on contra aid are confined to references to "slippery slopes," alleging that such aid constitutes the first step toward another Vietnam. While such dire warnings may carry some emotional appeal, they also reveal paucity in thinking about credible alternative policy directions.

Many Democrats attack the Reagan Doctrine for allegedly twisting anti-communist ideological objectives into the primary rationale for U.S. support of freedom fighters in Nicaragua, Angola, Cambodia and Afghanistan. Yet many of their calls for a change in emphasis in the direction of realistic self-interest betray an overriding concern for tactical expediency rather than strategic necessity. Oftentimes, there is less a calculation of national interest than an obvious political desire to avoid any intervention in situations where success may entail costs. But U.S. interests cannot be determined exclusively or in major part by assessed degrees of difficulty of U.S. involvement and/or tactical alternatives. Efforts to reduce national interests to simplify the task of maximizing gains while cutting costs merely avoid the difficult issue of defining U.S. interests in Third World countries. Calls for noninterventionism seldom reflect a clear appreciation of interests and power.

Regardless of party, however, the next president will have a unique opportunity. America's global position has changed radically since 1945, but a new administration can translate the rebuilding of the 1980s into a period of major and positive accomplishments. I would stress the following objectives.

We will need a general strategy that outlines clear-cut criteria for measuring Soviet actions against our legitimate security concerns. The test of our next president's policy will be his ability to define precise criteria for progress toward peace and stability, and to test Soviet intentions against those criteria. The test of Gorbachev's intentions must be his actions, not the growing sophistication of his public diplomacy.

Effective arms control will be an important element of that testing. It will remain both a necessary price of our continuing security, and a potential danger to it. It must not become a diversion from strategy or a substitute for defense planning, or be allowed to obscure the realities of the military balance, and the actions necessary to correct it.

Our alliance system must be sustained and strengthened as the basis for a coalition strategy; a new and more equitable distribution of burdens must be worked out. And we must obtain allied cooperation in attempting to relate concerns about arms control and the settlement of regional threats to our mutual security.

Both political parties have an obligation to participate in a continuous assessment of America's strategic interests. While no one can dispute the necessity of tactical caution, it alone cannot answer the policy dilemma as to the appropriate balance between strength and prudence. Many efforts to redefine or constrict our strategic interests merely mask a reluctance or unwillingness to contemplate the use of military power. A redefinition of or retreat from military commitments should not be confused with a policy designed to protect and promote U.S. national interests.

The administration that is sworn in on January 20, 1989, will inherit a far stronger, safer and more durable position in the world than Mr. Reagan did in January 1981, with the frustration of Iran and the shock of Afghanistan. Not only is our foreign policy sound and our international position greatly improved, but we are also pursuing an active dialogue with our adversary, on the basis of the strength necessary to defend our interests—and all without the agony of a foreign war.

Senator RICHARD G. LUGAR of Indiana was Chairman of the Foreign Relations Committee in 1985–86.

A Democrat Looks
at Foreign Policy

Arthur M Schlesinger, Jr.   WINTER 1987/88

Michael Dukakis For President pin, 1988.

This brace of articles revives a venerable custom. Sixty years ago Foreign Affairs published a similar exchange in which Ogden Mills, later Herbert Hoover's secretary of the treasury, spoke for the Republicans and Franklin D. Roosevelt for the Democrats. Such eminent precedent should establish the proposition that foreign policy is a legitimate party issue—though this proposition hardly needs legitimation in a republic where foreign relations have been a subject of vehement debate ever since Hamilton and Madison disagreed over George Washington's neutrality program. Still the old saw "politics stops at the water's edge" expresses a familiar misconception. The impression occasionally arises—and is always encouraged by whatever administration is in office—that debating the conduct of foreign policy is indecent or unpatriotic. Yet clearly nothing in a democracy is more entitled to uninhibited discussion than decisions of peace and war.

What follows is not a party statement. "I belong to no organized party," as Will Rogers said. "I am Democrat." No one can speak for the Democratic Party until a candidate is nominated and a platform adopted in the summer of 1988; the consequent mandate runs to the first Tuesday after the first Monday in November, and the ticket will be good for that journey only.

II

In the judgment of this free-lance Democrat, the foreign policy of the United States has been on a radically misconceived course since President Reagan took office in January 1981. This is not to lay all blame for foreign policy failure on the Reagan Administration nor to reject everything that Administration has done in its conduct of foreign relations. The continuities of U.S. foreign policy are greater than European critics of the United States (and American critics of democracy) understand. Geopolitical imperatives fall impartially on Republican and Democrat alike. All American administrations, no matter how much they differ, will act to preserve a balance of power in Europe and to prevent extracontinental annexations in the Americas.

Even in the shorter run, the roots of Reagan's national security policy (misdirected, in this writer's view) as well as of his human rights policy (steadily improving) lie in the Carter Administration. It was Carter who, for better or for worse, advanced the movement away from the concept of mutual assured destruction toward a war-prevailing strategy, who approved the MX missile, who expanded American security commitments in the Third World and whose Carter Doctrine defined the Persian Gulf as within the zone of U.S. vital interests. And it was Carter too who placed human rights on the world's conscience and agenda—for which Reagan roundly condemned him in the 1980 campaign, holding Carter's human rights preoccupation responsible for the "loss" of Iran and Nicaragua. In abandoning the Philippines' Ferdinand Marcos and Haiti's Jean-Claude Duvalier half a dozen years later, Reagan unabashedly adopted the policy for which he had so righteously denounced Carter in the cases of the shah and the Somozas.

Within this broad framework of bipartisan continuity, however, the Reagan Administration has carried forward historic differences between the Republican and Democratic parties, differences delineated by Ogden Mills and Franklin D. Roosevelt sixty years ago.

The salient difference is that the Republican Party has been in recent times the vehicle of unilateral action in world affairs and the Democratic Party the vehicle of international cooperation. Ogden Mills, an eastern, Wall Street Republican, had little sympathy for the defiantly isolationist William E. Borah-Hiram Johnson wing of his party. Yet even Mills emphasized the unshakable Republican commitment to the nation's "traditional policy of independence in foreign affairs" and dismissed the legacy of Woodrow Wilson as one "under which our independence of action might be subordinated to the decision of other nations." F.D.R.'s 1928 article, on the other hand, saluted the League of Nations as "the first great agency for the maintenance of peace and for the solution of common problems ever known to civilization."

The Reagan Administration has now given the G.O.P.'s unilateralist tradition a global application. No administration in recent times has paid less heed to the views and interests of allies, has more systematically scorned multilateral forums or has taken greater pleasure in being able to say, as Reagan said after an American plane forced down Palestinian hijackers over Italy in 1985, that we did it "all by our little selves."

Reaganite unilateralism, moreover, is inspired by a messianic conviction that the American destiny is to redeem a fallen world. It is inspired by a crusading anti-communism of a sort not seen in the United States since the high noon of John Foster Dulles. Where presidents from Truman to Carter saw the cold war as a power struggle, Reagan saw it as a holy war. He regarded the Soviet Union as unchanged, unchanging and unchangeable and found communist deviltry at the root of most of the world's troubles.

The presidential tone, it is true, has moderated as the years have passed. We hear less these days about the "evil empire," nor has the president recently repeated the remarks of his first press conference in 1981 ("The only morality they recognize is what will further their cause, meaning they reserve unto themselves the right to commit any crime, to lie, to cheat")—perhaps because people might think he was talking about his own National Security Council staff.

Crusades generally exaggerate the menace of the enemy, and this one is no exception. Most of the world sees communism today as a burnt-out faith and the Soviet Union as a weary, dreary land filled with cynicism and corruption, beset by insuperable problems at home and abroad, finally (and sullenly) accepting reform as the only hope of assuring survival as a great power. The Soviet Union can trust neither communist China to the east nor communist satellites to the west, and the Red Army, which the Pentagon tediously tries to scare us about, cannot after eight years defeat ragged tribesmen fighting in the hills of Afghanistan. Yet for Reaganites the Soviet Union remains a fanatic state carrying out with implacable zeal, cunning and efficiency a master plan of world domination— except when they see it as so frail that a couple of small pushes will shove its ramshackle economy into collapse.

Global unilateralism driven by an anti-communist crusade wobbles the Administration's sense of reality. Local conflicts become tests of global resolve. Stakes are raised in situations that cannot be easily controlled, threatening to transmute limited into unlimited conflict. We are encouraged in the fallacy, one we share with the rival superpower, that we know the interests of other nations better than those nations know their own interests—that we understand remote and exotic problems more clearly than the countries most directly involved, most directly threatened and most familiar with the territory. Unilateralism breeds the arrogance of ignorance, and ignorance breeds bad policy.

III

Reagan's Nicaragua policy is a spectacular example of unilateralism in action. From the start, the Administration took little interest in Latin American assessments of the situation. Yet Latin American countries are a good deal more endangered than the United States is by a Marxist Nicaragua; they are a good deal closer to the scene and a good deal more knowledgeable about it, and their leaders are just as determined as the United States is on their behalf to resist their own overthrow. Most Latin American governments feel that Reagan's military remedy is far more likely to promote than to impede the progress of Marxist revolution. But Reagan, in his determination to make the Sandinistas cry uncle, has methodically disparaged and sabotaged the Latin American search for a political solution—first the Contadora effort, then the peace plan presented by President Oscar Arias of Costa Rica.

Lebanon, another example, should have proved to us forever the dangers of random meddling in the Middle East, a part of the world in which we have had far less experience than we have had in Latin America and of which we have far less knowledge—a part of the world, moreover, so bedeviled by ancient religious and tribal hatreds that it defies not only Western management but Western comprehension. We did not have the slightest understanding of the historical tangle we were getting into when we sent the marines to Beirut and claimed that their mission was to save the Middle East. Nor has the Reagan Administration appeared to learn much from the massacre of the marines. Raising once again the standard of invincible ignorance, it then plunged unilaterally and mindlessly ahead into a larger mess in the Persian Gulf.

Let us recall the Reagan roller-coaster policy in the Gulf. Iraq initiated the war against Iran in 1980. The Reagan Administration first followed a policy of neutrality; then veered toward Iraq, a policy culminating in the restoration of diplomatic relations in

1984; then courted Iran with arms shipments on the grounds of Iran's supreme geopolitical importance to American security; then, in order to recover Arab confidence and to preempt the Soviet Union, veered toward Iraq again, despite the Iraqi assault on the U.S.S. Stark and the death of 37 American sailors.

Then Reagan decided to raise the military stakes in the Gulf against Iran—the very country he had been secretly arming a short time before. This was a decision taken without consultation with America's allies and with only sketchy notification to Congress. There was no evident effort to think through next steps, and the U.S. Navy did not even have the capacity to protect itself against Iranian mines. The reflagging of Kuwaiti tankers—again no consultation with allies—goes far to place the United States in the hands of two countries, Kuwait and Iraq, that have an obvious interest in drawing us into the war against Iran. "American naval forces in the Gulf," as a Senate Foreign Relations Committee staff report put it in October 1987, "are now, in effect, hostage to Iraqi war policy." An Iranian victory over Iraq would plainly be against the interests of the West, but the United States cannot do much by its little self to prevent it. Only as a last resort has the Administration turned to the international instrument it should have used from the start—the United Nations.

Sometimes the American government is wiser than other governments. Sometimes it is not. In any event there is no harm in taking other governments into account, especially when they are more intimately involved in the problem than we are. The realists who wrote The Federalist Papers understood this obvious fact of international life, which is why the 63rd Federalist called on the newly established American government to pay "attention to the judgment of other nations. . . . Particularly where the national councils may be warped by some strong passion or momentary interest, the presumed or known opinion of the impartial world may be the best guide that can be followed."

Unilateralism breeds something more than ignorance: it breeds illegality. Consider Central America again. President Reagan has pursued his policy of overthrowing the Sandinista regime in Managua in violation not only of congressional prohibitions but of nonintervention pledges repeatedly made to the Organization of American States ever since the Montevideo Conference of 1933, when the United States first subscribed to the declaration that "no state has the right to intervene in the internal or external affairs of another"; in violation too of the U.N. Charter and of customary international law. After Nicaragua appealed to the World Court, the Reagan Administration, having failed in challenging the court's jurisdiction, walked out of the courtroom and refused to argue the case on its merits.

In 1983 Reagan despatched an expeditionary force against the island of Grenada, an action undertaken without warning, without congressional authorization and in presumptive violation of the charters of the United Nations and of the Organization of American States. Though he was invading a member of the British Commonwealth, he did not bother to consult or even to alert his most loyal supporter among world leaders, the British prime minister. The pretext—the rescue of American citizens—had ample standing under international law, but the real and unconcealed purpose was to destroy an obnoxious regime. The people of Grenada and neighboring islands welcomed the invasion, but the legal fig leaves notably failed to impress the British prime minister or the U.N. General Assembly.

The net result of these instances, and recently of the far less justified intervention in Nicaragua, is that never before in our history have we had fewer friends in the Western Hemisphere than we have today. . . . We are exceedingly jealous of our own sovereignty and it is only right that we should respect a similar feeling among other nations.

So F.D.R. wrote in Foreign Affairs sixty years ago; plus ça change. . . . If a real crisis arises, Roosevelt added, it is not the right or the duty of the United States to intervene alone. It is rather the duty of the United States to associate with itself other American Republics. . . . Single-handed intervention by us in the affairs of other nations must end; with the cooperation of others we shall have more order in this hemisphere and less dislike.

IV

The climax of the present Administration's self-arrogated right to intervene single-handedly everywhere in the world is the famous Reagan Doctrine. Once again unilateralism breeds bad policy. The Reagan Doctrine exhorts people to take up arms in order to over-throw communist regimes. "We must not break faith," Reagan said in 1985, "with those who are risking their lives on every continent, from Afghanistan to Nicaragua, to defy Soviet-supported aggres-sion." Reagan's cry recalls the prizefight manager in the old cartoon urging his battered and bleeding pug into the ring for one more round: "Go on in there. They can't hurt us."

Obviously it is one thing to help people who, on their own, are resisting a foreign invasion, as in Afghanistan. Indeed, a Demo-cratic administration initiated this policy. It is something quite dif-ferent to create an insurgency in order to overthrow a government, such as Nicaragua's, recognized by most of the world, including ourselves. The contras are a wholly owned CIA subsidiary. When we organize a rebellion ab initio, does this not imply a moral obli-gation to those whom we spur on to risk their lives? Suppose their efforts are inadequate to the task. Having urged them into the breach, have we not incurred a responsibility to make sure that they succeed? If the "freedom fighters" we have invented fail on their own, are they not entitled to expect that we will send in our own troops to win what we have told them is our fight too? Or are we to "break faith" and ignobly abandon them? In the end the Rea-gan Administration will probably abandon the contras rather than send in the marines, as the Nixon-Ford Administration abandoned the South Vietnamese and the Kurds. Here, as elsewhere, the Rea-gan Administration takes the first step without having thought through the last step or calculated the consequences, political and moral, of failure. We Democrats, I trust, have learned these grim lessons the hard way—in the Bay of Pigs and in Vietnam.

Reagan claims sympathy for those fighting for freedom as a cherished American tradition. "Time and again," he has said, "we've aided those around the world struggling for freedom, democracy, independence and liberation from tyranny." But the men of the old republic drew a bright line between sympathy and intervention. As John Quincy Adams put it:

Wherever the standard of freedom and independence has been or shall be unfurled, there will [America's] heart, her benedictions and her prayers be. But she goes not abroad, in search of monsters to destroy. . . . She has abstained from interference in the concerns of others, even when conflict has been for principles to which she clings, as to the last vital drop that visits the heart.

President Reagan, on the contrary, seeks monsters, and, in stalking them, he risks what J. Q. Adams predicted—the involvement of the United States "beyond the power of extrication, in all the wars of interest and intrigue, of individual avarice, envy, and ambition, which assume the colors and usurp the standard of freedom. The fundamental maxim of [America's] policy would insensibly change from liberty to force. . . . She might become the dictatress of the world. She would no longer be the ruler of her own spirit." Given the existing balance of forces, the dictatorship of the world is not a likely outcome. Corruption of our own spirit is.

The Reagan Doctrine has made covert action its chosen instrument and has thereby made secrecy, deceit and mendacity the foundation of American foreign policy. The very adjective "covert" is a misnomer. Covert action is often easy to detect, always hard to control and in its nature illegal and immune to normal procedures of accountability. Covert action, moreover, is a weapon of marginal consequence in the scale of things. Its importance in the conduct of foreign affairs is greatly overrated. It appeals, as John Le Carré observes, to declining powers, who place "ever greater trust in the magic formulae and hocus-pocus of the spy world. When the king is dying, the charlatans rush in."

In January 1961 President Eisenhower's Board of Consultants on Foreign Intelligence Activities, a group of eminent citizens with

Robert A. Lovett taking the lead on this question, told the president after a review of the CIA record: "We have been unable to conclude that, on balance, all of the covert action programs undertaken by the CIA up to this time have been worth the risk or the great expenditure of manpower, money and other resources involved." Nothing the CIA has done in the quarter-century since gives reason to alter this considered verdict.

Covert action should never become, as it became in the Reagan Administration, a routine instrument of foreign policy. One is interested to note that this thought belatedly dawned on Robert C. McFarlane, the former national security adviser, as he prepared for the Iran-contra hearings. "It was clearly unwise," McFarlane told the joint congressional committee, "to rely on covert activity as the core of our policy. . . . You must have the American people and the U.S. Congress solidly behind you. Yet it is virtually impossible, almost as a matter of definition, to rally public support behind a policy that you can't even talk about."

Once again, unilateralism breeds illegality. "Support for freedom fighters," Reagan opines, "is self-defense, and totally consistent with the O.A.S. and U.N. Charters." This is a perilously elastic interpretation of self-defense and not one that legal scholars or allies are inclined to endorse. The Soviet Union asserted a similar right of global intervention in support of "wars of national liberation." Americans did not hail the principle when Khrushchev announced it a quarter of a century ago. Does it really sound better on the lips of an American president?

Under Reagan the United States now vies with the Soviet Union in proclaiming its right to act as a law unto itself around the planet. An especially obnoxious example is the Administration's effort to reinterpret the Anti-Ballistic Missile Treaty of 1972—a unilateral interpretation contrary to the "original intent" (so heartily acclaimed by Reagan in other contexts) of the officials, both American and Soviet, who negotiated the treaty and of the senators who ratified it; a reinterpretation contemptuous both of international law and of American constitutional practice;

a reinterpretation, moreover, that undermines the principal superpower arms control agreement and the foundation-stone for future arms control. "What is missing from all this," as Senator Daniel Patrick Moynihan (D-N.Y.) has commented, "is the sense we once had that it is in our interest to advance the cause of law in world affairs." Does the American interest really lie in imitating the Soviet Union—or does it lie in opposing the Soviet model with the idea of a world of law?

To deny that the United States has a profound stake in the operation of law in international affairs is more than a rejection of American tradition and a disservice to longer-term American interests. It is also to embark on a course that in harder cases than Grenada (i.e., involving more American casualties), Congress and public opinion will not long accept. "A policy is bound to fail which deliberately violates our pledges and our principles, our treaties and our laws," Walter Lippmann wrote after the Bay of Pigs. "The American conscience is a reality. It will make hesitant and ineffectual, even if it does not prevent, an un-American policy."

Still worse, the Reagan Doctrine carries illegality from foreign relations into the domestic polity. Founded as it is on lawbreaking, deception and lies, covert action imports very bad habits into a constitutional democracy. There is no need here to rehearse the squalid story revealed in the Iran-contra hearings. One has only to note that the Reagan Doctrine led on to actions that violated both the Constitution President Reagan swore a solemn oath to uphold and the laws he was pledged to execute. Of course the "neat idea" advanced by Lieutenant Colonel Oliver North was a dumb policy. But the issue is not the Rube Goldberg scheme to get the ayatollah to subsidize the contras, nor even its mode of execution, which seems to have been devised by Inspector Clouseau. The issue is whether the president of the United States is above the Constitution and the laws.

"When the president does it," as Richard Nixon inimitably put it, "that means that it is not illegal." Ronald Reagan's White House seems to share this view. Throbbing through the testimony of

Arthur M Schlesinger, Jr.

Colonel North and Rear Admiral John Poindexter is ill-concealed envy at the Kremlin's capacity to act as it wills without obstruction, restraint or disclosure. But the theory of the divine right of presidents finds little sustenance in the American Constitution.

When pressed, defenders of the Imperial Presidency redivivus, like Colonel North, invoke the case of United States v. Curtiss-Wright Export Corp. in 1936. Those who do so could not have read the decision. For what the Supreme Court did in Curtiss-Wright was to affirm the power of Congress to impose an arms embargo and further to affirm the right of Congress to delegate to the president the power to institute such an embargo. As Justice Robert H. Jackson later put it, Curtiss-Wright "involved, not the question of the president's right to act without congressional authority, but the question of his right to act under and in accord with an Act of Congress." The decision sanctioned presidential action within a framework ordained by Congress. It did not sanction independent presidential action.

It is true that Justice George Sutherland, who wrote the opinion, indulged in imaginative historical asides in order to distinguish the delegation of power in foreign affairs the Court was approving in 1936 from the delegation in domestic affairs it had struck down when it invalidated the National Recovery Administration in 1935. Sutherland's asides were dicta, bad history and not part of the Court's holding. The Court has never sustained the proposition that the president has an extraconstitutional source of power in international relations.

The Reagan endorsement of unilateral presidential power in foreign affairs comes oddly from an Administration whose attorney general lectures us so often about "the jurisprudence of original intention." For the framers of the Constitution explicitly rejected the idea that foreign policy was the private property of the president. The foremost proponent of executive energy in the Constitutional Convention was Alexander Hamilton, and Hamilton himself wrote in the 75th Federalist: "The history of human conduct does not warrant that exalted opinion of human nature which would make it wise in a nation to commit interests of so delicate and momentous a kind, as those which concern its intercourse with the rest of the world, to the sole disposal of . . . a President of the United States."

The Reagan version of unilateralism gives the Republican tradition a novel and ominous twist. The Reagan policies have been characterized—far more than those of the Nixon Administration, for example—by a studied subordination of diplomatic to military methods and remedies. The National Security Council staff has been effectively taken over by men whose experience has been in the Pentagon and in the armed services. The Foreign Service has been purged and humiliated. Professional diplomats occupy today a smaller proportion of ambassadorial posts than at any time in recent history. Reagan's budget reflects his priorities: spoiling the Department of Defense, starving the Department of State. The budgetary stringencies created by the defense budget have led to the cutback of State's budget by $185 million in 1986–87, with another $84 million scheduled to go this year. The result is the closing of consulates and even embassies around the world, the retirement of experienced diplomats and the weakening of America's diplomatic resources—all for the cost of a B-1 bomber.

The Reaganite assumption is that, in the words of the Financial Times of London, "military might would provide answers to political questions." Military action becomes a first, not last, recourse.

V

Reagan rode to power determined to rescue the United States from what he had peculiarly called Carter's policy of unilateral disarmament. In fact the arms buildup began with Carter, whose last Five-Year Defense Plan called for nearly as much spending as Reagan actually accomplished. Citing inflated Defense Department estimates of Soviet defense spending (estimates later refuted by the more scrupulous CIA), Reagan periodically proclaimed that the United States had fallen behind the Soviet Union—which, if true, represented a stirring presidential tribute to the superior efficiency and productivity of a collectivized economy. The Soviet generals engaged in comparable lamentations, each side announcing that the other was ahead in order to get bigger budgets for itself. As President Kennedy once put it, "The hard-liners in the Soviet Union and the United States feed on one another." It is difficult to figure how anyone could take these self-serving wails from the Pentagon seriously, especially around budget time.

But Congress did. It will have lavished nearly two trillion dollars on the Pentagon during the Reagan years. For much of this period Pentagon spending was deemed sacrosanct, and Pentagon megalomania was unbridled. Recall, for example, the award of 8,612 medals after the glorious American victory over Grenada, a small island without army, navy or air force, though we never had more than 7,000 troops on the island. This prodigality did not deeply impress veterans who had earned medals in the Second World War or Korea or Vietnam. But it was typical of an army that had more generals in peacetime than it had in 1945, when it was six times larger and fighting a world war.

In these years, the military budget was annually presented by our secretary of defense as a sacred text, not a line of which could be altered without incalculable harm. It finally took the minor outrages of overpriced coffee pots and toilet seats to awaken a complaisant Congress. But the major waste came in the enormous outlays for weapon systems so complex and delicate that they rarely worked in tests and are most unlikely to work in combat. The much vaunted MX cannot reliably land in the target zone. The much vaunted B-1 bomber turns out to have a befuddled electronic brain. The armed forces, The New York Times reported this summer, were "so short of spare parts that they must cannibalize some airplanes to keep others flying."

As for the $485 billion spent on the wonderful 600-ship navy, much went for aircraft carriers, fine for movies like Top Gun but sitting ducks in case of serious war, while the Persian Gulf intervention found the United States with only three operational minesweepers, all of Korean War vintage, and reduced American destroyers to the humiliation of being convoyed by the unarmed tankers they were charged to protect. There has been, I gather, real improvement in the quality and morale of the armed forces. But too much of the taxpayers' money has disappeared down a black hole, leaving a military establishment rich in glamorous but brittle high-tech gadgetry and poor in such mundane matters as combat readiness, stockpiles of munitions and equipment, depot maintenance, sea and air transport, not to mention minesweeping. The abiding Reagan theme has been overemphasis on nuclear weapons at the expense of conventional capabilities.

The culmination of the science-fiction approach is President Reagan's dream of "Star Wars"—an impenetrable defense shield to be erected over the United States like an astrodome. Star Wars has been presented in a succession of models, some designed to replace, others to reinforce, deterrence. All require the solution of problems of extraordinarily technical complexity by means scientists have yet to discover. Ultimate effectiveness depends on inordinately complicated systems working together in perfect unison under conditions of ultimate stress. Does no one remember the Challenger?

Most Democrats agree with former Under Secretary of State George W. Ball that Star Wars is not only a fantasy but a fraud. Few scientists think it likely to work in the long run. Its short-run effect will inevitably be to prevent agreement on the reduction of strategic weapons and, more than that, to rekindle the nuclear arms race. For the Soviet military establishment will seize upon it as an excuse to demand from Gorbachev more intercontinental ballistic missiles to overwhelm the space shield and more cruise missiles, bombers and other low-flying weapons to rush in under the shield. Since countermeasures are technically simpler than construction of the shield and cost far less, they will be relatively easy to sustain. And the arms race will roar on.

Reaganites defend Star Wars, or the Strategic Defense Initiative, precisely as a means of bringing the Soviet Union to the negotiating table. Maybe so, though this contention has been denied

371

by no less an authority than Andrei D. Sakharov, who adds: "To the contrary, the SDI program impedes negotiations." Surely the deeper reason that inclines Gorbachev to cut back the arms race—and would have so inclined him whether or not Reagan had ever dreamed of Star Wars—is his need to transfer capital, materials, scientists and engineers from military tasks to the modernization of the Soviet economy.

The militarization of foreign relations has had further effects. From the start the Reagan Administration has regarded arms transfers as a major tool of diplomacy if not as a substitute for it. The result has been to pour American weapons into the most explosive parts of the world—Central America, the Middle East, the Persian Gulf, South Asia. Given chronic instability and an unpredictable future, a good many of these weapons may be turned against the United States before the century is over—as has already happened with arms sent to China in the 1940s, Vietnam in the 1960s and Iran in the 1970s.

The ultimate premise of Reagan's foreign policy is that military power creates political and diplomatic power. It seems more likely, however, that the subordination of diplomatic to military interests has diminished American influence around the world. A foreign policy dominated by military men and ideological zealots degrades the role and narrows the scope of negotiation. Thus 13 South Pacific nations, led by Australia, recently proposed in the Treaty of Raratonga to make their part of the world a nuclear-free zone. Australia made a particular effort to ensure that the treaty did not compromise American interests. But the Pentagon objected and the United States refused to sign, causing vast irritation throughout the area over what the Australian foreign minister called the "clumsy" way Washington handled the matter.

The obsession with military buildup and military remedy has exacted a damaging price. The vain quest for American military leadership has resulted in the loss of American political and economic leadership. The combination of colossal defense spending with a major tax cut produced unprecedented peacetime budget deficits, an overvalued dollar and the transformation of the United States on Reagan's watch from a creditor nation to the world's number-one debtor. The concentration of America's science and technology on military research has held back American productivity and further endangered America's competitive position in world markets. "American scientists," The Economist observes, "are in a bind. Their research must aim either to deter the Russians, or to compete with the Japanese. No longer can they expect a single contract from the Pentagon to achieve both goals." Reagan's military priorities have accentuated America's financial and industrial vulnerabilities.

We have seen in recent months—well before the Iran-contra scandals—an ebbing of faith, first in American skills, latterly in American intentions. Ian Davidson, the foreign affairs columnist of the Financial Times, summing up the situation in a valedictory column in the summer of 1987, concluded that Reagan "has probably caused more damage to the European-American relationship in the Atlantic Alliance than any of his predecessors. What is more, he probably does not even realize it." Reagan's unilateralism is Gorbachev's most potent weapon. A recent Gallup poll showed that 56 percent of European respondents thought that Gorbachev was contributing to world peace; only 12 percent thought Reagan was. "The outside world almost unanimously views us with less good will today than at any previous period." This was F.D.R. in 1928 during another time of Republican unilateralism.

The infirmities of the Reagan foreign policy are not redeemed by the belated prospect of the treaty eliminating intermediate-range nuclear missiles. This would unquestionably be a useful, if limited, step forward; nor can one be much impressed by the claim, urged by Democratic as well as Republican conservatives, that the agreement would leave Western Europe naked before Soviet conventional force. Unless one dismisses the three-to-one superiority that offense is required to have over defense, assumes the loyalty and efficiency of the Soviet satellites, forgets the deterrent power carried by American submarines and bombers and believes that the invasion of Europe is on Gorbachev's agenda, Western Europe is safe enough. It could be rendered safer by negotiated limitations on conventional forces and by parallel reduction in Western nuclear artillery and Soviet tanks. But the supreme question—stopping the strategic arms race—is still ahead. Nor can any progress be expected here so long as the American government regards Star Wars as nonnegotiable.

VI

It remains a tough world filled with intractable problems, and it is reasonable to inquire what the Democrats would do differently. There is, at least in advance of the convention, no party line. George McGovern and Jesse Jackson on the party's left and Senators Bill Bradley of New Jersey and Sam Nunn of Georgia on the right have very different views on such issues as aid to the contras and Star Wars. Yet these four able men might agree on a broad reaffirmation of the Democratic Party as the party of responsible internationalism.

This does not mean, as Ogden Mills affected to fear, subordination of our independence of action to the decision of other nations. Neither Wilson nor Roosevelt, Truman nor Kennedy nor Johnson, was notably averse to asserting the national interest. But it does mean a recognition of interdependence as a prime fact of international life. It means a sensitivity to the interests of other nations, a readiness to consult with allies and to negotiate with adversaries. It would mean U.S. support for Latin American peace initiatives in Central America. It would mean reinvigorated American use of the United Nations and other multilateral agencies. It would end the unlovely spectacle of the United States careening around the world as a law unto itself and restore the historical American conviction that a world of law is in the national interest.

If Gorbachev and his reforms survive, a Democratic administration will believe—as most Democrats who have visited Moscow already believe—that the time has come to take Gorbachev seriously. A Democratic president will not dismiss the new Soviet look as propaganda or disinformation or, in the Reaganite cliché, "cosmetic." The changes under way in the Soviet Union hold out the hope of tranquilization in world affairs. Gorbachev needs an international respite to carry forward his program of domestic modernization.

His speech of September 17, 1987, printed in Pravda, apparently signals an extraordinary departure in Soviet policy, a dramatic shift in direction from unilateralism toward collaboration. Still, the Soviet record since 1917 justifies skepticism when a Soviet leader starts talking about strengthening the United Nation's peacekeeping responsibility, establishing a U.N. force to protect Persian Gulf shipping, accepting the compulsory jurisdiction of the World Court, giving the United Nations new authority in human rights and disclaiming the pristine Soviet commitment to world revolution. The Democratic response to these overtures will not be to spurn them but to test them. The world faces a historic opportunity to bring the cold war to an end, or at least to reduce it to considerably less dangerous dimensions. The American task is to seize the Gorbachev challenge and to translate his words into constructive and enduring agreements.

In particular, the possibility now exists to end the nuclear arms race. The bargain is there; if we renounce the Star Wars fantasy/fraud, we could complete a deal tomorrow. How long will the door remain open? A Democratic president, if he keeps his faith with Woodrow Wilson and Franklin D. Roosevelt, will not miss the chance. He will have, I hope, a bold and generous vision of the world's possibilities when humanity begins to devote its energy and ingenuity to cooperation rather than to conflict. In this spirit the 21st century may yet see the realization of F.D.R.'s world of the Four Freedoms.

To move the republic in this direction, a Democratic president would aim at the resurrection of diplomacy, the revitalization of the State Department and the restoration of competence and coherence to the management of foreign relations. The process by which the government made foreign policy under Reagan could hardly have been worse. "Is it not your view," Senator Paul Sarbanes (D-Md.) asked the secretary of defense about the Iran-contra decisions, "that it's an inexcusable and deplorable way to conduct the policymaking process of the government?" Even the indefatigably loyal Caspar Weinberger responded, "Yes."

The Reagan method has been to treat foreign policy as the president's personal property, to be conducted without undue regard for the laws and the Constitution and to be concealed, if necessary, not only from Congress and the American people but even, on occasion, from his own secretaries of state and defense. A Democratic president would recognize the futility of trying to run foreign policy in a democracy on any other basis than consent. He would especially recognize the necessity of restoring Congress to its constitutional partnership in the making of foreign policy. As a great American—and Democratic—diplomat, Averell Harriman, once put it: "No foreign policy will stick unless the American people are behind it. And unless Congress understands it the American people aren't going to understand it."

In a properly organized administration the national security adviser should see his duty as the coordination and clarification of choices presented to the president. He would have a small, crack staff and would not try to replicate the State Department in the basement of the White House. A Democratic president would be well advised to choose a secretary of state who has served in Congress as a way of strengthening the executive-legislative relationship. He would send out as ambassadors both Foreign Service officers and non-professionals qualified by knowledge, experience and stature to represent the United States abroad. He would place the CIA under vigilant oversight, executive as well as legislative, and direct it to concentrate on what its founders saw as its essential job: the collection and analysis of intelligence. He would regard diplomacy as the weapon of first resort, put covert action well down the list and use military force as the weapon of last resort.

In the field of national security a Democratic president would, I hope, appoint a strong secretary of defense equipped to regard

Pentagon budget submissions with due and informed skepticism. He would shift priority from the elaboration of nuclear systems to the modernization of conventional capabilities and to the application of high technology to conventional warfare. In the nuclear field he would certainly not pursue costly busts like the B-1 bomber and the MX, but would go ahead with small missile-launching submarines, the Stealth bomber and, more cautiously, with the single-warhead, silo-based Midgetman. I suppose he would accept a research program for Star Wars; astute subcontracting, at home and abroad, has created a vigorous lobby, and Star Wars remains a bargaining chip for arms control. But he would respect and extend the Anti-Ballistic Missile Treaty of 1972, negotiate limits on testing in space and stop babbling about early deployment (deployment of what?). Nor would he permit Star Wars to block a comprehensive test ban—a high priority—or the sharp reduction of nuclear weapons. He would reorganize the system of defense contracts and procurement. He would do his damnedest to reduce the defense budget.

Lack of total reverence for defense strikes some members of my party as, even if sound on the merits, politically hazardous. They fear, especially in the south, that the Democratic Party has acquired a reputation for keeping the United States weak, and they do not want to be taken for unpatriotic wimps. Reagan's flag-waving act, they fear, has cast a spell on the nation. Emphasis on the limits of American wisdom and power, they think, might offend the deluded electorate.

Possibly there is something in this, though polls show that most voters are skeptical about the military, prefer peace to war and arms reductions to arms races. The bloodthirstiness of our countrymen can be exaggerated, and their intelligence can be underestimated. I think most Americans take the point President Kennedy made more than a quarter-century ago:

We must face the fact that the United States is neither omnipotent nor omniscient—that we are only 6 percent of the world's population— that we cannot impose our will upon the other 94 percent—that we

cannot right every wrong or reverse each adversity—and that therefore there cannot be an American solution to every world problem.

VII

The day of the messianic foreign policy, the United States as the
redeemer nation commissioned by the Almighty to rescue fallen
humanity, is coming to an end, for a while at least. A modesty more
akin to the mood of the Founding Fathers may be taking over: "a
decent respect to the opinions of mankind." Reaganism is running
its course, the cycle is turning, and the time impends for a sharp
change in the national direction.

Democrats will continue to stand, as they always have, for national strength. They will never hesitate to use force when force is
required to defend the national interest. But they will remind the
nation that strength in the modern world has economic as well as
military dimensions. The impending crisis for the United States is
rather more likely to be in the banks than on the battlefield. We are
instructed incessantly about the deadly threat of Marxist Nicaragua (population 2.8 million). But the damage Nicaragua can do to
U.S. interests is nothing compared to the devastation that a large-
scale repudiation of the Latin American external debt—now approaching $400 billion—can wreak on the already shaky U.S.
banking system.

Our great international vulnerability today is economic rather
than military. Should a Democrat be elected president in 1988, he
would be prudent to devote his first State of the Union message to
a sober inventory of the national condition. He would recall America after the Second World War: a nation with a capital surplus, an
export surplus, 40 percent of the gross world product, 22 percent
of world trade, and every indication of continuing technological
and financial supremacy. He would draw the dread contrast 40
years later: the huge budget deficit; the huge trade deficit; the huge
bubbles of public debt, private debt, external debt; the decline in
America's ability to compete in world markets; the stagnation in
America's productivity; the shrinkage of America's industrial base;

the decay of America's infrastructure; the dissipation of capital in mindless speculation, mergers and leveraged buyouts; the increasing dependence on capital flows from abroad; the transformation of the United States into the largest debtor known to history. America, the new president could properly say, is at the mercy of international economic forces as never before. To avert disaster, America must work out modes of international collaboration as never before.

In the age ahead, economic power will be quite as significant as military power—a fact Gorbachev has recognized, though Reagan has not. Secretary of the Treasury James A. Baker 3d has done his best to call this Administration's attention to the Latin American debt, overhanging American banks like the sword of Damocles; but the president prefers to fume about the Sandinistas. The debt question would be high priority for a Democratic administration. Its containment would require debt relief for the Third World in exchange for the promotion of growth, conversion of debt into equity investment and an increase in international capital flows through wholehearted support of international institutions—the World Bank, the International Monetary Fund, regional development banks.

No issue has more perplexed Democrats than the classical argument between free trade and protection. Opening U.S. markets to Latin American exports, for example, would help considerably to alleviate the debt problem. But such a policy encounters understandable resistance at home from those whose livelihoods and communities are wasted by imports from abroad. Protection is a bad answer, but it signifies a real problem.

Free-trade purism at the expense of jobs and lives is irrelevant to a world already cluttered with obstacles to free trading. The Reagan Administration has done some good things, like this year's agreement with Canada. But it has undercut free-trade sermons by protectionist actions. And its deeper failure has been its refusal to support its aspirations toward an open trading world with the domestic measures necessary to make the policy work. It is inhuman to place the burden of transition on the workers and communities least able to pay the price.

A Democratic administration would take active responsibility for the domestic consequences of an open trading world. It would provide assistance to communities and retraining for workers during the ordeal of transition. It would increase national investment in the modes of education essential for a high-technology future. It would establish standards for plant closings. There is, I believe, a case for emergency tariffs during the lifetime of existing workers. There is a case for preserving industries vital to national security and technological growth, like the automotive, space, steel and machine tools industries, if protection is accompanied by tough standards for modernization. There is a case for government-to-government negotiations on trade matters. There is a case for tools in our kit to facilitate retaliation against closed foreign markets. There is no case for general long-run protection. No country can afford a beggar-thy-neighbor world. Because the Democratic Party has earned the trust of workers and their unions, it is in a far stronger position than the Republican Party to negotiate the tricky currents and shoals of trade policy.

Whether the question is diplomatic, military, political or economic, the choice today is not all that different from the choice of 1928: Republican unilateralism or Democratic internationalism. We have had seven years of a unilateralism militarized, ideological, messianic foreign policy, and look where it has got us.

As Franklin D. Roosevelt concluded his Foreign Affairs piece sixty years ago:

> In the simplest terms, this is the argument for a policy different from that of the past nine years. Up until then most of our history shows us to have been a nation leading others in the slow upward steps to better international understanding and the peaceful settlement of disagreements. During these nine years we have stood still, with the unfortunate effect of earning greater or less ill will on the part of other civilized peoples. . . . The time is ripe to start another chapter.

On that new page there is much that should be written in the spirit of our forebears. If the leadership is right—or, more truly, if the spirit behind it is great—the United States can regain the world's trust and friendship and become again of service. We can point the way once more to the reducing of armaments; we can cooperate officially and whole-heartedly with every agency that studies and works to relieve the common ills of mankind; and we can for all time renounce the practice of arbitrary intervention in the home affairs of our neighbors.

A free-lance Democrat, remembering America in glory and in shame from the 1930s to the 1980s, can only say: Right on, F.D.R.! Let the Democratic Party keep sailing ahead on its historic course.

ARTHUR M. SCHLESINGER, JR., is Albert Schweitzer Professor in the Humanities at the Graduate Center of the City University of New York.

The 1988 Election

U.S. Foreign Policy at a Watershed

George McGovern   AMERICA AND THE WORLD 1987

Bush and Dukakis debate, 1988.

A s we approach the 1988 election, we may be at the end of an era in American foreign policy. Since World War II the driving force behind our policy has been anticommunism, accompanied by containment of the Soviet Union with an ever more costly arms outlay. For more than four decades this policy has rested on the assumption of a bipolar world dominated by Washington and Moscow. New realities now demand fundamentally different policies if the United States is to remain an effective power.

This is not to suggest that communism is more acceptable today than it was forty years ago. Indeed, even the major communist states—the Soviet Union and China—are turning away from once accepted practices of communism. Without argument, the United States must maintain a sound national defense. But so clearly is communism neither the wave of the future nor the major challenge to American security that our anticommunist orientation has become irrelevant and obsolete. The two major powers—Washington and Moscow—are alike in this regard: they share an urgent need for new policies and priorities at home and abroad. Both must understand that the criteria of power and influence in the world are changing.

Ronald Reagan may represent the end of the line for the bipartisan cold war policy. The president seems to have taken, at least until recently, the most anachronistic aspects of that policy—an excessive reliance on arms, an obsessive anticommunism and an imperial, unilateral behavior at odds with our constitutional democracy—and carried them to the breaking point. However inadvertently, the Reagan Administration has dramatized the inadequacy of policies no longer relevant to the real world. Mr. Reagan has believed he was presiding over "morning in America"; we are about to experience the "morning after."

Unfortunately, the Reagan presidency has taken its toll also on the intellectual and political acuity of the party in opposition. If the ambivalent foreign policy actions of Congress and early presidential campaign performances are indicative, the Administration's obsession with the rhetoric, symbols and trappings of military power has, with some notable exceptions, suffused even a Democratic Party which has traditionally brought a broader perspective to the concept of American national security. In what some have labeled the "geo-economic era," this focus is dangerously outmoded.

Jacques Attali, an economic historian and top adviser to French President François Mitterrand, wrote:

> A great transfer of power is taking place in the world economy. The center of economic power is shifting away from America. When the core nation loses economic hegemony, it has to adjust the global security responsibilities it assumed at the height of its dominance. This is what finally happened to Great Britain in 1967, but it took 20 years from the end of World War II for them to finally conclude that they couldn't afford troops east of Aden.

George McGovern

II

In this crucial election period and beyond, do we have the will and the wisdom to develop a more realistic foreign policy, backed by better management of our economy to avert the further weakening of our position in the world? Will we face the need to shift from an excessive reliance on military power to the political, economic and moral sources of power in an interdependent global economy? Do we understand that even a great and powerful nation can no longer function unilaterally without regard to friend or foe? In this bicentennial of our constitutional democracy, can we profit from the lessons of the Iran-contra scandal and recognize anew the time-tested wisdom of the Founders?

The current economic difficulties of the supposed superpowers serve only to underscore a long-standing truth. Since the late 1940s both powers have overemphasized military and ideological factors and underplayed economic and political opportunities. The painful paradox that now confronts both Washington and Moscow is that the more they spend on armaments, the weaker and more insecure they become. The larger the number of nuclear weapons each side targets on the other, the more certain it is that in the event of war, Americans and Russians would be the first to disappear from the planet. Meanwhile, heavy arms spending deprives the two countries of the resources needed to strengthen their economies, participate competitively in the international economy and enhance their leadership in the developing world.

The economic costs of a permanent war economy and an interventionist foreign policy have for years been a focus of "liberal" concern. But even the most ardent of American conservatives must now recognize that the dangerous decline of U.S. industries owes much to a major portion of our business and scientific talent having been absorbed in war production for a single buyer—the Pentagon—instead of meeting the growing economic competitiveness of the modern world.

Japan and Germany, the defeated military powers of World War II, are challenging the preeminent status of the erstwhile victors, not by competing with them militarily, but by recognizing that the real arena of world power is not war games but hardheaded business leadership. The most serious enemy of America is not Russian tanks and rockets, or the Nicaraguan government or Cuban leader Fidel Castro. Our enemies are the bankrupting arms race, our mounting foreign debt (after years as the world's greatest creditor), the unpayable debts of the Third World held by U.S. banks, our lack of competitiveness in world trade and our consequent inability to play a more influential and constructive role in Third World development.

Power in the future will be determined increasingly by economic, political and moral factors. The arms race and an excessively interventionist, unilateral foreign policy have weakened those fundamental sources of American power.

It is possible that American military might prevented a Russian takeover of Western Europe in the wake of World War II. At that time an American-led containment strategy seemed logical. But if a Soviet move across Europe was ever imminent, it was in the years when Europe was still devastated by war. That is when the Marshall Plan's economic help and the military power of the NATO shield made the most sense.

Today conditions in Europe, the United States, the Soviet Union and the rest of the world have changed drastically. Western Europe is now strong and prosperous. Its population, material resources, productivity and industrial strength all exceed that of the Soviet Union.

Not since the 1961 Berlin crisis has Moscow engaged in any serious provocation against Western Europe, and even that was an act of political and economic weakness. Paradoxically, the Soviets followed the most belligerent line in those years when the United States either had a nuclear monopoly or at least overwhelming superiority. But as Moscow has moved toward nuclear parity with Washington and increased its dealings on arms control, trade and cultural exchange, it has tended to favor a policy of accommodation with the West.

This tendency has reached an apex in the person of Mikhail Gorbachev, who now emphasizes that in the future Soviet foreign policy will be driven by domestic economic needs. He and other realists in the Kremlin seem far more interested in trading with Europe, encouraging joint economic ventures with European firms and mutually reducing nuclear weapons than in fighting Europeans on the battlefield or exchanging bombs and missiles with them from the skies.

Russians may be notoriously averse to admitting mistakes to the outside world, but it takes little reading between the lines of Mr. Gorbachev's domestic and international speeches to discern his recognition that the Soviet economy has been so warped by its focus on arms production that it is incapable of meeting the needs of its people for modern housing, industrial goods, productive agriculture and scientific-technical breakthroughs for its future development. Gorbachev has left little doubt that he knows his country cannot lift its standard of living so long as it is bogged down in an ever-escalating arms race with the United States and Europe.

The Soviet leader has also signaled his belief that big-power interventionism in the emerging Third World is a hazardous and self-defeating policy. The bitter and frustrating experience of the Russians for the last decade in Afghanistan was doubtless in Gorbachev's mind at the Communist Party Congress in February 1986, when he forcefully contended that "encouraging revolution from outside, and doubly so by military means, is futile and inadmissible." It does not take an expert Kremlinologist to see that Gorbachev is saying something new.

On the arms control front, Moscow seized the initiative in 1985 by announcing and implementing a unilateral ban on all nuclear weapons testing. At the arms control discussions in Reykjavik with President Reagan, the Soviet leader seemed willing to make or accept even the most sweeping proposals for the reduction or elimination of nuclear weapons. More recently, in signing with President Reagan the treaty that would eliminate intermediate-range nuclear weapons from Europe, Gorbachev agreed to unprecedented access to Soviet military production and basing facilities for on-site inspection. Arms control offers can be propaganda, but a breakthrough verification regime to monitor the total dismantlement of Soviet SS-20s means there is extraordinary substance here as well.

As we move to shape the American election issues of 1988, the key question is whether we can begin to define foreign and defense policies that are more relevant to the realities of today's world. Can we meet the energetic and forceful challenge of Mikhail Gorbachev's Russia with intelligence, courage and realism? Can we muster the will and wisdom to see that the issues of the future cannot be resolved by a bigger arms race and more military interventions in Central America, Africa or Asia? Can we put forward a new range of policies to end the waste of an obsolete arms race, reduce the shameful deficit that is weakening our economy and our position in the world, safeguard the physical environment that sustains life on our planet and invest our resources more wisely in strengthening our families and educating our children?

We cannot analyze with certainty the motivations and tendencies of the Russian leaders, nor can we anticipate every development in other parts of the globe. But I offer the following propositions for debate in the 1988 election campaign. They are, I believe, consistent with the realities of our time.

III

First, we should replace our obsolete cold-war policy with a concerted effort to identify mutual interests with the Russians—trade, arms reduction, joint environmental efforts, shared exploration of outer space and cooperative efforts in the fields of health, education and cultural exchange. In such trouble spots as the Iran-Iraq war, the Arab-Israeli conflict, Afghanistan and Nicaragua, we should seek out the possibilities of Soviet and American initiatives for settlement.

The current shipping problem in the Persian Gulf stemming from the Iran-Iraq war represents an ideal example of a challenge the two superpowers should meet cooperatively rather than confrontationally. Both Moscow and Washington have an interest in ending the war between Iran and Iraq. Neither Washington nor Moscow has any interest in disrupting the shipping of the Persian Gulf or spreading the Iran-Iraq war further into that area.

The Reagan Administration naïvely committed our flag and our fleet to the Kuwaitis as a knee-jerk reaction to information that the Russians had responded in a very limited way to Kuwait's request for protection of tankers. Clearly, the Administration was also moved by a desire to regain credibility squandered mindlessly through arms sales to Iran. It would have been far wiser, however, to make our policy judgment on this matter only after careful consultation with all of the Gulf states, with our NATO allies and Japan and, most important, after full consultation with Congress. Then, if all signs indicated the need to protect shipping, the United States might have joined in a multinational escort force in concert with our allies, the Russians and some of the Arab states—perhaps under the aegis of the United Nations.

The Arab-Israeli-Palestinian conflict is another prime candidate for energetic and sustained cooperation by the United States and the Soviet Union in seeking a practical and just solution. Such other regional problem areas as Central America, Afghanistan and Southeast Asia could also be appropriate matters for Soviet-American consultation. Serious initiatives to cooperate with Mr. Gorbachev might prove more productive than we have accustomed ourselves to expect.

Second, we should join the Soviets in a complete ban on all nuclear testing, press ahead on the mutual elimination of medium-range nuclear weapons from Europe as provided for by the recently signed treaty, and agree to continued compliance with the Anti-Ballistic Missile Treaty—which means confining the Strategic Defense Initiative to research—in return for a mutual reduction of 50 percent in strategic nuclear weapons. Gorbachev has signaled his willingness to negotiate such a formula.

The major sticking point on this promising agenda for arms reduction is Mr. Reagan's insistence on the right to engage not only in research, but also testing and development of the SDI system—a position Mr. Gorbachev rejects. Most members of Congress and most arms control authorities, including those who negotiated the 1972 ABM treaty—as well as the Russians—believe that the 1972 treaty precludes anything beyond research and laboratory testing of missile defense systems. A major portion of the scientific and arms control community also believes that Mr. Reagan's concept of a kind of protective astrodome to make America invulnerable to nuclear attack is a destabilizing, frightfully costly fantasy. Former Under Secretary of State George Ball—a man of considerable experience in international affairs and arms issues—has described the so-called Star Wars system as "a fraud," but a very costly fraud that could consume upward of a trillion dollars.

SDI would depend almost entirely on computers and would require, by some estimates, ten million lines of computerized programming to make the system operable. Given the inevitable margin of error and malfunctioning in such an elaborate system, the danger is enormous that it might involve us in a nuclear exchange by mistakes in programming or interpretation. Given these concerns, would it not be better to move ahead on an agreement that will eliminate half of the missiles that Moscow now has targeted on us rather than living with Mr. Reagan's "dream" that we can some day build a shield that will make us safe in the event of nuclear war? I would urge that we confine work on SDI to research alone for a period of years while we proceed now with arms negotiations. As a practical matter, many technical questions must be resolved by research over the next few years before we can even speculate intelligently on whether it makes sense to go forward with SDI.

It has been argued by former Secretary of State Henry Kissinger and others that we are endangering the United States and Europe by eliminating intermediate-range nuclear weapons and cutting strategic nuclear weapons in half before dealing with conventional forces, where the Soviets are said to be relatively stronger. I would agree that we need to get the issue of conventional forces on the negotiating table, but this need not delay the next proposed step to reduce nuclear weapons as envisioned by Reagan and Gorbachev. Even with the 50-percent cuts called for in the tentative outline, each side would retain some 6,000 strategic nuclear weapons, including 4,900 ballistic missiles, with an average destructive capacity of 300,000 tons of TNT in each warhead. Since the only practical purpose of such weapons is to deter the other side from attacking, 6,000 nuclear monsters will serve the purpose as well as 12,000. Either force level is capable of eliminating most if not all of the life on our planet. Certainly we are no safer today with double the number of weapons targeted on our cities than we would be after the proposed second-stage agreement on strategic arms reductions.

Reagan and Gorbachev have both indicated their awareness of the need to move more purposefully on conventional force negotiations. Over the next decade, in close consultation with our allies, we should seek to negotiate with the Soviets mutual reductions in conventional forces that would enable us to draw down our 300,000 troops in Europe as well as the 40,000 now in South Korea. Obviously, the timetable for these withdrawals should depend on the scale and timing of Soviet reductions in troops, tanks and conventional units. Careful mutual arms control reductions, both nuclear and conventional, with proper verification can lessen tensions and fears. In turn, these steps also reduce the risk of war—which, of course, is the best defense of all in the nuclear age.

Third, if we can improve relations with the Soviets, reduce nuclear arms and draw down our forces abroad, we will have set the stage for a major reduction in U.S. military spending. We are now devoting 60 percent of our military budget to the projection of our power abroad and the defense of other countries, most notably our NATO allies and Japan, against a supposed Soviet or Chinese threat. But the countries we are defending are prosperous and moving steadily into a stronger economic and political relationship with the Russians and the Chinese. Does it make sense for the United States to pay over half the cost of NATO when the European states are as prosperous as we are and engage in more trade and joint ventures with the Soviets than we do?

It is now costing the United States approximately $150 billion annually to provide for the defense of Western Europe and Japan. This is roughly the dimension of our current annual fiscal deficit. For many years we have devoted a much higher percentage of our budget and our GNP to defense than have Japan and the nations of Western Europe. These countries are now pressing us hard to reduce our deficit in the interest of a more stable world economy. One way to do that is for us to cease carrying such a disproportionate share of the collective defense burden. We would be a stronger and a more prosperous nation with greater influence in the world if we shifted over the next ten years at least 30 percent of our military spending into deficit reduction, education, family support, environmental protection, rebuilding our public infrastructure and our railways, assisting our family farmers, upgrading the training and productivity of our industrial workers and strengthening the development of the Third World.

Fourth, while standing clear of Third World military struggles, unless conditions virtually demand our military involvement, we should support in every other reasonable manner democratic centrist forces in developing countries that are caught in power struggles between the hard right and the hard left. American political party professionals, labor union organizers, social activists, religious and public interest groups—all of these and more are needed to train, advise and organize those in the developing countries who seek democracy and justice. We should not hesitate to affirm abroad our active commitment to human rights and democratic ideals. Our 200-year-old experiment with constitutional democracy is the kind of good news we need to proclaim in the developing world.

The time is long overdue for us to recognize that even those countries in the Third World which happen to displease us ideologically are not beyond constructive American influence if we exercise that influence intelligently. We seriously negate that possibility, however, by following too rigidly a policy of economic and diplomatic boycott. It has long seemed to me that our policy of trying to isolate Cuba (to say nothing of earlier covert hit-and-run attacks and assassination attempts against Castro) has been ineffective and self-defeating. The quick decision in the opening stage of the Castro revolution to apply an economic and diplomatic embargo has inadvertently paralyzed American influence in Cuba and maximized Soviet power and influence there.

The same arguments can be made with reference to Vietnam and Angola. More than a decade has passed since the end of our bitter involvement in Vietnam. If that long and costly intervention was a mistake, is it not also a mistake to delay further the process of reconciliation and reconstruction of the country where we not only suffered such grievous losses, but where our arms took such a frightful toll of Vietnamese life and property? In a lengthy conversation with Premier Pham Van Dong in 1976, I was told that Hanoi desperately wanted American diplomatic recognition plus economic, medical and food assistance. The Vietnamese leader also made clear an eagerness to trade with the United States and even to open offshore oil resources to American development.

I found much the same kind of eagerness for U.S. recognition and cooperation in Angola during a visit there in 1978.

Why is it considered prudent and wise for us to carry on diplomatic and trade relations with the communist giants, China and the Soviet Union, while we boycott the little communist states— Cuba, Vietnam and Angola? Has the time not come to end this curious double standard?

There may be instances where it makes sense to employ economic and diplomatic boycotts, but on the record those methods no longer serve our best interests in dealing with the small revolutionary communist states. We have followed a much wiser and more productive course with communist Yugoslavia, notwithstanding the fact that it is in closer proximity to Soviet power than Angola, Vietnam or Cuba. Obviously there are other factors and differences involved, but our long-term approach to Yugoslavia may suggest a more productive approach to other communist states than the one we are now pursuing.

We are also not without influence in some of the Third World countries that are ruled by rightist governments. However belatedly, the Reagan Administration demonstrated that such right-wing leaders as Ferdinand Marcos in the Philippines and Jean-Claude Duvalier in Haiti were subject to local political action combined with American support and encouragement. The Pinochet regime in Chile is a classic example of a rightist government with a bad record on human rights that ought to feel constant diplomatic, moral and economic pressure from the United States.

In the Middle East, the United States understandably feels a special obligation to back the state of Israel, which we helped to create in the wake of the terrifying holocaust of Adolf Hitler's Nazi regime. But here as elsewhere we would be well advised to heed George Washington's warning against "inveterate antipathies" and "passionate attachments." The Arabs after all did not create the holocaust. They are not our enemies. Indeed, they actively seek our friendship and cooperation. Nor does it follow that Israeli objectives are synonymous with ours, including their 1982 invasion of Lebanon, their preference for Iran over Iraq, their support for the South African government and their hostility to the concept of a Palestinian homeland. We should continue to support Israel, but the time is long overdue for America to stand for self-determination for Palestinians as well as Israelis. Instead of closing the Palestinian Information Office in Washington, we should be talking to the Palestinians. Instead of foot-dragging on the proposal for an international conference on Middle East issues, we should be leading the way for such a conference.

It is possible that we may be faced with circumstances that leave us no honorable course except military intervention. I believe that during the genocidal campaign of the crazed Pol Pot against his own Cambodian people in the late 1970s the United States should have taken the lead at the United Nations in promoting a strong multilateral intervention. Perhaps as many as two million innocent

Cambodians were slaughtered in this totally irrational and barbarous orgy. Ironically, it was the unilateral intervention of the hated Vietnamese that finally halted the mass killing of Cambodians by their own government.

The bankruptcy of a policy that continues to view the Third World through the prism of an East-West cold war competition is dramatized by the current U.S. stance on Cambodia. The United States now recognizes and supports at the United Nations Pol Pot and his allies, instead of the Vietnamese-backed regime in Phnom Penh—certainly not on the merits, but on the basis of our opposition to Hanoi and Moscow.

There may be other instances in the Third World where we have no acceptable alternative except armed intervention. But for the most part, our power can best be demonstrated with nonmilitary means. We should think of armed intervention as a costly and high-risk measure of last resort and one that we should make every effort to carry out in concert with other nations—not unilaterally.

Improved relations with the Soviet Union and other communist states and substantial mutual arms reductions would not only help in getting our budget and trade deficits under control; they would also enable us to cooperate better with our standing partners in stabilizing the world trade system. We would be in a much stronger position to work with nations such as Mexico, Argentina, Brazil, Egypt and Israel in getting their debts under control and their economies in better shape. Instead of being the major supplier of arms to the Third World, we should seek to strengthen its economic health, not only because this is morally right but because a healthy Third World will be our major market in the future.

Fifth, there are two additional global concerns that lend themselves especially to American political, scientific and technical leadership: halting the degradation of the physical environment and ending human hunger. In concert with other nations and the U.N. system, we should lead the way in halting the pollution of the oceans and waterways, the erosion of the soil, the loss of forests, the contamination of the air and the disruption of the life-preserving ozone.

The alarming destruction of our planet by environmental deterioration may constitute a more serious threat to humanity than nuclear weapons. An international effort led by the United States to protect the world's environment could well be our first line of defense and national security.

Closely related to environmental concerns is the urgent need to win the struggle against hunger. Here again the United States is the best-endowed nation on earth to lead the effort to end starvation and malnutrition. We have the technical capability, the agricultural abundance and the shipping to lead the way to a world free from hunger. A more imaginative use of our surplus food in the short term and a greater effort to improve the agriculture of the developing world in the long term is the kind of internationalism that will give new force and respect to America's role in the world.

These environmental and hunger concerns present opportunities for closer cooperation with our allies, the Soviet Union and the developing world.

Sixth, it seems increasingly clear that our national and international concerns are deeply intertwined. There is, for example, little hope of ending our huge annual deficits unless we can bring the arms race under control. Nor can we correct the alarming U.S. trade deficit and the decline of some of our industries, including agriculture, that are dependent on exports unless the Third World, as the largest potential market for American goods, is able to improve its economic health. A further illustration of our inextricable involvement with Third World problems is the scourge of destructive drugs flowing into the United States. The peasants in such poor countries as Bolivia, Peru, Mexico and Colombia survive in considerable part by selling cocaine and marijuana to the American market. Equally poor farmers in Southeast Asia and Turkey supply us with heroin. In short, the poverty, underdevelopment and desperation measures of the Third World spill over into America to feed the most destructive social evil in our society.

The economic, political, environmental and military challenges around the globe demand international cooperation rather than unilateral action by single nations. For all practical purposes, isolationism and unilateralism are inadequate foreign policies in the world of today and tomorrow.

This means, I believe, that we must make increasing use of the United Nations system as a vital foreign policy vehicle. No American administration since World War II has given the United Nations the preeminent position it should have in the policies of a major world power. The Reagan Administration has been especially weak if not outright hostile in its attitude toward the United Nations. It is embarrassing that the current delinquency of the United States in paying its assessed contribution to the United Nations has made it necessary for smaller countries including Canada to pay their future assessments in advance so that the United Nations can meet its payroll obligations.

In our efforts to build better relationships with the Soviet Union and China, to address the massive problems of debt, development and hunger in the Third World, to meet the dangers of terrorism and the conflicts of the Middle East, to respond to the new scourge of AIDS—all of these and numerous other concerns challenge us to make greater use of the forum and the machinery of the United Nations. The U.N. Development Program and the U.N. World Health Organization have mounted a global effort against AIDS that is deserving of full U.S. support and participation. It should be noted that it was under the direction of the World Health Organization that smallpox was virtually ended worldwide.

IV

If bringing our relationship with the global community including Moscow up to date in the light of today's realities is the most urgent foreign policy challenge of 1988, the second and equally important challenge is squaring the conduct and substance of American policy with our historical national values. In the bicentennial of our Constitution, it is important that we renew our commitment to the vision of the Framers who drafted the Declaration of Independence and the Constitution.

We have painfully learned again from the Iran-contra fiasco that secretive, illegal or antidemocratic operations abroad are not compatible with the values and needs of our democracy. If I were permitted just one line of advice to the president elected in 1988 it would be: "Heed the Constitution." The only oath we require of our president is that he "preserve, protect and defend the Constitution of the United States" and "take care that the laws be faithfully executed."

Unfortunately, several of our presidents since the end of World War II have violated their inaugural oath. These violations were invariably defended in the name of national security. Most were schemes hatched in secret by a handful of people around the president. Most were not only illegal, but also mistaken ideas that embarrassed the nation.

Congress should act to do what former President Harry Truman recommended in his later years—limit the CIA and other intelligence or security agencies of the United States strictly to the gathering of intelligence. Setting up mercenary armies, mining international harbors, assassinating local officials, overturning governments, using arms dealers to circumvent the laws and our announced foreign policy—all such activities should be terminated by law. This will not, of course, stop a president determined to break the law, but it will, at least, make such actions plainly illegal. That is a step toward constitutional government and a revival of credibility and respect for our standing in the world.

Behind our covert activities of the past four decades has been the worship of "national security" and "the power of the presidency"—notions used to justify an interventionist foreign policy and a permanent war economy. But these concepts have an authoritarian quality that is alien to the founding ideals of our constitutional democracy.

At the heart of our Constitution is the separation of powers—the system of checks and balances. The president is the commander-in-chief of the armed forces and the conductor of foreign policy. But he carries out these activities under definite constitutional checks that give the Congress a strong role in the authorization and shaping of both military and foreign policy. It is the Congress which controls the granting of funds that determine the scope and substance of foreign policy and the size and mission of the armed forces. It is the Congress which declares war and determines whether and how American forces become involved abroad, and how long and under what conditions such interventions are continued. The Senate has a special responsibility to "advise and consent" on American treaty obligations and the confirmation of diplomatic officials, which means that its role in shaping our international obligations and our diplomacy was meant not to be ancillary but integral. The Framers of the Constitution sought to avoid an imperial presidency that would be free to direct the foreign policy and the armed forces unchecked by the people's elected representatives in the Congress.

It was not simply that the Framers distrusted unchecked power, which they clearly did; they also feared an interventionist foreign policy and large, permanent military forces. Washington, Jefferson and Madison were all willing to use military power when they saw no other reasonable alternative. But they all opposed the creation of standing military forces that went beyond emergency requirements, and they all despised an interventionist foreign policy that needlessly embroiled the United States abroad. Jefferson called for "peace, commerce, and honest friendship with all nations, entangling alliances with none." Washington, I repeat, warned against either "inveterate antipathies" or "passionate attachments" to other nations.

The Constitution that was hammered out in Philadelphia in 1787 sought to prevent reckless interventionism and rampant militarism by deliberately tying the hands of the president so that he could not raise huge military forces or involve the nation in foreign expeditions without congressional approval and close executive-legislative cooperation. Today, the postwar results of failing to heed the noninterventionist precepts of the Founders are painfully on view in the new fields of white crosses in Arlington Cemetery and on the black marble wall of the Vietnam Memorial. As a former World War II bomber pilot, I lament that many of my countrymen were dispatched in causes far less worthy.

If we are to "intervene" abroad, let us do so primarily with our political, economic and moral strength. A prominent example is the case of South Africa, where the American position should be clear and unequivocal. There is no place for apartheid in the modern world. We should follow a policy of steadily tightening diplomatic and economic pressure on South Africa in concert with other nations which share our rejection of national racism.

For most of our 200-year course as a nation we have been well served by the wisdom of the constitutional Framers. We have seen that document as both a body of principles and a living experiment that has enabled us to meet new and changing circumstances. But especially since World War II we have drifted far from the essential wisdom of the Founders and the constitutional process they bequeathed. This has led us into a series of ill-advised, bloody interventions abroad, a self-defeating arms race, disruptive economic costs at home, and a steady decline of real security and international influence. We are at a watershed, requiring a change in direction. In 1988, as at the beginning of the American nation, we need to build a foreign policy that is consistent with both the procedures and the substance of a genuine constitutional democracy.

V

If I may add a note of personal advice to the presidential contenders, I would warn them against making hasty pledges under campaign pressures that might hamper their capacity to make unfettered decisions in the White House. I blush when I think of a few of the commitments I made as the Democratic nominee in 1972, including a promise that if elected I would move the American embassy in Israel from Tel Aviv to Jerusalem. This might have pleased a few Israelis and a handful of American voters, but it would have been disastrous to our standing in the Arab world, seriously eroding our ability to serve as an "honest broker" of the Middle East conflict.

In 1960 Democratic nominee John Kennedy chided the incumbent Eisenhower Administration for not moving forcefully against Castro. Perhaps in this militant campaign rhetoric Kennedy, the candidate, was helping to set the trap for the Bay of Pigs fiasco that a few months later embarrassed Kennedy, the president. In 1968 candidate Richard Nixon implied that he had a plan to end the war in Vietnam. When the war dragged on for four more years, it produced a sense of betrayal that disillusioned millions of Americans. President Lyndon Johnson's pledge four years earlier that he was "not going to send American boys to do the job that Asian boys should be doing" was an earlier source of presidential credibility problems.

It is not necessary for presidential candidates to take a rigid stand on every one of the world's problems—especially those which carry domestic political lobbies demanding candidate commitments that are tempting to grasp but difficult to live with after the election. Indeed, a president's freedom of action is limited by the Constitution, by acts of Congress, by American public opinion and by the changing complexity of the global scene. Rather than glibly promising a neat solution to each of the foreign policy issues facing the country, a prudent presidential contender should pledge to seek basic policy objectives in consultation with the Congress and our allies, sometimes after negotiations with our rivals, but always within the spirit and the laws of our constitutional democracy. It is also still wise, I think, for an American president to form his final judgments and course of action "with a decent respect to the opinions of mankind."

Former Senator GEORGE MCGOVERN was the Democratic Party's presidential candidate in 1972.

American Foreign Policy: The Bush Agenda

Richard M. Nixon   AMERICA AND THE WORLD 1988

President George H.W. Bush is surrounded by a sea of U.S. military personnel as he greets troops following an arrival ceremony in the eastern Saudi Arabian city of Dhahran November 22, 1990.

I n 1945, a year before his speech in Fulton, Missouri, Winston Churchill sent a message to the new president, Harry Truman, about the ominous developments in Soviet policy: "An Iron Curtain is being drawn down over their front. We do not know what lies behind it. It is vital, therefore, that we reach an understanding with Russia now before we have mortally reduced our armies and before we have withdrawn into our zones of occupation." Churchill's advice went unheeded, and the West lost a historic opportunity to negotiate a favorable deal with the Kremlin when the bargaining leverage of the United States vis-à-vis the Soviet Union stood at its peak.

After almost half a century, the communist world's leader, President Mikhail Gorbachev, has undertaken dramatic changes within the Soviet bloc that give the free world's new leader, President George Bush, another historic opportunity to enhance the West's security and to effect a sea change in the U.S.-Soviet relationship. Gorbachev's policies of glasnost and perestroika have been hailed, even by some hard-line Western leaders, as heralding the end of the cold war. While his reforms give reason for a reappraisal of the West's policy toward the Soviet Union, we must bear in mind that the causes of the cold war-Moscow's domination of Eastern Europe and aggressive foreign policies around the world-still endure. Those who urge the West to "help Gorbachev" with low-interest loans and subsidized credits fail to realize that such actions are not in our interest until he makes an irrevocable break with the Kremlin's past policies.

An opportunity now exists to make genuine progress toward a more stable peace. President Bush can exploit this opportunity if he takes a hard-headed look at the Soviet Union under Gorbachev and devises a policy that presents the Kremlin leaders with intractable strategic choices. We must make Gorbachev choose between a less confrontational relationship with the West and the retention of his imperial control over Eastern Europe, between a continuing race in arms technology and arms control agreements that could create a stable strategic and conventional balance, and between access to Western technology and credits and continuing Soviet adventurism in the Third World.

II

Gorbachev has sparked enormous excitement in the West because he is perceived to be a new kind of Soviet leader. Dazzled by his "star quality"-the fashionably tailored suits, the polished manners and the smooth touch in personal encounters-reporters and diplomats alike have naïvely confused changes in style and rhetoric with shifts in substance and policy. I have met with three of the Soviet Union's principal postwar leaders-Nikita Khrushchev in 1959 and

1960, Leonid Brezhnev in 1972, 1973 and 1974, and Mikhail Gorbachev in 1986. Gorbachev is in a class of his own. He is their match in tenacity and forcefulness, but outstrips them in realism, quickness and intelligence. He deserves great respect for his boldness, his courage and his mastery of public relations. He is a different but, from the West's point of view, not necessarily a better type of leader. We must keep in mind that his talent and capabilities can just as easily make the world a more dangerous place as they can contribute to greater global security.

Gorbachev has launched his reforms and pursued a more conciliatory approach to the West because the communist economic system failed at home and the Soviet Union's foreign policy became counterproductive abroad. The centrally planned economy of the Brezhnev era has become a monument to corruption and inefficiency. Brezhnev's militarism and expansionism not only mobilized the West to strengthen its armed forces but also gave the Soviet Union a severe case of imperial indigestion after it gobbled up Third World countries. By the early 1980s, Moscow's clients in Afghanistan, Cuba, Nicaragua, Vietnam, Angola and Ethiopia cost the Kremlin at least $20 billion a year to keep in power. It is a mistake to think that only Gorbachev would have initiated a reform program, for these realities would have forced whoever came to power into rethinking Soviet domestic and foreign policy.

Unlike his predecessors, Gorbachev sees the world without ideological blinders. He has realistically assessed the Soviet Union's enormous economic, political, imperial and geopolitical problems. First, he recognizes openly that the Soviet economy has stagnated, with negligible or even negative growth rates since the late 1970s. Without economic reform and access to Western technology and capital, the Soviet Union will fall hopelessly behind the United States, Western Europe, Japan and-perhaps as early as the middle of the next century-China.

Second, Gorbachev initiated his economic reforms-perestroika-because he knows that the Soviet people can no longer be motivated with political slogans. The increased East-West contacts of the détente era and the revolution in mass communications have rendered futile the Stalinist strategy of isolation and ideological indoctrination. Today, the Soviet people are aware that their standard of living-cramped housing, endless food lines and empty store shelves-compares unfavorably not only with that of the West but also with those of the newly industrializing countries of the Third World. Gorbachev knows that only material incentives, not ideological exhortations, will induce the people to work harder. They will produce more only if they can actually purchase decent consumer goods with the additional rubles they earn.

Third, Gorbachev knows that economic failure and political repression have created seething unrest throughout the Soviet empire that could erupt at the slightest provocation. Time bombs lie just below the surface ready to explode, not only in virtually all his East European satellites but also in many of the non-Russian republics of the Soviet Union itself. Through glasnost, he has tried to create a safety valve to defuse this pent-up frustration, but by venting these angers he may have let the genie out of the bottle. He will find that demands for pluralism in Eastern Europe and greater national autonomy for the non-Russian peoples are difficult to control. Ironically, Soviet leaders used appeals to nationalism to expand their empire into the Third World. Now nationalism threatens to tear that empire apart.

Fourth, as Gorbachev surveys the global political scene, he must be struck by the fact that instead of improving the Soviet Union's position in the world, the Kremlin's foreign policy has managed to unite all the world's major powers against Moscow. The United States, Canada, Western Europe, Japan and China-which together account for over 60 percent of the world economy and which pose the threat of a two-front engagement in any world conflict-have cooperated actively for more than 15 years in opposing Moscow's traditional expansionist ambition. Moscow's old thinking led to a dead end, so Gorbachev has launched his "new thinking" in foreign affairs to loosen the bonds of, or break up, that anti-Soviet bloc.

Fifth, Gorbachev, as a communist, instinctively believes in the importance of the battle of ideas, but as a realist, he knows that the Soviet Union has lost that battle. Around the world-not only within the Soviet bloc but also in Africa, Asia and Latin America-Soviet socialism is perceived as the road to stagnation, not prosperity. It still appeals to those who want to seize and hold power but not to those who want to build a better life for their people. Through his reforms, Gorbachev seeks to create a new model and image for socialism and to give the communist ideology a second wind.

III

Gorbachev's goal is to reinvigorate his country's communist system, to make the Soviet Union a superpower not just in military but also in economic and political terms. Without sweeping reforms, he will not be able to afford the costs of the Soviet military establishment and of Soviet client-states, to provide the Soviet people with a better life, to create a model that can be competitive in the global ideological battle and to keep the Soviet Union in the front rank of world powers.

Gorbachev's reforms face three massive internal roadblocks that could derail his efforts. Despite his successes at the recent special party conference (June 1988) and his tours de force at the recent Central Committee and Supreme Soviet meetings, Gorbachev has not consolidated a firm political grip over the Soviet system. He can count only three or four of the 12 members of the Politburo as steadfast allies. While Yegor Ligachev, his apparent rival, may no longer be looking over Gorbachev's shoulder as the recognized number-two man, Ligachev's faction is waiting in the wings, ready to take over should Gorbachev falter. The last Soviet reformer-Nikita Khrushchev-met with an untimely political demise when he threatened too many entrenched interests.

Thus, we should make no concessions to Gorbachev that we would not make to the least progressive Soviet leader, for the chance still exists that the latter could come to power. While Gorbachev has been hailed as a superstar on the world stage, we must

405

remember that the stars that shine the brightest sometimes fade away the fastest.

In Gorbachev's four years in power, there has been a lot of talk but precious little progress. He has been unable to force the sclerotic Soviet party and state bureaucracies to abandon their Stalinist ways. He has the unenviable task of teaching old bureaucrats new tricks. It is one thing to tell a bureaucrat to do a certain task and another to order him to be creative and innovative. The former at least stirs him to action, while the latter evinces blank stares of total incomprehension.

Gorbachev's most profound problem is that he still believes in Marxism-Leninism. Even if he wins his political and bureaucratic battles, this handicap will ultimately doom his reforms to failure. Rapid, self-sustaining economic growth has occurred only in countries that respect the right of individuals to own private property and that allow unregulated prices and the laws of supply and demand to allocate economic resources. Gorbachev has expressed a willingness to grant farmers long-term leases for private farming and has stated that some prices will be decontrolled in the early 1990s, but he still wants to keep the party-state apparatus in firm command of the economy as a whole. While there have been several examples of economies moving from capitalism to communism, there are no examples of economies moving from communism to capitalism. No one has ever constructed a successful halfway house between a market-based and a command economy.

Gorbachev faces a profound philosophical dilemma: he can choose ideology or progress. If he chooses communism, he cannot have progress; if he chooses progress, he cannot have communism. Only by abandoning the ideology that is the bedrock of his power can he produce progress that will match that of the West.

Given the inefficient central planning system and the irrational pricing system, no foreign investor today has the slightest idea of how to judge which economic risks in the Soviet Union are worth taking. Making loans to the Kremlin is like laying down chips on the dice table; some bets may pay off but the odds are that in the long run the money will be wasted. In fact, it is not even in Gorbachev's interest for the West to provide economic assistance before fundamental economic reforms have been institutionalized. A banker does no favor to a borrower by making him a bad loan. We should not enable the Kremlin to borrow its way out of today's problems and thereby delay the inevitable day of addressing the causes of those problems.

Both American superhawks and superdoves overstate the impact Western policies can have on the Soviet Union. Superhawks argue that the West's arms buildup and its opposition to Soviet aggression in places like Afghanistan were the primary factors that prompted Gorbachev to launch his reforms. Those Western actions were vital on their own merits. But even without those actions Gorbachev would have had to initiate changes because the Soviet economic system was suffering from terminal illness. As a Chinese leader told me in 1985, without reforms the Soviet Union by the middle of the next century would "disappear" as a great power. That made internal change imperative, regardless of Western policies.

Superdoves, on the other hand, believe that we should do anything within our power to help Gorbachev in order to promote peace. But we must realize that whether he succeeds or fails ultimately depends on events and forces within the Soviet Union that we cannot affect. We cannot induce Gorbachev to cast aside his Marxist-Leninist obsession with keeping the state in charge of the economy. We cannot whip the Soviet bureaucracy into shape. We can hardly even make out the patterns of Kremlin political intrigue after the fact, much less lend a helping hand to those whose views and interests seem to parallel ours.

Above all, we must keep Gorbachev's reforms in perspective. He does not want to overturn the Soviet system; he wants to strengthen it. To paraphrase Churchill from another context, Gorbachev did not become general secretary to preside over the demise of the Communist Party. We have an interest in the success of his reforms only to the extent that they change the system to make it

Richard M. Nixon

less threatening to our security and interests. We should applaud glasnost and perestroika but not pay for them, for if his reforms do not irrevocably alter Soviet foreign policy we will be subsidizing the threat of our own destruction.

IV

Those who parrot today a fashionable slogan-"the cold war is over"- trivialize the problems of Western security. Gorbachev's public relations experts have made many Western policymakers forget that a more benign Soviet image does not mean a more benign Soviet foreign policy. As a result, the race to Moscow is already on. In recent months, Western leaders have jetted off to the Kremlin with planeloads of eager bankers and industrialists in tow, and Soviet leaders have gleefully lined up more than $10 billion in easy credit. Unless the West steps back and designs a coherent strategy, we will squander our leverage and lose the historic opportunity presented by events in the Soviet Union.

We should bear in mind a remark made to me in 1953 by Field Marshall Slim, then the British governor-general of Australia. In arguing for a dialogue between the United States and the Soviet Union, he said, "We must break the ice. If we don't break it, we will all get frozen into it so tight that it will take an atom bomb to break it." Today, the ice has broken even before the end of winter. We are witnessing the thaw that brings the promise of spring. While it is a period of great possibilities, we must tread carefully or risk falling into the icy waters.

We have to recognize that the situation we face now is infinitely more complex than the one we faced at the outset of the cold war forty years ago. At that time, the threat was as clear as Stalin's Iron Curtain and his belligerent rhetoric about the inevitability of war, all of which enabled President Truman to prevent a return to isolationism, adopt a policy of containment and win bipartisan support for entry into NATO and unprecedented levels of peacetime defense spending.

Gorbachev has brilliantly changed the game. In Europe, he has discarded the traditional Soviet tactics of diplomatic bluster and military threat and has mastered those of deceptive propaganda and political maneuver. He has substituted the wiles of diplomacy for the threat of force as his chosen instrument for foreign policy conquests. As a result, at a time when Soviet superiority in conventional military forces and in accurate land-based intercontinental ballistic missiles (ICBMs) is larger than ever before, he has made more progress toward the traditional Soviet objective of dividing the NATO alliance than any of his predecessors. We cannot counter his "peace offensive" simply by loudly warning about the military threat of Moscow's Red Army. Instead, we must launch our own political offensive to achieve our strategic and geopolitical objectives.

We will be pursuing those goals in what has become a multipolar world. Japan is already an economic superpower and will inevitably use its economic clout for political effect. Western Europe will become a unified economic market by 1992 and is beginning to intensify its cooperation in political and strategic matters. China, already a major nuclear power and fast becoming a major economic player, will emerge as one of the world's superpowers in the next century.

We can work with all of these new major powers more easily than Gorbachev can. Therefore, before the new administration holds a substantive summit with Gorbachev, it should conduct intensive discussions and meetings with our major allies and friends. We should do this not to present Moscow with an antagonistic and belligerent united front but to explore our common interests and to coordinate our policies where possible.

President Bush should continue to reject the advice of those who urge that he schedule a quick summit with Gorbachev in order to have a foreign policy "victory" early in his term. Gorbachev needs a summit far more than the president. Only when the Bush Administration has agreed on a strategy with our allies and has a definite program for making significant substantive progress on major issues should President Bush schedule an American-Soviet summit.

In formulating a strategy, we should begin by estimating what Gorbachev wants, then map out what we want, what trade-offs are possible, and what we can do to put pressure on him to agree to our terms. Most important, we have to recognize that linkage-the linking of progress on one issue to progress on another-is the key to any successful negotiations with Moscow. Kremlin leaders will always explicitly reject linkage, but they always implicitly accept it.

Without linkage, Gorbachev will string together a series of easy victories at the bargaining table. Each superpower has a greater interest in progress on some issues than on others. Gorbachev, for example, will press hard for access to Western capital markets and technology. The United States, on the other hand, has a greater interest in reducing Soviet influence in the Third World through settlements of certain regional conflicts that threaten our interests. Moscow will be more than willing to negotiate solely on the former. If we fail to pursue a determined policy of linkage, Gorbachev will dominate the agenda and make one-sided progress on his top priorities.

Linkage requires subtlety. An American president should not step before the cameras and announce that he intends to hold the next arms control agreement hostage to Soviet capitulation on one or another issue. Nor should the Congress make the mistake of publicly linking U.S. foreign policy objectives to Soviet domestic policy reforms. The Jackson-Vanik Amendment in 1973–74 was a case in point. Its purpose was to force the Soviet Union to increase Jewish emigration, but it had the opposite effect of drastically reducing it. We should vigorously press the Soviets in world forums to eliminate their human rights abuses. But we must allow them to appear to do so of their own volition rather than by clumsily making it look as if they did so only because of direct Western intervention in their internal affairs. No great nation can appear to allow its internal policies to be dictated by a foreign power.

We should link progress toward better East-West relations to restraint in Soviet global behavior. If we enter into agreements beneficial to Moscow despite direct or indirect Soviet aggression, we will in effect be giving the Kremlin a green light to assault our interests. If we pursue a determined strategy that includes linkage, we can further our strategic interests in Europe, in arms control negotiations and in the world's key regional conflicts.

V

Europe has again become the central focus of the East-West conflict, and our strategy vis-à-vis the Soviets must change to meet these circumstances. From 1945 to the early 1960s, the European continent was the principal arena of the world ideological struggle. From the early 1960s through the mid-1980s, after the division of Europe had become a settled political reality, the primary fields of conflict-Indochina, the Middle East, southern Africa, the horn of Africa, southwest Asia and Central America-were situated in the Third World. Now Gorbachev has made the Old World the central priority and target of his new foreign policy.

The traditional goal of Kremlin leaders has been to create political fissures between the United States and Western Europe in order to erode the strength of the alliance. Moscow has pursued this objective, at various times, through a strategy of confrontation that seeks to rattle European nerves and demonstrate the unreliability of America as an ally, or through a strategy of condominium with the United States that seeks to weaken European confidence by creating the impression that the superpowers are settling Europe's fate. Gorbachev has adopted the more straightforward tactic of appealing directly to the West Europeans. He has called for the creation of a single "European home" stretching from the Atlantic to the Urals-thus implying that the United States represents an obstacle to peace-and has sought to exploit the West European fatigue after forty years of East-West conflict.

The world of 1949, when NATO was formed, differs profoundly from the world of 1989. We need a new strategy in Europe-one that

411

enhances the Continent's stability not only through initiatives to revitalize the alliance in Western Europe but also through a sustained effort to foster peaceful change and positive political evolution in Eastern Europe.

The new administration should make Europe its top foreign policy priority. It should call for a major working summit-no black ties and no spouses-to hammer out a strategy for enhancing our collective security. First of all, we should articulate a common analysis of the nature of the Soviet military threat in Europe. Americans, and many Europeans, believe that the Soviet threat remains as great as or even greater than ever, especially because of Moscow's unrelenting buildup of conventional and strategic weaponry. But in recent years there has been a tendency among other West Europeans, especially but not exclusively those on the left, to view the Soviet Union as a stagnant society incapable of threatening the West or even to view Washington's calls for vigilance and readiness as a greater threat to peace than Moscow's armies.

Harold Macmillan once told me that alliances were held together by fear, not love. For many in Europe and the United States, the fear of the Soviet Union has waned, and what love may exist among economic competitors in the West is a very weak glue to hold an alliance together. It is therefore imperative that Western leaders issue a joint statement, in conjunction with its arms control proposals, that educates their publics on the nature and scope of the Soviet threat.

Second, we should agree on ways to defend common Western interests outside of Europe. In 1949 the West faced the threat of a direct Soviet military thrust into central Europe. In recent years, with the East-West competition in Europe focusing on the political plane, Soviet direct and indirect aggression has principally taken place in the Third World. The United States has borne the overwhelming share of the burden in countering Moscow's subversion and proxy warfare to protect regions such as the Persian Gulf, even though the Gulf is far more important to Western Europe than to the United States. Unless we devise a more equitable global security framework, it is inevitable that pressure will build in the United States for a significant reduction of the U.S. troop commitment to NATO.

Third, we should articulate a compelling rationale for NATO's nuclear deterrent and a joint approach for the next round of European arms control talks. At the Reykjavik summit, the Reagan Administration undermined public support for nuclear deterrence by advocating the idea of eliminating all nuclear weapons. We must renounce the Reykjavik rhetoric in unequivocal terms and explain to Western publics the realities of the nuclear age. We should pursue the so-called competitive strategies on the conventional level to undercut the significance of Soviet quantitative superiority and thereby raise the nuclear threshold. But nuclear deterrence, both strategic and tactical, remains imperative. Even if conventional arms control succeeds, NATO will have to maintain a residual, even if diminished, tactical nuclear capability in Europe, though the deterrent should be reconfigured to allay West German concerns regarding the bases and targets of these weapons. More important, NATO must arrive at a joint conventional arms control proposal that makes offensive warfare futile and that mobilizes public support for the Western negotiating position. A good beginning has been made in the recent NATO proposal for major cuts in the tank armies in Europe, though a public diplomacy offensive needs to be launched to sell it to Western publics.

Fourth, we must agree on a common approach to East-West trade. We should not provide the Soviet Union with technologies that can significantly improve its military forces. We should also create a joint institution for coordinating and regulating the Soviet Union's access to Western capital markets. It is not in our interest to have Western banks competing to provide the Kremlin with loans at below-market rates. Nor is it in our interest to repeat the mistakes of bankers in the 1970s who lent East European countries tens of billions of dollars that will never be repaid.

Fifth, we should design a common approach to the problem of Eastern Europe. The cold war began in Eastern Europe, and it will not end until Moscow's satellites receive their independence. In the past, it has always been in the West's interest, but not in Moscow's, to address the issue of Eastern Europe. Today, since Gorbachev needs East-West economic links and reduced tensions for perestroika to succeed, a new settlement is in the Kremlin's interest as well.

Without a political settlement in Eastern Europe, no stable, enduring improvement in East-West relations is possible. Postwar history is the story of continual attempts by the East Europeans to wrest their freedom from Moscow. The workers' uprising in East Germany in 1953, the popular rebellion in Hungary in 1956, the Prague Spring in 1968, the Solidarity movement in Poland in 1980, and the scores of other smaller incidents of open opposition all testify to the popular determination to be free. All these outbursts had to be suppressed directly or indirectly by Soviet arms, and all those interventions destroyed the prospects for an immediate improvement in East-West relations.

That pattern could soon recur. Eastern Europe has become an economic and political powder keg waiting to blow up. Today, the tectonic plates of East European nationalism and Soviet expansionism have built up enormous pressure as they have pushed against each other. We have seen the first tremors in the rise of East European dissident and reform movements. But a political earthquake is inevitable in the 1990s. If Moscow responds with military force, it will mean a return to sharper tensions in East-West relations and an abortion of Gorbachev's reforms.

If we want to avoid this grim scenario, we must work on three fronts.

First, the West should press for peaceful change in Eastern Europe. We should continue to exploit modern means of mass communication to break the grip of the East European regimes over their peoples. Radio Free Europe has been one of our most effective programs in the East-West struggle. In the 1990s we should establish direct television transmissions via satellite into these countries. We should also provide material support to those behind the Iron Curtain who are pressing for peaceful change, with Western trade union support to the Solidarity movement in Poland serving as a model.

Second, the West should continue its policy of differentiating between those East European regimes which demonstrate a willingness to enact reforms that move their countries toward political pluralism and those which do not. For those leaders who liberalize their regimes, we should make available economic credits, more advanced technology and debt rescheduling, while the others should be left to fend for themselves.

Third, the United States should put Eastern Europe on the U.S.-Soviet agenda. In Yugoslavia last year, Gorbachev signed a declaration that stated that "no one has a monopoly on truth" and that foreign powers had no "claim on imposing their notions of social development on anyone." We should insist that Kremlin leaders back up their words with deeds. We could even propose the neutralization of Eastern Europe along the lines of the Austrian Peace Treaty of 1955, with an interim agreement that leaves the military structure of the Warsaw Pact intact but that would allow the East European peoples to choose their own forms of government through genuine elections.

Eastern Europe is the natural field for political initiatives by Western Europe. Our allies' historical fatigue stems in part from the fact that for forty years their role has been defined by a negative mission-stopping further Soviet expansion. It can be cured by devoting energy to the positive mission of promoting peaceful change beyond the Iron Curtain. Holding the line against the Red Army has principally involved sacrifice and risk, but supporting the development of pluralism under the nose of the Red Army requires ingenuity and inspiration. It is a task that will not only enhance Western Europe's security but also help to restore its sense of purpose.

VI

Arms control should be treated as only one part of Western defense policy and not vice versa. Arms negotiations are a political imperative, indispensable in holding the NATO alliance together and for winning support in Congress for adequate defense budgets. For too long, however, many Western leaders have endorsed arms control as an end in itself, regardless of the impact that particular agreements would have on our strategic position. Moscow, on the other hand, has traditionally sought to use arms control to achieve political and strategic ends-to lull the West into a false sense of security, to limit developments in American weapons technology, and to preserve or increase Soviet advantages in weapons deployments. It is time for the United States to borrow a page from the Kremlin's negotiating handbook.

Since Soviet superiority in conventional arms represents the greatest threat to Western security, cuts in those forces should be the top priority of Western arms control strategy. Moscow's main goal is to reduce the numbers of strategic nuclear weapons and to stifle the Strategic Defense Initiative (SDI) while preserving its advantage on the conventional level, because that would maximize the political importance of its conventional superiority. Therefore, it is imperative that the United States link progress in the Strategic Arms Reduction Talks (START) to progress in conventional arms control negotiations.

Western conventional arms control proposals should focus geographically on the European central front, the most militarily congested territory in the world, and should seek to reduce those weapons that are most useful for offensive warfare. These should include at a minimum reductions in tanks and self-propelled artillery even beyond those proposed by Gorbachev at the United Nations. The weapons must be destroyed rather than pulled back into the Soviet Union; otherwise Moscow could redeploy them in a matter of days. In addition, military bases and supply depots should be relocated away from the front in order to make surprise attacks more difficult. NATO governments must insist in arms control talks that Gorbachev fulfill his pledge to accept "asymmetrical reductions" on the conventional level.

Gorbachev's rhetoric about reconfiguring Warsaw Pact forces to fit a "defensive" doctrine has been all talk and no action. His pledge in his recent U.N. speech to demobilize 500,000 troops and retire 10,000 tanks represents a significant symbolic gesture. But we must not pretend that it solves the security problem posed by the Warsaw Pact's tank armada (currently about 53,000).[1] Thus, if the 5,000 tanks withdrawn from East Germany, Czechoslovakia and Hungary are not destroyed but simply parked on the Soviet side of the border, they can be redeployed rapidly. Even if the tanks were destroyed, the Warsaw Pact's tank advantage would drop only slightly.

In addition to linking the strategic and conventional arms control talks, the new administration should redirect the U.S. approach to the START negotiations.

Our problem on the strategic level, which began in the mid-1970s and threatens to become much worse in the 1990s, is the growing vulnerability of our land-based missiles and command-and-control systems to a first-strike attack by the most accurate and powerful Soviet missiles. The Reagan Administration's effort to cut strategic forces by 50 percent focused too much on simply reducing the total number of strategic weapons instead of reducing the vulnerability of U.S. strategic forces and thereby enhancing strategic stability. The real test is not whether the treaty reduces the number of nuclear weapons but whether it reduces the likelihood of nuclear war. We must ultimately judge the value of any START agreement by whether it increases the security of our strategic forces and decreases the incentives for either side to resort to nuclear weapons in a crisis.

That is where the current START formula falls short. Under its terms, both sides would reduce their arsenals to 1,600 launchers including heavy bombers, ICBMs and submarine-launched ballistic missiles, and to 6,000 warheads, of which only 4,900 would be permitted on ballistic missiles. While such radical reductions might be politically appealing, close scrutiny shows that they actually increase the vulnerability of U.S. forces. Moscow would retain a land-based ICBM force composed almost entirely of the newer

Richard M. Nixon

SS-18, SS-24 and SS-25 missile launchers, all of which are first-strike weapons. At the same time, the cuts would reduce the number of targets inside the United States that would have to be destroyed for a first strike to succeed. Assuming that after reductions the United States would choose to retain its most accurate and modern weapons, the ratio of Soviet first-strike warheads to U.S. first-strike targets would grow drastically worse. In addition, the prospective reductions would restrict the deployment of our most capable and survivable force, the fleet of Trident II submarines, to no more than 17 boats. As a result, this force could well become vulnerable, for some number will always be in port or off-line, and the remainder, reduced to, say, ten boats, will be tracked by Moscow's fleet of 270 attack submarines.[2]

Some argue that these issues do not matter, because under the proposed START agreement we would be allowed to reconfigure our strategic forces to account for the new ceilings. They contend that we could build a new fleet of smaller submarines that would carry fewer missiles and a new generation of land-based missiles that would carry fewer warheads. This argument is flawed for two reasons. First, the START force reductions are to be carried out over seven years, while any programs to develop and deploy entire new strategic systems would take a decade or more. Second, it is totally unrealistic to think that Congress, which expects arms control to produce cuts in the defense budget, would vote to increase military spending by the tens of billions of dollars necessary to overhaul completely our strategic force posture.

Instead of seeking an arbitrary 50-percent reduction, the Bush Administration should consider adopting a two-part proposal, with the first level designed to meet minimum U.S. requirements and to produce a quick interim agreement and the second level directed to major reductions in first-strike weapons. In formulating our proposal for the first stage, we should calculate what kind of strategic force posture our security requires and propose launcher and warhead ceilings that could involve some reductions from present levels but would not impede the necessary U.S. weapons programs, particularly the mobile Midgetman missile. In addition, since the United States observed and the Soviet Union ignored the modernization restrictions of the treaties negotiated in the Strategic Arms Limitation Talks, this initial agreement would permit unrestricted modernization.

After the completion of the interim agreement, the two sides would focus on the far more difficult objective of increasing strategic stability by reducing the number of warheads on both sides capable of destroying hardened military targets in a first strike. Both superpowers would be allowed to retain an equal number of counterforce warheads. But the level of these most threatening weapons would be scaled back dramatically-far more than by the current START proposal. This should involve a 75-percent cut from the present level of such Soviet weapons and should also require reductions in planned deployments of comparable U.S. weapons, such as the MX, the Midgetman and the Trident II D-5 missiles.

This second agreement would also address the issue of strategic defense. As long as the Soviet Union possesses its formidable arsenal of first-strike weapons, the United States must press forward with SDI. Our position should be that research, development, testing and deployment of defensive systems is not negotiable. Only the extent of our deployments should be subject to limitation through mutual agreement, and those deployments should be calibrated to the extent of the Soviet counterforce threat.

A two-stage approach along these lines offers the best prospects for successful nuclear arms control. It would enable Presidents Bush and Gorbachev to conclude quickly an interim agreement capping the number of launchers and warheads, though unlike the current START formula the accord would not inhibit U.S. weapons programs needed to redress the asymmetry in strategic vulnerability and the imbalance in counterforce weapons. It would also create a stable foundation for a treaty to enhance strategic security by reducing the number of counterforce systems to levels that make a successful first-strike attack on the other side's strategic forces militarily in-feasible.

VII

The two regional conflicts requiring immediate presidential action, Afghanistan and Central America, represent opposite poles in American policy. Our program to aid the Afghan resistance has received bipartisan support, has operated continuously for almost a decade and verges on ultimate success. Our assistance to the Nicaraguan freedom fighters has been subjected to partisan bickering, has been at best episodic and has failed so far. In distant Afghanistan, we learned that a sustained, bipartisan program of large-scale assistance to anticommunist freedom fighters can produce major geopolitical gains. We should apply the same lesson to the nearby and strategically critical conflict in Central America.

In Afghanistan, as Moscow's tanks retreat, one round of the great game closes-but yet another begins. Our goal has been two-fold, to force the Soviet Union to withdraw and to restore the Afghan people's right to self-determination. Achieving the former does not automatically accomplish the latter. First of all, the communist regime in Kabul must be replaced. The best solution would be the removal of the Soviet puppet regime through the direct talks now taking place between Moscow and the resistance leadership. But should those talks stall or fail we must continue to provide whatever kinds of weapons the resistance requires to topple the Kabul regime. Since the character of the fighting has changed from guerrilla warfare to battles for taking and holding cities, the United States must upgrade its assistance quantitatively and qualitatively, particularly in terms of antiaircraft missiles, long-range mortars, and mine-clearing devices and equipment.

It does not serve American, or Afghan, interests for the United States to disengage before a political process is in place that will establish real self-determination for the Afghan people themselves. If the country collapses into a civil war with dozens of tribal warlords ruling their separate fiefdoms, the Kremlin will seize this as a lever to regain a measure of influence by supporting one or another group in the fighting or by declaring the need to keep forces in a "security zone" in northern Afghanistan. Therefore, at a time when our weapons pipeline still gives us influence, we need to address directly the critical issue of establishing, through the traditional Afghan means of a tribal assembly and through elections, a post-communist government that truly represents the people.

Central America poses far more difficult and, from the U.S. point of view, far more critical problems. Our interests are not threatened by Nicaragua simply because its government systematically violates human rights and spouts anti-American rhetoric. A dictatorship, even a totalitarian one, does not threaten our interests per se. Rather, the Sandinista regime threatens our interests only because Managua has forged links with the Soviet Union and has become a base for indirect Soviet subversion of other Central American states such as El Salvador. The problem is not that the Nicaraguan government is communist but that the communist government of Nicaragua is inherently expansionist. As the Sandinistas freely admit, and even boast, they seek "a revolution without frontiers" in Central America and insist on the right to aid communist guerrillas in neighboring countries.

At the first opportunity, the Bush Administration must impose linkage between the issue of Soviet access to U.S. capital, credits and technology and that of Soviet military assistance to Managua. Gorbachev must be made to understand that Nicaragua is a neuralgic issue for us. While academics might debate whether the Monroe Doctrine has become obsolete, the United States cannot allow the Soviet Union or any other foreign power to provide arms to a virulently anti-American and aggressive regime in the western hemisphere. Given the Soviet economy's pathetic condition, our economic power represents tremendous leverage. If we link these issues, we should be able to profit politically, as well as economically, from our economic relationship with the Soviet Union.

At the same time, we must recognize that the Sandinista leaders have made a mockery of the Arias peace plan, despite the cutoff of U.S. assistance to the contras. Managua permits fewer civil liberties and holds more political prisoners today than it did when the so-called process of democratization began. In its direct talks with the contras, it has in effect demanded surrender, rather than opening the way to a political compromise. Moreover, the Nicaraguan-backed communist guerrillas in El Salvador have dramatically stepped up their terrorist and military attacks.

The Bush Administration must determine, once and for all, the viability of the Arias peace plan. If the Sandinista-contra talks cannot achieve their objective, they should be ended. Since endless negotiations work to the advantage of the Sandinistas, the United States should undertake a final, 90-day effort to breathe life into the peace process. If that fails to produce a concrete, workable plan for genuine democracy in Nicaragua, the president should request from Congress a major military and humanitarian aid package for the contras. Coupled with the effort to cut off Soviet aid to Managua through superpower talks, this policy would represent a pincer movement against the Sandinistas, with Moscow putting the squeeze on one end and the contras on the other.

The United States today faces a clear choice: Do we oppose communist subversion in a series of protracted wars throughout Central America or at its source in Nicaragua? Managua's leaders are avowedly committed to supporting anti-U.S. insurgencies throughout the region. If Nicaragua becomes a safe haven and an arms conduit for communist guerrillas, we will be doomed to decades of facing the messy problems of advising our friends in counterinsurgency warfare.

VIII

Revitalizing the Western alliance, redirecting the arms control process, and resolving the critical regional conflicts in Afghanistan and Nicaragua should represent America's immediate foreign policy priorities. Gorbachev's admission of Soviet economic failure and his need for a breathing spell in the East-West competition so perestroika can take root creates an excellent opportunity for the United States not only to enhance the West's security but also to promote a more stable peace through a determined strategy.

This is not to say that Moscow's economic failures will make Gorbachev a pushover. His toughness and intelligence will more than compensate for his country's economic weakness, and his consummate ability in diplomacy and political maneuver will guarantee that he seldom winds up with the short end of a deal. If Western leaders want to avoid being taken to the cleaners, they must understand what Gorbachev wants and how the West should respond.

On his first priority, strengthening the Soviet Union's economy, he will seek free access to Western capital and technology. The United States, Western Europe and Japan must coordinate their policies so that the West exploits its economic power for political effect. We should go forward with unsubsidized trade in nonstrategic goods on a cash-and-carry basis. But until the Soviet Union overhauls its domestic economic system and discontinues its aggressive policies, it is not in our interest to bankroll reforms that will either squander our loans or bolster our adversary.

On his second priority, ending the Soviet Union's international isolation, Gorbachev will seek to separate the United States from Europe, particularly Germany, and to open a new relationship with China. We must undertake a new effort to reinvigorate the Western alliance and to infuse Western Europe with the positive purpose of fostering peaceful change in Eastern Europe. If Gorbachev satisfies China's "three obstacles," we should welcome a normalization of Sino-Soviet relations. We can be confident that, since China's top priority remains economic development, our relations with Beijing will continue to be closer than the Kremlin's.

On his third priority, arms control, he will seek new agreements that will reduce strategic weapons stockpiles but preserve the present Soviet advantage in counterforce capability. In order to reduce the main threat to the West-Moscow's conventional superiority-we must link progress in START to progress on conventional arms control. We must also recast our strategic arms negotiating positions so that a START treaty will enable us to restore the counterforce balance and eventually to enhance strategic stability.

Richard M. Nixon

On his fourth priority, prevailing in Third World conflicts, he will seek agreements that appear to settle the conflicts but that actually keep his client regimes in power. We possess the leverage necessary for the freedom fighters in Afghanistan, Nicaragua and Angola to prevail. We must never sign an agreement with the Soviet Union that undercuts, militarily or politically, those relying on our support, and we must exploit linkage to promote the retraction of the Soviet empire.

In the short run, we can sympathize with the thrust behind many of Gorbachev's aspirations. We both want to reduce military competition and the danger of nuclear war. We certainly should applaud those of Gorbachev's reforms that reduce, even marginally, the repression and poverty which plague the people of the Soviet Union. At the same time, we must keep in mind that in the long run the goals of the two sides diverge diametrically. Gorbachev wants reform because he wants a stronger Soviet Union and an expanding Soviet empire. We should support those reforms in the hope of making the Soviet Union less repressive at home and less aggressive abroad.

As the outpouring of sympathy and support for the victims of the Armenian earthquake so vividly demonstrated, there is a great well of friendship for the Russian people in the United States. The people of the United States and the people of the Soviet Union can be friends. Because of our profound differences, the governments of our two nations cannot be friends-but we cannot afford to be enemies. Gorbachev's historic challenge is to implement reforms that will remove those differences.

1 The Military Balance 1988–1989, London: The International Institute for Strategic Studies, 1988, p. 237.

The 1988 Election

Norman J. Ornstein
and Mark Schmitt   AMERICA AND THE WORLD 1988

Inauguration of George H. W. Bush, 1989.

In 1988 a Republican won the presidency for the fifth time in the last six tries, and for the seventh time in the last ten. In the past six presidential elections-over a quarter-century-Democrats have averaged approximately 43 percent of the national popular presidential vote. Over the past forty years Democrats have managed to exceed 50.1 percent of the popular vote only once, in 1964, in the wake of the Kennedy assassination.

The American public is sending a message with its voting behavior. Is it a profound message about what Americans want in their government at home and how they want America represented and projected abroad? Or are they separate messages for individual elections, unique reactions to specific circumstances that happen to mesh into a pattern of Republican hegemony? The answer is not at all clear, but which answer is correct matters less than which answer prevails in the interpretation of the 1988 vote.

The approach that each political party takes toward governing during the new administration comes down to whether the 1988 election is viewed as a seminal event involving a significant choice between two well-matched opponents, or a predictable and narrow victory for continuity over change. The more significance each party assigns to the outcome of the election, the more aggressive that party will be in the branch of government it controls.

Even before the results were in, the media seemed to decide the election was not important: "issueless," "personal," "trivial," "negative" were the usual expressions of disgust. There was a good deal of overstatement here, and it will take some time before we can fully understand the significance of 1988. In this essay we will try to put the election into context, examining the issues discussed and ignored, using the election to frame an analysis of the policy battles, options and outcomes ahead.

II

The analysis of American elections has become a cottage industry. Politicians, psephologists, pundits and press vie with one another first to predict election results and then to interpret them. One large school of analysis, bolstered by sophisticated mathematical models, believes that two simple factors can predict election outcomes: the state of the economy (measured by changes in real income levels) and presidential popularity. This school believed months before the campaign began-and without regard to what might happen through the fall-that George Bush would win by a very comfortable margin because of the economy and Ronald Reagan's public standing.

Another school of analysis believes that Democrats are losing presidential elections not because the results are predetermined by circumstances, but because the party is losing the battle of messages; the Democratic nominating process pulls candidates too far left of center, and they end up outside the acceptable range for a majority of voters. This school would accept George Bush's characterization of the campaign as a battle of values, which he won because of voter skepticism about the role of the government, fear of crime, belief in a strong defense and the need to project a strong American role in the world.

Yet a third school believes that Democrats lose presidential elections because they nominate amateurish candidates who run inept campaigns. For them, the ultimate irony in 1988 came when Michael Dukakis proclaimed the election to be not about ideology but about competence-and then ran an incompetent campaign. To these analysts, the Democratic Party has lost control of its nominating process and has appeared unable to get its act together-from Chicago in 1968, right up to Dukakis and his struggle with Jesse Jackson in 1988. They argue that the Democratic message would work, in other words, if the party could nominate somebody who could run an effective campaign and articulate that message.

There is truth in each explanation. Every American election is to some degree a referendum on current conditions. The innate American desire for change conflicts with the cautious yearning for continuity; the current status of peace and/or prosperity usually tips the balance one way or the other. With the economy recovering and the world at peace, voters in 1984 clearly preferred continuity, giving challenger Walter Mondale no realistic hope of unseating Ronald Reagan.

In 1980, by contrast, the deteriorating U.S. economy and concern over the hostages in Iran combined to provide a strong desire for change; as soon as Reagan, as Republican challenger, showed the American public that he was above the threshold of acceptability to be president, his victory over incumbent Jimmy Carter was assured.

This analytical model obviously holds better when an incumbent president is running for reelection, and the referendum on performance in office is clear-cut. When no incumbent is running, as in 1960 and 1968, simple indicators of economic performance and presidential approval do not work as directly, and the results are not so predictable. Eisenhower's popularity did not extend to Vice President Richard Nixon in 1960, and Vice President Hubert Humphrey was not buoyed by the healthy economy in 1968. Still, almost inevitably, the candidate of the incumbent party runs as a candidate of continuity. Vice President Bush was more successful than most of his predecessors in linking his fortunes to the outgoing president's popularity and to the strength of the economy.

In July 1988, when Michael Dukakis enjoyed a double-digit lead over George Bush, nearly three-fifths of Americans polled expressed the belief that America was heading in "the wrong direction." By September of 1988, when only 45 percent of Americans held that view, it was Bush who held a double-digit lead. (Over the same period, incidentally, Ronald Reagan's approval gained ten percentage points.) As one journalist noted, "the amount of peace and prosperity was the same in July as in October," but in fact public confidence in the prospects for continued peace and prosperity had dramatically improved, making the task of the candidate of change, Governor Dukakis, ever more daunting.

Daunting, but not impossible. Americans, after all, were divided right down the middle about the prospects for the country's future, and similarly split over the leadership qualities of Vice President Bush. Yet many voters who harbored misgivings about Bush ended up voting for him. Why? Values did make a difference. When Dukakis held the lead, Bush was notably lacking support among groups generically referred to as "Reagan Democrats" and "Reagan Independents." In a major post-election Gallup poll for Times Mirror, these groups-notably, "New Dealers" (older and more anticommunist and socially conservative Democrats) and "Disaffecteds" (middle-aged, unhappy and cynical independents)-had moved perceptibly to Bush, and in numbers nearly comparable to their support for Reagan. These voters were brought into the Republican presidential fold for the third consecutive time by perceptions that Dukakis would be weak on defense and crime and would be on the wrong side of social issues such as capital punishment, prayer in the schools and abortion.

On such values as anticommunism, religion and American exceptionalism, the Democratic Party at the national level may well be out of phase with mainstream America. But on other values-- e.g., social justice, tolerance toward the life styles of others and its approach to business-the Republican Party is just as likely to be out of step with the majority of voters. It was the hallmark of a competent Republican campaign that the values and issues that dominated in the fall were the ones where Democrats were vulnerable. The relentlessly negative and personal nature of the Bush campaign spotlighted the less popular values attributed to the Democrats and thereby kept the Democrats on the defensive, unable to shift the focus to Bush and the Republicans or exploit the G.O.P.'s vulnerabilities.

What was true of values was also true of certain issues. Consider defense. When asked which party can best maintain a strong defense, or deal with the Soviet Union, voters by a healthy margin picked the Republican Party. When asked which party can best keep the defense budget under control, voters by an equally wide margin chose the Democrats. When tensions between the United States and the Soviet Union are high, issues of strength tend to predominate and thereby provide an advantage to the G.O.P. But in 1988 Bush was faced with the ironic likelihood of being the victim of Reagan's success; Mikhail Gorbachev's glasnost and the Intermediate-range Nuclear Forces (INF) Treaty made the issue of a strong defense less salient and the bloated defense budget more so.

But with clever commercials and tough campaigning, Bush managed to shift the debate back to strength versus weakness, defining the issue much as it had been defined by Reagan in 1980. Bush managed to make Dukakis' perceived weakness on defense a major campaign issue, costing Dukakis votes and putting him on the defensive, forcing him to insist he was not weak on defense.

Dukakis' notorious ride in a tank was a direct response; it was so contrived that the film footage was used by the Bush campaign in one of its most pointed commercials. Moreover, while trying to prove his military toughness, Dukakis was unable to exploit the public's unease about defense procurement scandals or defense waste to drive votes from the Republican column into his own.

Since the 1950s polls have shown that the Republicans have an advantage on the question of which party is better able to maintain a strong defense; the Democrats have prevailed on the issue of which party would keep the nation out of war. During the Reagan years, the G.O.P. maintained its advantage on the first question and reversed the public view of the parties on the second, leaving the Democrats behind in public opinion in both traditional dimensions of foreign policy. But, as we have noted, neither of these issues was quite as salient in 1988 as in the past. Nontraditional dimensions of foreign policy began to emerge, dimensions in which the Democrats hold a solid advantage in public opinion. Defense waste, though a narrow issue, is one; economic nationalism, a much more far-reaching dimension, is another.

The early success of Missouri Congressman Richard Gephardt in the Democratic primaries was not simply a reflection of narrow protectionism among a small sliver of activist voters. Gephardt tapped into a considerable and deep unease among Americans about foreign competition-both the sense that we no longer control our own economic destiny, and the belief that we are being damaged by countries taking advantage of our commitment to free trade, playing by a different set of economic rules. In June 1988 an "Americans Talk Security" poll asked voters whether they considered "military rivals such as the Soviet Union or economic rivals such as Japan" to be greater threats to American security. Fifty-nine percent said the economic rivals posed the greater threat.

In a country overwhelmingly averse to new taxes, Times Mirror found 71 percent of Americans favoring tax increases to protect American jobs from foreign competition. Senator Bentsen made foreign competition the centerpiece of his campaign for the vice presidency and the focal point of his successful TV debate with his opponent, Senator Quayle. But Governor Dukakis was unable or unwilling to focus on this issue until the final weeks of the campaign, and even then he did so ineptly (he launched an attack on foreign ownership of U.S. industries at an automotive plant that no one had told him was owned by Italians).

On these matters, as well as on the drug issue, which became linked to foreign policy and the campaign through Panamanian General Manuel Antonio Noriega, the Republican Party and Bush were vulnerable, but the Democrats never exploited these vulnerabilities. The election became a referendum on the failed policies of the governor of Massachusetts, especially in his first term more than a decade ago, rather than on the performance of the incumbent administration or the leadership or judgment of the G.O.P. nominee.

It thus becomes difficult to separate the Democrats' vulnerability on values and issues from the competence of their presidential campaign. There is little doubt, on balance, that the Republicans and their candidate maximized their advantages and seized the initiative in the campaign, and that the Democrats, while facing the difficult task of persuading a complacent and satisfied electorate to take a plunge for change, forfeited a real opportunity for victory.

There is enough uncertainty and disagreement about the cause of the election outcome, though, to dissuade either party from full-scale, aggressive assaults on the other; each will be off-balance and unsure enough about its standing with voters, given both the 1988 outcome and the prospects for 1990, to proceed with caution despite calls for combat from activists. But each party will also be eager to claim policy leadership in 1989, to demonstrate that its people and principles, and the branch of government that each party controls, are leading the way while the other side founders.

The campaign itself did not provide the cutting issues that would have defined the competition for control of the agenda in 1989. Instead, the issues that dominated the campaign will scarcely be visible in the policy arena; other issues, downplayed in the campaign or emerging since the election, will be much more significant in the year to come.

III

Whatever the causes of the election outcome, the hallmark of the presidential campaign was its intensely personal character. American voters expressed dismay at the harsh nature of the campaign; many saw it as the most negative in memory. The issues that dominated public attention were the Pledge of Allegiance and prison furloughs for violent criminals; while these themes did indeed tap into significant underlying values, they were not the issues that commentators would expect to be the centerpiece of a presidential campaign.

The 1988 American campaign stood in dramatic contrast to two other national election campaigns conducted at approximately the same time in other countries. In Israel an overriding question-participation in an international peace conference-divided the two main political parties and served as the campaign's centerpiece. In Canada the election turned on the free trade agreement with the United States; surrounded by intense debates about nationhood and national identity, the parties divided so starkly on the bilateral free trade agreement that the election was a clear referendum on this one point.

There was nothing even remotely comparable in the United States. No crucial issues cut along party lines. The starkest differences between Democrats and Republicans, Dukakis and Bush, were on two issues barely discussed, aid to the Nicaraguan contras and the Strategic Defense Initiative (SDI). These were hardly at the level of a peace conference for Israelis, or a free trade pact for Canada, and they did not divide the parties nearly as sharply. Israel's Labor Party favored an international peace conference, while Likud was just as implacably opposed. In Canada the ruling Progressive Conservatives vigorously and totally defended the free trade agreement, while the Liberals and New Democrats completely opposed it. Compare those issues with aid to the contras: the Democrats opposed military aid but hedged their bets, supporting some humanitarian aid and the Arias peace plan; as for SDI, the Republican candidate hedged about rapid deployment and the Democrat criticized the concept, but supported continuing research.

The absence of deep partisan divisions on global controversies need not make for an "issueless" election, and a campaign that is not dominated by "big" issues can still shape the policy climate, decisions and outcomes for the next four years. Many of the real issues in the campaign were masked by the negative overtones and by the overall consensus on goals, if not means; indeed, in several respects, the 1988 election was not about what our government should do, but how it should do it. No candidate suggested ignoring the budget deficit, or resolving the deficit problem with a substantial increase in taxes. Both candidates pledged to extend government modestly to address the demand for health care, environmental protection, improved education, affordable housing and alleviating the drug problem. Neither candidate suggested abandoning the course of rapprochement with the Soviet Union; the question was how rapidly and extensively to proceed.

There were differences between the candidates, to be sure, on American-Soviet relationships-differences that were in fact debated in an enlightening fashion. Dukakis argued the view that changes in Soviet policy came about primarily because of the country's own economic problems; Bush contended that the Reagan Administration's arms buildup, and particularly the deployment of Pershing missiles in Europe, precipitated the most significant arms agreement in history. These differences reflected distinct policy choices; President Bush will be far more insistent than Dukakis would have been about continuing to fund nuclear weapons systems, and continuing to keep pressure on the Soviets by expanding American defenses, including SDI. But either candidate would have vigorously pursued further arms agreements with the Soviets, further cultural and economic ties, and an expanding dialogue and relationship with Mikhail Gorbachev.

The candidates also expressed very different approaches to the broader question of America's role in the world. By referring frequently to Grenada, Libya and the Persian Gulf, Bush suggested that his approach would resemble Reagan's-an assertive projection of America, the superpower, to protect its interests and the interests of the West wherever necessary, and sometimes by the use of force. By referring just as reflexively to the Contadora process, the Arias peace plan and the World Court, Dukakis expressed a preference for a muted American role, one predicated on prior agreement with our allies and partners in multilateral institutions and one governed by acute sensitivity to international law.

Sometimes the candidates did discuss these divergent approaches in their debates and speeches. But it would be a gross overstatement to suggest that the foreign policy differences between the candidates were a decisive aspect of the contest. George Bush's campaign managers fought vigorously to prevent one of the two debates from being completely dedicated to foreign issues, hoping to ensure that Michael Dukakis did not appear to be Bush's equal in command of international questions. For his part, Dukakis delivered very few speeches on foreign or national security policy, and he declined to offer a critique of American actions in Grenada, Libya and the Persian Gulf that might have shown how his foreign policy would differ from that of Reagan or Bush. Underlying this was Dukakis' apparent impatience with details in foreign policy; at a briefing on arms control, he reportedly insisted simply that we had too many nuclear weapons and showed little interest in the arcane specifics of how and where that number might safely be reduced.

Both candidates deliberately avoided underscoring their foreign policy differences in the general election campaign, while both had emphasized these topics far more in their campaigns for nomination. Why? One reason was the absence of international conflict or high tension. Under the circumstances, the foreign policy issues available for discussion were abstract and conditional-not subjects likely to grip swing voters in a ten-week general election period. For Bush, the broad theme of peace and prosperity, with an emphasis on prosperity, was more politically expedient than a detailed exposition of future strategic concerns.

During the party primaries, the tactics were different. Foreign policy issues helped Bush energize his party's conservative core, the leaders of which were mostly aligned with other candidates at the beginning. His strong support for SDI, including an openness to early deployment, and a skepticism that went well beyond Reagan's about swift movement of further arms control talks with Gorbachev, were intended to solidify his standing with these voters, who were not his natural base. If he had continued to stress these issues in the fall, Bush might have had to moderate his zeal about SDI or tone down his skepticism about Gorbachev, creating more potential problems with his party's core than gains among swing voters.

Dukakis similarly emphasized issues such as contra aid and South Africa in his campaign for the Democratic nomination, harshly and emotionally criticizing the Reagan Administration policies in order to generate activist support in Iowa and other early primary or caucus states. In the fall, though, Dukakis did not find these or other foreign policy issues to be particularly fruitful ground.

In the broadest sense, it was difficult for the candidate of change to argue for change when the public was satisfied with peace, the INF treaty and basic international stability. More specifically, most of the active opponents of contra aid were solidly in the Democratic corner; little new support could be mined by continuing to stress this issue. An emphasis on Gorbachev and arms control would have been more likely to underscore the achievements of the Reagan era than to help Dukakis make the case for change. Finally, a major focus on foreign policy would have called attention to Dukakis' lack of experience in that realm.

Dukakis had some success with voters where he tried to exploit foreign policy by focusing not on ideological or strategic differences but on specific instances of Reagan/Bush failures such as the Iran-contra scandal, Lebanon and Noriega. But his overall defensiveness in the campaign, forced on him by Bush's ability to dominate the agenda, made his jabs less potent and less salient to voters

Norman J. Ornstein and Mark Schmitt

than they might have been if the campaign had been defined in different terms.

IV

While the overt thrust of the Bush campaign was his attack on Dukakis, the campaign's broader message was, "If you've liked the last eight years, you'll love the next four." This naturally meant stressing areas of policy success, not engaging debate on major continuing or festering problems. There was almost no debate on Nicaragua and aid to the contras-an area Bush directly acknowledged had resulted in failure-and no serious or detailed discussion of the "twin towers," the budget and trade deficits. Bush's deficit reduction plan, playing on his broader message, contained no warning of problems or pain ahead, but rather was a combination of his "flexible" budget freeze and the oft-repeated refrain, "Read my lips: no new taxes." That refrain worked. But it may make a post-election resolution of the deficit problem much more difficult.

Bush's campaign reinforced the underlying public desire for continuity and resulted in a vote for the status quo at all levels. Even as Bush won 40 of 50 states, 98.3 percent of incumbents running for reelection to the House of Representatives won, and voters slightly enlarged the Democratic majorities in the House and Senate. As in 1984 any talk of a mandate by the newly elected president was diluted by his party's manifest lack of success in other contests.

Democrats, however, obtained scant comfort from their continuing success in American politics below the presidential level. Losing the top prize in American politics again, in an election that nearly all Democratic leaders believed they could have won-especially after Bush chose Senator Quayle as a running mate-left them bitter and disillusioned. Their frustrations were aimed first at their own candidate, but with Governor Dukakis back in Boston, Bush now faces their wrath. Democrats will have no interest in rescuing President Bush from his own campaign pledges, or in helping him out of politically embarrassing situations. With their control of Congress, Democrats have every incentive to advance their own agenda, and to turn Bush promises, e.g., to be "an environmentalist," to their own advantage.

Nor will the new president get much help from the Republicans in Congress. The countercyclical nature of American politics suggests that Republicans will lose congressional seats in 1990, the next mid-term election-a pattern that has held in every off-year contest (except 1934) since the Civil War. The initial euphoria of victory has already subsided for congressional Republicans; they are already looking to protect their flanks in two years. In the House of Representatives, the minority party is almost powerless, and 35 consecutive years of minority status has left the Republicans there deeply frustrated and increasingly bitter about their treatment at the hands of Democratic House Speaker Jim Wright and his colleagues. Every time President Bush works directly with the Democratic leadership in the House, Republicans will complain; but if he ignores that leadership and works instead with the Republicans, he will likely lose.

Faced with these constraints, Bush will have to adapt his presidency to fit the results and the conflicting messages of the campaign and election. In his first hundred days as president, he will need to do what he could not as a candidate-to establish not a mandate but something like an agenda, some objectives by which his administration can be evaluated and judged. Presidents who have defined their administrations by intense achievement in the first hundred days have generally stayed close to home; the New Deal, Great Society and Reagan Revolution all involved domestic enterprises. These presidents saved their international initiatives for subsequent years.

Bush will not have this luxury. A campaign predicated on preserving and extending current policies, combined with the relentless pressure of the budget deficit, eliminates any possibility of embarking on sweeping domestic initiatives. With the savings and loan catastrophe and the massive problems at nuclear weapons plants looming with hundred-billion-dollar price tags, any new domestic spending in a Bush Administration is likely to go toward cleaning up a mess, not promoting anything tangible or politically beneficial.

All presidents gravitate eventually to foreign policy, if only to escape the frustrations of continuing power struggles with Congress over domestic matters. But Bush, who would have little room to maneuver domestically even if Congress did not exist, will likely take an approach to the presidency that we have not seen in this century. If he is to put a strong mark on the presidency in his first year, he will have to do so in foreign policy.

V

President Bush is certainly better prepared than his recent predecessors to tackle foreign issues from his first days in office. He will be tempted, of course, to make his mark first in the American-Soviet arena, but he will also look for opportunities for action in Latin America and the Middle East. Still, it is difficult to see where or how he might turn to make a move as politically significant as Reagan's rapprochement with Gorbachev or Carter's Camp David accords.

Indeed, with most of the world's hot spots at least temporarily cooling down, the most promising area for the new president to launch some foreign policy initiatives might turn out to be in Washington itself. Conflicts between the executive and legislative branches over the conduct of foreign policy littered the Reagan years, and most of them remain unresolved. Part of the problem has been a continuing, festering lack of trust between the branches. The executive often ignored the legitimate prerogatives of Congress while challenging congressional power and purpose. For its part, Congress often went to undesirable extremes to impose its desires on the executive, distrusting his motives and capacity to carry out effective policy. If President Bush can clear up these problems early in his term, he will be able to act with more assurance later.

One focal point of this mutual distrust was the applicability of the War Powers Act, which became an element of controversy over Lebanon, Grenada, Libya and the Persian Gulf, among other places. Congress and the White House often found themselves in pointless and enervating debates about who was obliged to invoke the War Powers Act and when, devoting too little time and attention to revising the measure to make it acceptable to both branches. A modest effort on that score was begun in 1988; a presidential move to expedite that process would be good politics and good policy.

The Iran-contra arms scandal raised another area of congressional-presidential tension. Congress viewed the administration's defiance of the Boland Amendments limiting aid to the contras as a scandalous and illegitimate use of covert action. The executive viewed congressional micromanaging and meddling in foreign affairs, and congressional leaks of sensitive covert programs, as eminent justification for extralegal actions. The Iran-contra hearings did not resolve the tensions over covert actions, executive notification of Congress or congressional oversight.

The 101st Congress will start with some suspicion of George Bush in this area, given his well-known attraction to covert action. An initiative on his part to come up with an accord between the branches-perhaps a firm pledge on swift notification, in return for a smaller joint staff for the House and Senate Intelligence Committees, modeled after the respected Joint Taxation Committee staff, to cut down on congressional leaks and overactivism in the intelligence area-would be a major advance in inter-branch relations.

A third positive step would be to improve the dialogue between the branches on foreign policy, leading to a dialogue before decisions, not after-the-fact notification. A commitment by President Bush to meet regularly with a small, representative group of congressional leaders for a discussion of foreign policy would be an attractive olive branch. While no panacea, it would have the additional potential of building bipartisan and bicameral consensus in many areas, regional and otherwise, of foreign policy.

The next four years provide a rare opportunity for consensus on domestic as well as foreign policy issues. Few Democrats support opening the floodgates on federal domestic spending; most Republicans support modest federal initiatives in education, health, transportation, environmental cleanup and other domestic needs. Few Republicans oppose further arms talks with the Soviets; most Democrats support the concept and letter of the INF treaty and its logical extension. Countries whose governments once provoked partisan strife in the United States, such as Argentina and the Philippines, have become models of American bipartisan cooperation; the same can be said of South Korea and Chile. Few basic ideological or partisan divisions exist in American politics about policies toward the Middle East, Europe, the Pacific Rim, most of the western hemisphere and Africa. Even in trade the differences are more in style than substance. When it comes to the federal deficit there is a broad agreement that it matters, and must be reduced; the disagreements, over perhaps $20 or $30 billion in taxes in a $4.5-trillion economy and a $1.2-trillion federal government, are trivial.

The potential, then, exists for bipartisan cooperation on domestic and foreign policy issues. But that potential could go unfulfilled. The areas of agreement may be masked by partisan bickering, or the few disagreements might be exaggerated to gain partisan advantage, ultimately resulting in policy failure or gridlock.

There are more players in the game of governing than President Bush and the Congress. The intelligence, savvy, experience and judgment of Bush's officers and advisers, and the party leaders in Congress, will make a difference. Each side has some Washington veterans who are most comfortable cooperating in a bipartisan environment: James Baker as secretary of state and Brent Scowcroft in his second stint as national security adviser play this role for Bush; the Senate party leaders, newcomer George Mitchell (D-Me.) and veteran Robert Dole (R-Kans.), play this role on the Hill. Other officials are more combative partisans: John Sununu as chief of staff in the White House, Jim Wright as Speaker of the House. The balance of power among the conciliators and the partisans is likely to play a decisive role in how we face the dilemmas of the coming years.

And of course, we must take into account the political environment. The 1988 election was the first in twenty years without an incumbent running for reelection. In 1992, we are likely to return to the norm: a basic referendum on the incumbent's performance in office. The political components of that contest will be set in 1990, with the mid-term elections already preoccupying minds on Capitol Hill. How skillfully our policy leaders operate within this political context will determine how successfully we deal with the policy challenges and opportunities ahead.

NORMAN J. ORNSTEIN is a resident scholar at the American Enterprise Institute and co-director of the Gallup/Times Mirror survey of the American electorate. Mark Schmitt is a researcher at the American Enterprise Institute.

Foreign Policy and the American Character

Arthur M. Schlesinger, Jr.   FALL 1983

Ronald Reagan and Vice-President Bush meeting with Gorbachev on Governor's Island, New York City, 7 December 1988.

F oreign policy is the face a nation wears to the world. The minimal motive is the same for all states—the protection of national integrity and interest. But the manner in which a state practices foreign policy is greatly affected by national peculiarities.

The United States is not exempt from these unimpeachable generalities. As Henry James, an early American specialist in international relations, once put it, "It's a complex fate, being an American." The American character is indeed filled with contradiction and paradox. So, in consequence, is American foreign policy. No paradox is more persistent than the historic tension in the American soul between an addiction to experiment and a susceptibility to ideology.

On the one hand, Americans are famous for being a practical people, preferring fact to theory, finding the meaning of propositions in results, regarding trial and error, not deductive logic, as the path to truth. "In no country in the civilized world," wrote Tocqueville, "is less attention paid to philosophy than in the United States." And, when Americans developed a distinctive philosophy, it was of course the pragmatism of William James. James perceived a pluralist universe where men can discover partial and limited truths—truths that work for them—but where no one can gain an absolute grip on ultimate truth. He stood against monism—the notion that the world can be understood from a single point of view. He stood against the assumption that all virtuous principles are in the end reconcilable; against faith in a single body of unified dogma; in short, against the delusions of ideology.

Yet at the same time that Americans live by experiment, they also show a recurrent vulnerability to spacious generalities. This is not altogether surprising. The American colonists, after all, were nurtured on one of the most profound and exacting ideologies ever devised—the theology of Calvin—and they passed on to their descendants a certain relish in system and abstraction. The ideas of the Americans, as Tocqueville found in the 1830s, "are all either extremely minute and clear or extremely general and vague." The Calvinist cast of mind saw America as the redeemer nation. It expressed itself in the eighteenth century in Jonathan Edwards' theology of Providence, in the nineteenth century in John Calhoun's theology of slavery, in the twentieth century in Woodrow Wilson's vision of world order and in John Foster Dulles' summons to a holy war against godless communism. The propensity to ideology explains too why the theory of American internal society as expounded by some Americans—the theory of America as the triumph of immaculate and sanctified private enterprise—differs so sharply from the reality of continual government intervention in economic life.

This tension between experiment and ideology offers one way of looking at the American experience in world affairs. The

443

Founding Fathers were hard-headed and clear-sighted men. They believed that states responded to specific national interests—and were morally obliged to do so, if there were to be regularity and predictability in international affairs. "No nation," observed George Washington, "is to be trusted farther than it is bound by its interest." They understood, moreover, that the preservation of American independence depended on the maintenance of a balance of power in Europe. "It never could be our interest," wrote John Adams, "to unite with France in the destruction of England . . . . On the other hand, it could never be our duty to unite with Britain in too great a humiliation of France."

The Jeffersonians, though sentimentally inclined to favor France against Britain, were equally hard-headed when national interest intervened. "We shall so take our distance between the two rival nations," wrote Thomas Jefferson in 1802, "as, remaining disengaged till necessity compels us, we may haul finally to the enemy of that which shall make it necessary." And in 1814, with Britain waging war against America as well as France, indeed seven months before the British captured Washington and burned the White House, Jefferson watched Napoleon's European victories with concern. "It cannot be to our interest that all Europe should be reduced to a single monarchy," he wrote. "Were he again advanced to Moscow, I should again wish him such disaster as would prevent his reaching Petersburg. And were the consequences even to be the longer continuance of our war, I would rather meet them than see the whole force of Europe wielded by a single hand." In these arresting words Jefferson defined the national interest that explains American intervention in two world wars as well as in the present cold war.

I do not imply that the Founding Fathers were devoid of any belief in a special mission for the United States. It was precisely to protect that mission that they wished to preserve the balance of power in Europe. They hoped that the American experiment would in time redeem the world. But they did not suppose that the young republic had attained, in Alexander Hamilton's words, "an exemption from the imperfections, weaknesses, and evils incident to society in every shape." Hamilton urged his countrymen instead "to adopt as a practical maxim for the direction of our political conduct that we, as well as the other inhabitants of the globe, are yet remote from the happy empire of perfect wisdom and perfect virtue." If America was to redeem the world, it would do so by perfecting its own institutions, not by moving into other countries and setting things straight; by example, not by intervention. "She goes not abroad in search of monsters to destroy," said John Quincy Adams. If ever she did, "The fundamental maxims of her policy would insensibly change from liberty to force .... She might become the dictatress of the world. She would no longer be the ruler of her own spirit."

The realism of the revolutionary generation was founded in the harsh requirements of a struggle for precarious independence. It was founded too in rather pessimistic conceptions of human nature and history. History taught the Founding Fathers to see the American republic itself as a risky and doubtful experiment. And the idea of experiment, by directing attention to the relation between actions and consequences in specific contexts, implied a historical approach to public affairs. Yet—another paradox—the role of the Founding Fathers was to annul history for their descendants. "We have it in our power," cried Tom Paine, "to begin the world all over again"—a proposition quoted, by the way, by President Reagan in his recent address to the evangelicals at Orlando. Once the Founders had done their work, history could start again on a new foundation and in American terms.

So the process began of an American withdrawal from secular history—or rather of an American entry into what Dean Acheson once called "a cocoon of history." This process was sustained by the fact that the men and women who populated the new world were in revolt against their own histories. It was sustained, too, by the simultaneous withdrawal of the American state from the power embroilments of the old world. The realism of the revolutionary generation faded away in the century from Waterloo to Sarajevo when the European balance of power was maintained without American intervention. As the historical consciousness thinned out, ideology flowed into the vacuum. The very idea of power politics became repellent. The exemption from the European scramble nourished the myth of American innocence and the doctrine of American righteousness.

When America rejoined the scramble in 1898, it did so with an exalted conviction of its destiny as a redeemer nation, and no longer by example alone. The realist tradition by no means vanished. So William James protested the messianic delusion: "Angelic impulses and predatory lusts divide our heart exactly as they divide the heart of other countries." But this was for a season a minority view. When the United States entered the First World War for traditional balance-of-power reasons, Woodrow Wilson could not bring himself to admit the national interest in preventing the whole force of Europe from being wielded by a single hand. Instead he made himself the prophet of a world beyond power politics where the bad old balance of power would give way to a radiant new community of power. And he insisted on the providential appointment of the United States as "the only idealistic nation in the world," endowed with "the infinite privilege of fulfilling her destiny and saving the world."

So two strains have competed for the control of American foreign policy: one empirical, the other dogmatic; one viewing the world in the perspective of history, the other in the perspective of ideology; one supposing that the United States is not entirely immune to the imperfections, weaknesses and evils incident to all societies, the other regarding the United States as indeed the happy empire of perfect wisdom and perfect virtue, commissioned to save all mankind.

This schematic account does not do justice to the obvious fact that any American President, in order to command assent for his policies, must appeal to both reality and ideology—and that, to do this effectively, Presidents must combine the two strains not only in their speeches but in their souls. Franklin Roosevelt, the disciple at once of Admiral Mahan and of President Wilson, was supreme in marrying national interest to idealistic hope, though in the crunch interest always came first. Most postwar Presidents— Truman, Eisenhower, Kennedy, even Nixon—shared a recognition, alert or grudging, of the priority of power politics over ideology.

The competition between realism and ideology was complicated, however, by two developments: by the fact that the United States in the twentieth century became a great power; and by the fact that the balance of power in the twentieth century faced the gravest possible threats. There was in 1940 a very real monster to destroy and after 1945 another very real monster to contain. These threats demanded U. S. intervention abroad and brought the tradition of isolationism to a permanent end. But the growth of American power also confirmed the messianism of those who believed in America's divine appointment. And the fact that there were a couple of real monsters roaming the world encouraged a fearful tendency to look everywhere for new monsters to destroy.

II

The present Administration represents a mighty comeback of the messianic approach to foreign policy. "I have always believed," President Reagan said last November, "that this anointed land was set apart in an uncommon way, that a divine plan placed this great continent here between the oceans to be found by people from every corner of the earth who had a special love of faith and freedom." The Reagan Administration sees the world through the prism not of history but of ideology. The convictions that presently guide American foreign policy are twofold: that the United States is infinitely virtuous and that the Soviet Union is infinitely wicked.

The Soviet Union, Mr. Reagan has proclaimed, is an "evil empire," "the focus of evil in the modern world." Everything follows by deductive logic from this premise. The world struggle is "between right and wrong and good and evil." When there is evil loose in the world, "we are enjoined by scripture and the Lord Jesus to oppose it with all our might." Negotiation with evil is futile if not dangerous. The Soviet Union is forever deceitful and treacherous. The Soviet leaders erect lying and cheating into a philosophy and are personally responsible for the world's manifold ills. "Let us not delude ourselves," Mr. Reagan has said. "The Soviet Union underlies all the unrest that is going on. If they weren't engaged in this game of dominos, there wouldn't be any hot spots in the world." Not content with the orchestration of crisis in the Third World, the Soviet Union, once it acquires a certain margin of numerical superiority in warheads, can well be expected to launch a surprise nuclear attack on American targets. Safety lies only in the establishment of unequivocal military dominance by the United States, including a first-strike capability. If this means a nuclear arms race, that is Moscow's fault, not Washington's, because America's heart is pure. In any event nuclear weapons are usable and nuclear wars are winnable. We shall prevail.

The seizure of foreign policy by a boarding—party of ideologues invites a host of dangers. Most of all you tend to get things wrong. Where the empirical approach sees the present as emerging from the past and preparing for the future, ideology is counter-historical. Its besetting sin is to substitute models for reality. No doubt the construction of models—logically reticulated, general principles leading inexorably to particular outcomes—is an exercise that may help in the delineation of problems—but not when artificial constructs are mistaken for descriptions of the real world. This is what Alfred North Whitehead called "the fallacy of misplaced concreteness," and it explains why ideology infallibly gets statesmen into trouble, later if not sooner. The error of ideology is to prefer essence to existence, and the result, however gratifying logically and psychologically, undermines the reality principle itself.

Ideology withdraws problems from the turbulent stream of change and treats them in splendid abstraction from the whirl and contingency of life. So ideology portrays the Soviet Union as an unalterable monolith, immune to historical vicissitude and permutation, its behavior determined by immutable logic, the same yesterday, today and tomorrow; Sunday, Monday and always. We are forever in 1950, with a crazed Stalin reigning in the Kremlin and commanding an obedient network of communist parties and agents around the planet. In the light of ideology, the Soviet Union becomes a fanatic state carrying out with implacable zeal and cunning a master plan of world dominion.

Perhaps this is all so. But others may see rather a weary, dreary country filled with cynicism and corruption, beset by insuperable problems at home and abroad, lurching uncertainly from crisis to crisis. The Soviet leadership, three quarters of a century after the glorious Bolshevik revolution, cannot provide the people with elementary items of consumer goods. It cannot rely on the honesty of bureaucrats or the loyalty of scientists and writers. It confronts difficult ethnic challenges as the non-Russians in the Soviet Union, so miserably underrepresented in the organs of power, begin to outnumber the Russians. Every second child born this year in the Soviet Union will be a Muslim. Abroad, the Soviet Union faces hostile Chinese on its eastern frontier and restless satellites on the west, while to the south the great Red Army after three and a half years still cannot defeat ragged tribesmen fighting bravely in the hills of Afghanistan.

I don't want to overdo the picture of weakness. The Soviet Union remains a powerful state, with great and cruel capacity to repress consumption and punish dissent and with an apparent ability to do at least one thing pretty well, which is to build nuclear missiles. But there is enough to the reality of Soviet troubles to lead even the ideologues in Washington to conceive Soviet Russia as a nation at once so robust that it threatens the world and so frail that a couple of small pushes will shove its ramshackle economy into collapse.

The Soviet Union of course is ideological too, even if its ideology has got a little shopworn and ritualistic over the long years. It too sees the enemy as unchanging and unchangeable, a permanently evil empire vitiated through eternity by the original sin of private property. Each regime, reading its adversary ideologically rather than historically, deduces act from imputed essence and

Arthur M. Schlesinger, Jr.

attributes purpose, premeditation and plan where less besotted analysts would raise a hand for improvisation, accident, chance, ignorance, negligence and even sheer stupidity. We arrive at the predicament excellently described by Henry Kissinger: "The superpowers often behave like two heavily armed blind men feeling their way around a room, each believing himself in mortal peril from the other whom he assumes to have perfect vision . . . . Each tends to ascribe to the other a consistency, foresight, and coherence that its own experience belies. Of course, over time, even two blind men can do enormous damage to each other, not to speak of the room."

By construing every local mess as a test of global will, ideology raises stakes in situations that cannot be easily controlled and threatens to transmute limited into unlimited conflicts. Moreover, ideology, if pursued to the end, excludes the thought of accommodation or coexistence. Mr. Reagan has instructed us that we must oppose evil "with all our might." How now can we compromise with evil without losing our immortal soul? Ideology summons the true believer to a jihad, a crusade of extermination against the infidel.

The Russians are in no position to complain about such language. It has been more or less their own line since 1917. Reagan is simply paraphrasing Khrushchev: "We will bury you." Still the holy war has always represented a rather drastic approach to human affairs. It seems singularly unpromising in the epoch of nuclear weapons. And the irony is that, while Soviet ideology has grown tired, cynical and venal, the new American crusade is fresh and militant; and the Washington ideologues thereby present the Kremlin with an unearned and undeserved opportunity to appear reasonable and prudent. In particular, the American dash into ideology promotes a major Soviet objective, the turning away of Western Europe from the alliance with the United States.

Having suggested the current domination of American foreign policy by ideology, let me add that this domination is far from complete. Mr. Reagan's world view is not necessarily shared even by all members of his own Administration. It is definitely not shared by the Republican leadership in Congress. In general, it has been more vigorously translated into rhetoric than into policy. The suspicion has even arisen that Mr. Reagan's more impassioned ideological flights are only, in Wendell Willkie's old phrase, "campaign oratory," pap for right-wing zealots to conceal the Administration's covert creep to the center in domestic affairs. And the prospect of a presidential election next year creates a compelling political need for the Administration to attend to public opinion—a concern that may be a force for restraint in Central America and that could conceivably drive the Administration into arms control negotiations well before November 1984. Still, Mr. Reagan is not a cynical man, and, whatever the tactical function of his speeches, they must also in some sense express sincere convictions.

The greater restraint on ideology comes from the nature of foreign policy itself. The realism of the Founding Fathers sprang from the ineluctable character of international relations. National interest in the end must set limits on messianic passions. This fact explains the Administration's tendency to march up the ideological hill and then march down again, as in the case of the pipeline embargo. For the United States does not have the power, even if it had the wisdom, to achieve great objectives in the world by itself. Because this is so, a responsible foreign policy requires the cooperation of allies, and allies therefore have it within their power to rein in American messianism.

The pipeline embargo is only one example of the modification of ideology by interest. Ideology favors a blank check for Menachem Begin in Israel, but interest argues for the comprehensive approach to a Middle Eastern settlement that Reagan set forth on September 1, 1982, in the most impressive speech of his presidency. Ideology calls for the support of Taiwan at the expense of mainland China. Interest argues against policies tending to unite Chinese and Soviet communism. Ideology calls for the support of South Africa against black Africa. Interest argues against a course that leaves black Africa no friends but the Soviet Union. Ideology calls for the excommunication of socialist regimes. Interest sees benefits in cheerful relations with France, Spain, Italy, Portugal, Greece and Sweden. Ideology calls for chastisement of the debtor nations in the Third World. Interest leads to an additional $8.4-billion contribution to the International Monetary Fund.

III

Yet there remain sectors of policy where ideology still holds sway. One, for the season at least, is Central America. No one can be too sure over the longer run because the Administration has marched up and down this particular hill more than once in the last two years. During the vicariate of General Haig, insurgency in Central America was deemed a major Soviet challenge demanding a mighty American response. Then, in the first tranquilizing days of Secretary Schultz, the impression was allowed to spread that perhaps the troubles had ample local origins and, despite allegations of extracontinental instigation, might be amenable to local remedies. Subsequently Secretary Shultz caught the ideological flu, and by mid-1983 we were back at the global test of will.

Unquestionably the United States is facing tough problems in Central America. Nor does it meet the problems to observe that they are, in some part, of American creation. Twenty years ago the Alliance for Progress set out to deal with poverty and oligarchy in Central America. But the Alliance changed its character after the death of President Kennedy, and American policy abandoned concern with social change. When revolution predictably erupted in Central America, ideology rejected the notion of local origins and decreed that the Russians were back at their old game of dominos.

Ideology, it should be noted, offers a field day for self-fulfilling prophecies. If you shape rhetoric and policy to what you regard as a predestined result, chances are that you will get the result you predestine. Having decided a priori that the Nicaraguan revolution was a Soviet-Cuban conspiracy, Washington gave the Sandinistas little alternative but to seek support from the Cubans and Russians. The French wanted to sell Nicaragua arms and send in a military mission. Washington, instead of welcoming a democratic presence that would have been reliably alert to Soviet deviltry, exploded in indignation. When the CIA does its best to overthrow the government in Managua, we express unseemly shock that this government dare take measures to defend itself. Maybe it would have happened anyway, but the ideological policy makes insurgent anti-Americanism inevitable.

The present Washington disposition is to raise the stakes and to militarize the remedy. We are trying to provide the government of El Salvador with sufficient military aid to defeat the insurgency and to provide the insurgency in Nicaragua with sufficient military aid to defeat the government. If we don't act to stop Marxism in Central America, the argument runs, dominos will topple, and the Soviet Union will establish a bridgehead in the center of the Western Hemisphere. "Our credibility would collapse," Mr. Reagan has said, "our alliances would crumble, and the safety of our homeland would be in jeopardy." In April 1983 he denied any "thought of sending American combat troops to Central America." By June the thought had occurred, and he now cautioned, "Presidents never say never."

Other views are possible. The historian is bound to note that unilateral military action by the United States in Latin America is nearly always a mistake. Another by-product of ideology, along with the self-fulfilling prophecy, is the conviction that the anointed country, whether the United States these days or the Soviet Union in all days, understands the interests of other countries better than they understand their own interests. So in 1967 President Johnson sent Clark Clifford on an Asian tour, charging him to get the states of the South East Asia Treaty Organization to increase their contributions to the forces fighting communism in Vietnam. Clifford was astonished to discover that other Asian countries, though considerably more exposed to the danger, took it less tragically than the United States did and saw no need to increase their contributions. When he thereafter became Secretary of Defense, Clifford did his best to wind down American participation in the war.

453

If a Marxist Nicaragua (population 2.7 million) or El Salvador (population 4.5 million) is a threat to the Hemisphere, it is a more dire threat to Mexico, to Costa Rica, to Panama, to Venezuela, to Colombia than it is to the United States. These nations are closer to the scene and more knowledgeable about it; they are a good deal more vulnerable politically, economically and militarily than the United States; and they are governed by men just as determined as those in Washington to resist their own overthrow. When Latin American countries don't see the threat as apocalyptically as we do, only ideology can conclude with divine assurance that they are wrong and we are right. Are we really so certain that we understand their world better than they do?

In any event, ideology is a sure formula for hypocrisy, if not for disaster. Mr. Reagan says righteously that we will not "protect the Nicaraguan government from the anger of its own people." A fine sentiment-but why does it not apply equally to the government of El Salvador? Why do we condemn Nicaragua for postponing elections until 1985 while we condone Chile, which postpones elections till 1989? Would the Administration display the same solicitude for elections and rights in Nicaragua if the Somozas were still running things?

Ideology insists on the inflation of local troubles into global crises. National interest would emphasize the indispensability of working with Latin Americans who know the territory far better than we do and without whose support we cannot succeed. Let Mexico, Venezuela, Colombia and Panama—the so-called Contadora Group—take the lead, and back them to the hilt. Only if all agree on the nature of the response will intervention do the United States more good than harm in the Hemisphere. If it is too late for a negotiated settlement and our Latin friends reject military intervention, then we may have to resign ourselves to turmoil in Central America for some time to come—turmoil beyond our power to correct and beyond our wisdom to cure.

IV

Another sector where ideology still controls policy in Washington is, alas, the most grave and menacing of all—the nuclear arms race. It is in this field that the substitution of models for reality has the most baneful effect. War games these days are played by general staffs with such intensity that they come to be taken not as speculations but as predictions. The higher metaphysics of deterrence, by concentrating on the most remote contingencies, such as a Soviet first strike against the United States or a surprise invasion of Western Europe, makes such improbable events suddenly the governing force in budgetary, weapons and deployment decisions. History shows the Soviet Union to be generally cautious about risking direct military encounters with the United States; but ideology abolishes history. Reality evaporates in the hallucinatory world where strategic theologians calculate how many warheads can be balanced on the head of a pin. Little seems to me more dangerous than the current fantasy of controlled and graduated nuclear war, with generals calibrating nuclear escalation like grand masters at the chessboard. Let us not be bamboozled by models. Once the nuclear threshold is breached, the game is over.

I do not dismiss the Soviet Union as a military threat. We have noted that one thing Russia apparently does well is to build nuclear missiles. But we must keep things in proportion. Ideology, here as elsewhere, encourages exaggeration. Moreover, the professional duty of generals is to guarantee the safety of their countries; and the professional instinct of generals is to demand enough to meet every conceivable contingency. As old Lord Salisbury once wrote, "If you believe the doctors, nothing is wholesome; if you believe the theologians, nothing is innocent; if you believe the soldiers, nothing is safe." Like ideology, defense budgets need ever more menacing enemies.

In Washington Pentagon officials take masochistic pleasure at regular intervals in declaring that the Soviet Union is now stronger than the United States. These recurrent Pentagon panics, ably recalled by Robert H. Johnson in the Spring 1983 issue of this journal, range from the "missile gap," promulgated by the Gaither Report 25 years ago, to the "window of vulnerability," announced by Secretary of Defense Weinberger in 1981 and slammed shut by the Scowcroft Commission in 1983. One doubts that defense officials really believe their own lamentations; at least, I have never heard any of them offering to trade in the American for the Soviet defense establishment. When asked in Congress recently whether he would exchange places with his Soviet counterpart, the chairman of the American Joint Chiefs of Staff replied succinctly, "Not on your life." The ideologues achieve their dire effects by selective counting—by comparing theater nuclear weapons, for example, and omitting American superiority in the invulnerable sea-based deterrent. I would not take the lamentations too seriously, especially around budget time.

The irony is that the Pentagon and the Soviet Defense Ministry prosper symbiotically. There is no greater racket in the world today than generals claiming the other side is ahead in order to get bigger budgets for themselves. This tacit collusion, based on a common vested interest in crisis, remains a major obstacle in the search for peace. As President Kennedy remarked to Norman Cousins, the editor of the Saturday Review, in the spring of 1963, "Mr. Khrushchev and I occupy approximately the same political positions inside our governments. He would like to prevent a nuclear war but is under severe pressure from his hard-line crowd, which interprets every move in that direction as appeasement. I've got similar problems . . . . The hard-liners in the Soviet Union and the United States feed on one another."

The existence of Soviet military might obviously requires effective counterbalance. It requires nuclear deterrence capable of retaliation against a first strike, and this the West has. It also requires conventional force capable of discouraging Soviet aspirations in Europe, and this the West may presently lack. The need is to remove European defense from the delusion of rescue through limited nuclear war. The European democracies must understand that reliance on the bomb to save Europe no longer makes sense in the age of nuclear stand-off. However destructive conventional war can be in modern times, it is infinitely less destructive than nuclear war would be. And the sure way to make the improbability of a Soviet attack across rebellious satellites on Western Europe even more improbable is to leave no doubt that the costs, even without nuclear response, would be intolerably high. This lies within the power of the European democracies to do.

V

But what of the bomb itself? For we live today in a situation without precedent—a situation that transcends all history and threatens the end of history. I must confess that I have come late to this apocalyptic view of the future. To set limits on the adventures of the human mind has always seemed—still seems—the ultimate heresy, the denial of humanity itself. But we always recognized that freedom involves risk, and the free mind in our time has led us to the edge of the Faustian abyss. "Man has mounted science, and is now run away with," Henry Adams wrote more than a century ago. "Some day science may have the existence of mankind in its power, and the human race commit suicide by blowing up the world."

I had always supposed that, with the nuclear genie out of the bottle, the prospect of the suicide of the human race would have a sobering effect on those who possessed the tragic power to initiate nuclear war. For most of the nuclear age this supposition has been roughly true. Statesmen have generally understood, as President Kennedy said in 1961, "Mankind must put an end to war or war will put an end to mankind." I saw how after the Cuban missile crisis a shaken Kennedy—and a shaken Khrushchev, too—moved swiftly toward a ban on nuclear testing and a systematic reduction of international acrimony.

I no longer have much confidence in the admonitory effect of the possession of nuclear weapons. The curse of ideology is that as it impoverishes our sense of reality, it impoverishes our imagination, too. It enfeebles our capacity to visualize the Doomsday horror. It inhibits us from confronting the awful possibility we can no longer deny: the extermination of sentient life on this planet.

Under the hypnosis of doctrine, ideologues in Washington today plainly see an unlimited nuclear arms race not as an appalling threat to the survival of humanity, but simply as a fine way to do the Russians in. Either they will try to keep up with us, which will wreck their economy, or they will fail to keep up, which will give us the decisive military advantage. To have an arms control agreement, they believe, would be to renounce our most potent weapon against the empire of evil.

I continue to find it hard to suppose that either superpower would deliberately embark on nuclear war ab initio. But it is not hard to foresee a nuclear overreaction to the frustration or embarrassment of defeat in conventional warfare. It is still easier, with 50,000 warheads piling up in the hands of the superpowers and heaven knows how many more scattered or hidden or incipient in other hands, to foresee nuclear war precipitated by terrorists, or by madness, or by accident, or by misreading the flashes on a radar screen.

The stake is too great to permit this horror to grow. For the stake is supreme: it is the fate of humanity itself. Let me say at once that the answer to the nightmare cannot conceivably be unilateral nuclear disarmament. The likely result of unilateral nuclear disarmament by the West would not be to prompt the Soviet leadership to do likewise but to place the democratic world at the mercy of Soviet communism. History offers abundant proof that mercy is not a salient characteristic of any communist regime.

Neither the arms race nor unilateral disarmament therefore holds out hope. What we must do rather is to revive the vanishing art of diplomacy. American officials these days like to strike Churchillian poses. They remind one of Mark Twain's response when his wife tried to cure him of swearing by loosing a string of oaths herself: "You got the words right, Livy, but you don't know the tune." Our road-company Churchills lack one of the things that made Churchill great: his power of historical discrimination.

"Those who are prone by temperament and character," Churchill wrote in The Gathering Storm, "to seek sharp and clear-cut solutions of difficult and obscure problems, who are ready to fight whenever some challenge comes from a foreign Power, have not always been right. On the other hand, those whose inclination is . . . to seek patiently and faithfully for peaceful compromise are not always wrong. On the contrary, in the majority of instances they may be right, not only morally but from a practical standpoint." So, in the spirit of Churchill, let us not prematurely abandon the quest for peaceful compromise.

The reciprocal and verifiable nuclear freeze on the production, testing and deployment of nuclear weapons and delivery vehicles is backed today, according to polls, by more than 80 percent of Americans. The freeze is the most promising beginning, or so it seems to me. More must come. A joint Soviet-NATO command post, where each side could monitor the other side's radar screens and to which all war rumors would go for resolution, would do much to reduce the chances of accidental nuclear war. Deep cuts in nuclear stockpiles must follow, perhaps by each superpower delivering an equal number of nuclear weapons of its own choice for destruction by an international authority, a procedure that would minimize the theoretically destabilizing effect of reduction by fixed categories. Mankind has no choice but to find ways to crawl back from the edge of the Faustian abyss and to move toward the extinction of the nuclear race; better this, with all its difficulties, than the extinction of the human race.

VI

What the world needs to bring this about is above all deliverance from ideology. This is not to suggest for a moment any symmetry between the United States and the Soviet Union. In the United States, ideology is a lurking susceptibility, a periodic fling, fooling some of the people some of the time but profoundly alien to the Constitution and to the national spirit. Washington's current ideological commotion is the result, not of popular demand or mandate,

Arthur M. Schlesinger, Jr.

but of the superficial fact that in 1980 the voters, unable to abide the thought of four more years of what they had, had Reagan as the only practical alternative.

In the Soviet Union ideology remains the heart of the matter. It is not a susceptibility but a compulsion, inscribed in sacred texts and enforced by all the brutal machinery of a still vicious police state. Yet even in the Soviet Union one senses an erosion of the old ideological intensity until a good deal of what remains is simply a vocabulary in which Soviet leaders are accustomed to speak. Let not a spurt of American ideologizing breathe new life into the decadent Soviet ideology, especially by legitimizing the Russian fear of an American crusade aimed at the destruction of Russian society.

In the end, ideology runs against the grain of American democracy. Popular elections, as the Founding Fathers saw long ago, supply the antidote to the fanaticism of abstract propositions. High-minded Americans have recently taken to calling for a single six-year presidential term on the ground that Presidents, not having to worry about reelection, would thereby be liberated to make decisions for the good of the republic. This assumes that the less a President takes public opinion into account, the better a President he will be—on reflection, a rather anti—democratic assumption. In the instant case, the best things Mr. Reagan has done—his belated concern about racial justice, about the environment and natural resources, about hunger, about women, about arms control—have all been under the pressure of the 1984 election. He might never have cared if he had had a single six-year term. It may well be that Presidents do a better job when politics requires them to respond to popular needs and concerns than they would if constitutionally empowered to ignore popular needs and concerns for the sake of ideological gratification.

Ideology is the curse of public affairs because it converts politics into a branch of theology and sacrifices human beings on the altar of abstractions. "To serene Providence," Winston Churchill wrote an American politician nearly 90 years ago, "a couple of generations of trouble and distress may seem an insignificant thing. . . .

Earthly Governments, however, are unable to approach questions from the same standpoint. Which brings me to the conclusion that the duty of governments is to be first of all practical. I am for makeshifts and expediency. I would like to make the people who live on this world at the same time as I do better fed and happier generally. If incidentally I benefit posterity—so much the better— but I would not sacrifice my own generation to a principle— however high—or a truth however great."

In this humane spirit we may save not only our generation but posterity, too.

ARTHUR M. SCHLESINGER, JR., Albert Schweitzer Professor in the Humanities at the City University of New York, is working on a book about Franklin D. Roosevelt and the coming of the Second World War. This article is adapted from the Cyril Foster Lecture delivered at Oxford University in May 1983. Copyright (c) 1983 by Arthur Schlesinger, Jr.

After the Election

Foreign Policy Under Reagan II

Henry A. Grunwald   WINTER 1984/85

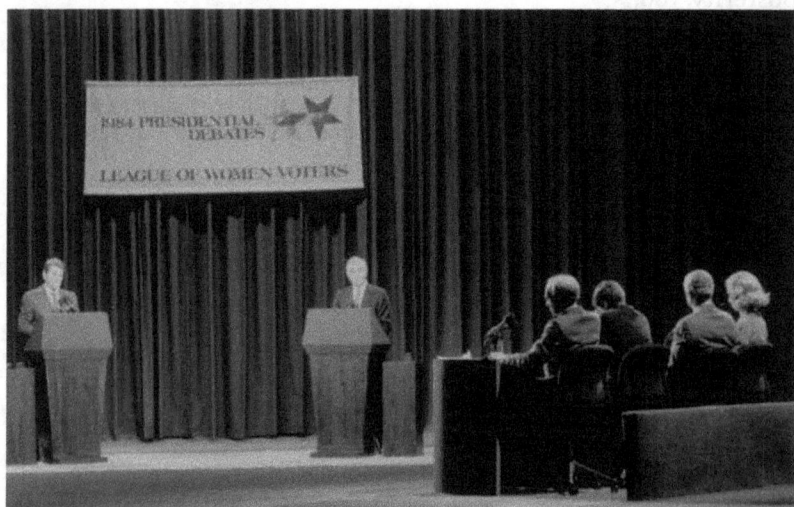

Reagan and Mondale debate.

The second Reagan Administration has a rare opportunity to reshape American foreign policy. The opportunity obviously springs from President Reagan's overwhelming election victory, which, if he remains in office for four more years, will make him the first full two-term president since Eisenhower. This victory has further strengthened his already impressive capacity for political leadership, reinforcing his authority to deal with the factions of his own party, with the feuding wings of the bureaucracy, and with foreign countries. The question is whether he will seize that authority and will know how to use it. Which Reagan, and which group of Reagan advisers, will dominate the second term? Will it be the stubbornly hard-line or the flexible President, the "ideologues" or the "pragmatists" among his counselors?

That distinction is, of course, somewhat oversimplified; the divisions within, and around, the President are not quite so clear-cut. There are apocalyptic and rational ideologues; there are very tough and semi-tough pragmatists. Still, the familiar labels do describe a genuine conflict, and in the first term, the evolution of that conflict was quite evident: from ideology to pragmatism.

The Administration started out by confronting the world with a hard-line, aggressive and Manichean set of policies, or pronouncements, that in nearly every instance gave way to compromise and at least outward accommodation. This was true of attitudes toward the Soviet Union, arms control, Central America, the European allies, and support of the International Monetary Fund, among others. The retreat and reversal on the Soviet-European gas pipeline issue was typical of this trend. These accommodations happened only after bitter bureaucratic infighting, and in response to various outside pressures: public opinion, politics, allied complaints, the risk of diplomatic debacles.

The need to compromise was symbolized by the resort to more or less bipartisan commissions: the Scowcroft panel on the MX missile, the Kissinger group on Central America. These commissions did extremely useful work and produced sound, generally centrist recommendations, which by no reasonable standard could be described as weak. What remains to be seen is whether, in the second term, these and similar policies will prevail, demonstrating in effect a learning experience by the Administration, or whether the right-wing "true believers" will succeed in dismissing them as mere temporary, tactical adjustments and will try to reassert the ideological super-hard line. A great deal depends on the answer, including the possibility of reaching at least the rudiments of a new national consensus on foreign and defense policy.

Henry A. Grunwald

II

In fairness, it should be said that, up to a point, the hard line was a useful corrective for weak and confused policies of the past and was welcomed in many quarters as a sign of a new American assertiveness. Administration critics almost automatically preface "ideology" with "right-wing." But there is liberal or left-wing ideology too, and its reading of Soviet intentions and of the causes of Third World instability often has been just as simplistic as right-wing interpretations, if not more so.

Besides, the Reagan Administration, often reckless in rhetoric but cautious in action, did have its successes. One of them was the championing of American military power. The arms buildup may have been excessive, and ill-advised in some particulars; very little was done to reform the armed services. But the buildup was plainly necessary and, despite much bickering, it was essentially supported by Congress and the public. It constitutes the most important single "foreign policy" action by Reagan so far.

Another clear achievement, of course, was the deployment of the Euromissiles for NATO, in the teeth of all-out Soviet opposition. In dealing with China, despite some early ideological rumbles and despite the baggage accumulated during decades of a deep Republican commitment to Taiwan, the Reagan Administration acted prudently and professionally. The same may be said, at the risk of considerable disagreement, about the Reagan policy toward South Africa. In other instances, policy was muddled through lack of skill and understanding, as in the Middle East.

On balance, the Reagan Administration often proved itself quite capable of realistic and largely nonideological policies, but they did not fit into any unified concept. Thus "more pragmatism" is not a sufficient foreign policy prescription for Reagan II. A pragmatism that merely and artificially splits the difference between sharply opposing views, or cobbles together a compromise for political and public relations effect, is hardly what we need. What is required is pragmatism within a framework of principle; firm assertion of American goals combined with a recognition that there are different ways of attaining them, and that some may be unattainable in the near future; a realization that, especially in foreign affairs, passion without skill can be worse than skill without passion. Reagan II, one would hope, will recognize that toughness, while indispensable, can take many forms. On the whole, the Administration has been deficient in seeing that strength has political and diplomatic components, that charging head-on at an objective is not necessarily the best way to reach it, and that guile and the ability to maneuver are every bit as important as muscle.

III

In perspective, the Reagan Administration's difficulties in dealing with the Soviet Union are familiar, almost traditional, even though pushed to extremes. From the outset, the Administration had difficulty coping with what can only be called the yes-but formula, which has been advanced for the last three decades by just about every specialist in the field: Yes, we must be strong, but at the same time flexible. Yes, we must understand that the Russians are relentless foes, but at the same time we must seek ways of coexisting. And so forth. As a general proposition, this formula is so obvious that it is no longer worth debating; the question is how it is to be applied specifically. Yet almost every new Administration comes into office paying lip service to the yes-but principle, while actually believing that a fresh start, a new approach—either softer or harder—will permit escape from the painful and laborious double track.

The Reagan Administration was particularly determined to reject the yes-but formula, which requires the ability to hold two opposite ideas at the same time (the mark of a first-rate intelligence, according to F. Scott Fitzgerald). This runs against the American tendency to see the world as good or evil, a mind-set not invented by Reagan, and to believe in solutions; the yes-but formula implies that U.S.-Soviet strains are not a problem to which there is a solution, but a more or less permanent condition that can only be alleviated, not cured.

In fact, each Administration sooner or later has been disappointed in its hope that these constraints can be escaped, the only exception being the Nixon Administration which knew better from the start. The fact is that the Reagan Administration is being pushed toward something that, by any other name, is still détente. Indeed, détente is constantly being reinvented, redefined or relabelled (as in Richard Nixon's afterthought, "hardheaded détente"). As long as it can be protected from the utopian left, which sees it as institutionalized brotherhood, and from the triumphalist right, which sees it as institutionalized surrender, and defined as no more or less than controlled conflict, it remains the inescapable intellectual framework for American policy.

It has been eloquently argued that arms control has been made to bear too much of the burden of U.S.-Soviet relations, and that there can be no hope for significant progress on arms control unless a degree of trust can be restored or created between the superpowers.[1] The notion brings to mind the observation by Salvador de Madariaga, writing about the 1930s in his memoirs, that "nations don't distrust each other because they are armed; they are armed because they distrust each other. And therefore to want disarmament before a minimum of common agreement on fundamentals is as absurd as to want people to go undressed in winter." It is hard to quarrel with this insight, and yet it is equally hard to see how the United States and the Soviet Union can retrieve even a few clothes of confidence unless there is at least a possibility of moving, however slowly, toward an accord on nuclear arms.

In short, the argument is circular and irresistibly leads back to the imperative of arms control. Its achievements in the past have been modest at best. Progress has been glacial, and exaggerated expectations have been aroused by the process. But there is simply no convincing alternative to it.

IV

The Reagan Administration has often acted as if any arms control proposal that might be acceptable to the Soviets must be automatically flawed, when in fact the Soviet Union, like the United States, will naturally accept only proposals it considers to be in its own self-interest. This negative attitude, plus the open contempt for arms control expressed by some members of the Reagan circle, plus the unrealistic proposals for cuts offered at the outset of the Strategic Arms Reduction Talks (START), has obscured a central fact: the major source of the problem lies in the Soviets' own aggressive nuclear buildup and their excessive view of what they require for their own security. It is therefore entirely possible that even a "reformed" Reagan Administration with a more tolerant approach to arms control may not get anywhere with the Soviets. There are certain concessions beyond which no administration can or should go in order to win an agreement. At the same time, President Reagan seems to have disavowed the possibility that America can permanently restore any significant nuclear superiority over the Russians. What is at issue is an acceptable but more realistic definition of parity.

It has become fashionable to say that arms control is virtually dead. This view is held not merely because of the acrimonious breakdown of both the intermediate-range nuclear forces (INF) and START negotiations, but, more importantly, because it is argued that technology keeps outpacing the negotiators. While advancing technology immensely complicates arms control efforts, it is not beyond the reach of negotiated agreements.

Politically, of course, one of the vast problems about arms control and nuclear strategy is their complexity and the inability of the public—or of most politicians—to grasp the issues in any detail. Much of the arms control debate seems like a scholastic exercise about how many warheads can dance on the head of a missile. This frightful air of unreality has much to do with the desire both on the left and on the right, in a curious mirror image, to escape these dilemmas and to find simple and understandable solutions.

On the left, the desire to escape takes the form of a utopian belief in good will or in unilateral actions. (The widely proposed "mutual and verifiable" freeze would not assure balance and would take extensive negotiations.) On the right, it takes the form of a search for "superiority," in the belief that we can outspend the Soviets and outdo them more or less indefinitely in technology. The Administration's Strategic Defense Initiative ("Star Wars") is an elaboration of this view.

The Star Wars program has a certain appealing plausibility: defense is better than offense, safety behind a shield in the sky is better than the "balance of terror." Professional analysts of course do not commit such oversimplifications, or at least not obviously. Lieutenant General James A. Abrahamson, head of the Strategic Defense Initiative research program, admits that no system the United States deploys will ever be entirely foolproof. But he argues that a less than total but highly efficient defense, which might mean anywhere from 50-percent to 99-percent effectiveness, depending on the scale of the system deployed, would make it impossible for the Soviets to plan a first strike with any high degree of confidence. That circumstance will enhance deterrence. Furthermore, even a partially effective defense would be bound to save lives in the unlikely event of an attack.

For the moment, the Administration has committed itself only to a research and development program which the Department of Defense says will require about $26 billion over the next five years. Even the more optimistic scenarios see continued need for new offensive weapons, which would only gradually be reduced. And even the most sophisticated and cautious advocates of space-based defense seem to harbor the hankering for a short-cut to safety. They too seek somehow to transfer the task of peacekeeping from the precarious calculus of threat and counterthreat, from the area of human will, to a more or less automatic regime of laser beams and mirrors in orbit.

Technological feasibility aside, the opponents of Star Wars seem to have the better case. The prospect of one side more or less safe while the other side is open to attack is untenable in the nuclear age. Moreover, in the absence of a new bargain with the Soviets, such a situation is bound to be relatively short-lived. We have seen in the past that sooner or later the Soviets can catch up with

American technology, the most notable example being multiple independently targetable reentry vehicles (MIRVs). All of this would mean great instability during a development period that might run for 20 years and, eventually, instability at a much higher and more complicated level of weaponry.

But this does not mean that development of a defensive system should be banned independently of what is done about nuclear weapons in general. The Soviets seem genuinely afraid of a technological race with the United States in space defense. This fear should be used as a major bargaining chip for an overall arms control agreement.

After an initial test of its low-altitude anti-satellite system (ASAT), which is not part of Star Wars but which the Soviets want to include in any talks about space weapons, the United States should offer a temporary suspension of further tests. This should be followed by negotiations that would tie any arrangements for space weapons to the rest of arms control. If it is too late for a total ban on space-based weapons, a possible outcome could be to permit relatively small defense systems for both sides, tied to an arms control agreement (reductions) in offensive weapons.

V

Despite the breakdown of arms control talks, the elements of an agreement for offensive weapons exist. They are summed up in the phrase, "off-setting asymmetries"—in other words, the recognition that the Soviets will not make any significant cuts in their principal arsenal of ground-based missiles unless the United States makes certain concessions in an area where it is particularly strong, namely bombers, cruise missiles and, increasingly, submarine-launched ballistic missiles. This principle is recognized in various schemes, including the so-called framework approach advanced by the State Department in August 1983 but never adopted by the Administration and in the so-called double build-down scheme. This last was put forward in the summer of 1983 by a somewhat shakily bipartisan group of Senators and Representatives which in effect forced it on the Administration. Advanced at the START talks without full conviction or complete details, the double build-down was quickly rejected by the Soviets as a mere repackaging of old, unacceptable American proposals.

The concept underlying these schemes, no doubt subject to a great deal of tinkering with the numbers, should become the basis for the Administration's arms control negotiating position. Despite its great complexity and uncertain beginnings, it remains a promising approach.

All this, of course, assumes that the Russians will allow themselves to return to the bargaining table, despite their earlier vow that they would not do so unless the United States halts deployment of Euromissiles. There is strong evidence that the Russians regret having backed themselves into that particular corner and want to come out of it. (It is interesting to recall that in 1979 the Soviets said they would not even negotiate on INF if NATO adopted the "two-track" approach, but they did in fact come to the table by 1981.) The conditions for improved relations reiterated in October 1984 by Konstantin Chernenko, in his interview with The Washington Post, did not include any reference to INF, and seem to offer enough room for maneuver to resume talks without undue advance concessions by the United States.

The verification problem, of course, presents an extremely difficult obstacle. But given determined research, it is hard to believe that "national technical means" could not be steadily improved. The Russians have made some forthcoming noises about on-site inspection, but it is doubtful that this could provide a significant overall solution. At any rate, those who believe that verification problems vitiate arms control fail to say how the situation would improve without arms control; both sides would still be dependent on the fullest possible information about the armaments of the other side but without the (admittedly incomplete) help on verification that arms control agreements do and can provide.

Movement, if any, is likely to be excruciatingly slow. No big breakthroughs should be expected. At all events, what is needed is a merger or at least a link of INF and START negotiations plus space-defense negotiations. The talks need not be fully integrated right away; they could begin separately and be linked gradually. The drawbacks of such a procedure are all too familiar: complexity and, through INF, the problem of how to bring the allies into the picture without either compromising their sovereignty and independence or else allowing them a role in the START area where they do not belong.[2] Despite such difficulties, it is impossible to see how anything can be accomplished without ultimately treating the issues of nuclear arms and arms control in their entirety. There is simply not enough room for bargaining and trade-offs if things are to be fought out separately in different arenas.

The foregoing would represent a fairly drastic change in the Administration's position on arms control—at least in its earlier phase. But it would be necessary if the President really hopes to make progress in the area during his second term, and there is much evidence that he does. His sincerity would not be the issue. The question is one of intellectual capacity and will. To achieve anything he will have to become personally involved in the process, understanding it far better than he has so far, or else put policy and execution into the hands of a really trusted, high-level associate with the power to enforce his views.

The President will have to crack down hard on the guerrilla war between various parts of the Administration, an action that would go very much against his grain. Some bureaucratic infighting and genuine competition between ideas cannot and should not be prevented. But thanks to certain single-minded and obsessive positions on the civilian side of the Pentagon and elsewhere, throughout the first Reagan term, "negotiability" with the Russians was not the issue, but rather negotiability within the Administration.[3] This situation can only be ended by a firm and decisive President and very likely by a change in some of the principal cast of characters.

VI

While arms control is thus at the center of U.S.-Soviet dealings, it must not be allowed to distract us from the world of politics and

Henry A. Grunwald

psychology surrounding the enclaves of missiles and warheads. In that larger context, Reagan II would do well to take certain precepts to heart. One is that we have only very limited means of influencing events inside the Soviet Union. As has been amply observed, fierce rhetoric certainly will not do it. (During the past year, and especially during the last few weeks of the election campaign, the Administration's harsh language gave way to a much softer style, downright reminiscent of Beethoven's introduction to Schiller's Ode to Joy—"Not these tones, my friends, but let us raise more agreeable ones. . . .")

Criticism, of course, must not cease, but the United States must also be very cautious in linking condemnation to practical policy, or in suggesting, as has been done by members of the Administration, that peace requires drastic changes in the Soviet regime. A lesson from pre-Reagan days, but still applicable, involves one of the most destructive actions of U.S. foreign policy, which was championed by the usually very wise late Senator Henry M. Jackson: the attempt to force liberalization of Jewish emigration from the U.S.S.R. by denying Russia most-favored-nation treatment. Focusing on Jewish emigration as distinct from any other, possibly worse abuses in the Soviet system was not only arbitrary, it was clearly counterproductive.

The Reagan Administration also needs to get better at matching means and ends, as is suggested, for instance, by its reaction to the imposition of martial law in Poland. The means were at hand for a much faster and more forceful reaction, notably suspension of the then still running INF talks and calling in the Polish debt to the international banks. But if for whatever reason it was decided not to react in that way, the mere denunciations and attempts at economic sanctions were futile. In fact, it can be argued that imposition of martial law was the minimal reaction that could have been expected from the Soviets and that no Communist state could ever permit an organization like Solidarity to subsist.

But aligning means with ends does not imply ceding anything to the Soviets that need not be ceded—and certainly not without exacting a price. True, the Soviet Union is a superpower with global interests that cannot be totally denied. Those who urge a last-ditch stand against Soviet influence in every corner of the globe, a sort of Churchillian resistance sometimes suggested by apocalyptic right-wingers, overestimate both our will and our resources. America must differentiate, without of course publicly drawing a map, between areas and situations of the first or second or fifth importance. Pressure on the Soviets and their surrogates should be applied everywhere, constantly, but in varying degrees. Above all, pressure should not cease without a quid pro quo, very likely in some other area.

Certain basics are beyond compromise. But many policies can and should be stopped or moderated in exchange for something else. American aid to resistance fighters in Afghanistan, for example, should continue. The embarrassment and material and human losses suffered by the Soviet Union in Afghanistan are of course beneficial to the West. But eventually there may come a point when the Soviets might be willing to curb certain actions elsewhere in the world in exchange for Western accommodation over Afghanistan. In such situations, there is always the risk that we will be outmaneuvered by the Soviets. But, despite such dangers, the willingness to deal at the right moment is essential.

This very much applies to an especially neuralgic area, Eastern Europe, currently in a state of considerable political restlessness. Any blunt, open political intervention there would be extremely, perhaps intolerably, provocative to the Soviets. But there should always be unpublicized, indirect probes, to be eased or stepped up in reaction to restrained or aggressive Soviet behavior elsewhere.

VII

Certain other areas require specific consideration because they will continue to test the Administration in special if quite disparate ways. They are the North Atlantic Alliance, the Middle East and Central America.

Obviously, NATO is by far the most important to America's position in the world and to its permanent contest with the

Soviets. The Administration started out on the wrong foot with the allies. Somewhat paranoid in the best of times, West European leaders and intellectuals were panicked by Reagan's rhetoric and image, by some of the rather casual if actually routine references to nuclear war, and especially by the attempt to veto the Soviet pipeline, which seemed to impose economic sacrifices on the West Europeans when the United States was lifting its grain embargo. Since those days of anger and suspicion, the atmosphere between the United States and the allies has improved considerably.

Today, NATO is widely proclaimed to be in crisis. The litany is familiar. Militarily, NATO strategy is seen in disarray: inadequate conventional forces to resist a possible Soviet attack, and a less than credible nuclear deterrent. Politically, Britain, Holland and West Germany harbor strong, more or less neutralistpacifist forces which want to opt out of the East-West conflict—and, some would say, out of history. These forces are in the minority, but majority governments (which may not be in the majority forever) cannot afford to ignore them. West European countries tend to press for American accommodation with the Soviet Union, sometimes, it seems, at any price, refuse to support or understand American responsibilities in the Third World, and still take for granted the American defense of their territory.

Either in sorrow or in anger, various remedies or retaliations are being advocated and pressed on the Administration. These include what Richard Burt, Assistant Secretary of State for European Affairs, calls "global unilateralism" (i.e., reducing forces in Europe so as to enhance U.S. flexibility to act in other regions) and "Atlantic reconstruction" (threatening withdrawal from NATO to provoke the allies into doing more for their own defense). The leading reconstructionist, Senator Sam Nunn (D-Ga.), has called for American troop reductions in Europe unless the allies meet a detailed and sophisticated list of requirements to improve NATO's military footing. But the threat of troop withdrawal in the near future is likely to be counterproductive. The NATO commander, General Bernard W. Rogers, evangelizes tirelessly for larger European conventional forces to be equipped with dazzling new high-tech weapons. But the price tag is estimated to add a one-percent increase in defense spending to the three-percent pledge the allies have already made but few have kept.

Various military thinkers are advancing new strategies, including mobility and counterattack, to avoid what The Economist has called a Maginot Line mentality without a Maginot Line. But such schemes make the Europeans highly nervous. Henry A. Kissinger has advanced an imaginative plan for restructuring the Alliance, with an American secretary general and a European commander, to emphasize the need for greater responsibility by the Europeans for their own defense.[4] The plan was welcomed as highly thought-provoking, which presumably was its purpose, but few leaders in NATO countries are likely to do anything about it any time soon.

The Administration attitude toward much of this agitation about NATO was summed up by Burt, who conceded the need for improvements while adding: "There must also be limits to our departures" (his own version of "Surtout, pas trop de zèle").[5] That may not be a bad prescription for American policy toward the Alliance in the second term. A top priority must be to undercut and contain the potentially disastrous left-wing neutralist movements. This is best done through a stable, realistic policy toward the Soviets, including arms control. The Administration should continue to press for greater European defense contributions in various forms, even though this contribution is considerably more significant than popularly understood in the United States.[6] The Administration should encourage any proposals for greater military cooperation among European countries, including that ever-elusive goal, standardization of equipment.

Reagan II should also continue to press for greater cooperation to prevent the transfer of military technology to the Soviet Union, for greater solidarity in major East-West crises, and for more of a role by European countries in "out-of-area" contingencies. As always, these efforts will be frustrating and often futile. We will have to accept the fact that the European view of the world, and of the

Soviet Union, is different from ours. We will continue to be lectured on proper global conduct by nations which achieved their present peaceable outlook not through wisdom or virtue, but through exhaustion, after hundreds of years of waging their own wars. But we will have to continue, even at great cost, to help hold the indispensable Alliance together. With much patience, some diplomatic skill, the quieter kind of public relations-and the almost always dependable help from the Soviet Union in the form of political overkill—the task is not beyond us.

A major problem between the United States and Western Europe lies in the economic area. There are major joint concerns about growth in an increasingly interdependent industrialized world, including policies toward the developing countries. The Europeans keep complaining about high American interest rates resulting from the deficits. While these complaints are justified, they are also excessive and tend to overshadow the Europeans' own responsibility for outmoded and ineffective trade and industrial policies. Fortunately there is a growing realization in Western Europe that central economic control and welfare statism are no longer working very well. It is not yet clear, however, what is to take their place.

As far as the developing countries are concerned, the debt crisis has been at least temporarily alleviated by the International Monetary Fund, backed by a somewhat reluctant United States and other Western industrialized states. Longer-range solutions remain elusive. There is a healthy realization among many Third World countries that prospects are very dim for achieving a "new international economic order" and the pieties of the Brandt Commission, all pointing to massive wealth transfers from the industrialized developing countries. The Reagan Administration's Third World prescription of capitalism, entrepreneurship and market incentives is theoretically sound, as has been acknowledged, indirectly, even by China. But in many developing societies, these prescriptions standing alone will not mean much or will be politically destructive. They will have to be part of a mixed economic system. Without going into details here, it is obvious that the Reagan Administration has a major opportunity in the economic area, including the international exchange system. It would also be useful if Reagan II could quietly abandon such dubious missionary efforts as trying to impose certain views about population control and abortion on other societies.

VIII

In the Middle East, the Administration has swung from overactive and ill-conceived involvement (former Secretary of State Alexander M. Haig's whirlwind attempt to rally the area for an anti-Soviet "strategic consensus") to extreme caution bordering on inactivity. The attitude in the second term should be somewhere in between.

The Administration can base itself on one solid conceptual piece of work, the Reagan peace initiative of September 1982, essentially a distillation of many earlier comprehensive peace plans. But the Administration never followed through with further diplomatic action. Instead it got lost in maneuvers to bring about a settlement in Lebanon, having failed to keep the Israelis from invading, if not actually having condoned the move. Today there are some new factors in the area which offer some modest opportunities.

Israel has a new coalition government, however shaky, whose prime minister and Labor Party members hold somewhat more moderate views on West Bank policy and other issues than the Likud governments of Menachem Begin and Yitzhak Shamir. Virtually all factions now want the Israeli army out of Lebanon, provided some kind of halfway reassuring security arrangements for South Lebanon can be achieved. Syria, enjoying the new prominence which it snatched from the jaws of defeat thanks to Soviet resupply and inept American diplomacy, is in no hurry to let the Israelis go. But it is finding its role as peacekeeper in Lebanon somewhat sticky. The ever-cautious King Hussein of Jordan has taken the very bold step-for him-of resuming diplomatic relations with Egypt while continuing his public refusal to have anything to do with the peace process. It is conceivable that Iraq may eventually follow Hussein in his move toward Cairo.

The United States should encourage what has already, if prematurely, been called the Egyptian-Jordanian axis. At the same time it must deal with Syria, treating it less as a Soviet dependency than as a regional mini-power with local interests and fears of its own. A tacit arrangement between Syria and Israel to stabilize the situation in Lebanon seems quite possible. That is a long way from a point at which Syria might stop vetoing any significant peace move, but under the circumstances in the Middle East one must be grateful for small mercies.

Some analysts argue that, ever since the Lebanese invasion, the Palestinians are no longer the key to the Middle East. The suggestion is that the Palestinian problem can be ignored with impunity.[7] It is obvious that the Palestine Liberation Organization has been shattered, with one part merely a Syrian puppet organization and another part, under Yassir Arafat, a cause in search of a home. It is also true that among Arab states both the sympathy (always conditional) for, and the fear of, the PLO has been greatly overshadowed by a new concern with Islamic fundamentalism. Nevertheless, the Palestinian issue cannot be put aside permanently. The Administration should pressure the Israeli government to improve conditions on the West Bank and to place a freeze on new settlements. Prime Minister Shimon Peres may be receptive to this.

In U.N. Security Council votes and in other ways, the Administration should also attempt to restore at least some image of even-handedness toward Israel and the Arab states. The Reagan peace initiative should be pursued behind the scenes, avoiding big public efforts that are too likely to end in disappointment. Meanwhile the Administration should look for every opportunity to take small bilateral steps to improve the situation and ease the atmosphere. In a postmortem on Lebanon, Richard W. Murphy, Assistant Secretary of State for Near Eastern Affairs, put it well: "We must work on the margins to protect our interests." He continued on this sobering note: "Lebanon reminded us that we cannot remake society, that we can work for peace but we cannot impose it. It also reminded us that the commitments we undertake must be ones that we as a government and as a people can sustain over time. We did not do well in that regard. Hence the need for both pragmatism and fortitude."8

IX

Nothing is more futile or arid than the debate between those who argue that the chief cause of Third World insurgencies is economic and social injustice, and those who argue that it is interference by the Soviets or their surrogates. Obviously both forces are at work, reinforcing each other, and both must be coped with. The Reagan Administration has balanced the two approaches—the stress on force and the stress on development—more successfully than it is generally given credit for.

The Reagan team undoubtedly started with an excessively apocalyptic view of the situation. But it was essentially right in believing that a successful communist revolution in El Salvador, or neighboring countries, no matter how seriously driven by the thirst for social justice, would be an American defeat. It can be argued reasonably that such revolutions are not preventable at acceptable costs, but it cannot be maintained that, in the Central American context, they are not against American interests.

The Reagan Administration often gave the impression that it was unconcerned about human rights in the area, and that it regarded dealing with this problem as a sort of moralistic luxury that could not be indulged in the midst of a civil war. U.N. Ambassador Jeane Kirkpatrick's now celebrated analysis distinguishing between irreversible totalitarian regimes and reversible or improvable authoritarian ones is impeccable in theory. In practice it does not answer the question, crucial in many parts of the Third World, about just when an authoritarian regime, no matter how strong its anti-communist credentials, becomes so corrupt and unpopular that it loses all legitimacy and, in fact, opens the door to totalitarianism. This almost always involves excruciatingly difficult decisions. Under Carter these decisions were made too naïvely, and human rights policy was too simplistic and patronizing. But such phenomena as the death squads in El Salvador had to be coped with for the most practical of reasons.

For some time now the Reagan Administration seems to have understood this and has in fact used a great deal of influence to curb the squads' worst abuses. Without such progress, the election of President José Napoleón Duarte would have been impossible. This election was something of a turning point—and incidentally one that would not have occurred had the Administration followed the counsel of those congressmen who, since 1981, have sought to condition continued military aid to the Salvadoran government on the commencement of indiscriminate negotiations between the government and the guerrillas, which would have led to "power-sharing." The election had significant impact on foreign countries. In 1981, France and Mexico had issued a joint statement calling the Salvadoran rebels "a representative political force," which implicitly equated their legitimacy with that of the government; such a statement would hardly be issued today. Last July, on the occasion of Duarte's visit, the Bonn government resumed aid to El Salvador. An extremely useful move would be the repeal of the Helms Amendment, which bans U.S. aid to land reform in El Salvador.

It is painfully obvious that Duarte's position remains highly fragile. The slight improvement in the performance of the Salvadoran army may not last. The far right may yet succeed in sabotaging Duarte's regime, especially if he pursues his dialogue with the guerrilla leaders. Moreover it is far from clear what can come of this dialogue since, from the beginning, the guerrilla leadership has not been interested in the success of a moderate, reformist regime like Duarte's, but in revolution. There are signs that the guerrillas are flagging militarily, and that they are more than ever split into hostile factions. It is premature to hope that they will put down their arms, trusting in the government's security guarantees, and take part in elections. But that is in effect what happened in Venezuela in the late 1960s, as well as what is beginning to happen in Colombia today, and the prospect of a similar outcome in El Salvador is at least somewhat more plausible than it seemed a year ago.

The situation in Nicaragua is more complicated and less hopeful. In considering that situation one should, at the outset, discard a great deal of cant about nonintervention. President Anastasio Somoza was overthrown, at least in part, thanks to American intervention. The Sandinista regime is clearly supported from the outside with arms as well as thousands of Cuban, Soviet, East German and other East Bloc advisers who constitute a significant influence in a country of 2.9 million. The claim that the Sandinistas were forced into kicking out their democratic political partners and lining up with Cuba because of American hostility is plainly wrong. By January 1981, the Carter Administration had allotted to the Sandinista government $117 million in aid, the largest amount from any single country. In its first two years, the new government in Managua received five times more U.S. aid than Somoza received in his final two years. But it is now evident that the Sandinistas planned to build an enormous army (by Central American standards) long before the United States turned hostile.

Still, with all this conceded, it is not clear what the United States hopes to or can accomplish in Nicaragua. The choices for Washington are painfully limited. Much can be said in defense of aid to the counterrevolutionaries, or "contras." They are not simply mercenaries or holdovers from the Somoza National Guard, but a genuine anti-communist movement, and it is not absurd to call them freedom fighters. Yet there is no serious prospect that by themselves they could overthrow the Sandinista regime, much as that would be in the American national interest. But they have proved important as an instrument to make the regime more malleable; there is little evidence to support the opposite view, namely that they solidified the regime. By cutting off aid to the contras, Congress irresponsibly deprived the United States of an important bargaining counter.

Contadora can be useful, depending on how it is handled. The provisions of the original proposal are potentially farreaching. As applied to Nicaragua they could, in effect, amount to interference in the country's internal affairs, in order to change and democratize

481

the regime; and could, if pushed to their maximum, provide for the removal of Cuban and other foreign forces, prevent foreign bases, and eliminate arms assistance to other revolutionary forces elsewhere in the area.

But the problems are several. First, some of the language in the treaty drafts seen so far is slippery. Second, it is far from clear how effectively the provisions could be enforced. Third, barring special unilateral arrangements, the Contadora provisions could mean a cutoff of American military help to the Duarte regime and other democratic forces in Central America. A deal has been suggested whereby the Sandinistas promise to stop aiding the guerrillas in El Salvador in return for cessation of American support for the contras. In view of the congressional cutoff of funding for the contras, that may be academic; but at any rate it does not seem like a very advantageous deal for the United States. In general, the United States should continue working with Contadora, but press for foolproof enforcement and maximum interpretation of its provisions (including the rejection of the November Nicaraguan elections as legitimate). This may mean a lengthy delay, but America should not let itself be pressured into accepting a premature and incomplete agreement. Standing on principle and playing for time may not be the worst policy here. Obviously, the appearance in Nicaragua of sophisticated offensive weaponry could change the equation.

X

Ultimately, the most important foreign policy goal for Reagan II lies in domestic politics: to achieve at least some measure of consensus on foreign and defense issues, especially regarding the Soviet Union.

Unfortunately, the more or less bipartisan approach to foreign policy that prevailed from World War II till Korea—some would say till Vietnam—was neither typical nor natural. In a functioning democracy the major issues of how a country deals with other countries, how it copes with questions of war and peace, cannot for long be excluded from the political process. For these matters are close to a nation's sense of self, its perception of its values and its meaning. In most elections, including the last one, it is simply unrealistic to ask both sides to throw away a major weapon, namely the argument that the opposing side is wrongheaded about the world—naïve or villainous, weak or reckless. And this is not a matter of cynicism, or at least not primarily. The more sincere the disputants, the more implacable. Yet there are special moments—this may be one—when the normal partisan quarrel over foreign affairs can be muted if not suspended.

It will be very difficult, putting it mildly, to persuade the fervent ideologues in the Republican Party of this. They are riding high, and they see the election as a clear mandate for the hard-line Reagan and for their more extreme goals. Nor will the right wing necessarily hesitate to attack the President if it considers him too weak.[9] While victorious, President Reagan will also increasingly be a lame duck. Nevertheless, he remains a hero to a majority of Americans, and thus a huge asset to the party; the right-wingers will have to be careful not to go against him too blatantly. Besides, he benefits from what might be called the Nixon-China syndrome: his anti-communist credentials are so strong that the country at large would have a hard time accepting the notion that he had gone soft.

The experience of the first term has shown that extreme hard-line positions not only fail to work with the Russians, but fail to work in domestic politics as well. An analysis of preelection polls and the election returns themselves makes clear that voters liked Reagan's patriotism, his emphasis on American strength and even rearmament. Especially blue-collar workers liked his macho image. But at the same time, voters wanted far more serious effort in arms control and peaceful diplomacy. The fact that President Reagan moved in that direction in recent months neutralized the peace issue, which was one of Walter Mondale's big potential assets, and helped increase the Reagan landslide.

The race for 1988 has already begun. If the President wants to play to history, leaving a legacy of better relations with the Soviets, as well as gain a serious chance of another Republican victory in

1988, everything indicates that he must follow more or less centrist policies. The best hope for the Democrats would be a Republican candidate and a set of policies to revive the "warmonger" fear of the earlier Reagan days. Moreover, despite his huge victory, Reagan will have to deal with a Democratic majority in the House of Representatives, where the Republicans made only modest gains. And even if North Carolina's Senator Jesse Helms were to assume the chairmanship of the Senate Foreign Relations Committee, President Reagan would not have clear sailing for his policies in the Senate (in fact, he might occasionally need Democrats to protect him from Helms' more outrageous positions). Thus, for political reasons as well as for idealistic ones, Reagan has every incentive to reach out to the Democrats in search of consensus.

Would the Democrats have any incentive to meet him even halfway? There is a strong case that they do. They have learned that the peace issue is highly complicated. Just as Reagan had to move to the center, they did too. Although there was much emotional support for a nuclear freeze and for the notion of banning nuclear weapons from outer space, voters did not favor positions they suspected might mean unilateral U.S. concessions. And if Reagan II is at all successful in restarting arms control talks and in otherwise improving U.S.-Soviet relations, the Democrats will have very little to gain from the issue. They would either have to come in on the left of the Republicans or else follow a me-too line, both politically highly unattractive. Thus they would have considerable reason to ease the peace issue out of politics, concentrate their 1988 strategy on the economy, and earn at least some of the credit that would derive from bipartisanship.

The Democrats would have to disown the quasi-isolationist and quasi-pacifist positions of many liberals (which Walter Mondale did only partly toward the end of the campaign). Similarly, Reagan would have to continue distancing himself from the far right. As the preceding pages suggest, there is a lot of room for him to do that without in any real sense "going soft." He can argue with reason that he is now able to negotiate from strength. A tough but realistic position on arms control may well win bipartisan approval. (A formally constituted, bipartisan body to deal with Soviet policy, which has been proposed, sounds excessively bureaucratic, but if it is necessary to get Congress involved, it should be tried.)

Agreement might be harder on issues like Central America and the military budget. But among the things Reagan could safely concede would be some further reductions in the defense budget combined with overall reform of the armed forces. Defense expenditures growing at a somewhat slower but sustainable rate backed by bipartisan consensus would be far more impressive to the Soviets than higher defense expenditures, which are probably not sustainable and at the mercy of congressional or partisan politics. One of the greatest boons to the Soviets over the years has been American inconsistency and the chance of playing Democrats off against Republicans. To avoid this and to achieve at least partial consensus would be worth a great deal.

HENRY A. GRUNWALD is Editor-in-Chief, Time Incorporated.

1   See Robert W. Tucker, "The Nuclear Debate," Foreign Affairs, Fall 1984.

2   See James A. Thomson, "After Two Tracks: Integrating START and INF," The Washington Quarterly, Spring 1984.

3   See Strobe Talbott, Deadly Gambits, New York: Alfred A. Knopf, 1984.

4   Time, March 5, 1984.

5   Address to the Time Conference on the Atlantic Alliance, April 1983, Department of State Bulletin, August 1983.

6   See Secretary of Defense Caspar W. Weinberger, Report on Allied Contributions to the Common Defense, Department of Defense, March 1984.

7   Robert W. Tucker, "Our Obsolete Middle East Policy," Commentary, May 1983.

8   Richard W. Murphy, "The Response from the United States to Current Political Developments in the Middle East," American-Arab Affairs, Spring 1984.

9   See Norman Podhoretz, "Appeasement by Any Other Name," Commentary, July 1983.

The First Term

From Carter to Reagan

Coral Bell   AMERICA AND THE WORLD 1984

Jimmy Carter with Ronald Reagan.

Analysts of President Reagan's reelection landslide have made much of the point that it was not necessarily a mandate for tougher policies: the voters' endorsement should be seen as primarily an enthusiastic expression of hope for continuance of the state of economic well-being and patriotic euphoria in which Americans, by and large, found themselves in late 1984. Be that as it may, it does seem quite clear by contrast that four years earlier Jimmy Carter lost votes on foreign policy issues. If Washington's relations with the outside world are going well, they may not be a decisive vote-getter, but the sense that they have gone badly can be a decisive vote-loser. Nothing fails like failure.

In my view, however, the two successive foreign policies have differed more in the images they have created at home and abroad than in their substance. Furthermore, in Mr. Reagan's case, ironically and surprisingly, words have proved an effective substitute for deeds in much of international politics, and maybe even of defense policy.

There is, of course, a difference between "operational" and "declaratory" policies and the signals both send to the outside world. The distinction was well traced in the pages of Foreign Affairs by Ambassador Paul Nitze in January 1956. Between what a government actually does and what it says or implies are its objectives and intentions lies some degree of divergence, sometimes a small gap, sometimes more of a chasm. These divergences do not mean that declaratory policy can be simply dismissed as bluff or hypocrisy. Nor are such differences always to be deplored, since they make possible a degree of flexibility. The French have a saying, "The soup is never eaten as hot as it is cooked." We might say that the hot soup of declaratory policy, as it emerges from the kitchen of the ideological cooks who prepare it, is always cooled a little by pragmatism before it is served up in the real world, which seldom matches the world of the ideologists' wishes.

While operational signals first require actual decisions by the Administration (in major cases by the President himself), declaratory signals emanate from a variety of sources, some entirely nonofficial. Presidential rhetoric provides one source of declaratory signaling, of course—during Ronald Reagan's years an important one. But another source is the spoken and written words of people who come into office with the President, as distinct from the permanent bureaucracy.

The outside world makes its assessments of the international stance of any given administration from the mix of signals it receives from all U.S. sources, weighing operational against declaratory. In Moscow there is an entire learned institute to interpret these signals, and every foreign office has an "American desk" trying to do much the same thing in smaller ways. Some of Washington's troubles with

Western allies during recent years, incidentally, have arisen from the diversity of sources of signals. London, Paris and Bonn are not disconcerted by changes of America's chief decision-maker; they change their own prime ministers and presidents and chancellors with reasonable regularity. But there is no precise equivalent in those capitals to the arrival of the new presidential entourage of policymakers; their own policymakers are well-entrenched permanent officials. Moreover, the Reagan circle tended to seem more "Reaganite" than the President himself, just as the Carter men had seemed more "Carterite" than that President. This is not surprising, since those who have been in electoral politics for many years (as tends to be the case for the persons who actually secure the nominations) have usually had the sharpest edges of their ideological stances blunted by the rough and tumble of political life.

The obvious differences in political philosophy between Presidents Carter and Reagan camouflage some basic points of distinct similarity. Each perceived and presented the conflicts of international politics in largely moral terms. Both implied that the moral assumptions of American foreign policy are not only important in themselves, but provide useful weapons in the American diplomatic armory. And both adhered to the notion of American "exceptionalism": U.S. society as the "shining city on a hill," its values a beacon for all the world.

In all that, both Presidents are heirs to a long-standing American tradition. Moralism and legalism have been central strands in American diplomacy from the earliest years of America's emerging consciousness of the United States as a power in a world of powers. To some analysts those strands have seemed the source of the disasters of U.S. policy making; to others the source of its major accomplishments. To the outsider both points of view have evidence to back them up. Some major disasters (like the involvement in Vietnam) and some major successes (like the process of European recovery stemming from the Marshall Plan, or the Japan Peace Treaty) were rooted in both strategic calculation and moral feeling among the policymakers of the time.

Though it may seem a little cynical to say so, the real differences do not seem to have been in either quantity or content of the moral assumptions. The basic point, at least on the evidence of the turn-about of American sentiments, seems to be that moral feeling is unlikely to "stay the course" when the strategic calculations that go with it prove unsound. The process of disenchantment, once it starts (as with Vietnam in 1967–68), sweeps away the original moral assumptions that went into policy. Thus the moral components that go into policymaking have to be judged not only on their own merits but on whether they conduce to realism in the strategic assessments that go with them.

II

Declaratory signals may sometimes look, at first glance, as if they were operational. The Reagan defense budget, for example, may be considered a strong declaratory signal—a statement of intent about the future balance of forces—rather than a transformation of the existing balance of the 1980s. The almost universal popular impression is that President Reagan has achieved—not merely proposed—an unprecedented rate of increase in U.S. military muscle. But I would argue that since the image of U.S. military weakness was created chiefly by words (mostly from the Reagan camp from the Republican nomination fight of 1976 onwards) it is logical that more words from the same sources should have been effective in readjusting that somewhat distorted image to reflect the reality of effective (though asymmetrical) superpower parity.

President Carter also made potent use of words, but it would be quite unfair to attribute all the troubles of U.S. foreign policy in the four Carter years to his own declaratory signals. Even without such signals, an adversary assessment in Moscow or elsewhere could reasonably have perceived a window of low-risk, low-cost opportunities. The general signals from American society as a whole, and from the liberal foreign policy establishment in particular, had been conveying a message of dwindling opposition to other countries' adventurism ever since 1975. National battle-fatigue, progressively increasing from 1968 and overwhelming by 1975, made the foreign policy mood of the early Carter years inevitable, and impossible to conceal from adversary policymakers. Even before Carter, in fact, Congress had sent the world a very loud declaratory signal in the Angolan resolutions of 1975–76 that the American political mood would be enough to block any operational policy of a tough-minded sort for the immediate future, even though the Administration may have wanted it. In that political mood of 1976, part of Jimmy Carter's appeal was the moral reassurance he provided during a time when American values and traditions were still under heavy attack at home and abroad. He encapsulated in his political image traces of an earlier, more innocent America and of small-town values.

To stand for virtue reasserted is probably always an asset in domestic politics. In international politics, however, a reputation for conspicuous virtue is likely to be construed as meaning that the new man is naïve. The saying "nice guys finish last" originated in U.S. sporting circles, but a rather similar estimate is implicit in the conventional wisdom of diplomats. And that was an image that Carter could hardly escape, given his status as a Christian fundamentalist, a Sunday school teacher, and particularly his espousal of Wilsonian values in world affairs.

Woodrow Wilson is still, no doubt, a hero to many Americans. But that is not really so in the outside world, except among a few remaining left-liberal and Third World optimists. In the Soviet Union, Wilson is remembered for the interventions of 1918 and as the standard-bearer of a theory of international politics competitive with Lenin's. In the chancelleries of Europe his name tends to be associated with high-minded ineffectiveness, failure to get the United States to take on the responsibilities of membership in the League of Nations, and unrealistic insistence on introducing notions of national self-determination in areas where they were bound to disrupt the chances of viable settlements. The hearts of European policymakers tend to sink at the thought of Wilsonian preachings from the White House. President Carter's version of moral rectitude in international politics was centered on human rights rather than national self-determination, but the human rights concept was even more disruptive to some of America's allies in the late 1970s (such as Iran) than the notion of self-determination had been for some of America's European allies in Wilson's time.

In fact, the case of Iran seems to indicate that well-amplified U.S. declaratory signals can begin to erode a fragile personal autocracy even before their author is in power. According to various observers, including Sir Anthony Parsons, who was British ambassador in Teheran at the time, the Shah's self-confidence began to crumble from the time of the Carter election campaign, and this damage does not appear to have been retrieved even by the considerable support in actual operational terms he received during the early Carter years.

III

The first four Reagan years bore an almost eerie similarity to the years 1949 to 1954, when the concept of "negotiation from strength" had a previous airing. In 1949, as in 1979, serious and respectable analysts were seeing a phase of major danger about five years ahead, with a "window of vulnerability" developing, because of a perceived major change in the underlying strategic balance. In 1949 the change was a true strategic milestone: the first Soviet atomic test. Along with the additional jolt of the Korean War, the West embarked on a major countervailing reaction: an ambitious NATO arms buildup, with U.S. defense expenditures reaching more than 14 percent of GNP by 1953 (twice the rate of the Reagan years). Then, as now, a technological "quick fix" to restore the original Western advantage glimmered in the minds of policymakers. Then it was the replacement of fission weapons by fusion; now it is the Strategic Defensive Initiative (SDI) or "Star Wars" image.

A powerful sense of déjà vu hung over the early 1980s for anyone who was once preoccupied with the early 1950s. Andrei A. Gromyko (the only major policymaker at a more or less similar level of influence in both patches of history) ought to be particularly haunted by it, because then, as now, there was a long drawn-out Soviet succession crisis which affected his personal fortunes. Then the succession was to Stalin, now the succession is still really to Brezhnev. Secretary of State John Foster Dulles then, like President Reagan until mid-1984, was given to combative but not always convincing declaratory signals, for instance, the doctrine of "massive and instant retaliation" in 1954.

Robert Murphy, one of Dulles' chief aides in that earlier phase of "negotiation from strength," once said that some of his master's signals had to be taken with "a whole warehouse full of salt." The question remains whether that level of skepticism can be retrospectively justified for the Reagan years. But we must start with a point whose importance is seldom conceded in European analyses, or liberal Democratic ones. Despite the general souring of relations between Washington and Moscow during the Reagan first term, there was not in fact a serious adversary crisis between the superpowers in that period.

A serious crisis between the United States and the Soviet Union has to be defined as one that produces not merely an exchange of insults but a measurably increased risk of actual hostilities. By that criterion, no such crisis can be discerned. The nearest approach, perhaps, was the shooting down of the Korean airliner in September 1983. Commentators who should have known better invoked the memory of Sarajevo, but the very evocation of that flashpoint makes it clear how remote the two great adversaries of the contemporary world were from that brink of an earlier era. This is reassuring, for it means that the crisis-management techniques and other factors which have built some stability into the central balance of power over the past 40 years have remained workable, even after several years of robust and continuing asperities between the superpowers.

To say this is not, of course, to deny that relations between Moscow and Washington by 1983 were at their lowest point since the death of Stalin 30 years earlier. One may fully assent to that proposition, and agree also that the situation had disastrous consequences for some areas of international life (especially the effort toward arms control), and yet still hold that the basic mechanisms for preserving the peace, such as they are, do not appear to have been much impaired. In fact, perhaps the contrary.

The many crises which were already on stream before January 1981 have not been visibly mitigated, and some have probably been marginally worsened. Poland, Afghanistan, the Persian Gulf war, the Middle East, Central America and the Caribbean, southern Africa, Vietnam and Kampuchea—all bear their normal tides of human misery along the accustomed pathways. I am not proposing an unduly rosy view of international politics during these past four years, merely pointing out that all was actually quiet, save on the rhetorical front, in the central confrontation between the superpower adversaries.

A potential explanation for this state of affairs can be found on the Soviet side of the confrontation. President Reagan's first term spanned the final decline of Leonid Brezhnev, the quasi interregnum as his death approached, the brief rule of Yuri Andropov, and the early months of another ailing veteran of the Politburo, Konstantin Chernenko. The decisions made in Moscow during those four years were those of men who (like their elderly though sprightly counterpart in Washington) all had good reasons to be conscious of their own mortality. Elderly, ailing men (ayatollahs may perhaps be excepted) are not usually given to bold adventures in foreign policy.

Not only were the decision-makers in Moscow declining in health during the Reagan first term; the Soviet policy machine had too many problems on its hands to take the sort of initiatives which might create more. Afghanistan and Poland, the needs of useful allies in Cuba, Vietnam, South Yemen, Syria and Ethiopia appear to have left few resources even for marginal and faltering allies in Angola and Mozambique, much less for taking on major new commitments. One might also argue that the domestic difficulties in the Soviet sphere of power, largely the results of economic failures, impose their own constraints. Or, less optimistically, one could say that there appears in Soviet policy an alternation, accidental or deliberate, of periods of "forward policy" (as 1976–79) and of relative pause while the gains of the forward policy are consolidated or digested. On that interpretation, the comparative quiet of the first Reagan term could be seen as a natural consequence of Soviet activism in the Carter years. President Reagan, in other words, enjoyed the good fortune of President Carter's bad fortune. If so, the relative immobilism of Soviet policy would have to be seen as a short-term phenomenon, not likely to persist for four more years.

Other possible explanations focus on the American side, and involve the distinction between operational and declaratory signals. The contrast between the Reagan and Carter years seems particularly illuminating. It owed more to contrasts in what the two Presidents and their respective entourages said than to any vast differences in what the two Administrations actually did.

Indeed, it is difficult to think of any major operational differences at all, save the sharper and more combative stance during the Reagan years in the Caribbean and Central America and a greater skepticism on arms control (though I would be inclined to put arms control proposals into the sphere of declaratory policy anyway). If one looks at the basic substance of the major operational policies— continuance of support for NATO; continuance of a wary cultivation of China; continuance of support for Israel, along with as much or as little cultivation of moderate Arab governments as is compatible with the Israeli connection; a continuing consciousness that the security importance of Japan outweighs any economic rivalries; continuing orientation to the Association of South East Asian Nations and to the Pacific, including ANZUS pact countries Australia and New Zealand; a continuing restraint of the basic hostility to Vietnam and Iran—on all these it is difficult to see more than marginal change.

Observing these continuities in operational policy and contrasting them with the differences in media images, and the differences also in the overall international fortunes of the two

Administrations, it becomes difficult to resist the inference that President Reagan's declaratory signals have been, on balance, useful to his purpose, not only electorally but internationally, and that the opposite was true for President Carter. Perhaps this outcome is as yet more clearly visible in Carter's case, when we remember that the mildness of his initial declaratory signals left him derisively (and unfairly) still seen at the end as a "terminal case of meekness," despite actual operational policies in some respects tougher than any so far in the Reagan period.

IV

To substantiate this assessment, let us look at a small cross-section of policy issues during the Reagan years and compare the declaratory and the operational signals that have been associated with them: China, Lebanon, the Persian Gulf, Poland, the Korean airliner, and the trans-European gas pipeline.

On China policy, the difference between the early declaratory signals that seemed to establish President Reagan as a dedicated friend of Taiwan and his actual operational policy, following precisely the path taken by Presidents Nixon and Carter to the Great Wall, is so obvious as hardly to need demonstrating.

Lebanon offers a more subtle and complex pattern, but one, to my judgment, of much the same meaning. Initially the Reagan Administration approach seemed to promise a discarding of earlier U.S. mediatory efforts in favor of something both more ambitious and more in line with stated neoconservative positions. In March 1981 Secretary of State Alexander Haig told the Senate Foreign Relations Committee that the objective was to "establish a consensus in the strategic regional sense among the states in the area," all the way from Pakistan to Israel and Egypt. But during the episode of Syrian antiaircraft missiles in April 1981, the Israeli bombing of the Baghdad reactor in June 1981, and the initial phases of the Israeli invasion of Lebanon in June 1982, the true operational message seemed to be that Washington was leaving the direction of events in the hands of the local actors.

Then there were the commitment of the marines in August 1982 and the Reagan Plan initiative in September: both ambitious declaratory signals of what was desired and desirable. But that did not really entail a new operational commitment, save in the diplomatic time and energy of U.S. envoy Philip Habib and other policymakers, mostly somewhat below the topmost level. Even the commitment of marines was at a token level. When President Eisenhower put marines into Lebanon in 1958, he used about 14,000 and left them there until the political objectives of the U.S. government had been secured, for the time, and for good or ill. The small detachment that President Reagan put in did not have a military purpose but a diplomatic and political one; it was a declaratory signal. When the marines suffered the casualties of October 1983, the President declared that the United States had "vital interests" in Lebanon. And Secretary of State George Shultz said, "We are in Lebanon because the outcome will affect our whole position in the Middle East. To ask why Lebanon is important is to ask why the Middle East is important." Again, strong declaratory signals.

A few months later, in February 1984, the marines were simply taken out. Congressional opposition, 259 deaths and the opening of election year were enough to make declared vital interests subject to reassessment. By late 1984 Lebanon had in effect been divided into Israeli and Syrian spheres of influence. The Maronite Christians, whose position of dominance in Lebanese internal politics had so long been sustained by the West (first the French and then the Americans), seemed to be losing ascendency to the Muslims. I offer no criticism of that outcome in itself; indeed, I think it may conduce to the chances of long-term stability. My point is merely the disparity between the declaratory signal: "This is interpreted by us as a vital interest," and the operational message that the United States can ultimately sail away. The Eisenhower Doctrine, by late 1984, appeared no longer operative in Lebanon. And to a chorus of surprise, Richard Murphy, the U.S. assistant secretary of state for Near East and South Asian affairs, could proclaim the Syrians to be no longer "Soviet puppets" as had been assumed so confidently earlier by Reagan spokesmen. On the contrary, the Syrians could be quite "helpful," Murphy told a congressional committee in July 1984, apparently endorsing their role in security and stability. In other words, the declaratory signal by then matched the operational signal: the Reagan Administration, far from being more ambitious in the area than its predecessors, was less ambitious and more prepared to leave local events in local hands.

In the Persian Gulf, one might argue similarly that the Carter Doctrine proved to be non-operative in President Reagan's time. Again the initial declaratory signals were strong: the transformation of the Rapid Deployment Force into the Central Command, and its fleshing-out with assigned forces such as carrier battle-groups and airborne divisions and fighter wings to a total of almost 300,000 men. But though a major war was in progress in the Gulf throughout the four years of the Reagan first term, there was hardly more than a hint of American intervention, even when tankers were subject to missile attacks. And when mines were laid along the tanker routes, the Western powers merely swept them up, with a bit of Soviet cooperation. On the evidence one would say that there has indeed been a tacit understanding between Washington and Moscow that each would limit its intervention in the area, on the assumption that the other continued to do so.

Again, no one in his or her right mind would complain. The point is just that there was in this case also a chasm, rather than a mere gap, between what the expectations had been back in 1980 of what the Reagan policy would be in the event of local hostilities threatening the Gulf oil routes to the West, and what actually happened. Or, more precisely, did not happen. For the world has in fact proved able to shrug off a major war, now into its fifth year, in which both sides have threatened or damaged oil installations or oil tankers in and around the Gulf. The oil glut persisted despite those events. OPEC has not only been unable to raise oil prices; it had by late 1984 seen the real price of oil fall, as cuts in production had to be made to keep the nominal price hovering somewhere near $29 per barrel. Present U.S. policy in the Gulf looks uncommonly like a tacit acquiescence in the Nixon Doctrine—that local powers must learn to fend for themselves in local crises.

In the Polish crisis, already under way when President Reagan came into office but reaching its decision-point only with the declaration of martial law in December 1981, the pattern hardly varied from earlier East European crises. The rhetoric was vehement, and the debate expressed U.S. outrage, but the actual sanctions against the Soviet Union were exceedingly mild. In particular, grain sales under existing agreements were not restricted; the United States continued to participate in the Helsinki review talks and the Geneva negotiations on arms control; a scheduled meeting between Haig and Gromyko was allowed to proceed. In fact, aside from the suspension of Aeroflot services and some restrictions on high technology purchases, it is difficult to see anything in U.S. operational policy that could have caused much wincing in Moscow. The unfortunate Poles themselves were rather more the true victims of any clampdown, suffering suspension of food aid and other economic blows for a time. Overall, American policy seemed a clear continuation of the tradition of well-signaled U.S. restraint in East European crises, which again dates right back to Dulles in 1953.

Washington's reactions to the shooting down of the Korean airliner in September 1983 were almost a carbon copy of the reactions to the declaration of martial law in Poland less than two years earlier. Again the level of rhetorical denunciation reached a new crescendo, again there were symbolic gestures of outrage—declaratory signals—like the denial of landing rights for Gromyko's plane when he sought to make his customary visit to the U.N. General Assembly. But again operational policies were not exactly severe. The grain deal was not rescinded. The Madrid meeting (essentially a continuance of the Helsinki Conference on Security and Cooperation in Europe which Reagan had so often denounced) was not only allowed to proceed but was chosen as a venue for a low-key meeting between Shultz and Gromyko. Shortly after the incident the arms control talks were suspended, but that was a Soviet declaratory signal against the Pershing II and cruise deployments, not Washington's choice.

The Soviet gas pipeline provides an example of a different sort of crisis, an intramural crisis of the NATO alliance. The declaratory signals were as usual fierce: talk of sanctions against America's closest and most necessary allies. And Washington did have a case; dependence by the West Europeans on Soviet sources for even a small segment of their energy supplies does not seem a good idea, nor does the provision of a new source of hard currency to the Soviet Union. But the Europeans also had a point: their vulnerability to Middle East oil producers is so great that their total level of risk is not more than marginally increased, if at all, by some shift of energy dependence to the Soviet Union. And the Russians need to be able to sell commodities to the West if they are to buy Western goods in return. The advantages of détente, economically but also in human terms, are too great for the European powers to be willing to relinquish them, especially not at the instance of an American Administration as little credited with understanding Europe as that of President Reagan. So the Europeans dug their toes in and ignored the Washington rhetoric. The gas now flows westward, and hard currency eastward; U.S. sanctions have not exactly been overwhelming. Again the contrast was between a tough initial declaratory policy and an ultimate operational policy of shrugging the whole thing off.

Arms control (or the lack of it) provides the most complex example of declaratory signals. Formal proposals were made, such as those presented in the Strategic Arms Reduction Talks and intermediate-range nuclear forces negotiations, but there were informal but perfectly clear indications, evident even before he came to office, that Mr. Reagan was unlikely to be an enthusiast for arms control treaties, judging by all he had said about Strategic Arms Limitation Talks (SALT I and SALT II). And then there were his defense proposals, clearly likely to amount to a major rearmament effort, mostly in advanced nuclear weapons.

It is not totally impossible to combine a belief that the United States by 1981 needed to upgrade its nuclear capacity in some fields vis-à-vis the Soviet Union with a belief that arms control treaties have merit in promoting the stability of the general strategic relationship with the Soviet Union. But to formulate policies giving weight to both objectives takes more specialized knowledge of the field than even his aides would claim for the President. Given the necessities of the arms buildup, the nature of some of the arms control appointments made, and the actual process of the negotiations, no one reasonably conversant with the issues could have been surprised at the outcome, or lack of outcome, of the formal initiatives in the first Reagan term. An air of "doing it for the record" (ingenious though the proposals were) hung over them from the first. Nevertheless, and despite Reagan's earlier denunciations of SALT II, that unratified treaty seems to have remained operational. And despite heavy hints that the Anti-Ballistic Missile Treaty might be discarded, it has so far been preserved.

V

These instances seem to add up to reasonably solid evidence that on the whole the diplomatic bark of the Reagan Administration has been considerably fiercer than its bite; that is, the pattern has been one of declaratory signals a good deal sharper than the operational ones. There is one obvious area where policy may be seen as an exception to that rule: Central America and the Caribbean. In Nicaragua, the Administration has tried to see what some very heavy-handed declaratory signaling could accomplish. Possibly that will prove a mere prelude to actual combat operations. But perhaps the general Reagan pattern will be maintained, that of declaratory signals fiercer than operational policies, at least as compared with Eisenhower's 1954 covert intervention in Guatemala, Kennedy's Bay of Pigs fiasco and Johnson's 1965 use of marines in the Dominican Republic.

The point of real interest, however, is not in which areas the Administration's bark has proved fiercer, but whether it can be argued with any plausibility that the fierceness of the signaling has precluded the necessity for action. Could it be that the rhetoric has raised assessments in Moscow of a higher level of risk in any kind of Soviet forward policy, making the "correlation of forces," the central concept in a Leninist analysis, look less favorable? Factors against adventurism stemming from the Soviet side were, in any case, strong. Even a slight extra weight of assessed risk, created by U.S. declaratory signals, might have proved substantial enough to tip the scales.

If we compare that putative payoff from one kind of declaratory policy with the misfortunes of the Carter period when an alternative kind of declaratory policy was in force (though the operational policies were not all that different), it seems to suggest a revised view about the general relationship between declaratory and operational signals—a view possibly applicable beyond this eight-year stretch of American experience.

Both sets of signals contribute to the expectations which the superpowers have of each other. Those expectations in turn are incorporated into the assessments of costs and risks which determine actual policy decisions on both sides of the central balance. But there is an important distinction between declaratory signals and operational signals that is particularly relevant to the present and the most recent past (the last two decades, more or less). The powers have for these 20 years or so had independent means of seeing for themselves, with the aid of satellites and such, what the capabilities of the other side are. So the ambiguities from which have traditionally arisen the miscalculations that precipitate crises, and sometimes wars, are no longer in the field of relative capabilities. They are almost exclusively now in the field of will; sometimes the will of a society as a whole, sometimes the will of its dominant political elite, but more often the will of the chief decision-maker and the small group of policymakers who immediately surround him.

And of that small group's will, in a situation of crisis, no satellite can provide direct observation. Operational policy does provide some signals bearing on will, of course, but in this particular field declaratory policy—speeches and such—provides the most direct guide to mood, and thus cannot safely be discounted by an adversary as a signal of will. In other words, declaratory signals may be a rather more important component of the total mix of signals now than they were before the age of surveillance (i.e., before about 1965) because the remaining ambiguities of the power balance are in the area of will rather than capacity, and declaratory signals tend to determine the image of will which each group of adversary decision-makers forms of the other.

In summary, a general war in the nuclear age is more likely to come from miscalculation than from deliberate challenge, and miscalculation, in the age of surveillance, is more likely to derive from uncertainties about the will of the chief decision-maker in the adversary camp than about the strategic capacities of the two systems. Khrushchev's apparent miscalculation about Kennedy offers a parallel: he is reported to have come away from their Vienna meeting in 1961 convinced that the young new President was "too liberal to fight." The genesis of the Cuban missile crisis, undoubtedly the most dangerous war-threatening crisis of the entire nuclear period, may in part be seen in that assessment. Carter was perhaps, because of his initial declaratory signals, in some danger of accidentally engendering that same kind of calculation or miscalculation; Reagan is clearly not. The preservation of peace rests, unfortunately, on nothing more substantial than the system of expectations in Moscow and Washington as to how the decision-makers in the other capital will react in the event of policies unacceptable to them. So one would not wish any kind of dangerous illusion to creep into those sets of expectations, such as the illusion that the other side had "no option but détente." Disillusion is no doubt very embittering. Illusion, however, is a great deal more dangerous in international politics. If either adversary has no option but détente, why should the other pay any price to preserve the détente? Soviet policy in the late 1970s might be taken as partial evidence of that mood, so Soviet reassessments, after the Reagan inauguration, were therefore useful rather than damaging to the basic mechanism that keeps the peace, in the sense of helping disperse any such illusion, and thus reducing the chance of some lethal miscalculation.

VI

It probably would be too optimistic to believe that noisy declaratory signals—i.e., hostile rhetoric—can become a substitute for more destructive international behavior. That would mean that the two superpowers had been sensible enough to adopt the technique of gorillas deep in their respective patches of jungle, loudly beating their respective chests—not as a prelude to fighting but because they want to avoid doing so—these declaratory signals being an established ritual for ensuring that their respective interests are not unacceptably encroached upon. Still, at least in the Western world and especially in the hands of a professional "communicator" like Ronald Reagan, rhetoric and gesture do seem to have been adequate substitutes for operational toughness with most of his supporters.

At this point, one final feature of the Reagan foreign policy, the popularity of the Grenada invasion, becomes illuminating. The wresting of that tiny island from the group of erratic left-wing thugs who had murdered the prime minister and half his cabinet seems to have been justifiably popular on the island itself, and I have no quarrel with the view that the upshot will enhance the Grenadians' chances for life, liberty and the pursuit of happiness. But in terms of geopolitical realities it was no big deal. The nationalist enthusiasm for the success of U.S. forces does seem rather on a par with proudly lauding a steamroller for its success in cracking a walnut.

What might, however, be said in approval of the Grenada operation was that as a declaratory signal of a dramatic sort it worked very well indeed. It focused the attention of the entire world, at least for a week or two, on that tiny patch of land, and on Washington's will (no one doubted the capability) to do something about developments it did not like in the Caribbean. The President even

Coral Bell

picked up a bonus when Suriname, having seen what happened in Grenada, sent its own Cubans packing. So, in effect, Mr. Reagan secured some inhibition on the growth of Cuban influence in two areas for the price of one, as well as a great deal of popularity with the U.S. electorate. He is an intuitive politician, and his intuitions were clearly on target in the decision to launch the Grenada operation at the time of the marine casualties in Lebanon.

Any such apparent payoffs from the Reagan policies must of course be balanced against costs. The chief debit, undoubtedly, in the eyes of most observers was the "opportunity cost" of the failure of arms control efforts. I would not myself rate this so high as many commentators, because I doubt that the early 1980s could have been a good period for arms control even if Jimmy Carter had been returned to power. The rows over the Pershing II and cruise missiles would have been the same; the ambivalence of the Europeans would have been the same; the felt need for NATO to stick to its 1979 resolution would have been the same. The rate of increase in military spending might perhaps have been somewhat less than President Reagan has secured, but in fact the Carter proposals on the MX (the most controversial item) were a great deal more extravagant both on numbers and basing than the program that the Reagan policymakers have apparently settled for, bowing to the recalcitrance of Congress: no vastly expensive mobile basing system, and probably less than half the numbers. Even attitudes on the nuclear freeze and the arms control "build-down" ideas might not have been all that different, since the freeze in particular is the sort of notion easier to go along with in opposition than in government.

Ought one then to say that the chief costs have been in the level of irritation at various Reagan declaratory signals among the policymakers of his major allies? But whether NATO has been seriously damaged—beyond what it might have been if Jimmy Carter had stayed in power—seems to me again quite doubtful. NATO conduces so solidly to the respective national interests of its European members, and is so well understood to do so by the foreign policy elites currently in power in those capitals (and even by their domestic political opposite numbers), that it will take a great deal more than harsh words about gas turbines to really shake the alliance. And though European policymakers and analysts sharpen their considerable wits on both varieties of American foreign policy moralism, on the whole they probably see the more real danger in President Carter's kind of Wilsonianism, especially in respect to the West's fragile relationship with the Third World. (The reverse is true, of course, of left-liberal critics and also of many Third World elites. They tend to respond sympathetically to the Wilsonian value-system, at least until they work out what national self-determination might imply in the cases of their own national minorities, and what any serious observance of human rights might do to their own authority structures.)

One might make a better case for true damage to U.S. credibility in the Middle East, with certainly a reduction of assumed U.S. capacity to control events, whether one is thinking of Lebanon or the Gulf. The Saudis have been irritated by the neglect of the Fahd Plan and by the U.S. debates over the supply of aircraft and missiles. Kuwait and Jordan have been irritated enough to purchase Soviet missiles. Morocco has contracted its improbable marriage of convenience with Libya, a government ranking almost equal with the Soviet Union in the demonology of American neoconservatives. Syria has undoubtedly advanced its status and sphere of influence, not only vis-à-vis Lebanon but also the United States, and even apparently Israel. And the Soviet Union, which had been successfully excluded from real (as against titular) power in Middle Eastern crises might be deemed to be back now, as the shadow behind Syria. All the Arab countries, even Egypt, have obviously been irritated by the strategic cooperation agreement with Israel.

Yet even assuming some loss of U.S. influence in the Middle East, I am not sure one ought to go on to assume reduced prospects of reasonable stability there. Actual settlements may be out of reach in the foreseeable future, but paradoxically, a more viable balance of conflicts seems to be emerging from the increased Syrian ascendancy, a rearrangement of alliances in the Arab world, and the Israelis' recognition of the limits of their capacity to operate in Lebanon. Again paradoxically, the strategic cooperation agreement would thus prove a prelude to some Israeli retreat, not an increase in dominance.

VII

Finally, we must look at what will probably seem an insuperable objection to any policy that allows a substantial gap between declaratory and operational signals: that the gap is bound to be noticed after a while and thus the credibility of future declaratory signals will be diminished, not only among allies and in the Middle East and Central America, but much more importantly, in Moscow. True, but what that means chiefly is that the Administration will need a new policy for the new term. In a wildly optimistic moment, one might hope that some such thought, along with the simple cynical electoral calculation, was among the reasons for the universally noticed Reagan change of rhetorical style in the last year of his first term. The true nature of that change, in the terms we have been using, was that the declaratory signals were softened to match the continuing mildness of the operational signals. Obviously, in the second term the original gap could easily be restored by a new sharpening of the declaratory signals, or the two could be kept in tandem, so to speak, by a sharpening of both.

It is, however, difficult to see what exactly would be the advantage of such a course, either for the President personally, or for his Republican Party backers, who will want to continue keeping Democrats out of the White House, and who will presumably continue to remember that the war issue was the one on which their man came closest to being vulnerable. Moreover, though Mr. Reagan was able to campaign in 1980 and during his first two or three years in office on the alleged deficiencies in his predecessor's defense policies, that will hardly do for his fifth and subsequent years in power. From 1985 any further talk of American strategic weakness will imply a reflection on his own past policies.

Thus it has become logical for the Administration instead to imply (as was done in the September 1984 U.N. speech) that the "strength-building" part of the negotiation-from-strength concept is already adequately under way. Therefore the phase of negotiation may be approaching. If the President can successfully make this transition, he might even manage to avoid the difficulty which defeated the policymakers who propounded the same strategy in the early 1950s: the difficulty of choosing the moment when the optimal chance of diplomatic progress has been reached. During that earlier historic phase, the best situation for the West in terms of potential negotiating leverage seems in retrospect to have been late 1953, with the Soviet decision-makers still in the phase of post-Stalin disarray, and while the impetus of the first NATO rearmament effort still looked strong. But that moment was lost, and by 1956 a new and rather incautious Soviet decision-maker, Nikita Khrushchev, was in control, and a new upswing in Soviet strategic capacity was under way.

That cycle does not have to be repeated, though all the conditions that make it likely already exist. The parallel with the early 1950s could be bleakly completed with a new rise in the level of danger as the Strategic Defense Initiative research begins bearing fruit, and perhaps an early 1990s crisis to parallel 1962.

That could happen, but sufficient intelligence applied to U.S. policy could prevent it. There is a case for assuming that on both sides of the balance a new phase of detente and arms control looks possible and desirable. On the Soviet side, the only interpretation which makes sense of Mr. Gromyko's decision to come calling before the election is that the decision-makers in Moscow had by September 1984 concluded that they were stuck with Mr. Reagan, little as they liked him, for another four years, and must pursue a damage-limiting strategy by trying to re-create enough détente to take the impetus out of the SDI research, if possible. Otherwise they would have to try and match it: a very expensive decision for their faltering economy. Once they had decided on that strategy, it became tactically logical to make the bid before the election, when the Administration's incentive to appear conciliatory was at its strongest.

It may be objected that while the Russians had nothing to lose by such an approach, President Reagan will be in severe danger of losing the ideological support of neoconservative "true believers" if he continues the softened declaratory signals of election year into the new term, and particularly if his operational signals indicate an actual move toward negotiation and détente. There are indications already of some loss of faith in the President among the sharper-tongued gurus of this group.

But in his second term President Reagan obviously has to worry about how he will stand with history rather than about the support of groups once tactically useful, but now certainly no longer necessary. There is reason to be skeptical that he is a typical neoconservative: he seems to lack the urbane sharpness, the pessimism and disillusion, and the worries about theoretical consistency that distinguish the more notable members of the intellectual clique who developed that doctrine. Many of them are people for whom Soviet policy, especially in the Middle East and Eastern Europe, has been a source of true emotional trauma, especially if they were liberals or radicals to begin with. That gives them some piercing insights, but it does not give them much in common with an easy-going, relaxed Californian of Irish Protestant background, with a sunny optimism of temperament and a rather short attention span. So there appears psychological scope for a parting of the ways.

If the President does lose the neoconservatives, or they him, it will make relations with his European allies a good deal easier. The thoroughly conservative foreign policy establishments of the European powers tend to regard American neoconservatives with a jaundiced eye, because the neoconservatives tend to picture the Europeans as hovering perpetually on the brink of Finlandization. That is seen as a very real insult by the European policymakers concerned, since it implies stupidity as well as cowardice.

Of course only the second term will determine which way the choices will go, but the auguries for renewed dialogue and perhaps even eventual gains in the field of arms control appeared promising as 1985 began. Soviet alarm over the potentialities in the Strategic Defense Initiative has already been heavily signaled, and appeared a major incentive for Moscow to try further shifts in tactical positions. The need to bring the deficit, and therefore the arms budget, under control had almost the same effect for Washington. The pressure of grassroots feeling about nuclear dangers and the discontents of their respective allies bore on both superpowers, though asymmetrically. A reason for arms control still better than any of those is, or should be, present in the minds of decision-makers on both sides: the pressing need for reinforced crisis stability at a time when the balance between offensive and defensive weaponry may be liable to sudden change. There are not many arms control objectives of equal urgency and importance for both sides, but crisis stability is one, and it could provide the guiding thread through the labyrinth their arms control negotiators are about to enter.

As a final paradox, one might note that despite the fact that Presidents Carter and Reagan were both foreign policy moralists in their respective ways, their contrasted experiences appear splendidly to exemplify Machiavelli's reflections on the roles of fortuna and virtu in political life. Fortune has certainly been with Mr. Reagan so far, in comparison to his recent predecessors. Unlike those who came to office in 1969, he had no disastrous war to wind up. Unlike Mr. Carter, he was not borne into office on a wave of liberal guilt and loss of U.S. self-confidence. On the contrary, he has benefited domestically and internationally by the swing of the pendulum back to nationalist buoyancy. As a patch of historical experience, it tends to reduce an analyst to reflections about the luck of the Irish. But from the point of view of the theory of foreign policy, the greater importance of declaratory over operational signals in an age of surveillance may be the idea to be noted.

CORAL BELL is Senior Research Fellow at Australian National University. She is the author of *The Diplomacy of Détente* and editor of the series *Agenda for the Eighties*.

The First Term

Four More Years: Diplomacy Restored?

Leslie H. Gelb
and Anthony Lake   AMERICA AND THE WORLD 1984

Reagan in Minneapolis, Minnesota, 1982.

Nineteen hundred and eighty-five begins as a year of promise in world affairs. The Soviet Union has returned to the bargaining table with the United States after a year's hiatus. The Middle East is relatively quiet despite the violence in Lebanon. The situation in Central America is unhappy but seemingly stalemated. Nowhere are American forces engaged in combat. No catastrophes hover over President Reagan as he begins his second term.

Nineteen hundred and eighty-four marked a passage of sorts for the Reagan Administration. After three years of stifling rhetoric and inaction, the White House and the State Department returned to more traditional diplomatic forms—moderate words that allow for compromise, and actual engagement with adversaries previously shunned. Of equal importance, President Reagan and Secretary of State Shultz assert that the Administration has restored America's position and power in the world, and that on this basis they are ready to pursue diplomatic ends.

As always, however, the picture is decidedly mixed. On the plus side, Mr. Reagan has generally succeeded in generating positive perceptions of the United States, of a nation on the move while its chief adversary is in decline. For the most part, nations are treating the Reagan Administration with respect and looking to it for leadership.

Uncertain still is how much the Administration has actually improved American military and economic power. Upon closer inspection, America's gains in these categories over the past four years may turn out to be less impressive and enduring than they are commonly portrayed. Likely, they fall far short of the position of strength the Administration may feel it requires in order to compel others to bend toward American desires. And on the negative side, the Administration will find that the world it now wants to engage presents a frozen diplomatic landscape. This is due in part to the lack of Reagan diplomatic accomplishments and in part just to the way the world is, filled with enduring animosities and real conflicts of interest, and with circumstances where leaders are in fact seldom strong enough to impose their wills or resolve their differences.

Of more immediate and practical concern is whether the Administration, its new promises notwithstanding, is sufficiently led, organized and disposed to the sustained attention and kinds of compromises necessary to the conduct of more traditional diplomacy. Mr. Reagan's staunchest conservative supporters are arguing that his first term was right on course, and that he should stick with it. Better no agreements with adversaries than agreements that compromise American principles and interests, they contend. Besides, they are saying, the United States is still inferior militarily to the Soviet Union, and the Administration is not yet ready to negotiate from strength.

But the conflicts of the world will not stop or stop compounding until the United States is prepared to resume the role of peacemaker. Mr. Reagan can count himself fortunate thus far that he has not faced the difficult choices of his predecessors. But he cannot count on such continued good fortune. For the kinds of achievements the President now insists are his most cherished goals, he will have to turn his back on some of his most basic professions of faith.

II

The Reagan philosophy, as the President explained it in 1980 and 1981, represented a radical departure from the foreign policies of the previous decade. Presidents Nixon, Ford and Carter had consistently, albeit in different ways, conducted foreign policies that were adjusting to the changed world. Each pursued an active diplomacy to compensate for the diffusion of international power that had become so evident by the late 1960s. Ronald Reagan reversed the logic: Washington's policies should not have to adjust to the world—a strong reassertive America could make the world adjust to Washington.

To understand how sharp the Reagan departure was, one must recall the evolution in American thinking about foreign policy during the 1960s. In the halcyon years of unequaled American power after World War II, the United States had essentially pursued policies of deterrence through the threat of force. Diplomacy with the Soviet Union was subordinate to simple deterrence. President Eisenhower was periodically intrigued by new diplomatic opportunities, but Secretary of State John Foster Dulles slowed the progression of such policies, and Eisenhower then ran out of time.

Presidents Kennedy and Johnson were more prepared to deal with the Soviets. There was some progress after the Cuban crisis, and a limited nuclear test ban treaty was achieved. But the impulse for diplomacy, either with Moscow or in troubled regions, was increasingly diverted by the demands of the Vietnam War. When Lyndon Johnson called on others to reason together with us, his audience was his opponents in Vietnam. He could not find a larger diplomatic stage on which to operate. Foreign policy had become Vietnam policy.

Yet throughout the 1960s, more and more analysts were finding in Vietnam a fundamental conceptual error in American foreign policy. It was time, they argued, for America to recognize that the world had changed. Our strength was newly limited, not by a loss of American will, but by a profusion of new nations and a diffusion of military as well as economic power. This called, they argued, for adjustments, both in defining a more careful hierarchy of our interests and in how we pursued them.

It was not only liberals who were thinking these thoughts. Henry Kissinger wrote in 1968:

For most of the postwar period, America enjoyed predominance in physical resources and political power. Now, like most other nations in history, we find that our most difficult task is how to apply limited means to the accomplishment of carefully defined ends. We can no longer overwhelm our problems; we must master them with imagination, understanding and patience.

In 1969, Richard Nixon well understood the point Kissinger had made. He proclaimed the end of the postwar era in international relations, and laid out a series of new policy directions in which a new emphasis on diplomacy would help compensate for a reduction in America's relative strength. No longer possessing a preponderance of power, the United States would maneuver within a sustained balance of power. And under President Nixon important diplomatic achievements were attained: in the Strategic Arms Limitation Talks (SALT I) agreements, in the opening to China, in the disengagement of Egyptian and Israeli forces in the Sinai.

President Nixon was struggling not only with changed international realities, but with basic changes in the domestic politics of foreign policy as well. Ever since World War II, the American public had insisted that its presidents' foreign policies successfully serve two goals: containing the spread of communism and Soviet influence, and keeping America at peace. Of course, the two goals were sometimes contradictory. But any politician who failed to promise both, and any president who could not produce both, was penalized at the polls.

Mr. Nixon found his way between the Charybdis of war and the Scylla of appeasement by winding down American participation in Vietnam while proclaiming policies of peace with honor. He was able to avoid reaction on the right to his recognition of a new era largely through his wars with the left. The attacks on him by the anti-war movement helped shield him from suspicions of softness. His tough rhetoric and emphasis on a sustained balance of power strengthened the shield.

Nevertheless, when Mr. Nixon was gone and the war was over, hard-liners who found Henry Kissinger's policies of adjustment at best distasteful, and at worst un-American, went on the attack. To accommodate either our goals or our diplomacy to a changed world would become a self-fulfilling admission of weakness, they argued. The attack on Mr. Kissinger within both the Democratic and Republican parties focused on his historical pessimism and his acceptance of the view that we could not order the world in the way we wished. For the Democrats, it was his lack of concern about the internal policies of other governments and their human rights abuses. For conservative Republicans, it was his willingness to negotiate and thus compromise with the Soviet Union: if we are all that is good and they are all that is evil, then to compromise with the devil is sin. So in 1975 and 1976, Gerald Ford bent to the winds from his right in the Republican Party, abandoned the pursuit of a SALT II agreement and banished the word "détente" from his Administration's lexicon. Policies of adjustment were put on hold. Serious diplomacy would wait.

Jimmy Carter came to office presenting a picture of the world in 1977 similar to that described by Richard Nixon in 1970. The challenge for American foreign policy was to adapt to and shape processes of change abroad. Certainly, there was more emphasis on human rights and less on containment than there had been with President Nixon; more effort at achieving regional solutions to

regional problems and less on constraining the Soviets through détente and linkages. But like Nixon and Kissinger, Carter and Secretary of State Cyrus Vance pursued policies of diplomatic
engagement. And, again, important results were achieved: in the
Camp David accords, in normalization of relations with the People's Republic of China, in the negotiation of a SALT II agreement, in the Panama Canal treaties and in helping to achieve a
settlement in Zimbabwe.

Unlike Richard Nixon, Jimmy Carter left office with his foreign
policies largely discredited. Part of the reason was his failure ever
to fashion a coherent policy toward the Soviet Union. Another was
the way in which the Iran hostage crisis came to symbolize what
was perceived as a weak presidency. It laid bare the limitations to
American power, and the American public did not like it. Perhaps
most important was a signal difference from the Nixon approach:
while the former President had presented policies of adjustment in
the rhetoric of national power, Mr. Carter presented them in the
rhetoric of adjustment (except when it came to human rights). It
was honest, but it alarmed both the American public and our allies.
The containment imperative had been violated. In 1980, when his
rhetoric shifted, his anti-Soviet tough line was more confusing
than convincing.

As the pain of Vietnam receded in the national memory, Americans were ready for a return to the security of the 1950s. Ronald
Reagan promised to achieve this. His was not the rhetoric of diplomacy; it was the rhetoric of supremacy, and it tended to exclude
diplomacy.

III

President Reagan painted a picture of the world which was both
more dangerous but also potentially much easier to shape to our
interests and in our image than the world described by Presidents
Carter and Nixon. The Soviets were more menacing than
Mr. Carter had said they were, at least before 1980. But in the Reagan
view we did not face a jumble of complex and intractable problems

Leslie H. Gelb and Anthony Lake

which required an American foreign policy of maneuver and adjustment. The problem was not a complex world; it was simply the will of America. Restore our spirit and our strength, and we could reverse the adverse growth of Soviet military power over the past decade. Restore America and there could be be a restoration of the "postwar era" whose obituary President Nixon had written in 1970.

From this followed a more expansive definition of American interests. If a failure to stand up to the Soviets anywhere would encourage further aggression, and if the Soviets were the source of radical challenges to the status quo almost anywhere in the world, then every trouble spot posed a vital threat to American interests. This required, in turn, a massive military buildup. As Robert Osgood wrote in a Foreign Affairs review of President Reagan's first year:

The overriding goal of the Administration's foreign policy was to make American and Western power commensurate to the support of greatly extended global security interests and commitments. There was no disposition to define interests more selectively and no expectation of anything but an intensified Soviet threat to those interests. Hence, the emphasis on closing the gap between interests and power would be placed on augmenting countervailing military strength. . . .

With new military strength would come two kinds of solutions to our foreign challenges. First, we could negotiate with the Soviet Union from a position of strength. The threat of an arms race which the Soviets could not hope to win would force Moscow to negotiate arms control agreements on terms less generous than those conceded by American negotiators in the SALT I and SALT II agreements.

In addition, new American military strength would also deter Soviet trouble-making around the world. Nixon's "era of negotiation" would be replaced by an era of American might. Secretary of State Alexander Haig, speaking in 1981, described the "four pillars" of the President's foreign policy: restoration of America's economic and military strength; reinvigorated alliances; progress in the developing countries; and a relationship with the Soviets "marked by greater Soviet restraint and greater Soviet reciprocity." Unlike such listings of goals and means by the Nixon and Carter Administrations, there was no separate pillar for policies of diplomatic engagement in the world's conflicts. President Reagan would create an era of deterrence without diplomacy.

This was Mr. Reagan's vision. It worked well in domestic politics, in allied and friendly capitals and, to a degree, with the Soviets as well.

The American public responded well to his pictures of the world, not only during the campaign but throughout his first term. Some have interpreted this as a sign that the American people are therefore prepared for foreign policies of reassertion—that the Vietnam analogy is dying, that the containment imperative is once again dominating the peace imperative in our political debates. It is more complicated than that.

President Reagan was not promising, in either the 1980 or 1984 campaigns, policies of global activism, a return to the impulse of engagement of a John F. Kennedy. He was promising a foreign policy that perfectly matched what seemed to be the national mood: a new, comfortable nationalism which was not so much assertive as narcissistic; a mood, in Stanley Hoffmann's phrase, of "happy self-contemplation." After the nightmare of Vietnam and the humiliation of the hostages in Iran, Americans wanted desperately to feel that they were again "Number One." They thrilled to the happy notion of national supremacy and the glowing terms in which the President promised it. But they did not want that supremacy to come at a serious cost. Mr. Reagan did not suggest that we bear more burdens or pay much of a price—except in defense spending. If we were economically and militarily strong, the world would be better behaved and we need not become involved in actual conflicts.

Thus one explains a contradiction in the polling data from 1984: the voters approved of Reagan's overall foreign policy leadership— but disagreed with him on the substance of such paramount issues as arms control, Central America and defense spending, as opposed to strong defenses. They applauded his rhetoric, for it promised "peace through strength," a kind of cost-free containment. They responded to the images and slogans he and his supporters used: "Go for the Gold," America as Number One. They loved the 1984 Olympics in Los Angeles. They were concerned, however, with the prospect of military entanglements in Central America or the deficits that paid for the defenses. It was a kind of cinematic nationalism; you could find in the images of supremacy an escape from reality.

Through his first term, the President was able to avoid a reckoning. As William Schneider has shown, he was a decisive leader in the terms of this national mood. The invasion of Grenada was a triple success: the military objective was achieved; it was over quickly; and the costs were small. But the President, Schneider argues, also exercised popular leadership in Lebanon. He acted decisively to get out once the costs of his policy became real. Schneider writes:

During the Vietnam trauma, pollsters regularly asked Americans if they preferred a "hawkish" or a "dovish" policy in Southeast Asia. The answer they got over and over was, "We should win or get out." What people didn't want was endless, pointless, escalating involvement. Well, what did Reagan do as President? In Grenada we won. In Lebanon we got out. So much for the Vietnam syndrome.

The President's rhetoric and emphasis on rearmament was welcomed not only at home, but among leadership groups in allied nations. Like the American public, they recoiled when the President went too far in attacking the Soviets, or showed a proclivity for unilateral action, or seemed insouciant about nuclear war, or pursued policies which implied future costs and dangers. And certainly there were major strains created by Washington's proclivity for unilateral action.

But European leaders responded positively to his vision of America reborn and his sense of optimism about the future. They admired the American economic progress of 1983–84 and welcomed accelerated U.S. defense spending. They found in the style of his leadership echoes of "America the Liberator." It was a rerun not only of the protected days of the immediate postwar era; it recalled the American strength of World War II itself. Thus the success of the imagery of Reagan's celebration in Normandy of the 40th anniversary of D-Day.

The Reagan approach may also have succeeded, in one sense, with the Soviets. While diplomacy between Washington and Moscow was rocky throughout his first term, as it had been in Jimmy Carter's last year, it may be that the Soviets were deterred from foreign adventures by Reagan's posture, although such a proposition is impossible to prove. The proportions of image and real intention mixed into Reagan's posture of toughness can be debated, but even images matter. There was a new appearance of American strength, and, as John F. Kennedy once noted, appearances contribute to reality. Without access to the councils of the Kremlin, there is no way of knowing whether America redux actually deterred contemplated Soviet moves. It is a fact, however, that Mr. Reagan was right when he said there had been no new Afghanistans on his first watch.

Thus, by 1984, there was an impression, at home and abroad, of a renewed America. And so, at the beginning of the year, President Reagan and Secretary Shultz could begin to speak of new policies of diplomatic engagement. It was good politics, but it also flowed from the initial premise of 1980: first restore America, and then move on to bargain. Addressing the American Legion on February 24, 1984, the President declared that the two "essential preconditions of a strengthened and purposeful foreign policy" had now been met: the restoration of a strong domestic economy and the "rebuilding of our foundation of our military strength." Mr. Shultz, in a speech before the Trilateral Commission on April 3, noted that: "We have rebuilt our strength so that we can defend our interests and dissuade others from violence." He went on to say: "A foreign policy worthy of America must not be a policy of isolationism or guilt but a commitment to active engagement."

In that speech and elsewhere, Secretary Shultz described the world and American diplomacy in terms much different from the traditional Reagan rhetoric. He told the Trilateral Commission that:

> ... evolution of the international system was bound to erode the predominant position the United States enjoyed immediately after World War II. But it seems to me that in this disorderly and even dangerous new world, the loss of American predominance puts an even greater premium on consistency, determination and coherence in the conduct of our foreign policy.

This statement could well have been made by senior officials in the previous three Administrations.

In some respects, Mr. Shultz went even further than his predecessors in opening the door to a stable arms control process with Moscow. To a Los Angeles audience on October 18, he announced that the Administration would not link progress in arms control to Soviet good behavior around the world. The arms control process and arms control agreements were good in themselves and should not be jeopardized, as they had been before, by differences in other areas. This went beyond the statements of Secretary of State Vance, who argued against a policy of linkage but acknowledged that linkage existed as a practical matter in American politics. That is, even if the Carter Administration wanted to keep arms control immune from Soviet conduct, political pressures would not allow it. The Shultz speech was a repudiation of the Nixon-Kissinger policy of explicit linkage, which maintained, in effect, that arms control was at least in part a reward for Soviet good behavior.

Despite the encouraging public statements, however, there were two levels of reality at the end of the first Reagan term. On one level, there were improved atmospherics, a sense that the strategic tide was now moving in an American direction, a positive response from foreign allies and perhaps greater caution on the part of adversaries—and the promise of a new American approach in the second term. On the other and more tangible level, there were three problems to be addressed: the actual state of the American military and economy; continued conflict on the Administration's bureaucratic battleground; and the frozen diplomatic landscape.

IV

Has there actually been a dramatic improvement in America's military and economic position? The real military picture is cloudy. There is little question that America is stronger and has been getting stronger militarily for the last eight years, with the expenditure of well over a trillion dollars. The Reagan Administration itself has spent about $800 billion in four years. But military experts hotly debate whether the country has gotten its money's worth. One must wonder whether key members of the Administration, though they publicly claim great improvement, are all that confident that this is so.

The Administration has substantially increased spending on the readiness of American forces. Yet, by standard measures, the improvement is slight or nil. The percentage of combat units judged to be in the top two categories of readiness has gone up by only one percentage point in the last four years. Progress shows up only in two areas: overall quality of personnel (attributed mainly to the economic recession and pay increases) and naval aircraft readiness. The number of main-line tactical aircraft for the air force, navy and marines has grown by only three percent, from 2,996 to 3,092. Main-force navy ships have gone from 479 to 524, but the air force actually ordered more tactical aircraft during the Carter years than under Reagan. To be sure, there is a much higher percentage of modernized aircraft, for example, F-15s replacing the older F-4s. And overall, the conventional forces are more capable. But it is hard to argue that there has been a good total return on the large expenditures in readiness.

It is harder still to argue that, if there was a strategic nuclear window of vulnerability in the first place, the Administration has done anything to close it. Initially, it was a cardinal tenet of the Administration that the most pressing military problem for Washington was to do something about the Soviet ability to launch a few hundred of its big land-based missiles and destroy virtually all of the American land-based nuclear forces. But, in four years, the Administration has done nothing to reduce that theoretical vulnerability. The new MX missile, whose future is in doubt, is to be based in "vulnerable" silos and not in a survivable mode. The small, mobile Midgetman missile is still years from deployment. The Administration is interested in a ballistic missile defense system to protect the land-based missiles, but that is even further in the future—leaving aside questions of feasibility, cost and the impact on arms control.

The President's Commission on Strategic Forces, also known by the name of its chairman, retired Lieutenant General Brent Scowcroft, did the White House the favor of closing the theoretical window of vulnerability by a simple proclamation. The commission stated that for all practical purposes it is not now open. Senior Administration officials have stopped talking publicly about this infamous window, and that in itself is a good sign. But the idea dies hard and still lives on in some quarters of the Administration.

Nor can the Administration credibly claim that the overall gap it said existed in strategic nuclear capabilities has been narrowed. For the first time, the United States is now behind the Soviet Union in the total number of ballistic missile warheads, by about 7,000 to 8,000. The United States is also further behind the Soviet Union in gross megatonnage and missile throw-weight with the decisions to retire the aging Titan missiles and older B-52 bombers. Not that we believe that these particular calculations are of central consequence, given the tremendous overall nuclear capabilities possessed by both sides and the fact that the United States continues to lead in the total number of deliverable strategic warheads and bombs. But there are many in the Administration who have maintained over the years that the numbers concerning heavy missiles and throw-weight, and the attendant perceptions of relative Soviet-American strength, are of critical importance.

Perhaps Administration leaders are calmer about these numbers today in the knowledge of future American capabilities. Perhaps they think that the Trident submarines and Trident II missiles coming on line, the new force of cruise missiles now being deployed, and American superiority in the technology of antisatellite and space-based weaponry are sufficient to correct the presumed imbalances. Perhaps they draw the necessary comfort and confidence from the trends. But that is not reflected in the private statements of many officials as new Soviet strategic programs plunge ahead as well.

The balance of nuclear forces in Europe is also a subject of mixed feelings. On the one hand, the Administration can take justifiable pride in having held the alliance together to bring about the deployment of the Pershing IIs and ground-launched missiles. About 100 are now available in West Germany, Italy and Britain. Deployments scheduled in 1985 for Belgium and the Netherlands will be a problem. On the other hand, the Soviet Union has more than doubled its lead in modern medium-range nuclear missiles since Mr. Reagan took office. The number of operational SS-20s now stands at 378 with 1,134 warheads, compared to 140 with three warheads each four years ago (and other SS-20 sites are under construction). Moscow has also increased the number of forward-deployed battlefield nuclear weapons. The Soviet Union now has more nuclear warheads of all types in Europe than the United States, some 8,000 to about 6,000. These numbers can mean much or little, depending on one's perspective on nuclear power, but they are unlikely to give real comfort to the Reagan team.

It is far from clear that the Administration is at peace with itself on these questions and on defense policy matters and the use of force generally. If anything, the disparity between commitments and capabilities has grown under this Administration, largely because commitments have been extended. In his annual posture statement to Congress in 1983, Secretary of Defense Caspar Weinberger stated that, "given the Soviets' capability to launch simultaneous attacks in the Persian Gulf, NATO, and the Pacific, our long-range goal is to be capable of defending all theaters simultaneously." Thus, instead of closing the gap between commitments and capabilities by cutting back on commitments, as did President

Nixon, President Reagan has expanded both commitments and capabilities—and the former faster than the latter.

After the elections, in late November 1984, Mr. Weinberger confused matters further in a speech to the National Press Club detailing the standards which should guide American military intervention. He said the territory or the issue should be "deemed vital to our national interest," without defining this in any way; that involvement must command public and congressional support, with clearly defined political and military objectives; and that the Administration must be determined in advance to win or not get involved at all. The Pentagon portrayed the speech as both an effort to sharply limit American military interventions and a rebuke to Secretary Shultz for being willing to use force too readily for fuzzy diplomatic ends. Mr. Shultz had spoken in September of the need to use force against terrorists and states sponsoring terrorism, even at the risk of innocent civilian casualties and further military involvement. In general, the pattern has been that Mr. Shultz and his State Department aides have been more willing to use military force, as in Lebanon and Grenada, than Mr. Weinberger and the Pentagon. It seems as if Secretary Weinberger believes that having more American arms will speak for itself, deter challenges and obviate the need to actually use force in the first place.

All of this tends to cast doubt on whether the Administration is in fact united behind Secretary Shultz's recent statements that the United States has succeeded in restoring the military balance and now will move forward to negotiate. There remains a powerful segment of the Administration which continues to argue that the United States is still behind the Soviet Union. Centered in, but by no means limited to, the Pentagon, this group fears that the combination of budget-cutting pressures plus the lure of arms control will erode support for necessary further large increases in military spending.

These budget-cutting pressures are the consequence of some hard economic truths. The abundant confidence the Reagan team had in the American economy throughout most of 1984 now seems generally in shorter supply, and with some reason, as 1985 begins. Beyond the domestic dilemma of how to reduce deficits while not raising taxes, there is the fact that the United States is becoming a debtor nation for the first time since World War I. Whether having foreigners invest more here than Americans do abroad will be helpful or harmful in the long pull is not known, and that uncertainty has caused considerable unease. Beyond that, the $130-billion trade deficit causes outright distress. Protectionist pressures, resisted by the Administration in the first term, will be harder to blunt now. More basic and distressing still is the growing realization in the Administration that deficits will not be conquered by higher and higher levels of economic growth. Administration leaders know they will be embroiled in a continuing struggle among themselves and with Congress over what to do about budget cuts and tax reforms. All of which means that Mr. Reagan will have to spend a lot of time once again on the economy, and that he will not have as much time as hoped to devote to foreign affairs or be able to act with quite the expected economic clout when he does.

V

These problems are exacerbated by another harsh reality: the President has apparently been unwilling or unable to create peace within his own government. Every administration has been torn by internal conflicts. Under every president, some high officials have opposed making deals with communists and some have always insisted on best bargains or nothing. Other high officials were willing to risk compromises with adversaries, communist or not, on the grounds that such risks were less painful and costly than the alternatives. It is unlikely that any administration could or should be free of such internal disputes. But from the Nixon Administration on, presidents were able to exercise the necessary leadership within their administrations to achieve realistic diplomatic agreements.

President Reagan has not done this. The problem is not that he faces divisions between the Department of Defense and Department of State or between the State Department and White House staff that are greater than in previous administrations. In fact, the philosophical divisions are far fewer in this Administration than in the Carter Administration: there was a greater distance to travel between Cyrus Vance and Zbigniew Brzezinski than there is between Mr. Shultz and Mr. Weinberger.

The problem, at least in part, is that the right wing in the Reagan Administration is further to the right and less willing to countenance compromise than the right in previous administrations. When it came down to it, National Security Adviser Brzezinski and his allies either actually favored or were willing to back SALT II, the Panama Canal treaties and the Camp David accords, to name a few. Mr. Weinberger and his allies have not been so flexible. When a powerful group in any administration is flatly against compromise, it is very difficult for a president to make concessions without substantial political vulnerability. But it can be done, if a president is in as strong a political position as is Mr. Reagan.

The problem is that the President has rarely chosen decisively, in particular situations, between contending factions. So, one week Lebanon is vital to American interests and the next, the marines are withdrawn. So, one day Moscow is told the Administration is prepared to be flexible and the next, Mr. Reagan decides against compromises at a cabinet meeting. So, at one meeting he orders compromises only to have the bureaucracy continuing to fight as if no decisions had been made.

Thus, on foreign policy, the Administration has been in almost perpetual disarray, or worse, profound internal stalemate. Mr. Reagan could have cut through this by removing the anti-diplomacy group. But he did not, and there is every reason to believe thus far that he will not in his second term. Perhaps these officials reflect his own true ideological beliefs, or perhaps he finds it impolitic to remove them.

Nor has the President established a steady middle path of his own, as Robert McFarlane, the national security adviser, has tended to recommend. Mr. McFarlane does not have that kind of clout in the White House and has not proven himself a match for the two departmental elephants. The President could have taken an active and intimate part in the internal debates and gained the necessary knowledge to impose his own position. But, again, he did not. He has not mastered the substantive issues, if his news conferences and news stories are to be taken as evidence. Whether he is disposed to do so now remains a central question. For without mastery, or at least a solid working knowledge, of foreign cultures and the intricacies of arms control issues, it is highly doubtful that this or any Administration would feel comfortable making compromises. In the absence of such intellectual control, the natural tendency is to put matters off, to refer the problems back down to the middle levels of the bureaucracy for further study, in search of elusive and magical consensus, while using comforting slogans and rhetoric as a substitute for substantive policy.

Policy statements by the Administration, to be sure, have become more or less consistently moderate during the past year, but everything else is seemingly unchanged. Nor is there appreciably less skepticism about the value and necessity of compromise if diplomacy is to produce agreements. In the upper echelons of the State Department, there may be more talk about using diplomacy to manage differences with other governments—but even here, the effort to resolve disputes is made more through rhetoric and highly visible diplomatic encounters with adversaries than through hard and politically risky compromise. Promises and prospects essentially come down to White House assurances that the President is determined to achieve diplomatic successes in his second term, especially in arms control, and now feels he is in a position to do so.

It is difficult to assay those assurances or how the President perceives his political circumstances. Does he believe the right wing of the Republican Party is now more powerful and independent of him than before? Will Republican conservatives in Congress be more or less cooperative? Does he think that freedom from running for reelection will permit him to become more philosophically pure or more pragmatic and independent of unwanted and narrow political pressures? These are critically important questions, but highly speculative ones.

VI

Less speculative is the frozen quality of the international diplomatic landscape which the President now surveys, as he considers new policies of diplomatic engagement and new efforts at arms control.

The diplomatic agenda contains four crucial problems: Central America and the Caribbean; the Middle East; southern Africa; and relations with the Soviet Union, including notably the achievement of "meaningful arms control." In each case the legacy of the past four years is one of no catastrophic failures but no concrete and positive diplomatic accomplishments.

In Central America and the Caribbean, the Administration in 1984 stepped up both diplomatic and military activities. Gone was any talk of going to "the source" in Cuba. Gone also was the earlier total opposition to talking with the Sandinistas and Salvadoran guerrillas. The United States began talking regularly to the Sandinistas. The Salvadoran government and the Salvadoran guerrillas started meeting face to face, at the initiative of Salvadoran President José Napoleón Duarte and, initially, against Administration wishes. The Contadora group had produced a draft treaty to settle matters between and within Nicaragua and El Salvador, but the Administration found its terms too vague and provisions for verification inadequate. The draft was shunted aside. There was, in sum, diplomatic communication throughout the region, but the parties to the various disputes seemed no closer to compromise than before. The real talking was still being done on the battlefield.

That may be the only place in the region where the Administration believes satisfactory outcomes are possible. Washington will not countenance any power-sharing arrangement between the Salvadoran government and the guerrillas. Nor is it likely to find any agreement made with the Sandinistas to be acceptable as long as the Sandinistas remain in power by virtue of that agreement. The prevailing view in the Administration still seems to be that, inevitably, left-wing revolutionaries will refuse to honor negotiated agreements—and by that time, the American people may not want to become reinvolved to stop them.

It would not be stretching what is known too far to say that the Administration's real aim is to unseat or substantially dilute Sandinista power in Nicaragua and to make the Salvadoran government sufficiently strong to eschew compromise. Some Administration officials argue that progress has been made toward these ends; the weight of expert opinion is otherwise. The indubitable fact is that the adversaries in the region are more heavily armed than ever, with still more weapons on the way. Increased fighting is the most likely prognosis for the coming year.

The American position and the prospects for negotiated settlements also dimmed in the Middle East, beginning with the virtual collapse of American policy in Lebanon in the first three months of 1984. As fighting exploded among the various Lebanese factions, Mr. Reagan reassessed his position and decided to withdraw the marines and the offshore naval presence. The immediate effects were a realignment of power within Lebanon favoring Syria, and as a consequence, Lebanese President Amin Gemayel's decision to renounce the 1983 peace treaty with Israel.

This experience will not be lost on Israel when and if the Administration starts pushing Mr. Reagan's plan for Jordanian-Israeli negotiations on the West Bank and Gaza Strip. But in the meantime, Israel was overwhelmed by internal economic difficulties and was forced to declare its intention unilaterally to withdraw its forces from Lebanon. So the Administration's main aim, to bring about withdrawal of Syrian and Israeli forces from Lebanon, collapsed. Syria, it appears, is the winner in Lebanon after having been defeated by Israeli forces on the battlefield. The losers are Israel, the United States and serious hopes for diplomatic progress.

This kind of outcome seemed almost foreordained by an Administration that never appeared to know what it wanted in the

Middle East—or at least, how to get it. First, it wanted a "strategic consensus" of Israel and the moderate Arab states against the Soviet Union. When that proved unattainable, it switched its focus to Saudi Arabia. The Saudis proved not to be the key to peace in the area. Then, when Israel attacked Lebanon, the Administration condemned the action, and relations with Jerusalem were deeply strained. Just as suddenly, the Administration altered course once again and began emphasizing its ties to Israel.

There is every indication now that Mr. Reagan's diplomatic position in the region is in a shambles. The Administration has all it can do to help the Israelis restore their economy and withdraw their forces from Lebanon, without trying to convince Jerusalem to compromise on the West Bank as well. King Hussein of Jordan has shown himself unwilling or unable thus far to chance negotiations with Israel, and he is to be the linchpin of the Reagan peace plan. And while the Administration busied itself with new strategic conceptions every year and with the Reagan plan, it allowed the one diplomatic track that had proved successful—the Camp David process between Egypt and Israel—to languish, if not die. Egypt now has little to do with Israel, and Egypt and Jordan are pushing for a return to a U.N.-led Middle East peace effort. As Mr. Reagan begins his second term, he will have no alternative but to start all over again.

Southern Africa is the one area where Administration policy has been quite constant and where it has pursued policies of sustained diplomatic engagement. Instead of pressuring South Africa as President Carter did, Mr. Reagan chose a policy of "constructive engagement" with Pretoria. In theory, this improved relationship would, in turn, be used to wheedle concessions from Pretoria on the role of blacks in South Africa and on granting independence to Namibia. Political repression has not lessened in South Africa, and at year's end, a sudden outburst of political protests in Washington helped produce a rare criticism of Pretoria's policies by President Reagan.

There have been active discussions on the future of Namibia, but the Administration complicated the chances for a settlement there by tying South African departure from that territory to the withdrawal of Cuban troops from Angola. Despite some give and take, Angola and South Africa remain at odds on this issue. The Angolans are also demanding that all aid be stopped by Pretoria and others to the insurgency led by Jonas Savimbi. At the end of 1984, the Administration claimed that it was moving in on a settlement—but it had been making such claims for two years or more.

VII

It was in the area where diplomacy matters most—relations with the Soviet Union and the negotiation of limits to the arms race— that the Reagan Administration encountered the greatest difficulties in its first three years. Then in 1984, Soviet-American relations went from bad to worse to, suddenly, just before the November elections, better. By most indications, the almost four-year deterioration seems to have ended.

In November 1983, Moscow kept its promise and walked out on the talks on intermediate-range nuclear forces in response to the first deployments of American Pershing II and cruise missiles in Europe. At the time, Soviet officials insisted they would not return to the table until the missiles were withdrawn. In a related move, Moscow refused to set a date for the resumption of the December 1983 round of Strategic Arms Reductions Talks. Unless Soviet leaders were substantially detached from reality, they must have realized that there was no chance Washington would agree to remove the new missiles from Europe. Thus, they deliberately painted themselves into a diplomatic corner and put an end to the offensive nuclear arms talks until after the American elections.

Perhaps the Politburo had painted itself into a domestic political corner as well, and the Soviet leaders felt they could not back down for internal reasons. At the same time, however, they seemed to be sending a message to the American electorate: there could be no genuine arms control while Reagan remained President. They steadily denounced him in the first six months of 1984 as a dangerous militarist, a man who might cause a nuclear war. Trying to influence the American elections was a gamble, to be sure. But it was not a ludicrous calculation at the beginning of 1984. Mr. Reagan was ahead in the public opinion polls, yet he did not have a commanding lead and much could have happened in an election year to jeopardize his reelection. Also, the Russians were having troubles of their own with the death of their leader, Yuri Andropov, in February, and his replacement by Leonid Brezhnev's protégé, Konstantin Chernenko.

Meanwhile, the more intransigent and dyspeptic Soviet rhetoric became, the more conciliatory was Mr. Reagan's. In January 1984 alone, he gave two major speeches, one of them the State of the Union address, calling for a new "dialogue" with Moscow and for improving relations between the two superpowers. Moscow countered that it was all election-year propaganda. While the polls showed that many American voters were skeptical about Mr. Reagan's sincerity on arms control, they also showed that most Americans were blaming the Soviets for failure to return to the bargaining tables. The same reaction held when Moscow decided in May to boycott the summer Olympics in Los Angeles. Instead of making Mr. Reagan look warlike, Moscow's strategy boomeranged and made the Soviet Union into the villain.

By June, any significant hope of defeating Mr. Reagan in November had vanished, and Moscow began to soften its stance. In late June, Mr. Chernenko proposed a new Soviet-American negotiation aimed at preventing the militarization of outer space, including a moratorium on the testing of antisatellite weapons. The United States had just successfully downed one missile in space with another—the first time this had been accomplished by either superpower. Also, Washington was getting ready to test an antisatellite system more sophisticated than the older and unreliable Soviet one. Soviet leaders may have reckoned there was some chance Mr. Reagan might agree to negotiate on Soviet terms, if only to prove to the electorate that he was serious about arms control. If, on the other hand, Mr. Reagan rejected the Soviet offer, perhaps this would weaken his credibility with the American electorate on arms control issues generally.

Once again, however, Soviet leaders outsmarted themselves and Mr. Reagan outmaneuvered them. He "accepted" the Soviet proposal for talks on space weapons, but refused to concede in advance that their aim would be to prevent the militarization of outer space. That kind of judgment, he responded, could be made only if and as the two superpowers also agreed to address once again the subject of offensive nuclear forces. In other words: no talks on defense without resuming talks on offense. Mr. Reagan also continued to argue that the two sides should reconsider the value of space-based defense and even offered to share American technology in this field. He was ready, he said, to send his delegation to Vienna in September or October or after the election as the Soviets had proposed. Not willing to accept talks on American terms and give Mr. Reagan a major political victory as well, Moscow let the matter drop, publicly at least.

But Soviet leaders were already making their policy shift toward the Reagan Administration. In July, a Soviet delegation came to Washington and quietly initialled an agreement upgrading the hotline, or crisis communications, pact between the superpowers. Other agreements and arrangements were proffered by Washington and accepted by the Kremlin: resumption of talks on cultural exchanges and building new consulates, restoration of Soviet fishing rights, and initiation of talks on a boundary dispute in the Bering Sea. All of these were below the political threshold, but the signal was clear.

There was no mistaking this in September when it was announced that Soviet Foreign Minister Andrei Gromyko would meet with Secretary Shultz at the United Nations later that month, and then would meet in Washington with Mr. Reagan for the first time. Even though Mr. Gromyko arranged to visit also with the Democratic challenger, Walter Mondale, the game had obviously changed.

In his speech to the U.N. General Assembly on September 24, 1984, Mr. Reagan said that the two superpowers had "to extend the arms control process to build a bigger umbrella under which it can operate—a road map, if you will, showing where in the next 20 years or so these individual efforts can lead." He made this same kind of presentation to Mr. Gromyko at the White House on September 29, and reportedly stressed that he would be willing to "consider" restraints on antisatellite weapons testing if the arms control process as a whole, including, especially, offensive arms, were to be renewed. Then, on November 22, it was announced in both capitals that Mr. Shultz and Mr. Gromyko would meet in Geneva on January 7–8, 1985, in "new negotiations" to discuss space weapons, medium-range missiles and intercontinental-range nuclear forces.

As a result of this meeting, the two superpowers agreed to conduct one "umbrella" negotiation with working groups in the three main areas. Mr. Shultz did not convince his Soviet counterpart of the potential virtues of defensive systems; nor did Mr. Gromyko convince Mr. Shultz about the dangers of an arms race in space. They did agree, however, that there would be "an interrelationship" among the different negotiations. But the meaning of this relationship, that is, whether progress on offensive weapons would depend on progress on defensive systems as well, was left ambiguous. In the end, the overriding message of this Geneva meeting was not so much that the two sides were now ready to make serious progress on arms control, but that they were prepared to improve overall relations and reduce tensions between them.

It has taken a full year and more for the two superpowers to get back to where they were in November 1983. Even that was not a notable high point in bilateral relations, either in managing political disputes or in arms control. The two sides were far apart then and, by most indications, neither has altered its substantive positions since. Most of the blame for the hiatus in bargaining has to rest with the Soviet leaders. They walked away from the table. Their excuse for this, that the Administration was not negotiating seriously, did not wash with the Western audience they sought to influence.

Nonetheless, the Administration bears a heavy responsibility for the diplomatic stalemate in Soviet-American relations and many other areas as well. There have been two reasons for this. First, Administration leaders have displayed an attitude of almost anti-diplomacy. It was as if they felt that to engage with adversaries, or sometimes even friends, would mean being tainted or taken. Also, diplomacy requires knowledge of foreign leaders, cultures and issues, qualities which have not been in overabundance around the cabinet table. Above all, diplomacy entails compromise, and this does not come easily to those in the Administration who equate compromise with capitulation.

VIII

The intractability of the central diplomatic challenges which confront the Administration is not a consequence only of its own performance or the policy decisions of other governments. The problems are complicated by a fact almost completely beyond American control or even influence: few of the current leaders in pivotal nations are powerful enough internally to make important concessions externally.

Under the best of circumstances, personal courage and solid domestic backing are required before a leader can put together an internal coalition to make compromises. Instead of Mr. Brezhnev, who seemed to be the unchallenged leader, there is Mr. Chernenko, a man who apparently must operate by strict consensus. Instead of President Anwar el-Sadat of Egypt and Prime Minister Menachem Begin of Israel, we have Hosni Mubarak and a coalition government led by Shimon Peres. Governments in Japan and Western Europe operate with slim majorities. It is doubtful that President Duarte of El Salvador can go very far without approval from his armed forces. Only Deng Xiaoping of China appears to have the authority of his immediate predecessors, at least on strictly domestic matters.

Domestic political weakness is reinforced in almost all cases by military stalemate. While an essential balance may be a prerequisite to arms control agreements, military stalemates tend to work not only against accepting diplomatic compromises, because there is not much fear of losing, but against escalating conflicts as well, for there is not much prospect of winning. For the next year or two or more, the Sandinistas are not strong enough to eliminate the contras (counterrevolutionaries), and vice versa. The same kind of balance holds between guerrillas and governments in El Salvador, Namibia and Angola. The Arab states have no real military alternative for some years against a clearly superior Israeli military force. Neither Iran nor Iraq seems able to mount a convincing offensive to end their war. The Khmer Rouge and Vietnam appear at a standstill, as do the Soviets and the Afghan resistance. Thus, Mr. Reagan faces situations where neither side is in a position to force a settlement on the other, and yet the prospective costs of escalation are not forcing a compromise on both.

IX

We do not quarrel with Mr. Reagan's sincerity about being flexible and wanting to settle disputes through serious diplomacy. We do question whether the present East-West military balance will be enough to satisfy Administration supporters and hard-liners, whether the Administration is sufficiently united and disposed toward the hard compromises necessary to reach agreements, and how well the Administration will do when it comes up against the stubborn realities of world affairs and regional conflicts. Our concern is that after an initial period of efforts which bump into these realities, the pressures and temptations to recoil, to go back to temporizing measures and to rhetoric that disguises inaction, will be enormous. What will Mr. Reagan do when the Russians do not capitulate or give him what he may now expect, or when diplomatic efforts in Central America or the Middle East do not yield early results?

Our hope is that he will persist, and our belief is that the President has powerful incentives to do so.

First, he is almost uniquely in a position to bring American power to bear and get things accomplished. He has a better chance than any of his post World War II predecessors at quelling opposition from the right. He has succeeded in creating the impression that the United States has turned the tide against the Soviet Union in broad strategic terms. Allies feel he will defend Western interests, and adversaries fear him. He would have the support necessary to make agreements and to press those who would violate the terms of agreements. In fact, from both domestic and diplomatic vantage points, he is better positioned than Presidents Nixon and Carter when they made their breakthroughs on arms control, the Middle East and, in Mr. Carter's case, the Panama Canal treaties. They faced diplomatic stalemates and intractable regional conflicts comparable to those that exist today. And they managed to deal with them at a time when American power was ebbing and Soviet power seemingly rising.

Second, if he does not succeed diplomatically, the problems will get worse. The nuclear competition between the Soviet Union and the United States is at a crossroads. Both sides are developing and testing new technologies—antisatellite weapons, antisubmarine warfare, terminal guidance for warheads, space-based defensive systems and the like. When and if these are all deployed, possibly in the next 10 to 15 years, the essential calculus of deterrence—that no matter which side strikes first, both sides lose—could be undermined. In times of crisis, leaders on both sides could come to believe that they might be able to strike first, destroy almost all the other side's assets, and blunt the small retaliatory attack. Steps must be taken to curtail this new competition now.

If the Administration's optimistic predictions prove false and the situation in Central America deteriorates, an escalation in the fighting and decisions about possible American intervention could follow. Nor can continued stalemate be taken for granted in the volatile Middle East. Even without diplomatic progress, a diplomatic process there is critical to offering the parties an alternative to violence and maintaining an American role.

Third, if the problems get worse, President Reagan will no longer be able to avoid the domestic political dilemma that undid many of his predecessors—the choice between military intervention or foreign defeat. Thus far, events in Central America, the Middle East and elsewhere have not posed this dilemma in stark and inescapable terms. But time and luck could run out.

The assets which Mr. Reagan has developed can turn quickly to gossamer—if the American economy deteriorates, if defense budget increases are unduly and increasingly slashed, and if, above all, the Administration does not move to demonstrate that it is as wise in the ways of diplomacy as it has been determined to restore American power. The fact that the problems are difficult does not absolve the Administration from trying to reconcile differences and keep conflicts under control. For the stalemates of today can turn into the opportunities and explosions of tomorrow.

LESLIE H. GELB is national security correspondent for *The New York Times*. He was director of the Bureau for Politico-Military Affairs at the State Department, under Secretary Vance (1977–79).

ANTHONY LAKE is Five College Professor of International Relations at Mount Holyoke College. He was Director of Policy Planning at the State Department during the Carter Administration.

The First Term

The Reagan Road to Détente

Norman Podhoretz   AMERICA AND THE WORLD 1984

A September 12, 1990 file photo shows former U.S. President Ronald Reagan holding a hammer and chisel next to the Berlin Wall on Poltsdammer Platz in East Berlin.

T he conventional wisdom has it that Ronald Reagan was elected to his first term in 1980 largely on the strength of economic considerations. Yet there can be no doubt that a good many voters supported him because they had been growing increasingly worried about the decline of American power and resolve in the face of the growing power and aggressiveness of the Soviet Union. Nor is there any doubt that these voters included a significant number of life-long Democrats (I myself among them), who saw in the Carter Administration—and especially in Mr. Carter's announcement shortly after taking office that it was becoming less and less necessary to contain Soviet expansionism—evidence that the Democratic Party was still in the grip of the neoisolationist forces that had captured it in 1972 behind the candidacy of George McGovern.

It was true that after the Soviet invasion of Afghanistan Mr. Carter had repented of his conversion to McGovernism and emerged as a born-again Truman Democrat. Confessing that the invasion had effected a "dramatic change" in his view of "the Soviets' ultimate goals," he even went so far as to proclaim a new presidential doctrine, reminiscent both in spirit and substance of the doctrine bearing Truman's name which had originally committed the nation to the policy of containment in 1947. The new Carter Doctrine of 1979 warned the Soviet Union that "an attempt . . . to gain control of the Persian Gulf region" would be "regarded as an assault on the vital interests of the U.S." and would be "repelled by use of any means necessary, including military force."

But the new Carter did not confine himself to drawing a line in the Middle East; he also began reversing course in Central America. Earlier in his term, demonstrating that he really had overcome what still earlier he had dismissed as "that inordinate fear of communism which once led us to embrace any dictator who joined us in that fear," Mr. Carter helped topple an already tottering Somoza regime and enthusiastically threw his support to the new government in Nicaragua despite the fact that it was dominated by the openly communist Sandinistas. Now, when the Sandinistas began acting like communists by moving to eliminate all political opposition, the new Carter cut off American aid; simultaneously he sought to bolster the junta in El Salvador in its struggle against the guerrillas there who were linked to the Soviet Union through their Cuban and Nicaraguan supporters. Here too, then, a line was being drawn.

Finally, Mr. Carter combined these gestures with a heightened enthusiasm for military spending on the one hand and a correlative diminution of enthusiasm for arms control on the other. Having come into office in 1976 with a pledge to reduce the defense budget by at least five billion dollars, Mr. Carter three years later called for a five-percent increase in the defense budget; and having spent an enormous amount of time and energy pressing for the signing and ratification of the second Strategic Arms Limitation Talks treaty (SALT II), he now withdrew it from consideration by the Senate (where not even a Democratic majority could produce enough votes for ratification).

Welcome though all this was to dissident Democrats like myself, many of us interpreted it as an election-year accommodation to the new political climate in the United States which had first shown itself in the outburst of patriotic sentiment during the bicentennial celebrations of 1976 and which had erupted into blazing visibility after the seizure of the hostages in Iran and the Soviet invasion of Afghanistan. In any case, in Ronald Reagan, a former Democrat, we thought we had discovered a more legitimate heir to the mainstream Democratic tradition in foreign policy—the commitment to containment running from Truman through Kennedy, Johnson and Senator Henry M. Jackson—than Jimmy Carter, let alone Mr. Carter's leading Democratic rival, Senator Edward Kennedy. Whereas the Democrats of 1980 seemed to have lost the heady faith in American power expressed by Senator Kennedy's older brother John in 1960, Mr. Reagan wanted to "get the country moving again." In fact, Mr. Reagan could have run under that very slogan without striking a discordant note, since he was calling for the same kinds of policies that it had symbolized for Kennedy in 1960: repair of a military imbalance (the "missile gap" then, the "window of vulnerability" now); a tougher policy toward Soviet expansionism (beginning with this hemisphere—Cuba then, Central America now); and a more assertive American role "to assure," as Kennedy put it in his inaugural address, "the survival and the success of liberty." And when, in office, Mr. Reagan gave key positions to Democrats like Jeane Kirkpatrick, Eugene V. Rostow, Elliott Abrams, Richard Perle and Richard Pipes—all of whom had in one way or another been associated with Senator Jackson—he seemed to be forging a living link between the old Democratic mainstream and his own administration.

II

If, however, a good many of his Democratic supporters saw in Mr. Reagan the hope that the Republican Party would now assume the responsibility for containing Soviet expansionism that had originally been shouldered by the United States under Democratic leadership but that the Democrats since Vietnam had been increasingly eager to evade, others regarded him as the carrier of a quite different political tradition, and one more indigenous to the Republican Party. This was the tradition that regarded containment as a species of appeasement and that advocated a strategy aimed at the "rollback" of Soviet power and the "liberation" of its East European satellites.

It must be acknowledged that those who either hoped or feared that Mr. Reagan meant to pursue such a strategy had reasonable cause. Two decades earlier, in converting from a Democrat to a Republican, Mr. Reagan had thrown in his lot with the most conservative elements of his new party, first coming into public prominence with a speech in support of Barry Goldwater at the 1964 Republican National Convention, and then succeeding Goldwater as the leader of the Republican right. And while in his 1980 campaign the loudest echoes from the past came from the John F. Kennedy of 1960, in his early statements as President Mr. Reagan sounded rather more like John Foster Dulles and the Richard Nixon of 1950—the Nixon, that is, who had denounced containment as a "cowardly" policy and who, like General Douglas MacArthur in Korea, believed that the only alternative to victory over "international communism" was defeat.

Thus, speaking very early in his Administration from the same platform from which Jimmy Carter had declared that containment was growing obsolete, Mr. Reagan referred to communism as a "bizarre chapter in human history whose last pages are even now being written." Naturally, in turning the tables on the old Marxist prophecy that capitalism would eventually perish of its own internal contradictions, Mr. Reagan did not suggest that he had any intention of helping the process along by going to war.

Nevertheless, the echoes of the liberationist rhetoric of old were inescapably there.

More surprisingly, given the more conciliatory posture Mr. Reagan began to adopt toward the Soviet Union during the 1984 campaign, these echoes were sounded again both by the President himself and his secretary of state, George Shultz, at the very height of that campaign itself. The United States, declared Mr. Reagan in August of 1984, "rejects any interpretation of the Yalta agreement that suggests American consent for the division of Europe into spheres of influence," and a week after, declaring that "the tide of history is with us," Mr. Shultz added: "We will never accept the idea of a divided Europe." Again a note of caution was struck to ward off any suggestion that military means were under consideration ("We may not see freedom in Eastern Europe in our lifetime. Our children may not see it in theirs"). But if the hands here were the hands of Shultz, the voice was the voice of Dulles.

It was in statements like these, coming on top of Mr. Reagan's characterizations of the Soviet Union as an "evil empire" and a "focus of evil," that the Soviets themselves professed to detect an ominous turn in American policy. As one observer, writing in 1984, summarized it after extensive conversations with Soviet officials: "All this sounded to Soviet ears very much like the revival of . . . 'rollback' [and] contributed to the impression that the U.S.S.R. was dealing with a new phenomenon—an Administration that seemed truly and unprecedentedly committed to the goal of doing the Soviet Union in"—or at least of rolling back the Soviet system "right to the gates of the Kremlin itself."

Surely, however, to take such professed Soviet impressions of the Reagan Administration at face value was to fall victim to a campaign of disinformation. Perhaps the Soviets had some grounds for apprehension when Mr. Reagan first assumed office, but by 1984, after watching his performance as President for three years, they had no reason whatever to believe that he was trying to resurrect the dream of rollback. On the other hand, they had every reason to pretend to such a belief. For by simulating alarm over the rhetorical belligerency of the Reagan Administration, they could—and did—help to provoke a clamor both in the United States and Europe against the minimal steps the Administration really was taking to shore up a Western position that had deteriorated badly during the years of détente.

Indeed, in any effort to understand the foreign policy of the first Reagan Administration, the beginning of wisdom is to recognize that its overriding purpose was to prevent the balance of military power, and the "correlation of forces" generally, from tilting irreversibly toward the Soviet Union. Mr. Reagan and his people not only said but genuinely believed that the Soviets had been allowed by the misguided policies of the past three Presidents (two of them, of course, Republicans) to achieve a net military superiority over the United States; that this had already spawned political consequences in the form of an increase in Soviet adventurism first in Africa and the Middle East and then in Central America; that unless the United States moved rapidly, both in the military and political spheres, it would be unable to restore a safer balance; and that arms control negotiations would at best retard the ability of the United States to move fast enough and would at worst lock it permanently into a position of inferiority and therefore of extreme vulnerability.

From this assessment of "the present danger," it followed that the first order of business must be to close the military gap by an immediate refurbishing and modernization of the American military arsenal, both nuclear and conventional, and by the deployment of intermediate-range missiles in Western Europe to match the growing force of Soviet SS-20s. About this Mr. Reagan himself was absolutely clear and steadfast. Against enormous pressures, often coming not only from his Democratic opponents but also from within his own party as his budget deficits mounted, he refused to cut back significantly on military spending. He successfully resisted comparable pressures both within the United States and in Western Europe to back away from deployment of the Pershing II and cruise missiles. He adroitly avoided (though not without considerable help from the Soviets) arms control negotiations that might have jeopardized his military programs. He used the prestige of his office to fight against newly fashionable proposals such as the nuclear freeze and the doctrine of no first use of nuclear weapons which would have prevented both the modernization of the American arsenal and the deployment of intermediate-range ballistic missiles in Europe. And finally, he authorized further research on and development of a system of strategic defense in the hope that it would provide a better way than arms control to neutralize the threat of a Soviet first strike.

Clear and steadfast as he was in the matter of military hardware, Mr. Reagan recognized with equivalent clarity that the balance of power could not be repaired by hardware alone. It was also necessary to restore a willingness to use the military hardware that Americans were once again willing to buy. Here the main obstacle was cultural. Not perhaps since the 1930s in England had the idea of using military force fallen into such widespread disrepute as it did in the United States in the aftermath of the American experience in Vietnam. Whatever other "lessons" Vietnam might have been thought to yield, the one that seemed to take deepest root in American culture was that military force had become, or was at any rate on the way to becoming, obsolete as an instrument of American political purposes in the Third World.

This putative lesson had already been drawn by a number of prominent people in connection with the oil embargo of 1973, when a tiny and militarily powerless nation, Saudi Arabia, demonstrated that it could blackmail and exact tribute from a superpower like the United States. But it took the sight of American helicopters scrambling desperately out of Saigon almost two years later to drive the idea home. No matter that, strictly speaking, the United States had not been defeated militarily in Vietnam; the fact remained that the nation had poured virtually everything it had short of nuclear weapons into Vietnam in order to prevent a takeover of the South by the North, and it had failed.

When to these considerations was added the ever-mounting tide of nuclear pacifism—the belief that no rational purpose whatsoever could be served by the use of nuclear weapons—the Clausewitzian law that war is the continuation of politics by other means seemed well on the way to being repealed so far as the American political culture was concerned. The upshot was, as Meg Greenfield of The Washington Post observed, that even many Americans who insisted there were places where they would favor military action "never could seem to think of one this side of San Diego," and if American action meant using nuclear weapons, not even anything this side of San Diego would in their view be worth defending.

All this posed—and continues posing, as witness Secretary of Defense Caspar Weinberger's specifications this past November of the six conditions which must be satisfied before American troops can be committed to combat—a formidable obstacle to the resurgence of the American will to use military force under any circumstances, or even, ultimately, to threaten its use as a deterrent. Recognizing the problem, Mr. Reagan worked hard to cultivate and nourish the countervailing spirit of American nationalism (or "the new patriotism," as it came to be called), the earliest political consequence of which had been his own election to the presidency.

In pursuit of this purpose, Mr. Reagan made free and frequent use of patriotic language and engaged in an unembarrassed manipulation of patriotic symbols; he lost no opportunity to praise the armed forces, to heighten their morale, to restore their popular prestige; and he repeatedly announced as an accomplished fact that the United States was "standing tall" again. Although he disclaimed any intention of "sending American combat troops to Central America," or for that matter anywhere else, he said over and over again that the United States could be counted upon to honor its military commitments to its allies. When, finally, he did send American troops into action, in Grenada, he not only succeeded in his stated objective ("to restore order and democracy") there; he also helped to restore confidence here in the utility of military force as an instrument of worthy political purposes.

In offering this analysis, I do not mean to suggest that I agree with those who accused the Reagan Administration of "militarizing" the American conflict with the Soviet Union, and of seeking military rather than political solutions to the problems of Central America. It was simply preposterous to accuse Mr. Reagan of provoking an arms race when, after a decade of cutting its military expenditures as the Soviet Union—having already enjoyed a great advantage in conventional forces—first achieved parity and then began to pull ahead in its nuclear arsenal as well, the United States at last decided on a significant increase in defense spending in order to start catching up. So too with Central America, where under Mr. Reagan only one-quarter of the American aid and a similar proportion of the American personnel were military (the rest of the aid being economic and the rest of the personnel being journalists).

I would, however, concede that these tendentious charges of militarization contained this much truth: that Mr. Reagan and his people were much clearer and more consistent in dealing with the military dimension of American power than they were in defining the strategic objectives toward which American power was to be directed.

III

In the early days of his Administration, Mr. Reagan and his first secretary of state, Alexander M. Haig, Jr., reaffirmed the commitment made by Jimmy Carter to prevent a Soviet move into the Persian Gulf. They also declared that the United States would not tolerate any further extension of communism in Central America, and they called publicly on the Cubans and the Nicaraguans (and privately on the Soviet Union) to stop the flow of arms to the Marxist-dominated guerrillas in El Salvador. At the same time, going beyond his blunt and unusually harsh verbal attacks on the Soviet Union as an "evil empire" and a "focus of evil," Mr. Reagan attempted to seize the offensive in the ideological conflict between East and West.

In proposing this offensive, Mr. Reagan offered a sharp and salient contrast to the three Presidents who came before him. His immediate Republican predecessors, Richard Nixon and Gerald Ford (both working with Henry Kissinger), had tried to tone down the vivid ideological coloration which had been given to the U.S.-Soviet conflict by their predecessors, and to redefine the conflict in more traditional terms as a great-power rivalry. Jimmy Carter, Mr. Reagan's immediate Democratic predecessor, finding realpolitik in the Kissinger style deficient in the moral fervor he himself favored, sought to supply the lack by assigning to the United States a responsibility for protecting and establishing human rights everywhere in the world. Yet, far from reinvigorating the ideological passions that had once been aroused in the American soul by the struggle with the Soviet Union, the new emphasis on human rights tended to dilute such passions through diffusion and generalization. In practice it also diverted attention away from the Soviet Union itself and toward rightist dictatorships like Iran under the Shah and Somoza's Nicaragua, whose friendly relations with the United States made them all the more vulnerable to American pressures.

This diversionary effect was by no means an accidental or unintended consequence of Mr. Carter's foreign policy. On the contrary, it was entirely congruent with his belief that the struggle between East and West was growing "less intensive" and was being superseded in importance as a threat to peace by a world "one-third rich and two-thirds hungry." The focus, therefore, must now shift from East-West to North-South—away, that is, from the Soviet Union (except as a partner in arms control) and toward the Third World.

As against Mr. Carter's fixation on the Third World, Mr. Reagan tried to bring the East-West conflict back into the center of American consciousness. So far as he was concerned, Soviet expansionism remained the greatest threat to peace, and while he neither believed nor said that the Soviet Union was responsible for all the ills on earth, he did believe and did say that the Soviet Union more often than not was using its new global reach to exacerbate troublesome situations in Africa, the Middle East and Central America.

(As for the threat of a world "one-third rich and two-thirds hungry," Mr. Reagan proposed to deal with it not through a program of global redistribution but by encouraging the kind of capitalist enterprise that was generating prosperity in such countries of the "South" as Korea and Taiwan.)

In thus bringing the Soviet threat back to the center of his foreign policy, Mr. Reagan was reestablishing a link with the Nixon-Kissinger view of the world. But there was also a dramatic difference. As against the great-power realpolitik of Mr. Nixon and Dr. Kissinger, Mr. Reagan tried to redefine the East-West conflict once again primarily in ideological terms. Speaking to the British Parliament where, he said, was enshrined "the enduring greatness of the British contribution to mankind, the great civilized ideas: individual liberty, representative government, and the rule of law under God," he deplored "the shyness of some of us in the West about standing for these ideals that have done so much to ease the plight of man and the hardships of our imperfect world." Ronald Reagan had no intention of allowing the United States to remain in so shy a condition. Accordingly he called for a "campaign" to assist and further "the democratic revolution" that, he told the British Parliament, was "gathering new strength" all over the world—and even within the Soviet Union itself, not to mention its East European empire.

Yet, if the Soviets really interpreted all this to mean that the Reagan Administration "was truly and unprecedentedly committed to the goal of doing the Soviet Union in" and of rolling back the Soviet system "right to the gates of the Kremlin itself," they must have been utterly bewildered by the policies the Administration actually followed. Why, for example, would an Administration intent on "doing the Soviet Union in" lift a grain embargo which, while not exactly calculated to topple the communist system, was nevertheless helping to aggravate the very internal economic difficulties that Mr. Reagan cited as a symptom of instability and decline? More pointedly, why would an Administration committed to rollback fail to exploit an event like the Polish crisis of 1981–82?

When Hungary erupted in 1956, the foreign policy of the United States was in the hands of a man supposedly dedicated to the liberation of Eastern Europe, but John Foster Dulles stood by and watched Soviet tanks crush this heroic uprising because the only alternative seemed to be a military response by the United States that might have unleashed a third world war. The same fear restrained Lyndon Johnson when Soviet tanks went into Czechoslovakia in 1968: short of embarking on unacceptably dangerous military measures, there was nothing the United States could do, and so the United States did nothing but register verbal protests. By contrast, when martial law was declared in Poland—a step almost universally understood to have been taken as a substitute for a Soviet invasion to crack down on the Solidarity movement—the United States was in a position to do more than light candles on Christmas and produce a disapproving television program. Thanks to the inability of the Poles to pay the interest on their debts to Western banks, there was an opportunity to keep the crisis at a boil by declaring Poland in default. No risk of war was posed by such a policy, and yet from the haste with which the United States, and even more the West Europeans, shrank from it, one might have thought that they expected the Soviets to launch a nuclear strike if the West refused to roll over the Polish loans.

There were, of course, strictly financial considerations involved in this decision; moreover, the Reagan Administration was acting not alone but under severe pressure from the West Europeans (who carried the bulk of the Polish debt). Even so, the fact remained that, given an opportunity to do something neither imprudent nor reckless to further a process of disintegration within the Soviet empire, the Reagan Administration chose to go in the opposite direction. That is, it cooperated with the Soviets and their Polish surrogates in quieting the situation down instead of stepping aside and letting an internal rebellion against Communist rule (which, in contrast to the Hungarian uprising of 1956, the United States had done nothing whatsoever to encourage) take its course and work itself out.

Whatever the merits of this choice of rollover as against roll-back, there was simply no way it could be reconciled with the idea that Mr. Reagan was trying "to do the Soviets in." It was, however, entirely consistent with the so-called Sonnenfeldt doctrine, according to which the disintegration of the Soviet empire in Eastern Europe would be so dangerous, so pregnant with the risk of a general war, that continued Soviet control over those countries must paradoxically be considered a vital interest of the West.

So far as I know, it has never been suggested that this doctrine should be applied to other areas of Soviet imperial influence or domination like Afghanistan and Angola. Yet despite Mr. Reagan's praise of the "freedom fighters," as he did not hesitate to describe them, struggling against Soviet troops or their Cuban surrogates in those countries, the increase during his first term in the level of American military aid to the anti-Soviet Afghans was clearly not large enough to make a decisive difference; nor, to put it mildly, was there any visible increase in American diplomatic support for the anti-communist guerrillas in Angola.

But if Afghanistan and Angola were to be left more or less to the play of local forces, and there was to be no rollback in Europe, what about Central America, and specifically Nicaragua? Was rollback to be the policy there? Here it must be said that the Reagan Administration would in all probability have openly and proudly supported toppling the Sandinista regime if not for the Boland Amendment and similar congressional measures prohibiting such a policy (as against one merely aimed at preventing the flow of arms from Nicaragua into El Salvador or exerting pressure on the Sandinistas to honor their old promises of democratic reform). Under the circumstances, the Administration had to be content with circumventing these restrictions as best it could.

It is, however, important to recognize that even under the rules of détente the United States would not be required to acquiesce in the takeover of Nicaragua by a communist regime—certainly not one allied to Cuba and the Soviet Union and dedicated to sponsoring a "revolution without frontiers" in this hemisphere. Indeed, when the Reagan Administration attempted to deal with the communist threat to El Salvador and the growing aggressiveness of the Sandinistas in Nicaragua by issuing warnings to the Soviets and by hinting that new pressures would be brought against Cuba, it was acting in a way entirely consistent with détente as defined by no less an authority than Richard Nixon. That is, it was trying to correct a violation by the Soviets of the agreement to restrain third parties whose activities might bring the superpowers into direct conflict. Against this background, the invasion of Grenada assumed a greater significance than the size of that tiny country or the scale of the military operation might suggest. For it showed that the Reagan Administration was serious in serving notice to the Soviets that the United States meant to resume policing the "rules of the game," and that public opinion was no longer the insuperable barrier to the use of military force for this purpose that it had been since 1975.

Mr. Reagan, in short, may have dreamed of a democratic revolution in Eastern Europe, but he had no intention as President of the United States of sponsoring or even encouraging one. By the same token, if he could help it, the Monroe Doctrine, threadbare though it had grown, was not going to be replaced by the Brezhnev Doctrine in the Western hemisphere.

IV

Thus far, in everything but name, we have détente as Mr. Nixon now conceives it: a "hard-headed" détente, involving "strength of arms and strength of will sufficient to blunt the threat of Soviet blackmail." Mr. Nixon stresses the military element in order to distinguish his idea of détente from Mr. Carter's which he, like Mr. Reagan, evidently regards as scarcely distinguishable from appeasement. Yet the enormous irony is that in the economic sphere Ronald Reagan, the great critic of détente, whether of the Nixon or the Carter variety, and the man who as President was accused of trying "to do the Soviets in," did not even measure up to the standards of toughness required by Mr. Nixon's theory.

To be sure, questions have been raised about the degree to which Mr. Nixon himself lived up to his theory as President. But whatever Mr. Nixon's practice in office, his most recent theoretical prescription for hard-headed détente in the non-military sphere brings into play "a mixture of prospective rewards for good behavior and penalties for bad behavior that gives the Soviet Union a positive incentive to keep the peace rather than break it"—in a word, linkage. Mr. Reagan had endorsed this idea in his 1980 campaign and it was reaffirmed in office by Mr. Haig, who later defined it as "the concept that any improvement in relations between Moscow and Washington had to be linked to an improvement of Moscow's behavior in the world." Yet in his 1980 campaign Mr. Reagan had also promised American farmers to lift the grain embargo instituted against the Soviet Union by Mr. Carter in response to the invasion of Afghanistan. The two promises were contradictory, and in choosing to keep the one to the farmers rather than the one to the Soviets, Mr. Reagan demonstrated, as he would do even more unmistakably in the Polish crisis, that the Soviets had little to fear from American "penalties for bad behavior" and little to gain in the way of "prospective rewards for good behavior" that they were not already getting for bad.

With this, among other things, in mind, and friendly though he was to the Reagan Administration, the columnist George Will was moved to describe it as an Administration that loved commerce more than it loathed communism—a jibe that could with even greater justice have been directed at the West Europeans. Mr. Reagan at least tried to stop the Europeans from subsidizing the construction of a gas pipeline which would not only help the Soviet economy but make the Europeans vulnerable to blackmail in some future crisis: this while Soviet troops were still ravaging Afghanistan and while new Soviet missiles aimed at Western Europe were being added almost daily to an already overpowering arsenal. But here even Mr. Haig, the great believer in linkage, was willing to sacrifice it for other objectives—in this case alliance solidarity—and Mr. Reagan was persuaded to back down. Again the Soviets were taught that they had nothing to fear from linkage; and in the virtually inconceivable event that they were too dense or too irrational to absorb the lesson, it was spelled out explicitly by Mr. Haig's successor as secretary of state, George Shultz. Exactly four years after Mr. Reagan had said "I believe in linkage," Mr. Shultz repudiated it: "In the final analysis, linkage is a tactical question," he said. "The strategic reality of leverage comes from creating facts in support of our overall design."

If, then, Mr. Reagan often sounded like John Foster Dulles, he also exhibited the kind of caution which always marked Dulles' policies, for all the latter's liberationist rodomontade. (Dulles, said his French counterpart, Georges Bidault, "was always talking of 'calculated risks,' which in practice most often meant that he calculated a great deal and risked nothing.") Indeed, if we compare how the Administration in which Dulles served responded to a crisis in Lebanon with how the Reagan Administration reacted to a crisis in the same country, we find that in the use of military power Mr. Reagan was much more restrained than even his cautious predecessor. Under Eisenhower, the marines were landed in Lebanon to prevent a possible takeover by anti-Western Arab radicals tied to Syria and backed by the Soviet Union. Under Mr. Reagan, the United States gave half-hearted support to its Israeli ally in a war aimed at driving anti-Western Arab radicals, also tied to Syria and backed by the Soviet Union, out of Lebanon; and when the marines were sent in, the purpose was to prevent the Israelis from finishing the job. Worse still, in spite of all the talk about retaliation that came from the Reagan Administration, and despite the high priority it had always given to combating international terrorism, when those marines were attacked by terrorists, the United States did nothing.

Nor did the Reagan Administration ever follow through on its early efforts to forge a "strategic consensus" of pro-Western states in the Middle East that would include Israel and that would compensate for the loss of Iran as the "policeman" of Western interests in the region and the main bulwark against a Soviet move to control the Persian Gulf. This new approach—which had been endorsed by Mr. Haig, by the President's first national security adviser, Richard V. Allen, and then by the President himself—also meant the stationing of American ground forces in the region to serve as a "tripwire." But the first breath of Saudi opposition to the idea blew it away.

In allowing the Saudis to kill a bold and original initiative which might just possibly have circumvented the intractable Arab-Israeli conflict while shoring up a dangerously vulnerable vital interest, the Reagan Administration was—in a different set of circumstances but yet again—favoring commercial considerations over its anti-Soviet passions. The dangerous vacuum left by the fall of the Shah in Iran thus remained, and all that was left to address the Arab-Israeli conflict was a new Reagan version of the old Rogers Plan which, because it depended on Jordanian willingness to recognize and negotiate with Israel over the disposition of the West Bank, was doomed to failure as a nonstarter.

There was, finally, one other area in which Mr. Reagan's anti-communist passions were forced to give way, and that was in relations with China. Here, however, the pressures had little or nothing to do with commerce and everything to do with geopolitics. No doubt Mr. Reagan would have been happier to act as President on his old belief that Taiwan was the real China, and he even made a few feints in the direction of increased support for Taiwan after moving into the White House. But, before long, relations with China began to resume the course on which they had been set by another passionately anti-communist Republican President whose anti-communism had yielded to the opportunity presented by the Sino-Soviet split for playing one communist power against another.

If Mr. Reagan had been as great an ideologue as he was often said to be, he might have taken the position that the loss in clarity of ideological purpose entailed by this policy was greater than any advantage that so economically backward and militarily weak a nation as China could bring to the balance of power. But Mr. Reagan, while perhaps more swayed by ideological conviction than most professional politicians, showed in his first term (as he had already demonstrated, when governor of California, to those with eyes to see) that for better or worse he was more politician than ideologue.

As such he would go only so far, and no farther, against the pressures of public opinion, and the resistance of the media and the permanent government; he would wherever possible cut his political losses after doing anything risky or unpopular; and in the face of serious opposition, he would usually back down even from a policy to which he was personally devoted.

This at least partly explains why Mr. Reagan in his first term failed to steer the nation away from the course of détente on which it had been moving since 1972 and toward a new strategy of containment aimed, just as the original conception of containment had been, at a prudent encouragement of the forces of disintegration already operating entirely on their own within the Soviet empire. If Mr. Reagan had seriously tried to effect such a change of direction, he would have run into conflict not only with European opinion, but also with powerful interests in the United States; and this conflict would have entailed greater risks than Mr. Reagan the politician was evidently willing to take in supporting the convictions of Mr. Reagan the ideologue. As President, therefore, he was swept inexorably along by the conceptual momentum and institutional inertia of the recent past.

V

Campaigning for a second term, Mr. Reagan chose as his slogan "America is Back." The truth was that, as compared with what the country had become under the policies followed by the Carter Administration in its first three years in office, America was back—in at least the sense that it would no longer passively acquiesce in the achievement of an irreversible military superiority by the Soviet Union and that it was no longer prepared (in Mr. Haig's words) to "accommodate [itself] to the inevitable loss of the world to Moscow." Yet neither was the United States under Mr. Reagan prepared, as it had been only 20 years earlier under John F. Kennedy, to "pay any price, bear any burden, meet any hardship, support any friend, oppose any foe, to assure the survival and the success of liberty."

Of course Kennedy's nominal successors in the Democratic Party of the 1980s were even less prepared to undertake this commitment than the Republicans under Mr. Reagan (not to mention the so-called moderate or liberal Republicans who hoped to succeed him). To an unhappy dissident Democrat like myself, this meant that in 1984 Mr. Reagan, for all the deficiencies that showed up in his first term, was preferable to Walter Mondale or any of Mr. Mondale's rivals. As the Democratic Party was now constituted, a Mondale administration would in all likelihood have set out to undo even Mr. Reagan's minimal efforts to prevent the Soviets from consolidating the military superiority they have already all but achieved; it would have reversed even the inhibited attempt by Mr. Reagan to prevent the spread of Soviet-backed communist regimes in Central America; and it would have pushed the United States further in the direction of isolationism and appeasement.

But, if Mr. Reagan was preferable to Mr. Mondale, I see no point in self-deception about the likely course he will take in his second term. Here the earliest clue could be found in some of Mr. Shultz's statements during the campaign about the future of Soviet-American relations. The United States, Mr. Shultz said this past October, having in the last four years "put the building blocks in place" in the form of a restoration of the military balance, was now ready not for a more vigorous policy of containment or an even more forward strategy of victory, but rather for what "could be a most productive period in Soviet-American relations."

That this statement, like similar ones made by the President himself at the United Nations and elsewhere, was something more than an election-year reassurance became clear shortly after Mr. Reagan's great victory in November, when, despite the fact that the military balance had not yet been restored, he resumed arms control talks with the Soviet Union. But I believe that the

Reagan Administration's election-year rhetoric also pointed beyond arms control and toward a broader and more ambitious objective.

In his first term Mr. Reagan proved unwilling to take the political risks and expend the political energy that a real break with the underlying assumptions of détente would have entailed. Finally, however, overwhelmed by the pressures of the political present, and perhaps lured by seductive fantasies of what historians in the future might say of him as a peacemaker, Mr. Reagan seems ready to embrace the course of détente wholeheartedly as his own. Thus, upon being asked by a reporter at a press conference in January whether the Shultz-Gromyko meeting just concluded in Geneva "might lead to the new era of détente that Mr. Chernenko called for last November," Mr. Reagan replied: "Yes, we would welcome such a thing as long as it was a two-way street."

What this means is that we can expect negotiations with the Soviet Union not merely on arms control but toward an agreement along the lines of the Basic Principles of Détente of 1972. As Mr. Reagan himself explicitly put it in his post-Geneva press conference: "we very definitely are trying to arrive at a position in which we can settle some of the other bilateral and regional issues, and trade matters, that are at odds between us."

At the same time, Mr. Reagan seems to be heading toward a deal in Central America broadly modeled on the one that concluded the Cuban missile crisis in 1962. In that settlement, which foreshadowed the weakening and eventual abandonment of the Democratic Party's commitment to containment, the Kennedy Administration accepted a communist Cuba in exchange for the withdrawal of Soviet missiles from Cuban soil. Similarly, Mr. Reagan may well accept a communist Nicaragua in exchange for a promised withdrawal of Cuban and Nicaraguan support for the communist insurgency in El Salvador. Alternatively, the 1962 Declaration on the Neutrality of Laos might serve as the model for an agreement under the Contadora process calling for the withdrawal of all foreign forces from the area.

Yet there is no reason to believe that agreements of this kind will restrain the Soviets or their Latin American clients and surrogates any more effectively the second time around than they did the first. North Vietnamese forces were not withdrawn from Laos after 1962; détente did not prevent the Soviets from forging ahead both militarily and politically; and the missile deal set the stage for an active Cuban role in that very process of Soviet expansion. If, then, Mr. Reagan should move in this direction, he will cruelly disappoint those of us who once hoped that he might lead the Republican Party into assuming the responsibility for resisting Soviet imperialism that he himself had so often and justifiably attacked the Democrats for no longer wishing to carry.

NORMAN PODHORETZ is the Editor of Commentary. His most recent books are *The Present Danger* and *Why We Were in Vietnam*. Copyright © 1985 by Norman Podhoretz.

www.ingramcontent.com/pod-product-compliance
Lightning Source LLC
Chambersburg PA
CBHW050447270326
41927CB00009B/1640